Perspectives on Legal Aid

Perspectives on Legal Aid

An International Survey

edited by Frederick H. Zemans

Greenwood Press
WESTPORT, CONNECTICUT

Published in the United States and Canada by
Greenwood Press, Inc., Westport, Connecticut

English language edition, except the United States and Canada,
published by Frances Pinter (Publishers) Limited

First published 1979

Library of Congress Cataloging in Publication Data

Main entry under title:

Perspectives on legal aid.

1. Legal aid. I. Zemans, Frederick H.
K133.P47 362.5'8 79-883
ISBN 0-313-20986-3

Library of Congress Catalog Card Number: 79-883

ISBN: 0-313-20986-3

Printed in Great Britain

To Debbie, David and Marcia

Editor's Note

This book brings together various national perspectives on the provision of legal aid in contemporary society. The essays were originally written at the invitation of Professor Vittorio Denti of Pavia, Italy, who used them for his General Report on Accessibility of Legal Proceedings for the Underprivileged, Legal Aid and Advice at the International Congress of Procedural Law held in Ghent, Belgium in August 1977. The Work of Professor Denti and the organizers of the Ghent Conference is appreciated.

As the Introduction states, the provision of legal services and access to justice became a major theme at the Ghent Conference and it was felt by the contributors that it was important to share the data and information which had been collected in the national report. The editor, along with Professors Judd Epstein of Australia and Vincenzo Vigoriti of Italy agreed to assume responsibility for publishing a volume containing both Professor Denti's general report and the national reports. We received encouragement and assistance from many people and individuals in this endeavour which ultimately has become the responsibility of the editor.

I wish to express my appreciation to the administration and staff of Osgoode Hall Law School of York University, Toronto, Canada, for stimulating this project both with research money and support staff assistance. All contributors were helpful in expanding and editing their papers for the purpose of this publication. I was particularly fortunate in obtaining the assistance of Dr. Paula B. Weiss, as Assistant Editor, and Ms. Kathy Johnson as technical editor. Both Dr. Weiss and Ms. Johnson are experienced individuals who were then students at Osgoode Hall Law School. Their commitment to excellence facilitated the success of the project. Four of the papers were translated and the French paper was summarised by Dr. Weiss, José Herran-Lima and Ms. Helene Barbes. Mr. Derek Winnett, Ms. Johnson and Dr. Weiss all assisted in the editing of the manuscript and I was helped in the final proof-reading by our three children, Debbie, David and Marcia.

In conclusion I must express my thanks to the Institute of Advanced Legal Studies of the University of London and to the Social Sciences and Humanities Research Council of Canada who provided me with the opportunity to complete this book. The final responsibility for the publication of any book is that of the publisher. This is particularly the case in a scholarly endeavour. I was most fortunate to be able to work closely on preparing this manuscript with Dr. Frances Pinter and her colleagues who were at all times helpful and expeditious.

No balance sheet of gratitudes would be complete without mentioning my wife Joyce, whose assistance and encouragement is reflected in all my work and writing on legal services.

London, England,
February 1979

Frederick H. Zemans

Contents

Introduction

A doorkeeper stands before the Law. To this doorkeeper comes a man from the country, and he begs for admission into the Law. The doorkeeper tells him, however, that he cannot grant admission at this time. The man considers this, and then asks if he will be permitted to enter later. "It is possible," says the doorkeeper, "but not now." Because the door to the Law is standing open, as is usual, and the doorkeeper steps aside, the man bends to look inside through the portal. As the doorkeeper notices this he laughs, and says, "If it attracts you so much, try to go in without my permission. But be warned: I am powerful. And I am only the lowest of the doorkeepers. From chamber to chamber there are other doorkeepers, each more powerful than the last. Not even I can bear the sight of the third doorkeeper." The man from the country had not expected such difficulties. He thinks the Law should be always accessible to everyone. But when he looks more closely at the doorkeeper in his fur coat, with his large sharp nose and thin black Tartar's beard, he decides rather to wait until he is given permission to enter. The doorkeeper gives him a stool, and permits him to sit down at one side of the door. He sits there for days, and then for years. He makes many attempts to gain permission to enter, and he wearies the doorkeeper with his many requests. The doorkeeper frequently conducts little hearings with him, questions him about his home and about many other things, but the questions are impersonal, the questions that great men ask, and the result is always that he is not given permission to enter. The man, who had prepared himself for his journey with many provisions, uses everything, no matter how valuable, in attempts to bribe the doorkeeper. The doorkeeper accepts everything, but says, "I am only accepting this so that you will not think that you did not try everything." During the many years the man observes the doorkeeper almost continuously. He forgets the existence of the other doorkeepers, and this one seems to him to be the single obstacle to admission into the Law. In the first year he curses his luck aloud, later, as he grows old, he mumbles only to himself, he becomes childish, and since in the long study of the doorkeeper he has even come to recognize the fleas in the doorkeeper's fur collar, he even begs the fleas to help him convince the doorkeeper. Finally his eyes become dim, and he does not know if his eyes are failing him or if it is really becoming darker. But even in the darkness he can see a radiance which comes from the portals of the Law. He will not live much longer. Before his death, all that he has experienced in this time merges into one great question which he has not asked yet. He motions to the doorkeeper, since he can no longer raise his stiffening body. The doorkeeper must bend down low for the difference in sizes has changed, much to the man's disadvantage. "What do you want to know now?" asks the doorkeeper, "you are insatiable." The man says, "Everyone strives for the Law. How is it that in these many years no one but me has sought permission to enter?" The doorkeeper recognizes that the man is about to die, and in order to reach his failing hearing, he shouts at him, "Here nobody but you could be permitted to enter, for this entrance was intended only for you. I will go now and close it."

Kafka, *The Trial*

The first International Congress on the Law of Civil Procedure was held at Ghent, Belgium from August 27 to September 4, 1977. Some 300 participants from more than fifty countries gathered to discuss achieving a justice "with a human face". In his address at the official opening session, Prof. Dr. W. Delva, dean of the Faculty of Law, State University of Ghent, described the problems which surrounded the question of humane justice:

> Any practising lawyer, however, can see for himself in his daily work that the rules of Procedural Law require a more human dimension.
>
> These rules must be made more humane if Procedural Law is not to lead to injustice. If it is indeed a fact that
>
> –only the arrogant, querulous person is helped, not the shy person seeking justice,
>
> –only the trained person is in a secure position, not the unskilled person who needs help,
>
> –only a well-informed person can get along, not the desperate wretch for whom the judicial machinery appears as a mysterious sphinx,
>
> there must be something wrong somewhere.
>
> Furthermore, these formal legal laws also need a human application.

Because if it is a fact that;

—the judge inspires fear, instead of awe,

—the servants of the law are feared and not regarded as people who can help,

—there exists total distrust, if not hate, in the law, instead of reliance on it,

then something has gone desperately wrong.

Therefore, procedural law is, perhaps more than any other branch of law, susceptible of improvement, both in the field of a more humane phasing as in the field of human application.

A conference dedicated to pursuing the concept of a humane justice would have been incomplete without consideration of provision of access to the law for the underprivileged and poor, those who do not normally have unlimited access to legal services, but who are more often than not more in need of these services than their privileged brothers. This question was considered at the Congress under the heading "Accessibility of Legal Procedures for the Underprivileged; Legal Aid and Legal Advice". The Congress's general reporter for this area was Professor Dr. Vittorio Denti from Pavia, Italy, and national reporters from twenty different countries participated in the session and prepared national reports detailing the situation in their countries.

This edition is a collection of the reports on the accessibility of legal procedure, including Dr. Denti's general report, which was drawn from the national reports and the national reports from sixteen of the countries, many of which were revised and expanded for this publication. Some of the national reports were not available to us.

Most of the papers were received in an English version which was either prepared by the author or prepared for him by a translator. A few of the papers, however (those from Spain, Mexico, Germany, Poland, and Scandinavia), were received in the original language and translated in Toronto.

We have attempted to keep as much as possible to the original format of each paper and have therefore sought to make as few changes as possible in the texts. Where translations were involved, however, there was often a certain amount of rewriting which was done by the editors.

Although most of the original texts had numerous footnotes and suggestions for further research, we have decided to delete those notes which refer to material which would not be normally available in the United States, Great Britain, or Canada. While this decision might at times leave the reader wondering about the source of certain data, it was our feeling that the reports would be unnecessarily clogged by adding references in several different languages.

Publication of the national reports on legal aid was a project which was decided upon during the Ghent Congress. It was felt that the national reports represented a valuable cross-section of scholarship in comparative law and as such should be made available on a wider basis than Congress publications and individual journal publications could offer. It is hoped that this collection will be of value to a relatively large group within the legal profession. To the student of comparative law and of those areas of the law which are most often called law and poverty, it will serve as a reference text and a handbook which will offer information on social problems in a number of areas of the world and will indicate what legal responses have been taken towards evolving a solution to these problems. It is hoped that it will stimulate consideration of various potential solutions and serve as an impetus to further study and consideration. To the legislator and law reformer, the essays will serve as a compilation of innovative approaches which have been taken in various areas and which are directed at attempting to ensure equality before the law despite inequalities in societies which are generally made up of collections of unequal social groups. Because provision of legal services is a constantly evolving area, the approaches outlined in these reports may serve as an impetus to law reform and experimentation which will help provide access to justice for those parts of society who are now barred. The final member of the legal profession to whom this collection is directed is the practising lawyer; he is, perhaps, the most important member of the audience. As Jerold S. Auerbach, in *Unequal Justice. Lawyers and Social Change in Modern America* (Oxford, 1976) explained:

> A lawyer is a lawyer – but only to a point. There are significant differences among lawyers which, the evidence suggests, are neither random nor necessarily meritocratic. These differences have profound implications for the presumed fairness of the adversary process, for the adequate provision of legal services to all who need them, and for the capacity of the legal process to provide equal justice.
>
> If the practice of law is to become a public profession, not remain a private club, new values and voices are necessary. Justice should be defined not only by process but by product: is the result, measured by the interests of clients and the needs of society, fair? Legal services should exist by right to all citizens, not as a privilege to some. Substan-

> tial federal subsidies, supplemented by an excess profits tax on corporate law firms, can make this possible. But the prerequisite to reform is public regulation of the legal profession in the public interest. Otherwise, equal justice under the law will remain subservient to unequal justice among lawyers (pp. 3–4; 308).

There are changes necessary to the provision of legal services which must emanate from within the legal profession itself and cannot be imposed upon it from outside. It is our hope that this collection will offer the practising lawyer an overview of a problem whose importance may be forgotten on a day-to-day or case-by-case basis.

Discussion of the problem of provision of legal services or access to justice to the underprivileged is not possible without first defining those people who make up the underprivileged classes and what is involved in giving them access to justice.

Obviously the poor are among the underprivileged. In some countries, such as Korea, where there are no racial minorities, only the poor are underprivileged. But in most countries, the concept of "underprivileged" cannot be restricted merely to those whose disposable income does not extend to the purchase of legal services. In the context of these national reports, we must consider the underprivileged to be those people who experience physical, psychological, or financial difficulties in attempting to assert a right, make a claim, or present a defence.

Physical barriers to access to justice are the most noticeable and present the first barrier which must be overcome. They are also some of the easiest to combat for they are readily seen and identified and are capable of being eradicated. The most common example of such a physical obstacle is the fact that most lawyers have their offices in downtown areas or are at least located in cities or towns of some size. This presents a physical obstacle for those who live in outlying areas or sparsely populated rural areas. If a person is forced to make a journey of some distance in order to consult with a lawyer, he frequently must miss work unless he has a job with flexible working hours. Often these difficulties may prove insurmountable, and may result in leaving a large segment of society without legal services.

Psychological obstacles to access to legal services exist in most countries. These include every feeling that prevents a person from seeking legal services – a sense of fear, hopelessness, lack of information, ignorance, unfamiliarity. These problems operate most often with racial minorities and the poor, although they are not restricted to these groups. The state of mind of these groups was vividly described in Michael Harrington's

The Other America (New York, 1962) which dealt chiefly with the Negro minority in the United States:

> To belong to a racial minority is to be poor, but poor in a special way. The fear, the lack of self-confidence, the haunting, these have been described. But they, in turn, are the expressions of the most institutionalized poverty in the United States, the most vicious of the vicious circles.
>
> There is, in a sense, a personality of poverty, a type of human being produced by the grinding, wearing life of the slums. The other Americans feel differently than the rest of the nation. They tend to be hopeless and passive, yet prone to bursts of violence; they are lonely and isolated, often rigid and hostile. To be poor is not simply to be deprived of the material things of this world. It is to enter a fatal, futile universe, an America within America with a twisted spirit (pp. 71–2; 122).

Another of these psychological barriers is lack of information. At the National Conference on Law and Poverty held in Ottawa in 1971. John Ayotte, from the Greater Montreal Anti-Poverty Co-ordinating Committee, pointed out:

> We have amongst us some social workers and some lawyers. They have the tools of the trade – their education – from which they got information. Most poor people do not have the education, therefore they do not have the information. They are the living problem.

A person who is unaware of his legal rights and has no knowledge of the services available to him is in no better position than he would be if there were no such rights and services. One is reminded of the plight of Josef K. in Kafka's *The Trial*:

> "Can I look at the books?" K. asked, not from any special curiosity, but simply so that his visit would not be useless.
>
> "No," said the woman, and shut the door again, "that is not permitted. The books belong to the examining judge."
>
> "Ah, I see," K said, and nodded. "The books must be law books, and it is a characteristic of this judicial process that one should be ignorant as well as innocent when he is condemned."

Even where there exists knowledge about rights and services available, the legal process is unfamiliar to the vast portion of all nations. Unfamiliarity breeds fear, and fear prevents the underprivileged from seeking aid. Language also presents a psychological barrier. This can readily be seen in societies where there are large numbers of immigrants or indigenous minority groups such as the Australian aboriginals or the Canadian native peoples, groups that are not immigrants but who do not speak the same language spoken in the legal system. Even for those people who do speak the national language, the legal system remains a mystery filled with legal jargon which is incomprehensible to the uninitiated.

Financial barriers, like physical obstacles, are readily distinguished. When a person is poor, when his disposable income – that portion of income that is not spent for purchasing the necessities of physical life – is very small, he is incapable of paying for legal service of any kind. Court fees and lawyers' fees are expensive, and no country has yet socialized the legal profession to the extent that money proves no obstacle.

Thus although the group characterized as the underprivileged does contain the poor, it is not merely lack of money that makes a person underprivileged as far as access to justice is concerned. Ignorance, fear, and language difficulties also operate in producing a segment of society which for one reason or another is not provided with legal services such as are taken for granted by the privileged segments of society. How then are these people to be guaranteed access to justice? Martin Friedland, dean of the Faculty of Law of the University of Toronto, surveyed the problem of access to justice in Canada. In *Access to Justice* (Toronto, 1975), a study which arose out of his work for the Law Reform Commission of Canada, he stated:

> One obvious method of giving citizens access to the law is through lawyers. But even if it were practical to do so, it is surely wrong in principle to preserve the law in a form that only lawyers can find and interpret. We should not require high priests to keep the law (p. 6).

Most countries have developed a set of formal and procedural guarantees where access to the courts is concerned. Formal guarantees are more often than not declarations, frequently constitutional, aimed at proclaiming the existence of a substantive equality among all classes. Yet formal guarantees do nothing more than lay the groundwork for those provisions which actually operate to provide equality – the procedural guarantees. Declaring a right does not ensure that it will operate, nor does any amount of repetition of the statement that all men are equal guarantee equality before the court if one party has a lawyer and the other does not, if one party speaks the language and the other does not. Procedural guarantees function to equalize the situation where it can be equalized. They do this by providing a right to have a lawyer, a right to be heard in one's own language, even by permitting litigation in the first place. In 1963, the

American Supreme Court pointed out:

> In the context of NAACP objectives, litigation is not a technique of resolving private differences; it is a means for achieving the lawful objectives of equality of treatment by all government, federal state and local, for the members of the Negro community in this country. It is thus a form of political expression. Groups which find themselves unable to achieve their objectives through the ballot frequently turn to the courts. Just as it was true of the opponents of New Deal legislation during the 1930's, for example, no less is it true of the Negro minority today. And under the conditions of modern government, litigation may well be the sole practicable avenue open to a minority to petition for redress of grievances (*NAACP* v. *Button*, 371 U.S. 415 (1963), 429–30).

The importance of equality, formal and procedural, is a result of the character of litigation itself. In most legal systems, civil litigation remains an adversarial contest before a passive judge, and handicapped parties make poor adversaries. Dean Friedland was referring to criminal law when, at the National Conference on Law and Poverty, he said:

> In the field of legal aid, the adversary system demands strong advocacy on both sides of the case, and therefore not having a lawyer prejudices the case of the accused.

This statement is, however, equally true in the context of civil litigation.

Formal and procedural guarantees can go a long way towards creating an artificial equality before the court, particularly when the procedural guarantees contain a right to the advice and assistance of counsel. Where the right to counsel is firmly entrenched, the state is forced to provide such counsel to those who are unable to afford legal services. Still, in many countries, there is a growing feeling that while litigation is one method of providing access to justice, other methods exist or should be developed. Again the statements of John Ayotte from the National Conference on Law and Poverty are worthy of consideration:

> As far as I am concerned, the judicial system is a protection racket for the lawyers. An individual cannot go to court without a lawyer if he really wants to win his case, unless it's something too minimal to even mention. I've seen myself, I've seen others appear before judges without lawyers and get sentenced. If someone goes with a lawyer, he gets off with a very light fine, or he gets off completely. The only reason there is a conviction in a case where there is no lawyer, is simply because there was not a lawyer to defend that person, not because a lawyer could have done a better job of defending but because there just wasn't a rip-off.

Although the essays in this collection emphasize access to the court system, it is important to recognize that the poor, who comprise approximately one-third of the world's population, need much more than access to lawyers and the legal system, and more than reform of civil procedure to allow them to become effective and potent members of their communities. Some writers would go further and state that lawyers are the last group in society upon whom the poor should rely. Stephen Chapman, in a recent article in *The New Republic* entitled "The Rich Get Rich, and the Poor Get Lawyers", stated:

> . . . there are better ways to ensure that the poor have ways of settling their disputes and protecting their rights, such as eliminating the numerous restrictions that prevent competition among lawyers. An even more substantial and far reaching answer is to avoid reforms that encourage litigation and to nurture those that help people to avoid it, like no-fault insurance, arbitration, and mediation (September 24, 1977, p. 9).

Any evaluation of the provision of legal services to the poor must recognize that most innovations to court systems to assist the poor have actually reinforced their dependency on lawyers and other professionals for assistance. The lawyer remains the interpreter of statutes, the dispenser of services, the negotiator and the articulate spokesman in court. The tenant or welfare recipient who receives legal services perceives any success as that of his counsel, and not his own. The client gains little knowledge, little self-confidence from the process, and he remains unconvinced that the legal system is responsive to his needs.

If the tenant or welfare recipient is assisted in representing himself or herself, he or she is left with an understanding of the administration of landlord and tenant legislation or of the relevant welfare provisions. He or she is also left with a recognition that there can be some control over destiny and a capacity to make the system respond. If the tenant is counselled by a community advocate from a similar background, a community of purpose is recognized that is often lacking even with the most humane and compassionate lawyer. The tenant and his community advocate may recognize that a number of citizens have similar problems and suffer from a comparable plight which may provoke them to create a tenants' association and to take collective action.

Lawyers create corporate structures to encourage the accumulation of capital and human resources. Lawyers in private practice have similarly recognized that law clerks, legal executives and paraprofessionals are able to handle many of the routine and repetitive tasks in the practice of a lawyer. Similarly there is a need to assist the non-lawyer to represent members of the low income community and to participate in the education and resource development of the low income communities. The need to find court-workers and advocates from within the community and reserve is being recognized by the Native Indian communities of Canada and the United States. These physically and emotionally isolated communities seek to resolve their individual and community problems by finding assistance from within, rather than asking or pleading for assistance from without.

The transient, the immigrant, the unemployed, the injured worker have unique and difficult legal problems. The legal profession has a limited understanding of the legal and social problems of the low income citizen. Advocates, counsellors, and animators are needed to assist the citizen confronted by a bureaucratic system.

Representation, knowledge, and preventive legal aid are the rights of every citizen. These can be generated from within rather than from outside the community, and by others than the aristocratic legal profession.

If the judicial system is unthinkable without lawyers, then other methods are available to solve grievances. Informal tribunals with active arbitrators instead of passive judges provide a conciliation method that involves fewer of the barriers that make access to the court system difficult for the underprivileged.

True access to justice is achieved only when no person is deterred by financial, psychological, or physical barriers from seeking a legal solution for the assertion of a right, for making a claim, or for defending a civil claim or criminal charge. While the ultimate realization of this goal may indeed be Utopian, it can be partially achieved by making the path to the court, the normal dispenser of justice, easier for the underprivileged, by ensuring equality before that court, or by creating new methods of dispute resolution that do not embody the inequalities inherent in the adversarial court structure.

The provision of legal services and access to justice is a problem with no single solution. Just as the problem varies with the socio-economic make-up of a society, the solution must be tailored to the individual needs of the society. Furthermore, there is seldom any one solution to a society's needs: often several methods must be tried and introduced into heterogeneous social groups.

It is our hope that this collection will provide interesting information, increased understanding, and will stimulate readers to consider the area of provision of legal services to the underprivileged and seek solutions which will make the promise of equality a reality.

Frederick H. Zemans, *Editor*
Paula B. Weiss, *Assistant Editor*

FILIP REYNTJENS

Africa — South of the Sahara

1. Introduction

Research material, especially empirical data, on legal aid, the legal profession, and access to jurisdictions and administration in Africa is rather scarce. Except for the work done by the International Legal Aid Association,[1] the International Legal Center[2] and the Center for African Legal Development,[3] hardly any research has been performed. Moreover, legal texts do not always reflect the actual implementation of a system; and the available material is soon out of date (and not updated, since in Africa legal publications are rare). The information flow is thus very limited, which makes a survey a rather difficult enterprise. Not only is there a lack of relevant and up-to-date information about existing legal aid provisions in the countries under survey, but comparisons of a financial and economic nature are equally difficult because of variations in populations, national wealth, economic conditions and currencies. Figures are soon out of date because of inflationary trends and the lack of supporting sociological data.[4] The problems with which we are here concerned are so intermingled with social attitudes, the formation of national elites, and policymaking that this report can only be a brief general outline of specific problems involved in providing legal aid in Africa.

2. The rationale for a legal aid system in Africa

Part of the rationale for providing legal services for the poor in the developing countries is much the same as the traditional threefold rationale put forward in Europe and North America:[5] first, that effective legal services to the indigent are essential to the proper functioning and integrity of the machinery of justice; secondly, that such services are demanded for humanitarian and charitable reasons; and thirdly, that all citizens must have equal access to information about the legal system and to expert advice and service. These issues are, of course, relevant to the developing countries, but there are also other dimensions to the rationale for providing legal services to the poor that are unique to those countries.[6] In addition to the traditional elements, services to the indigent in developing countries can also contribute to the creation of a unified national legal system (which, as will be seen, does not always favour a ready access to justice); to more effective implementation of existing social welfare and regulatory legislation intended to benefit the poor; to greater public accountability of the bureaucracy; to greater public participation in the governmental process; and to strengthening the legal profession.[7]

I would agree with Metzger[8] that, apart from these traditional rationales, even an effective legal services programme can contribute only marginally to eliminating the poverty of lower income groups and that its contribution is, rather, towards distributive justice – the non-discriminatory operation of institutions with which citizens deal; but it is, on the other hand, accepted that ineffective legal services constitute a serious obstacle to economic development.[9]

3. The specific setting in Africa

A number of specific circumstances influence the possibilities of providing legal aid in Africa.

The high number of indigents

According to Western economic standards, the poor in Africa comprise the vast majority of the population. Eighty-five to 95 per cent of all Africans live outside the money-economy in a subsistence agricultural food-crop economy. This implies that nearly all of the African population should be in a condition to benefit from free legal advice and assistance if available.

The limited financial means of African states

Even in developed countries, which arè – at least by developing nations' standards – wealthy, there is frequent criticism of the cost and the real impact of legal aid schemes. If developed countries consider the burden too heavy, how can developing countries (especially African ones, many amongst the poorest in the world) cope with such costs, given the fact that they have extremely limited means for achieving their priorities? Legal aid, furthermore, is not considered in developing countries as a vital priority, although many governments have recognized the need for legal aid provisions.

The small number of lawyers

In most African countries under survey, the number of trained lawyers is minuscule. West Africa is often considered to be an area where the legal profession is well established. In Ghana, for example, the legal profession started to function in an organized way soon after the Supreme Court Ordinance Act, 1876. There were 564 lawyers in 1970, a large figure by African standards, which yielded a 1-15,000 lawyer/population ratio for the country.[10] The Luckham study shows, however, that this relative surplus exists only for a limited kind of practice in a restricted number of urban areas.[11]

The picture is gloomier for other parts of Africa. A recent study of the administration of justice in Uganda, quoted by Dunning,[12] shows a figure of 161 lawyers engaged in private practice for a population of some nine million (lawyer/population ratio of about 1-56,000). Of these, 120 were Asian lawyers, many of whom have had to leave the country, thereby reducing the ratio to, perhaps, 1 to 150,000. By the end of 1975 there were eighty-one advocates registered on the Roll in Tanzania. Of these, only fifty-three were in private practice, and half of those were situated in Dar-es-Salaam. The population of Tanzania mainland is about 12 million; the lawyer/population ratio is 1-240,000.[13] There appears to be, furthermore, a clear correlation between the establishment of law offices and commercial and plantation activities.[14] The 1972 Law Directory shows ninety lawyers in practice in Zambia, all (except for a handful) holding offices in Lusaka, Kitwe or Ndola; none had offices off the "line of rail".[15] The country has an area of about 200,000 square kilometres and a population (in 1972) of nearly 4.5

million – a lawyer/population ratio of 1-50,000.

Uganda, Tanzania and Zambia are quite well off, however, if one considers the fact that a country like Rwanda had in 1975 only about fifteen lawyers in all – a ratio of 1-300,000. Only four of these performed some part-time private practice, which results in an appalling lawyer/population ratio of about 1-one million!

The legal profession is generally poorly organized (if organized at all), lawyers earn rather modest incomes, ethical standards of professional conduct are sometimes poor, the quality of professional advice rendered is low and the impact on society – even the wealthy sector – is small.

The problem is thus not just to decide how to allocate the services of a tiny group of professionals in a society where the poor constitute the vast bulk of the population[16] but also to examine the means by which legal access can be provided.

The disparity of jurisdictions

People are often removed from access to judges because of the size of the area the judges have to cover in countries with extremely bad communications. Some countries have made considerable effort to create many small local jurisdictions; for example, Rwanda has installed some 100 cantonnal courts (dealing mainly with customary matters as described below) for an area of not quite 27,000 square kilometres, as compared with thirty-one similar jurisdictions in Malagasy for an area of 590,000 square kilometres.[17] This obviously raises the problem of staffing these lower courts with competent and decently paid personnel. Some countries have therefore created the institution of the *juge unique*[18] (for example, Zaïre by Law Decree of July 10, 1966, and the Central African Empire by the Act No. 65/75 of December 23, 1965); others have created circuit sessions of jurisdictions of first instance (cf. Article 205 of the Criminal Code of Malagasy, the Act of December 9, 1964, in Benin (formerly Dahomey), and Act No. 9-63-AM of May 10, 1963 in Upper Volta).

Unification and professionalization of the law

Before independence (and for a number of African countries, after independence), two systems of law and administration of justice existed together: the indigenous laws applying only to indigenous people, and the introduced laws applying to the non-indigenous.[19] Customary law was, and to a large extent still is, the base of African legal systems. It has not been replaced successfully and will not be in the foreseeable future,[20] certainly not in areas such as land law, succession and marriage. These are precisely the areas with which the ordinary poor African is most concerned.

In a move towards modernization and development, the African leaders are pursuing a policy of unification at both the national and the international level in order to remove the existing pluralism in the legal system and in the substantive law.[21] Only a few countries are implementing a policy of legal pluralism in the application of the law.[22]

This trend towards clarification and rationalization, implying the restriction of customary law, further limits access to dispute settlement by the ordinary litigant. Many of the disabilities poor and illiterate people face in their encounters with justice stem from the complexity, lack of adaptation, and centralization of the law and the courts.[23] This is so for several reasons.

First, it has been suggested by many that a fundamental characteristic of customary law is its emphasis on reconciliation of litigants rather than the establishment of liability.[24] This characteristic, which prevents actual litigation where parties usually need to be represented, will probably be lost as the process of westernization continues. Secondly, customary law is usually well known by the people, although they do not always agree on its content. This uncertainty as to the content of customary law is damaging to the urban financial community but is not so serious for the majority of ordinary citizens' problems; it apparently does not prevent justice among the majority of the population involved in disputes dealt with by customary law rules. This law is also better known by the judges in rural areas, especially because many of them have had little formal legal training. The neglect and the purposeful assimilation or destruction of the customary law will inevitably result in failure to deal with the problems of the great masses in the countryside. The problem is thus not only one of knowledge of the principles of customary law but also of a ready access to dispute-settling bodies (hardly perceived as "courts" in the occidental sense of the word; "threshold-fear" is as yet unknown in a large part of Africa). Thirdly, the integration of occidental and customary systems will inevitably lead to the professionalization of the judiciary and to the necessity for assistance to litigants by the legal profession. Both forms of professionalization of the judicial process are the result of the importation of a foreign legal thought and system, and the ensuing complexity of law and procedure. The professionalization of the judiciary ("professionalization" here meaning that a law degree is required) implies both high costs, which most African countries cannot afford if they want to establish a number of small territorial jurisdictions, and the risk of a growing gap between judge and ordinary citizen. Perhaps even more disturbing is the professionalization of legal advice and assistance. A bar is a dangerous thing in a poor country, for its creation always leads to an eventual monopoly on representation of litigants.[25]

An integrated law and court system is not only much more difficult for an unrepresented individual to deal with,[26] but it also increases the need of the poor for professional legal advice and representation. It provides more opportunities for monopolizing trends in the legal profession, when it becomes stronger; and the smaller this profession is, the more stringent the monopoly. There are not enough lawyers to support this development, and neither the people nor the state could afford to pay for their services.

This monopolizing trend is illustrated, for example, in Rwanda. Article 82 of the Code of Civil Procedure states that anyone can represent a party in all stages of the procedure, if the representative is in possession of a simple power of attorney (which may even be delivered orally by the person he represents). The government is now, however, seriously considering the creation of a Bar (in a country which had in October 1977 forty-five lawyers in all), with a far-reaching monopoly of representation in justice – thus wiping out traditional customary forms of representation such as *Kuhagarikira* (to sustain)[27] on which article 82 of the Code is based. The effect will be to deny any form of legal assistance to the vast majority of the population.

4. Existing legal aid provisions in Africa

A study on legal aid in Africa by Barbara S. Newman[28] concludes rather optimistically that "this survey establishes the significant fact that legal aid in some form exists virtually throughout the continent". The fact may appear significant on paper, but the actual implementation of legal aid – which was beyond the scope of her work – appears to be another and rather more disappointing story.

Statutory provisions for legal aid

The Newman study attempts to outline the legal aid systems of thirty-one African countries as noted in statutes, enactments and information gathered by the International Legal Aid Association.

The first group of countries provide only limited legal aid and have no plan for free or reduced-cost legal advice or assistance. These countries are Rwanda, Kenya, Namibia (formerly South West Africa), Sudan, Nigeria, Rhodesia and Swaziland; this group includes so-called rich and poor countries alike. Exemption of court fees is, however, possible in Rwanda, Namibia, Nigeria and Rhodesia. In some of these countries a lawyer can be appointed to act *pro deo* in criminal cases on a capital charge (Namibia, Sudan, Nigeria, Swaziland). In Namibia, Rhodesia and Swaziland, actions can be filed *in forma pauperis* in civil proceedings. Finally, in exceptional circumstances, the Law Society of Kenya can ask lawyers to represent poor persons. If a lawyer is provided, he is normally not entitled to remuneration, except in Sudan, and under certain limited circumstances in Rhodesia and Swaziland.

A second group provides legal aid only in criminal proceedings. These countries are Botswana, Gambia, Ghana, Liberia and West Cameroon. The assistance is provided in criminal proceedings in all courts in Botswana and Liberia. It is offered only to persons accused of capital offences in Gambia, Ghana and West Cameroon. If indigence of the accused is proven or reasonably assumed, the assigned lawyer receives a fee out of public funds in Botswana, Ghana and Liberia.

In a third group of African countries extensive legal aid programmes exist for civil and criminal cases, but no legal advice is offered. These countries include Angola, Burundi, East Cameroon, Ivory Coast, Malagasy, Malawi, Mali,[29] Mauritania, Mozambique, Niger, Senegal and Zambia. All these countries require proof of insufficient means for a litigant to obtain the services of a lawyer and to be relieved of payment of legal costs. This proof consists mostly of a certificate of indigence issued by a municipal or governmental authority, or an extract from the applicant's tax returns (or a certification of exemption from tax). Some of these countries (Ivory Coast, Malawi, Mali, East Cameroon, Mauritania, Niger and Senegal) require, moreover, that it must seem just to grant legal aid, or that the applicant has a *prima facie* cause of action or defence, which sometimes requires that the particulars of the other party's case must also be submitted (e.g. in Mauritania, Niger and Senegal).

The lawyer assigned serves without remuneration in Angola, Burundi, East Cameroon and Mozambique. He is paid in any case out of government funds in Malawi and Zambia. He receives a fee only if the assisted person is successful in the Ivory Coast, Mauritania, Niger and Senegal. Information on whether the lawyer receives payment is lacking for Malagasy.

The fourth group of African countries provides not only legal aid in civil and criminal proceedings, but also free legal advice prior to any court action. These are the Central African Empire, Benin (formerly Dahomey), Gabon, Mali,[30] Zaïre, Tanzania, Togo and Uganda. For both advice and representation, the applicant must show inadequate means, except in the Central African Empire, Benin, Mali, Togo and Uganda, where a lawyer will be appointed for the criminally accused regardless of his financial means. This provision applies only for very serious offences such as murder, manslaughter and rape. As far as proceedings are concerned, a number of countries (Benin, Gabon and Zaïre) again require that a good cause of action or defence be shown in addition to financial need. The assigned lawyer works without remuneration in the Central African Empire, Zaïre, Togo, Tanzania and Uganda (although for Tanzania the Legal Aid Act No. 21/69 provides that remuneration of the lawyer is determined by the presiding judge and shall be paid out of the general revenue). Mali's government pays the fee of the advising or assisting lawyer. And again, in Benin and Gabon, the lawyer may recover his fee in a civil case only if the assisted litigant is successful. It should be noted that legal advice and assistance in civil cases in Tanzania are made available only through the Tanzania Law Society, and for the capital city of Dar-es-Salaam only, which again stresses the gap between urban and rural areas.

Tables 1 and 2 give a schematic survey of legal aid provisions in criminal and civil cases as appearing in texts, not – *repetitio magister discipulorum* – in reality.[31] It should be stressed that these data are pre-1970 (taken from the International Legal Aid Directory).

The Newman study attempts to summarize in a few pages the systems of thirty-one countries. Such an approach is often superficial, and like statistics they can mean anything or nothing without supporting information. I cannot agree with the conclusion that legal aid in some form exists virtually throughout the continent. Akiwumi and Eshetu, in their *Report on Legal Aid in English-Speaking Africa*,[32] state that it appears that in almost every English-speaking African country the concept of justice as a public service has not been recognized either in legal texts or in practice. A. Boni, President of the Supreme Court of Ivory Coast, stresses the same point several times in his report for the same conference,[33] as did Ramangasoavina in an earlier paper.[34] A study of the administration of justice in Uganda, which is listed in the Newman survey as one of the African countries providing free legal aid and advice prior to any court action, suggests the impossibility for anything close to observance of this

Table 1
Criminal Proceedings

Country	*Aid available to*	*Nature of Aid*	*Financial provisions*	*Provided by*
Angola	nationals, resident and non-resident foreigners, stateless persons	all steps prior to proceedings, preparation of case, representation at proceedings, in all courts, in special courts, on appeal	court fees: all disbursements, fees, expenses; costs of expert witnesses	government: lawyers in form of free service
Benin (formerly: Dahomey)	nationals	same as Angola	same as Angola, but repayment to treasury may be required	government: lawyers in form of free or reduced-cost service
Botswana	same as Angola	preparation of case, representation at proceedings; only in proceedings where accused is charged with capital offense; available in all courts with jurisdiction to try capital cases; not available in special courts; available on appeal	court fees	same as Angola
Burundi	same as Angola	same as Angola	same as Angola	same as Angola
Central African Empire (C.A.E.)	same as Angola plus persons in other than individual capacity	same as Angola	same as Angola	same as Angola
Chad	same as C.A.E.	same as Angola	same as Angola	same as Angola
East Cameroon	same as Angola	preparation of case and representation only in supreme and assize courts; in all proceedings in supreme and assize courts; available in military courts but no other special courts; available on appeal		
Federation of Nigeria	same as Angola	in preparation of case where accused is charged with murder; an accused committed for trial upon an order of commital receives free copy of disposition; representation at proceedings; in assize courts and on appeal to supreme court; on appeals	court fees, all necessary disbursements	government
Gabon	same as C.A.E.	same as Angola	same as Angola	same as Angola

Table 1 continued

Gambia	same as Angola	all steps prior to court proceedings; in preparation of case; only before supreme court, court of appeals, privy council; on appeal	same as Angola, plus lawyers' fees in some cases	same as Benin
Ghana	same as Angola	preparation of case; representation at proceedings; only in high and supreme courts; on appeals; in practice, available only to one accused of murder	same as Angola, plus lawyers' fees	government
Ivory Coast	nationals	same as Angola	same as Ghana	government
Lesotho	nationals	preparation of case; representation at proceedings; only in cases where accused is charged with murder; in high court and court of appeals; on appeals	same as Ghana	government
Liberia	same as Angola	preparation of case; representation at proceedings; in all proceedings, in all courts with jurisdiction; in special courts; on appeal	same as Ghana	government
Malagasy	same as Angola	same as Angola	same as Angola	government
Malawi	same as C.A.E.	preparation of case; representation at proceedings; only in resident magistrate and high courts; available on appeal but only in certain criminal areas	same as Ghana	government
Mali	nationals	same as Angola	same as Angola	government
Mauritania	nationals	same as Angola	same as Benin	same as Benin
Mozambique	same as Angola	same as Angola, except for special courts	same as Angola	same as Angola
Niger	nationals	same as Angola	same as Benin	same as Benin
Rhodesia	same as Angola	preparation of case; representation at proceedings; available in high court and magistrate's court, but seldom granted in the latter	same as Ghana, but subject to approval of registrar of high court	same as Benin
Senegal	nationals	same as Angola	same as Benin	same as Benin
Sudan	nationals, resident and nonresident foreigners	same as Botswana, except available also in special courts	same as Benin	same as Benin
Swaziland	same as Angola	same as Botswana	same as Ghana	same as Benin
Togo	same as C.A.E.	same as Angola	same as Angola	same as Angola
Uganda	same as Angola	preparation of case; representation at proceedings; available only to those charged with murder, manslaughter, rape; only in high court or court of appeals; on appeal	no court fees in criminal cases; lawyers' fees	government
West Cameroon	same as Angola	same as Botswana, but available also in military courts	lawyers' fees	same as Benin
Zaire	same as C.A.E.	same as Angola	same as Angola	same as Angola
Zambia	same as Angola	same as Angola, except not in native courts	same as Ghana	same as Benin

Table 2
Civil Proceedings

Country	*Aid available to*	*Nature of Aid*	*Financial Provisions*	*Provided by*
Angola	nationals	all steps prior to proceedings in preparation of case, representation at proceedings; legal aid available in all proceedings, in all courts, in special courts, on appeal	court fees, all necessary disbursements, fees, expenses, costs of expert witnesses	government; lawyers in form of free services
Benin (formerly: Dahomey)	nationals, persons in other than individual capacity–only to public corporations or private organizations possessing legal personality whose purpose is charitable	same as Angola, plus aid available to enforce court decisions obtained with or without legal aid	same as Antola, but assisted may be required to repay such to treasury	government by temporary relief from costs; lawyers in form of free or reduced services; moneys recovered by those assisted in proceedings
Burundi	nationals, resident and nonresident foreigners, stateless persons	same as Angola		
Central African Empire (C.A.E.)	nationals, resident and nonresident foreigners, stateless persons, persons in other than individual capacities	same as Antola except aid not available in arbitration cases	same as Angola	same as Angola
Chad	same as C.A.E.	same as C.A.E.	same as Angola, plus no lawyer fee	same as Angola
East Cameroon	same as C.A.E.	preparation of case only in federal and supreme courts; representation at proceedings only in federal and supreme Courts; available in all but customary courts; available in no special courts other than administrative tribunals or military courts; available on appeal	same as Angola, but in supreme court some fees are payable by assisted person	same as Angola, plus monies recovered by assisted person in proceedings

Table 2 *continued*

Federation of Nigeria	same as C.A.E.	available in all proceedings, in all courts, in special courts, on appeal	exemption from court fees and other procedural expenses	same as East Cameroon
Gabon	same as C.A.E.	same as C.A.E.	same as Angola	same as Angola
Ivory Coast	same as Benin	same as Benin	same as Benin	same as Benin
Malagasy	same as Burundi	same as Angola	same as Chad	same as East Cameroon
Malawi	same as C.A.E.	same as Angola, but available only in resident magistrates' courts or high court	same as Chad	government; contribution from assisted person
Mali	nationals	same as Angola	same as Chad	government
Mauritania	same as Benin	same as Benin	same as Benin	same as Benin
Mozambique	same as Burundi	same as Angola, except not available in special courts	same as Angola	same as Angola
Niger	same as Benin	same as Benin	same as Benin	same as East Cameroon
Rhodesia	nationals, resident foreigners, stateless persons only if resident	same as Angola except available only in high court or magistrate court	court fees	government to extent that fees are remitted; lawyers by free services
Senegal	same as Benin	same as Benin	same as Benin	same as Angola
Swaziland	same as C.A.E.	same as Mozambique	court fees	same as Angola, but lawyer may recover fee from opponent of the pauper
Tanzania	same as C.A.E.	same as Angola	same as Angola, but assisted may have to make contribution	same as East Cameroon
Togo	same as C.A.E.	same as Angola	same as Angola	same as East Cameroon
Uganda	same as Burundi	same as Angola	None	same as East Cameroon, plus contributions from aided person
Zaire	same as C.A.E.	same as C.A.E.	same as Angola	same as Angola

norm, asserting that each year in the courts there are considerably more cases tried than there are lawyers actively engaged in private practice.[35] And that was before the hasty departure of the Asian lawyers!

In short, the situation of legal aid and advice in Africa is not as optimistic as the Newman survey suggests, at least as far as actual implementation is concerned. I shall therefore examine a few countries more closely (one in every group of the Newman survey) in order to assess the actual working of systems, and perhaps draw some lessons out of these experiences.

5. The Implementation of legal assistance in four African countries

Rwanda

Rwanda is classified in the Newman study among the first (worst) group of countries which provide only limited legal aid. It is asserted that Rwanda has no plan for free or reduced-cost legal advice or for legal aid in either civil adjudications or criminal proceedings. Rwanda, however, actually has quite a good legal aid system.

First, article 380 of the Code of Civil Procedure provides that the indigent party can be completely or partially exempted from procedural costs. The president of the jurisdiction establishes the fact of indigence and, in the case of a refusal of exemption from costs, a free appeal to a superior jurisdiction is available.

Secondly, Article 82 of the same code establishes (in line with the already mentioned traditional form of representation of Kuhagarikira) that a party may be represented or assisted in all courts by any agent, whose authority is established through a simple declaration by the represented party at the audience or in written form.

Thirdly, in every tribunal of first instance (of which ten exist, i.e. 1 for every 450,000 inhabitants), an *auditeur des requêtes* (auditor of petitions) is established, who plays a major role. He has several functions:

- He is entitled to receive all petitions on simple request (it is not necessary in Rwanda to serve a writ in order to summon the defendant).
- He helps people to formulate their demands or defenses in legal terms. If both parties come to him to ask what should be done, he may propose a conciliatory solution. If only one party appears, he usually asks the other to come to his office to determine what steps should be taken.

- If litigation seems inevitable, he indicates the procedural steps to follow.
- He advises parties on their chances of success in appealing a decision. If they decide to appeal, he indicates how to do so.
- He is even entitled, according to article 81 of the code and with the permission of the Minister of Justice, to represent parties "when they are incapable of defending themselves or to be represented otherwise." It should be added, however, that this permission has not been given since 1973 (the year of the military coup).

The importance of the auditor of petitions is thus obvious. In 1976, for instance, the tribunal of first instance of Butare, the country's second largest town, issued judgments on an average of forty civil and criminal cases per month; the auditor did the introductory work for one or both parties in half of the cases. The auditor advises an average of twenty people a day at his consultations. Of these twenty, only one in every five starts a procedure in the strict sense of the word. He thus not only performs a pre-trial role, but is an important informal conflict-solver as well, principally because of his power to convene both parties at his office in informal circumstances.

Fourthly, procedural forms are extremely limited and simple (I have already mentioned earlier that a party can be summoned to court by a simple request or petition or even orally), and judges tend to play a rather active role in the process, especially if one or both parties are unrepresented.

In conclusion, I submit that in Rwanda, although no "classic" legal aid scheme exist, the need for advice and assistance has been met in a rather effective way.

Ghana

Ghana is listed in the Newman study under group 2 (countries providing legal aid only in criminal proceedings). But even in criminal proceedings, the availability of legal aid is very limited. Statutory provisions entitle indigent persons to free legal aid under a scheme administered by the courts themselves; in practice aid is available only for the most serious criminal offences involving capital charges. If the aid is granted, the presiding judge assigns a lawyer who receives a fee out of public funds. This fee is, however, so modest that it is usually only attractive to young lawyers still striving to establish a practice.[36] Thus, not only are few people eligible for legal aid, but the number and the quality of lawyers prepared to work under this scheme is limited, diminshing even further the scope of actual legal aid. The contradiction between the ideal of free and equal treatment before the law and the unavailability of legal remedies to the poor and illiterate has been examined several times.[37]

The result is that legal aid in the statutory scheme is partially replaced by other methods by which practitioners can make their services available to those who could not otherwise afford them. Lawyers in Ghana tend to offer their services free of charge to those who appear to be in need of them. Table 3 shows that more cases are handled under this informal scheme than under assigned briefs in the legal aid scheme. One must note, however, that it is likely that lawyers may have overestimated the time they spent on purely charitable work.[38] The table shows, furthermore, that it is the less-experienced practitioners who tend in general to provide assistance and advice to the needy. A third way for lawyers to

Table 3[39]

Ghana – Proportion of lawyers' time spent on assigned briefs and free services to poor litigants

	None	*Up to 10%*	*10%–20%*	*More than 20%*
1 *All lawyers*				
(a) Assigned briefs	69,2	15,9	15,0	–
(b) Free Services	17,8	37,4	25,2	19,6
(c) Assigned briefs plus free services	14,0	31,6	26,3	28,1
2 *Lawyers who enrolled up to 1960*				
Assigned briefs plus free services	26,3	36,8	21,1	15,8
3 *Lawyers who enrolled 1961–70*				
Assigned briefs plus free services	9,5	31,0	27,4	32,1

offer some relief to indigent parties, described in the Luckham study, is to take cases on a contingency fee basis, charging clients only nominal consultation fees, and recovering from the proceeds of the successful claim or litigation. It is obvious that this arrangement is almost entirely confined to civil injury cases, but it makes the services of a lawyer – at least as far as these claims are concerned – more readily available to persons of modest means.[40]

It appears clear from this survey that, even in the restricted area where statutory provision regulate legal aid, other, more informal, procedures have developed to fill a small part of the gap between theory and reality.

It must be noted that in Ghana, as in Rwanda, members of the judiciary tend to redress the balance against unrepresented litigants, that problems of the poor are partly taken over by the resources of the extended African family, and that in the lower courts there is relatively little need of counsel. But given the fact that Ghana is not only a comparatively rich African country but that it has also (by African standards) a very good lawyer-population ratio (1-15,000 in 1970), the statutory legal aid scheme appears to be very inadequate, and, in fact, almost non-existent in practice. The growing complexity, centralization and formalization of the law and the courts increase the problem.

Zambia[41]

Zambia is classified in the third group of the Newman study – those countries providing extensive legal aid systems for both civil and criminal cases. The construction of the system is indeed a good one. Under previous experiments with more restricted legal aid schemes (Poor Prisoners Defence Ordinance, 1945, and the Poor Persons Defence Ordinance, 1957), the court decided whether or not to grant legal aid. If the answer was positive, the Law Society allocated the case to a practitioner on a list of those lawyers willing to handle legal aid cases against payment out of public funds.

The 1964 constitution laid down explicitly the principle of the right to legal representation. Accordingly, the 1967 Legal Aid Act (C. 546) set up a new system with a separate department of lawyers to provide legal aid. Because legal aid had not been readily available under the previous schemes, the government tried to ensure easier access, not only by creating this team of lawyers specially employed for the purpose, but also by providing that civil as well as criminal matters would be handled; by making the issuance of a legal aid certificate for poor people mandatory in a number of specified offences; and by enabling the applicant to apply for assistance directly to the Director of Legal Aid, as well as to the courts. The Director of Legal Aid has a number of legal aid counsel and legal aid assistants, all of whom are civil servants of the Ministry of Legal Affairs.

To ensure the access of the ordinary citizen in the villages to the services provided, legal aid committtees for every district of the country have been established. In 1972, the Legal Aid Department consisted of the Director, two senior legal aid counsel and eight legal aid counsel with six legal aid assistants (who were untrained). It is important to stress two points here: first, that this number of lawyers involved in legal aid is insufficient to cope with cases in such a large territory and such a great population, although a considerable number of cases are handled; and second, that much of the effective service is possible only through appointment of students of the Law Practice Institute, founded in 1968 to give a one-year postgraduate course to university law graduates seeking admission as practitioners. The students, as learner legal practitioners in the civil service, serve part of their time as legal aid assistants in the Legal Aid Department.

Table 4[43]

Zambia – Operating statistics of the Legal Aid Department, 1970

Criminal Cases	*Applications*	*Approved*
High Court		
Homicide	259	259
Other offences	185	185
Subordinate Courts		
Specified offences	340	340
Non-specified offences	162	136
Appeals to the High Court and Court of Appeal	490	116
Total	**1,436**	**1,036**

Civil Cases	*Applications*	*Investigations*	*Proceedings*
Fatal Accidents	63	42	21
Personal injuries	87	50	37
Employment	132	57	75
Other contracts	117	60	57
Divorce, affiliation	73	49	30
Other matters	151	90	54
Total	**623**	**348**	**274**

This programme of involving students in a clinical legal programme is extremely important in all countries suffering from a serious shortage of lawyers.

In criminal proceedings, a person who has insufficient means to engage legal assistance may apply for legal aid. The court must grant a legal certificate to a person committed by a subordinate court for trial by the High Court, and to a person charged before a subordinate court with certain specified offences such as rape, arson, forgery and rioting. In the case of other offences, the court has discretion to issue a certificate. When the court does issue a certificate, the Director of Legal Aid is obliged to provide legal aid; in any event, a person may apply directly to the Director, who has discretion to issue the certificate.

In civil proceedings, applications are not made to the court but to the Director or to a legal aid committee. The Director has discretion to grant legal aid; in practice, he first decides whether the applicant has a good chance of success in his cause of action or defence. The Director may even invite a person to apply for legal aid. If legal aid is to be granted, the Director assesses the means of the applicant and decides on the amount of the contribution necessary.

Table 5[44]

Zambia – Comparison of High Court cases taken by private practitioners and by Legal Aid, 1970–72

	1970	*1971*	*1972**
Total number of cases	1,379	1,314	954
Plaintiff legally represented	1,272	1,253	943
Plaintiff legally represented by private practitioner	1,239	1,210	912
Plaintiff legally represented by Legal Aid Department	33	43	31
Defendant legally represented	587	482	176
Defendant legally represented by private practitioner	575	470	164
Defendant legally represented by Legal Aid Department	12	12	12

*Note: Table includes civil cases only, excluding divorce proceedings through November 6, 1972.

De Mornay Davies's report, from which most of the data are taken, mentions also the interesting point of the costs involved in this rather extensive legal aid system. In 1971, out of a total national budget of $635 million (U.S.), $15 million (U.S.) was spent on social welfare, of which $145,700 was for legal aid. For the same year, the comparable figure for legal aid in Great Britain was $4 million (U.S.).[42]

As far as the actual operation of the system is concerned, the following tables show that the provisions have at least a quantitatively serious impact and that the great majority of applications (about 72 per cent) is approved (Table 4); but on the other hand, the parties represented under the legal aid scheme remain a tiny minority of all legally represented parties in the High Court (Table 5).

Tanzania

Although the Newman study listed Tanzania as a country providing free legal advice prior to any court action as well as legal aid in criminal and civil proceedings, legal aid here is "in a rudimentary state of development."[45]

Legal aid in criminal cases is administered by the courts. The Legal Aid (Criminal Proceedings) Act No. 21 of 1969 has extended the availability of legal aid considerably, compared with the previous scheme (under the 1936 statute, legal aid was, in practice, only available to those accused of murder before the High Court), to include all proceedings except those before a primary court. Apparently, however, regulations to implement this new legislation have not been promulgated.[46]

Matters are even worse, perhaps, in civil cases, where advice and assistance are available only through a plan organized by the Tanzania Law Society in 1962 and only effective in the capital city of Dar-es-Salaam. The system depends upon the voluntary participation of lawyers in private practice, who serve without remuneration. The deficiency of the plan is illustrated by the fact that despite steadily increasing applications in 1969 only sixty-three cases were handled under the Tanzania Law Society's programme.[47]

The role of the Tanzanian ombudsman as "poor man's lawyer and court" should be emphasized. The Permanent Commission of Inquiry, as the ombudsman's office is officially called, was established in 1966 to protect citizens against arbitrary or unfair exercise of executive power, given the creation of a one-party state. It was quickly observed, however, that the commission was doing more than what a *conseil d'état* or an ombudsman usually does. The commission has the power to require explanations from a court for delays in hearing suits and appeals, and to investigate why a court took no action; it can then take the appropriate steps to expedite the hearing. Because most people in Tanzania handle their cases without legal assistance, the commission thus acts as a "poor man's lawyer." The commission also provides an avenue for redress of grievances (at public expense) against the administration. Although these cases (such as a refusal to issue a licence, false imprisonment, and interference with individual property) could have been dealt with by the ordinary courts, most of them were brought before the commission, which acted thus not just as a poor man's lawyer, but as a poor man's court as well.[48]

6. The future for legal aid in Africa

A well-organized legal assistance and legal aid scheme of the classic Western type requires a number of conditions: a relatively small number of indigent people; a well-organized legal profession with a great number of members and a considerable impact on policy-making; a highly productive economy resulting in a high national income; a well-established tradition of a constitutionally strong judiciary – independent, respected by the executive, and bound by due process of law; and a tradition of social welfare and justice as a public social service. Even where these conditions exist (as they do in Europe), legal aid schemes face permanent criticism from both the concerned population and the legal profession. None of these conditions is present in Africa today.[49] It seems unrealistic to propose Western-style legal aid provisions, which would only serve a tiny fraction of the hundreds of millions of needy. A far more interesting and efficient approach would be to examine how the need for legal resources can be minimized by making the legal system easier to use for those without professional representation. A small-scale scheme for the provision of legal aid in the cases which require it should complement such an approach.

Before examining ways of achieving that goal, however, I should stress that we know too little about the legal needs of the mass of people in Africa, particularly if one defines legal needs in broad terms to include needs for intermediaries to deal with a wide range of government agencies and officials. We also know very little about the impact of continued modernization and professionalization of the court system. This social estrangement from the legal system may create new kinds of needs for social services.[50] These aspects of the problem should be examined in order to attain a more effective view on the subject covered here.

The active role of the judge

The (mainly French) European tradition, imported to Africa, decrees that initiation of the procedure lies with the parties. Some African countries have, since independence, considerably altered the passive role of the judge to that of an active participant directing the proceedings.

The degree of the judge's participation in the procedure depends on whether one considers that only the parties are concerned with the process, or that the application of justice is a fundamental responsibility of the state.[51] Even in France, notwithstanding its liberal tradition, greater judicial participation of the judge has evolved, in the interests of the parties, through the institution of the *juge chargé de suivre la procédure.*[52] In Algeria, the preparation of a case is now done by the judge, who is responsible for establishing the facts in the case.[53] This movement towards a more inquisitorial system and away from a system that allows the parties or their lawyers to direct the procedure is found in a number of mainly French-speaking African states, making justice quicker, cheaper and more accessible to unrepresented litigants.[54] It has sometimes been argued[55] that the quality of justice suffers from such an approach, but recent legal theory has advocated this approach, starting from the premise that the judge's task is not just the application of legal norms, but that he also has a creative role in the formation of the law. The American and Scandinavian realist movement, sociological jurisprudence, Josef Esser in Germany, the Dutch "Functional Jurisprudence", and Van Gerven and Storme in Belgium, among others, have also expressed this view.[56]

The active role of the judge also opens the possibility of conciliation in court. In Malagasy, for example, the judge has the power either on his own initiative or upon demand of a party to try to reconcile the parties.[57] In some countries special jurisdictions for conciliation have been created, for example in the Central African Empire, where the customary chiefs have retained this power.[58] In Benin, *les tribunaux de conciliation* assume this task[59] and in Guinea, so-called *tribunaux populaires* have been created.[60] In Mauritania, a judge on circuit may on his own initiative institute preliminary investigations on any matter. This tendency in some countries to confer wide investigatory powers upon the judge obviously facilitates access to justice by unrepresented parties. But although the usefulness of this trend is widely acknowledged, in practice most African countries continue the trend towards complexity, thrust upon them by what they consider to be the demands of modern life.[61]

Simplification of procedure and availability of jurisdictions

The judge can only play an active and direct role if the parties have found their way to the legal forum. It is therefore also necessary to simplify procedural forms and to create more jurisdictions, each covering a smaller area. In some of the countries under survey, court procedures have been considerably simplified compared with the metropolitan systems which served as models, resulting in shorter delays and reduction of procedural requirements. Thus, for example, a litigant can summon the opponent party by a simple written or oral request or statement before the clerk of the court (or before a specially instituted agent like the auditor of petitions in Rwanda; see *supra*) or even by simple appearance in court. This tendency, however, seems to exist only in francophone Africa (Algeria, Malagasy, Rwanda, Mali, Guinea, and Burundi). I have already mentioned earlier that widespread geographical distribution of jurisdictions is essential for ready access, especially in large countries with difficult communications. Measures such as the institution of the sole judge; the creation of small basic jurisdictions, not necessarily staffed with (qualified) lawyers, having jurisdiction in petty offences and small (mostly customary) civil matters and possessing extensive conciliatory and investigatory powers; and the organization of circuit sessions would not only enable people to get in touch more readily with the judicial agencies, but would also ensure better knowledge by the judge of the local customs, local circumstances, and the language of the area. I also believe that representation of litigants should not be allowed in these lower, mainly customary, courts, staffed by non-lawyers.

The legal profession

An eminent African magistrate[68] has expressed his astonishment at the fact that the attainment of judicial office does not, in African countries, require the possession of a law degree, whereas the possession of a university law degree has always been a prerequisite for admission to the legal profession, sometimes (as in Zambia) including a period of practical training. The effect of the monopoly of the legal profession, where it exists, is obviously more pronounced if the number of its members is small. The concern of the profession to limit access and to strengthen its monopoly should not prevent its growth and the maintenance of standards and integrity.

It is not certain that incorporating all lawyers into the civil service (as was done in Guinea) and assigning them to cases as required, at public expense, provides a solution. Such a measure takes away some of the stringency of the monopoly, but it raises another problem: that of the independence of these "civil servant lawyers" *vis-à-vis* the government, especially in actions brought against the state and in criminal matters.[63] Even when the need for legal resources is minimized as much as possible, legal advice and assistance by professionals or paraprofessionals will always be indispensable, and perhaps increasingly needed at least for a certain kind of litigation in the modern sector. This brings us to the question of financing these provisions and of the contribution of university-based legal clinical programmes.

Financing legal aid

There are several possible sources for the financing of legal services for the poor.[63]

(a) Traditional formal sources

Government sources: the government is the major source of finance for legal aid in most developed countries; the poorer the country is, the less effective is this service. The costs involved in a completely government-financed scheme are almost unbearable for underdeveloped countries, which assign a low priority to legal aid in any case. The limited extent of government support in developing countries is illustrated by the figure for Zambia (a country doing much in the area of legal aid, according to African standards) mentioned earlier: $145,700 (U.S.) for 1971, out of a total budget of $635 million (U.S.) (i.e., 0.02 per cent).

Non-government sources, such as charities and the legal profession: for example, New York lawyers provided over $400,000 (U.S.) to the New York Legal Aid Society in 1971. Moreover, the extent of the legal profession's undertaking of work without fee is unknown. This practice, accepted in Western countries as a traditional obligation attached to the right to practice, exists also in Africa (cf. my description of Ghana), but its scope is bound to be extremely limited, given the low number of lawyers engaged in private practice and their relative poverty.

(b) Novel existing sources

These are considered in the Purcell memo as being examples of previously untapped sources of funds.

Trade-union-provided legal aid: given the poor organizational state of the unions in Africa and the low number of employees, this source is as yet unused in Africa, but it may represent interesting opportunities in the future.

Group legal services, consisting of groups of people joined for the purpose of obtaining access to the courts. In the sense that these services incorporate a more or less formal method of collecting contributions for the defence of the members of the group, this principle might have some relevance in the context of developing countries, for instance within a co-operative, a village or an enterprise. It is in line with the traditional solidarity of a collectivity (extended family, village) in Africa.

Suitor's fund: this is a fund established to provide a source from which litigants can recover their costs in certain situations. For example, legislation can require that a sum of, for example, 10 per cent of all court fees to be collected by the state and paid to the fund. Another possibility is offered in Burundi and Rwanda. The Code of Civil Procedure (Burundi: Article 114; Rwanda: Article 383) provides that a proportional duty of 4 per cent is to be paid by the unsuccessful party to the state on every monetary judgment. It would be conceivable to pay, for example, one per cent of this proportional duty into a suitor's fund or into a more general legal aid fund.

(c) Potential sources of finance, as suggested by Purcell

The legal profession in developing countries is, as pointed out earlier, unlikely to be capable of making any significant contribution towards funding legal services by voluntary donations. There are, however, a number of ways in which the profession can be required to make a contribution, including the obligation to undertake legal aid work on a rotating basis as a condition of continuing practice (for example, assigning a few days per month for doing free legal aid work); the imposition of a fee on the issuance of practising certificates, to be paid into a legal aid fund (which would, however, given the small legal professions in these countries, not necessarily amount to a great deal); and the payment of fixed percentages of costs recovered from the other party into the fund.

Legal institutions (meaning here courts and government agencies) may levy a small charge on all court fees, on fines and penalties imposed by the courts, on administrative stamp duties or fees, on applications for licences, and so on. This would affect only the relatively wealthy part of the population.

Employers and other institutions and groups making available the services of lawyers to workers and members. It would be possible, for example, to demand that amongst employee benefits provided, the company should ensure that some legal services are made available.

It should be noted that the practice of waiving the payment of court fees and costs, which already exists in a number of African countries, must be generalized; it provides substantial relief at relatively low costs.

Any one of these devices is unlikely to produce adequate amounts to fund a legal aid scheme, but collectively the services may at least contribute to it.

University-based clinical legal aid programmes

Although it would appear that the best legal aid system for Africa would be one that minimized the need for formal legal procedures, it is necessary to mention a source of legal advice and assistance to indigent litigants: the law faculties. One must, given the African situation, put aside any vision of large-scale provision of professional legal services for the poor as financially unfeasible and incompatible with the acute need in the decades to come to use many African lawyers for other purposes.[65] An option might be to initiate legal aid programmes as a part of legal education.

Clinical legal programmes can provide mutually reinforcing benefits for participating law students, for the clinical legal schemes in which they work, and for the law school at which they study.[66] I shall emphasize in this context the contribution of such programmes to legal assistance, although the other aspects are important as well. Experience in a limited number of countries indicates that law students can assume a responsible role and make a significant contribution to the success of legal aid schemes. Students represent a cheap source of manpower, which in the presence of proper supervision reaches a standard at least equal to that of young qualified lawyers. They can do a great deal of preparatory work, and the responsibility conferred upon them makes them feel that no effort for the client is too great. They take considerable time to prepare a case, and they develop a deep appreciation of the importance of legal aid activities as well as a sense of personal responsibility.[67] The well-supervised use of law students will significantly ease the limitations under which most of the legal aid programmes in Africa now have to work; it is only through student programmes that there is any possibility in the near future for legal services becoming widely available to the poor.[68] In describing the Zambian system, I have already stressed the indispensable contribution the students of the Law Practice Institute make to the implementation of the existing legal aid scheme.[69] It is obvious that student participation reaches its greatest efficiency where students are entitled to appear in court and to represent litigants.[70]

One problem among many which I should finally mention here is the location of the universities: they have to serve – especially in developing countries – even much greater areas than jurisdictions and lawyers. A law faculty-population ratio is always 1 to several millions of people, since most African countries have but one faculty of law (if they are lucky enough to have even one). Law students might be sent into the country as a practical exercise as part of their curriculum; another solution might be to oblige all law students to act as legal aid advisers after their final year of study anywhere in the country before they can obtain their degrees. This would provide a relatively large number of widespread and qualified legal aid manpower, costing only the amount of the students' scholarships. The African countries are surely entitled to this free service of their new "elite", as they have financed their education.

7. Conclusion

I have stressed in this paper that none of the conditions for a successful legal advice and assistance system exists in Africa today. Some small-scale provisions may be developed and some financial means may be found to implement these, but I would suggest that the remedies for equal access to jurisdictions and for a relatively good distributive justice may be found elsewhere: deformalization (or rather, non-formalization) of the law and the courts; an active role for the judges; a readier access to the legal profession; a widespread distribution of easy-to-reach jurisdictions; avoidance of professionalization of the judiciary and representation in justice, except for the modern westernized segment of society; a selective use of law students and other extra-governmental resources; the preservation of some traditional dispute-settlement techniques and of customary law in matters regarding the ordinary citizen.

Most African countries, however, march along in the opposite direction in their striving towards modernization, unification, development and nation-building. They are, in so doing, destroying what was valuable without being able to replace it by something else. This, however, may not be surprising; even wealthy Western nations have yet to achieve a satisfactorily working system which allows justice for all.

Notes and References

1. 93 Jermyn Street, London SW1Y 6JE.
2. 866 United Nations Plaza, New York, N.Y. 10017.
3. Faculty of Law, Addis-Ababa University, P.O. Box 1176, Addis-Ababa, and Institut de Sociologie, Université Libre de Bruxelles, Avenue Paul Héger, 1050 Brussels.
4. T. Purcell, *Legal Services Finance Raising and Management*, ILC Memorandum, September 1973, p. i.
5. B. Metzger, Legal Services to the Poor and National Development Objectives, in: *Legal Aid and World Poverty*, Praeger, New York 1974, p. 4.
6. B. Metzger, art. cit., p. 5.
7. For a further description of these specific rationales, I must refer to Barry Metzger's paper I have mentioned in notes 5 and 6. His description is, however (as he himself admits), somewhat speculative.
8. Art cit., p. 7.
9. C. J. Dias, Research on Legal Services and Poverty: its Relevance to the Design of Legal Services Programs in Developing Countries, in: *Wash. Univ. Law Quart.*, 1975, pp. 7–15.
10. R. Luckham, The Market for Legal Services in Ghana, *Rev. Ghana Law*, 1976, p. 15.
11. See Tables 4, 5 and 9 in R. Luckham, art. cit.; and H. C. Dunning, Legal Systems and Legal Services in Africa, in: *Legal Aid and World Poverty*, op. cit., p. 22.
12. Art. cit., p. 22.
13. M. R. K. Rwelamira, *Report on Research on the Legal Profession in*

Tanzania, paper presented for the ILC-Conference on 'Legal Professions', October 25-27, 1976, p. 32.

14. M. R. K. Rwelamira, op. cit., p. 22 (see also his Table I: Distribution of Law Offices in Tanzania, on p. 21).
15. G. de Mornay Davies, Legal Services to the Poor in Zambia, in: *Legal Aid and World Poverty*, op. cit., p. 54.
16. As put by H. C. Dunning, art. cit., p. 22.
17. A. Ramangasoavina, La Justice dans les pays en voie de développement, *Rev. Jur. Pol.*, 1965, p. 516. The most recent statistics available to the author were 1965.
18. J. Bureau, L'Assistance judiciaire dans les Pays francophones, in: T. G. Verhelst (ed.), *L'Individu face à la Justice en Afrique*, Addis-Ababa, 1972, p. 270. References in this report will be to the French version of this work. An English version exists under the title: *Legal Process and the Individual. African Source Materials*, Addis-Ababa, 1972 (edited also by Thierry Verhelst).
19. On this plural system see for example: A. N. Allott, *New Essays in African Law*, Butterworths, London, 1970, pp. 9ff. and pp. 197ff.
20. See for example: E. Schaeffer, Aliénation-Réception-Authenticité. Réflexions sur le Droit du Développement, *Penant*, 1974, pp. 311-32.
21. For further information on this trend, I refer *inter alia* to: A. N. Allott, Towards the unification of Laws in Africa, *Int. Comp. Law Quart.*, 1965, pp. 366-89; idem., The Unification of Laws in Africa, *Am. Journ. Comp. Law*, 1968, pp. 51-87 and E. Cotran, The Unification of Laws in East Africa, *Journ. Mod. Afr. Stud.*, 1963, pp. 209-20.
22. A. Sawyerr, Application of Law in Tanzania: A "proper remedy" Approach to some problems of legal pluralism, *E. Afr. Law Rev.*, 1974, pp. 223-46.
23. R. Luckham, art. cit., p. 27.
24. H. C. Dunning, art. cit., p. 28. See, however: M. Gluckman (ed.), *Ideas and Procedures in African customary Law*, O.U.P., London, 1969, especially the essays of Van Velsen and Nkwambo Mugerwa, as well as the introduction by Allott, Epstein and Gluckman, who all argue that the establishment of liability appears to be a universal phenomenon. Generally, however, literature stresses the strong element of compromise in small-scale societies: compare S. Roberts, Law and the Study of Social Control in small-scale societies, *Mod. Law Rev.*, 1976, p. 676.
25. This process of building up professionalization, followed by monopolization is superbly described in H. Wilenski, The Professionalization

of everyone, *Am. Journ. Sociol.*, 1964, pp. 137-58. See also: E. Greenwood, Attributes of a Profession, *Social Work*, 1957, pp. 45-55.

26. H. C. Dunning, art. cit., p. 45.
27. See: A. Gille, Note sur une forme d'assistance en justice au Rwanda: le "Kuhagarikira", *Bull. Jur. Ind. et Droit Cout. Cong.*, 1946, p. 367.
28. B. S. Newman, To Further a System of Justice: Legal Aid in Africa, *Afr. Law Stud.*, 1970, pp. 97-110.
29. Mali is mentioned in groups 3 and 4 of the Newman study. It is not clear where this country belongs, neither is the reason for this double setting.
30. See note 29.
31. Source: B. S. Newman, art. cit., pp. 112ff.
32. Report for the Conference of African Jurists on the African Legal Process and the Individual (Addis-Ababa, 1971), reprinted in T. G. Verhelst (ed.), op. cit., pp. 245-57, at 246 and 257.
33. A. Boni, Assistance Judiciaire aux Individus, in: T. G. Verhelst (ed.), op. cit., pp. 238-44, at 239 and 243.
34. A. Ramangasoavina, art. cit., p. 512.
35. 1971 Report to the Attorney-General of Uganda, quoted by H. C. Dunning, art. cit., p. 30.
36. R. Luckham, art. cit., p. 21.
37. For example at the Fourth Bench, Bar and Faculty Conference; see: R. B. Turkson, The Fourth Bench, Bar and Faculty Conference, *Rev. Ghana Law*, 1975, p. 62.
38. R. Luckham, art. cit., p. 22.
39. Source: R. Luckham, art. cit., p. 23.
40. R. Luckham, art. cit., pp. 21-2.
41. For Zambia: see: B. S. Newman, art. cit., p. 106; T. G. Verhelst (ed.), op. cit., pp. 250-2; G. de Mornay Davies, art. cit., pp. 53-73; and B. Metzger, Legal Aid and the Law Student in the Developing Nations, in: *Selected Readings in Clinical Legal Education*, CLEPR and ILC, New York, 1973, pp. 349-51.
42. T. Purcell, op. cit., p. 2.
43. Source: Legal Aid Department of Zambia, Annual Report 1970.
44. Source: High Court Records.
45. H. C. Dunning, art. cit., p. 37.
46. H. C. Dunning, art. cit., p. 38.
47. *Problems of developing countries in starting and extending the scope of Legal Aid*, Int. Leg. Aid Assn. Memorandum for the Tokyo Conference, 1970, p. 11.

48. A. Kiapi, First results from the Tanzanian Ombudsman – First Annual Report 1966/67, *E. Afr. Law Rev.*, 1968, pp. 204-5.
49. H. C. Dunning, art. cit., p. 48.
50. Private communication by Dr. J. C. N. Paul, International Legal Center, New York, April 10, 1977.
51. J. Bureau, art. cit., p. 267.
52. Law Decree of October 30, 1935.
53. Code of Civil Procedure, Ordinance No. 66-154 of June 8, 1966.
54. H. C. Dunning, art. cit., p. 31.
55. For example by: J. Thibaut and L. Walker, *Procedural Justice: A Psychological Analysis*, Hillsdale, 1975.
56. See generally, M. Storme, The Active Role of the Judge, in: *Rapports belges au XIe Congrès de l'Académie Internationale de Droit Comparé*, Bruxelles, 1974, pp. 167-76, with references, and M. Cappelletti, Procédures Orales et Procédures Ecrites, in: *Rapports Généraux présentés au VIIIe Congrès International de Droit Comparé*, Milan, 1970, pp. 90-7.
57. Articles 145-148, Code of Civil Procedure.
58. Ordonnance Municipale, art. 155.
59. Law of December 9, 1964, and Decree No. 455 of November 26, 1966.
60. Law No. 58/AN/1962 of April 14, 1962.
61. Ben Slama, L'Assistance judiciaire en Tunisie, in: T. G. Verhelst (ed.), op. cit., p. 279.
62. A. Boni, art. cit., p. 244.
63. J. Gilissen and J. Vanderlinden, Essai de Synthèse, in: J. Gilissen (ed.), *L'Organisation Judiciaire en Afrique Noire*, Bruxelles, Editions de l'U.L.B., 1969, p. 53.
64. I shall follow here the categorizing of T. Purcell, op. cit. This paragraph is based largely on his paper.
65. H. C. Dunning, art. cit., p. 49.
66. B. Metzger, Legal Aid and the Law Student in Developing Countries, in: *Selected Readings in Clinical Legal Education*, op. cit., pp. 324-53.
67. B. Metzger, art. cit., p. 346.
69. See also: B. Metzger, art. cit., pp. 349-51 and G. de Mornay Davies, art. cit., pp. 68-70. –
70. As is the case in Rwanda, where a legal clinic has been created by the Law Faculty in the beginning of 1977.

JUDD EPSTEIN

Australia

The form and extent of the provision of legal assistance in Australia is a much debated topic. No conclusions have yet been reached. The central issues are much the same as those raised in most jurisdictions, though with some particularly Australian characteristics. It is generally agreed that the existing services, though they play a vital role in the provision of legal aid, are inadequate to meet the full range of legal needs experienced by disadvantaged people in the community.

Three major issues are still unresolved. Existing schemes emphasize representation for the individul client. Whether legal aid should effect changes in the economic, social and political status of the poor, educate the public in the use of law and assist the poor to organize themselves, is still an open question. Responsibility and control of the provision of services is also in balance. The federal government, state governments, legal profession and welfare organizations are all anxious to obtain control over or participate in the bodies administering the aid, but are far less willing to undertake to supply adequate funding for the services supplied. Presently the debate is focused upon the choice of delivery mechanisms – salaried lawyers or private practitioners.

The situation is very much in a state of flux. Decisions are being made daily. Even now the long term commitment of Australia to adequate access to legal proceedings for all its members is less than clear; whether the availability of legal aid and advice is expanding or contracting is still uncertain. Everyone, in theory, supports legal aid, and there is good will on all sides. Whether that is enough in the end is another matter.

The need for free or subsidized legal services

The provision of free or reduced price legal services in Australia is generally limited to those persons without adequate income or assets. At one time, it was envisaged that legal aid might be available to all as a universal welfare benefit provided by the state, but, due to limited funds, that aim is not being pursued seriously today.

There are people living in poverty in Australia. An independent, non-parliamentary Commission of Inquiry into Poverty in Australia was announced by the Prime Minister on August 29, 1972 and its main report was submitted on April 18, 1975.[1]

It identified the extent of poverty due to inadequate income. In doing so, it drew a poverty line at an austere low level and described as "very poor" those below the line and as "rather poor" those 20 per cent above it. In August 1973, the poverty line for a standard family was $62.70, or 56.5 per cent of average earnings at that time.[2] The overall measure of poverty, in terms of adult income units, showed that, on an annual income basis, 10.2 per cent were very poor and 7.7 per cent were rather poor. Given the costs[3] of legal services provided by the private legal profession, it was concluded that those living in poverty could not afford to utilize lawyers or courts in the absence of free or reduced-cost legal aid.

A survey was conducted which attempted to ascertain the use that the poor make of the legal system, and their legal needs were categorized.[4] The general conclusions drawn were that the poor underuse the legal system, fail to perceive their legal problems, and have limited access to the courts.[5] In general, the poor seldom use lawyers, except in the conveyance of property and in connection with some marriage or family problems. The survey did isolate several areas of legal needs of persons living in poverty in which the legal system was underused. These included accommodation – especially payment of rent, repair or eviction from leased property; industrial accidents and automobile accidents; consumer problems, specifically hire-purchase and faulty or defective goods; money problems including borrowing, lending and bankruptcy; and family problems, including breakdown and custody.

In great part, the categories of the underprivileged with legal needs in Australia would be not unlike those in many other jurisdictions. These would include the disabled, the unemployed, single parent families, juveniles, and the aged. Their particular legal needs are known to most. Two special categories, however, present more unusual problems, and are dealt with in greater detail.

Aboriginals

There are approximately 130,000 full blood and part Aboriginals in Australia today. It has been estimated that "probably 90 per cent of the people of Aboriginal descent in Australia are living in poverty, some to a degree matched only in the most backward of the poverty-stricken areas of Asia, Africa and Latin America".[6] A survey in Brisbane, Queensland, showed 44 per cent of Aboriginals were very poor and a further 15 per cent rather poor, and it is likely that the incidence of poverty among rural Aboriginals would be even higher because of lessened prospects for regular or well-paid employment.[7] Approximately 67 per cent of the Aboriginal population is rural or migratory. Most of the Aboriginals' contact with the legal system is with the police and criminal courts; they are notorious underusers of lawyers and courts in civil matters. Yet, exploitation of Aboriginals in civil matters is well documented.[8]

Aboriginals are under special disadvantages in obtaining access to courts. They are unfamiliar with the English courtroom procedure and have difficulty with the English language. In many cases they are intimidated by the dress, behaviour and physical structure of the courts. Many lack the concept of time and numbers. Some distrust local lawyers, fearing them to be part of the administration.

Because a comprehensive approach was needed to bring legal education and participation in the legal system to the Aboriginal people, the government-funded Aboriginal Legal Services have been organized, and will be discussed later in this report.[9]

Migrants

A second underprivileged group which has difficulty in gaining access to the legal system is the non-British migrant. The last three decades have seen a massive influx of non-English speaking European migrants, especially Italians, Greeks and Dutch. According to the 1971 census, some 12 per cent of the population was born in a country in which the native language is not English. It has been discovered ". . . that to be a non-British migrant in Australia today means that you are more likely to be poor and socially isolated than the rest of the population, and your children are more likely to suffer educational disability than other children."[10] Australia's geographical isolation, unicultural and unilingual tradition has made it difficult for migrants to prosper. Access to the legal system has been especially difficult. Very few lawyers speak more than one language. Migrants have faced a dual disadvantage – they have little or no understanding of Australian commercial transactions and are faced with an entirely different legal system and set of rights and obligations. The *Legal Needs of the Poor*[11] survey showed non-British migrants knew very little about the availability of free legal aid, and failed to understand their legal rights or to appreciate that a lawyer might have been able to help them with their problems.

Many non-British migrants have immigrated to Australia without government financial assistance and have had to purchase many household goods upon arrival. They have been found to be disproportionately represented in complaints relating to the purchase of cars, other consumer items, and hire-purchase transactions. Housing poses particular problems; sale notes may be informal documents which the migrant does not realize are binding. Migrants have been found to be markedly less likely to make wills than are other members of the public.

In courts, as well, the non-English speaker is disadvantaged. In civil cases, the language of the courts is English. The migrant has no right even to an interpreter though the judge has a discretion to permit an interpreter to translate and to assist in putting questions to witnesses at the migrant's own expense.[12] Most courts have no official interpreters; parties must hire them privately. Evidence of witnesses may be translated as well, with the loser bearing that expense. Even with ample judicial goodwill this places the migrant at a disadvantage. Translation is often disfavoured as it hinders the effectiveness of the cross-examination, which is thought to be essential in the adversary system. Though there are several migrant welfare and friendship organizations in Australia which aid the migrant in his legal and other affairs, no legal aid scheme has been specifically set up, or special procedures adapted, to help the migrant.

Obstacles to the access of professional aid and advice

In general, to use effectively any of the ordinary courts in Australia, one requires access to a member of the legal profession. To the extent that professional assistance is unavailable, a citizen is at a considerable disadvantage in contemplating bringing, defending, or being involved in any litigation. Recourse to legal professionals is impeded in three ways – territorial unavailability, cost, and psychological obstacles, especially fear.

Australia is a vast land mass, approximately the size of the continental United States of America, thinly populated overall, with a high degree of urbanization. One particular electoral district in Western Australia has a land area over thirty times the size of Belgium and a population of only 2,100 adults. Lawyers are not uniformly distributed, but are concentrated in the commercial centres of the capital cities with far fewer offices in the suburbs and rural regions.[13] There are also fewer lawyers *per capita* than in many other nations; the current ratio of one lawyer per 1,400 persons is only one-third as many lawyers *per capita* as in the United States. These figures obviously have adverse implications for the population when they seek legal assistance. The Commission of Inquiry into Poverty found that the underprivileged in Australia were deprived of equal access to justice because those sections of the metropolitan areas where persons living in poverty were located, and some rural areas, were not adequately served by private practitioners. The assertion that clients require solicitors in their own residential areas and are unwilling or unable to reach the centre city area for consultation was disputed in an English context,[14] but may have greater relevance in Australia. Less available means of public transport, distance between suburbs and core city, and work habits here may make ready access more important. To take an extreme example, in the northern two-thirds of the state of Western Australia, an area several times the size of the entire British Isles, there is only one resident solicitor. This must impede access to justice.

Besides the territorial problem, there are severe psychological barriers which limit access to lawyers by the underprivileged. Entrance to the profession is limited, for the most part, to those who secure a place through the very limited quota system of the universities, often those graduating from private fee-supported secondary schools. Lawyers are uniformly chosen from a socio-economic class different from that of the underprivileged, and it is hardly surprising that some poor people are unwilling or afraid to deal with them.[15]

Many persons are unaware that their problem is a legal one or that a lawyer can be of assistance. There is an ethical ban on individual advertising by lawyers and little institutional advertising is provided. There is no specialist register, little group representation through trade unions or other organizations, and in the absence of referral agencies, many simply do not know which solicitor to use.

Closely related to the psychological obstacles is the problem of cost – the factor most responsible for denying persons access to the private profession. The cost of a lawyer (discussed below) is not publicly displayed, is difficult to ascertain, and, in many instances, is wrongly magnified by the potential client. The availability of low cost or free legal services is not widely advertised and is unknown to many; hence professional assistance may not be sought when needed.

Impediments to access to the courts

In most jurisdictions of Australia, there are three hierarchies of first instance courts for civil matters. In all ordinary courts, however, the plaintiff or defendant would be well advised to seek the assistance of a professional lawyer. The prinicpal reason for this is Australia's adherence to the adversary system. No duty is imposed upon any judge to assist the unrepresented client in the preparation or presentation of his case. In all first instance courts provision is made for the exchange of written pleadings, and processes whereby pre-trial discovery may take place. During the trial itself rules of evidence are enforced, including the taking of testimony, cross-examination, and consideration of objections to the proffer of proof. The documents exchanged during the proceedings must conform to legal rquirements and are well beyond the ability of most laymen to read or understand, much less draft.

This is not to suggest that individual judges or magistrates do not, upon occasion, attempt to assist individual litigants, or that an unrepresented litigant cannot obtain a fair hearing. Clerks of court may assist any litigant, though they are under no obligation to do so, and many would be unqualified. It is clear, however, that those litigants who enjoy professional representation are clearly advantaged.[16]

Retaining a lawyer for purposes of litigation requires the potential litigant to consider the costs of representation as well as court costs. In most states of Australia, scales of fees are established by the Rules of Court. These prescribe fees chargeable to a client both for the use of the court and many of the activities undertaken by his lawyer, such as drafting and engrossing documents, paying witnesses etc. The fees are lower in courts of lesser monetary jurisdiction, but otherwise do not vary according to the amount in dispute. The indemnity rule of costs is the general rule – the loser of litigation must pay the costs reasonably and properly incurred by the winner. The contingency fee is not permitted. The amount in cost that any litigant may be required to pay is unknown, even in broad terms, to the party when he is contemplating litigation. This uncertainty may tend to limit access to the courts, especially among the poor

Additional cost factors serve as obstacles. In some Australian states a divided profession may involve the client in the added expense of a second lawyer. When litigation is contemplated, the solicitor may well recommend the involvement of a barrister to settle documents, advise on evidence, and to make all representations in open court. The traditional English rules of two-thirds payment to a Junior when Queen's Counsel is retained, limitations of the procedural work done by Queen's Counsel, and the tendency to have counsel's opinion in negotiations all increase costs of litigation. In civil litigation the jury is still widely used in most Australian states, though often court rules provide for juries of four or six rather than twelve.

Two other miscellaneous factors which may limit access to the courts are worthy of consideration. While Magistrates' Courts (or Courts of Petty Session as they are known in other states) are well distributed geographically, the courts of higher monetary jurisdiction tend to be concentrated in the capital cities, though country sittings may be held. Delays are common wherever the case is held; hearings more than a year after the Certificate of Readiness for Trial is issued are becoming more common. While these may be said to be general problems of access, their effect upon the poor and underprivileged is more marked.

Provision of legal aid: constitutional requirements

Australia is a federal state with law-making power divided between the central government and the states. The Constitution of the Commonwealth of Australia contains no explicit grant of power to Parliament under which a nationwide legal aid scheme could be provided. Nor is there a "Bill of Rights" or listing of individual rights which guarantees any Australian equal access to the courts, equality before the law, a right to bring or defend legal proceedings, "due process", or any other entrenched "higher law" provision regarding legal rights.

Thus at first glance it appears that the provision of legal aid, in so far as it depends upon governmental action, must be initiated by the individual states. Indeed it was alleged that the Commonwealth's approach to the provision of legal services, the Australian Legal Aid Office (ALAO), was funded by an appropriation not sanctioned by any head of Commonwealth legislative power. Others submit that the governmental initiative is *intra vires*. They allege that the appropriation for legal services ia authorized under s. 81 of the Constitution – the appropriation or spending power. This submission depends upon an interpretation that the expenditure is "for the purpose of the Commonwealth".[17] Otherwise the government may, it appears, only justify appropriations, first for those persons for whom the Commonwealth has a special responsibility and for whom it can pass special laws and, secondly, in relation to things describable as "Commonwealth matters". The former includes aliens, Aboriginals, students, immigrants and Commonwealth pensioners,[18] while the latter includes such matters as matrimonial causes, insurance claims, pension claims, tax matters and some areas of consumer protection.[19] Section 51(39) grants Parliament the power to make laws governing matters incidental to the execution of any of the powers mentioned above. It is clear that under s. 122, the federal government may make any law providing any kind of service for people living in the territories, principally the Australian Capital Territory and the Northern Territory.

Broadly speaking, the Australian Labour Party, which was in governmend during the introduction of the ALAO, was convinced that the Commonwealth powers extended to such an appropriation while the Liberal-National Party coalition now in power, some state governments, and some private practitioners hold that the constitutional difficulties inherent in Australian federalism are such that it is unlikely that a federal salaried service could validly provide legal aid in areas of state jurisdiction. The current national government prefers to operate under s. 96 of the Constitution providing grants to states on such conditions and terms as the parliament decide, so as to allow each state to pass its own legislation for the provision of extensive legal aid.

Means of provision of legal aid

The widespread grant of free or reduced-price legal services to those unable to pay is a relatively recent phenomenon in Australia. Governments and lawyers' professional bodies have been actively involved only within the past decade. While developments in each state have occurred separately, they have been influenced by developments in sister states, and the differences between states are relatively minor. An impression of the general pattern in Australia, illustrated with examples drawn from various states, will be provided here.

The experience of South Australia is more or less typical of the other states. The South Australian government originally provided legal assistance through the Office of the Public Solicitor, founded in 1925, but this was disbanded in favour of services provided by the South Australian Law Society in 1933 which agreed to see that no person would be without proper assistance if he were deserving of such assistance and would be unable to obtain it without the help of the Society's members.[20]

All members of the legal profession were expected to participate in the scheme and were compensated, if at all, by the collection of such costs as were ordered against the losing unassisted party. A small reimbursement to practitioners was available from the Central Legal Assistance Fund, but the scheme virtually consisted only of the charitable contribution of practising lawyers. The state government, is conferring legislative sanction upon the scheme through the *Poor Persons Legal Assistance Act 1936*, also agreed to waive or reduce fees payable to the state for assisted persons.

The only other way of obtaining legal assistance in civil matters was through private charitable organizations, through *in forma pauperis* proceedings, or, in some states, through rudimentary state government salaried service schemes. Most of the latter, however, concentrated upon criminal matters.

Today the person without means is in a much better position throughout the nation. In all states there is a service provided by the professional bodies; the federal government provides a salaried service (the ALAO); the state salaried service in some jurisdictions is involved in civil matters; and both government-supported and independent voluntary services are actively involved in providing a wide range of legal and quasi-legal assistance.

The Law Society schemes

Each state in Australia offers legal assistance through a scheme administered by the Law Societies and authorized by state legislation.[21] Persons seeking free or subsidized legal assistance forward applications to a committee. This committee considers whether the applicant falls within the statutory eligibility requirements of the scheme, and whether sufficient funds are available to assist the applicant. If the applicant is successful he will be referred to a member of the private profession who will then enter into a standard lawyer/client relationship. The lawyer's fee will be paid, to an agreed upon percentage, from a fund administered by the committee. The committee members themselves do not represent applications in court.

While each scheme is funded independently of other schemes, all administer limited funds. In considering the operation of these schemes, two matters should be borne in mind. First, the relevant statute in each state, and regulations made pursuant to those statutes in some states, prescribe conditions for eligibility. A detailed analysis of the legislative provisions of the various states may be misleading, since the committees administering the funds find it necessary to narrowly interpret at times, and to ignore provisions or limitations at other times. Because the amount of funds available differs from year to year and state to state, all states require highly flexible administration. Secondly, there is a paucity of public figures on the expenditure of the funds, making an accurate assessment rather difficult. Each state is idiosyncratic in the data it supplies; it is next to impossible to draw meaningful comparisons between the state's schemes.

Structure of the schemes

In each state the Law Society schemes are administered by a committee which is either an independent statutory committee[22] or a subcommittee of the state Law Society.[23] These committees are responsible for the day-to-day administration of the scheme, including the receipt of applications, conduct of interviews, approval or rejection of applications, and assignment of the successful applicants to individual practitioners. In some jurisdictions there are regional committees which handle the applications in their area.[24] Members of the committees are almost exclusively lawyers practising within the jurisdiction. Some schemes which grant interviews and give advice will have full-time paid staff; most committees depend upon volunteers from the profession. In South Australia, laymen are used to conduct interviews; Queensland and Western Australia have members from the Attorney General's office (Justice Department) but no lay participation.

The schemes also differ on whether all private practitioners within the state are called upon and expected to participate in the schemes, or only those enrolled on panels who have indicated their willingness to participate. In general, those states in which the scheme grew from the professional duty, "charitable" model expect universal participation. In Western Australia where a panel is provided for under the legislation[25] particiption among the private practitioners is reported to be universal, as it is in Victoria and Tasmania where no panel is chosen and where all participate. Yet in New South Wales, applications to join the panel are disappointingly low and the expected increase in applications has never been fulfilled.[26]

Range of assistance available

All of the state Law Society schemes are oriented towards an individual client approach, rather than an attempt to use legal aid as an instrument for improving the position of the poor in society. None promotes social change through law reform, community legal education, or runs test cases. Even within the individual approach there are wide variations in the range of assistance available.

Three states appear to offer the broadest range of services – providing "legal assistance". The phrase is defined very widely in Tasmania[27] and Western Australia;[28] it is left undefined in South Australia.[29] In each of these states it includes representation (for those otherwise eligible) in all courts and tribunals for all matters, advice and assistance before or in the absence of litigation, and assistance in such non-litigious areas as conveyancing, drawing of wills, and grants of probate. Yet, in the absence of statistics enabling one to ascertain the amount of time and expense allocated to each, it is very difficult to estimate the quantity of assistance available other than for litigation. For instance, it is known that South Australia rarely grants assistance in non-litigious matters, and Western Australia's advice service is manned exclusively by volunteers. In other states, advice and assistance is either not included within the statutory ambit or is excluded through interpretation or administration. In Queensland, for example, a plan whereby officers of the Legal Assistance Committee are authorised to advise eligible clients for up to one hour for one dollar is theoretically available, but is so little publicized that it is next to unused.

Even in providing representation, the coverage is by no means all-inclusive. Some states exclude tribunals, others exclude even the ordinary courts of least subject matter jurisdiction.[30] Some will not grant assistance for certain disfavoured causes of actions such as defamation or breach of contract of marriage.[31] Legal aid for the preparation of appeals is often unavailable through the schemes.

Determination of eligibility

The funds of each scheme are inadequate to allow approval of all requests for subsidized legal assistance. No aid is given as of right. Regardless of the criteria provided by the various state acts, the balance in the fund at any one moment, the number of applications, and the resulting exercise of discretion or interpretaiton on the part of the administrator determines whether an application will be successful or not. The two criteria chosen to guide the exercise of this discretion are the means test and the requirement of legal merit.

There are basically two types of means tests used in Australia today – a detailed, specific limit on the permissible resources of the potential client,[32] and a flexible test, such as "unable to afford the normal cost of service required".[33] The various application forms used by each state require applicants to detail their income and assets regardless of the test ultimately employed. Where there is a specific limit, legal assistance under such a scheme will not be granted when it appears that the applicant is possessed of property of a total value of a given figure, say $1,000, exclusive of certain exempt property, including usually a dwelling house up to say $10,000, a motor vehicle up to a certain sum, wearing apparel, tools of trade, and household furniture, or an annual (or monthly) income that exceeds a specific figure, after calculating certain allowable deductions. With the flexible test, assets and income are analysed in much the same way with additional factors such as the estimated cost of the proceedings, the nature of the cause of action, amount in controversy, and anything else considered relevant to the person determining the application. Another factor, which is considered later in this report,[34] is the amount of contribution, if any, the applicant is expected to make towards the costs of the proceedings – Western Australia, in its scheme which expired on April 17, 1978,[35] had a very detailed means test with very modest limits imposed upon the applicants. Yet, like most schemes, it had a "hardship" clause built in, and its administrator reported that "eligibility restrictions under the Act are simply not used, and the Committee acts under its discretionary power".[36]

The test of legal merit must also be satisfied before an application is approved. The test is similar in effect in all states, though the mode of expression may differ. A committee must convince itself that the applicant has "reasonable ground for taking, defending or being a party to proceedings".[37] This is often measured by the United Kingdom yardstick "whether a prudent unassisted party who had adequate but not overabundant means of his own would choose to risk them by bringing or defending the action".[38] In practice, some states eliminate very few applications under this test. Tasmania does not reject unless the application is totally devoid of merit, while Western Australia basically reviews only whether the dispute is a legal matter (under the Act of 1967). Queensland will deny aid if the advantage is trivial or a solicitor would not normally be utilized.[39]

There is no well-developed procedure for contesting denial of legal assistance under any of the schemes. Three states do provide, in theory, an appeal from the decision rejecting the application, but in practice appeals are rarely, if ever, brought.

Procedure

Most schemes require a written application form. These are always available from the committee itself, and sometimes from referral services, welfare agencies, clerks of court or private practitioners. Most committees report that the bulk of applications originate from agencies or private solicitors. Almost invariably, when an application forwarded from a private practitioner to the committee is approved, it is returned to the referring lawyer, inviting him to serve as the lawyer.

Financial arrangements

The sources of finance for the schemes, and the amounts provided, vary from year to year, making forward planning a haphazard affair. In all the state schemes, other than Tasmania, a major source of funding is the interest drawn on solicitors' trust accounts. The underprivileged gain the benefit of interest accrued on monies that unassisted clients have deposited with their solicitors. Most of the schemes have benefited from occasional grants by their state government from consolidated revenue, while in more recent years the Commonwealth government has been granting money to the states, on a *per capita* basis, earmarked for use in the Law Society schemes.

Another major source of revenue for some schemes[40] has been contributions by the assisted persons. Some states, such as New South Wales, required a minimum contribution from everyone aided[41] (with a waiver in case of hardship); others, like Victoria and South Australia, usually require some contribution, while Queensland and Tasmania rarely require any contribution whatsoever. Interestingly, in Victoria, the contribution is expressed in $X per week, without specific time limit, and the amount the assisted party may eventually contribute could exceed the fees he would have paid had he arranged representation through a private practitioner directly. Still another source of revenue for some state schemes is the costs recovered from the losing unassisted party. Such costs may be directly payable to the committee, which has power to recover them in the name of the assisted person.[42]

The new wave – State Legal Aid Commission

The commonwealth government, elected in 1977, has expressed a preference for each state to create its own Legal Aid Commission which would co-ordinate all forms of legal aid provided within the state, and receive grants from the commonwealth government.

In response to this governmental initiative the states of Western Australia, South Australia, Queensland and the Australian Capital Territory (ACT) have passed legislation establishing Legal Aid Commissions.[43] In each instance the delivery of legal services within the state is to be organized under the relevant Act, replacing both the existing Law Society schemes and the Commonwealth Salaried Service – the ALAO. At the time of writing, only Western Australia had commenced operation.

While the state Acts vary in particulars, their overall outline and design is similar. The South Australian Act will be used here as the model.

The South Australian Act establishes a Legal Services Commission of ten persons. A chairman, nominated by the state Attorney-General, must be a judge or practitioner of five years' standing. The balance of the commission includes three nominees of the state Attorney-General, one nominated by the Commonwealth Attorney-General; one nominee to represent the interests of assisted persons, nominated by the state Attorney-General, after consultation with the South Australian Council of Social Services; three nominees of the Law Society; and a Director chosen by the commission itself.

The chief functions of the commission are to establish a Legal Services Office, to provide or arrange legal assistance, to determine eligibility criteria, to conduct research into legal needs, to promote public education on legal rights and duties, and to make grants to persons or bodies engaged in or promoting legal assistance.[44]

Section 11 of the Act specifically directs the commission, in exercising its functions, to take into account the need for legal assistance to be readily available to disadvantaged persons, the desirability of enabling all assisted persons to obtain the services of legal practitioners of their choice, and the importance of maintaining the independence of the legal profession.

The delivery of legal services will be undertaken by both commission officers, and by practitioners engaged by the commission. Applicants will apply for assistance to the Director. The Director will determine whether assistance is to be granted and, if granted, on what terms. An appeal from a denial of assistance or from a grant made on unfavourable terms lies to the commission.

The Western Australian Commission commenced operation recently; the others are not yet under way. Those Australian states that have not promulgated legislation are in the process of doing so. In Tasmania, the Committee of Inquiry into Legal Aid has completed its hearings and is preparing its report. The Attorney-General for Victoria has committed the state to the idea of a Legal Aid Commission and has sought submissions on its composition, responsibility, etc.[45] Legislation has been promised for the next parliamentary session though no draft Bill is yet available. New South Wales recently circulated a working paper outlining the scheme of the proposed Act to establish its Legal Service Commission. In the Northern Territory, an ordinance along the lines of the ACT is being prepared.

Commonwealth Legal Aid Commission Act

Legislation has been passed to establish a Commonwealth Legal Aid Commission.[46] That Act itself does not provide or deliver any legal assistance nor does it create a Legal Aid Commission independent of government as some had hoped. The Act has two relatively minor objectives. It creates a Legal Aid Commission which is to secure an overview of the activities of the proposed State and Territory Legal Aid Commissions, to keep statistics and to recommend additional methods of delivery of legal aid. Secondly, the Act seeks to preserve some of the rights of ALAO staff who transferred to state or territorial commissions. Some minimum terms and conditions are to be included in any arrangement for transfer of staff.

The Commission is constituted by a chairman, deputy chairman, two commissioners nominated by the Attorney-General, two commissioners nominated by the Attorneys-General of the states in which Legal Aid Commissions have been established, a commissioner nominated by the Law Council of Australia, and a commissioner nominated by the Australian Council of Social Services.

The members of the Commonwealth Legal Aid Commission have only just been announced, and it is not yet operational. The formal agreements between the Commonwealth and each state under which the Commonwealth will provide funds for the provision of legal aid in the federal area, have not yet been negotiated and announced. Until the content of these agreements are known, the shape and direction that this phase of legal aid will take remains conjectural.

Comments on the functioning of the law society schemes

The major limitation on the Law Society schemes, as their annual reports acknowledge, is that there is simply too little permanent funding to allow an adequate range of services to be provided to most people who are in need. While all are aware of the danger of the "bottomless pit" in providing legal assistance to those in legal need, the finance available for the schemes has been very limited indeed when contrasted with other forms of social welfare. The Law Societies often claim that, were the money the Commonwealth now spends on its salaried service placed into the Law Society schemes, they would provide a better overall service than both now provide.

Each scheme is administered through its own legislative provisions and regulations, and each has its own individual characteristics. The scheme operating in the state of Victoria administers much the largest fund and may be used as an example to comment upon the functioning of most of the schemes. From 1974 to 1975, there were approximately 178,400 defended civil cases heard in Victorian courts[47] while 6,529 applications for legal assistance in civil matters were approved,[48] so that one party was granted legal assistance from the Law Society scheme in about 3.6 per cent of civil cases heard. This figure must be regarded with caution. There are two or more parties to each civil matter. Many who were granted representation may have obtained approval on such harsh terms that they did not accept the offer. While 70 per cent of those who completed an application were granted aid, the figure of those in need of legal representation and unable to pay would have been several times the number of those who applied. Yet Victoria receives one application per 265 residents, whereas New South Wales receives only one per 1,235 residents, and rejects a higher proportion than does Victoria.

The current source of finance is inadequate, varies unpredictably from year to year, and cannot ensure that the poor are given access to legal proceedings.

The interest held on monies held in solicitors' trust funds has been the principal source of finance in Victoria, as in most states. Large defalcations by solicitors have diverted the use of this money.[49] Even in the absence of defalcations, in times of economic inactivity there is a danger that the money available will dwindle. The need for long term financial security is vital. While state government and Commonwealth government grants have been made in the past, these depend upon transitory legislative majorities. An unequivocal commitment to legal aid must be made and adequate recurrent sources must be found to ensure forward planning and direction.

In the absence of such government commitments, Victoria and others have had to depend upon costs recouped, and contributions by assisted persons. Many regard the Legal Aid Committee as no more than a source of extended time payment, rather than a supplier of subsidised legal services. Often deferred payments may be obtained through a private practitioner directly without the intervention of the Legal Aid Committee. Since the committee fixes a weekly sum to be repaid without definite time limits, a person may pay more than he would to a private practitioner.

Some 75 per cent of the expenditures from the fund are payments to the profession, at the rate of 80 per cent of normal fees. Many members of the profession are dissatisfied with the costs and fees allowed. About two-thirds of the payments to the profession are for solicitors, the remainder to barristers. Even with fees paid to solicitors only on scales of costs prescribed by regulation and for magistrates' courts,[50] and barristers paid the lowest amounts recommended by the Bar Council (e.g., Queen's Counsel brief-on-trial of action – A$600.00), as long as "fees for services" is used, only a small percentage of those in need may be aided.

Limits on accessibility to the society schemes

If schemes which employ lawyers in private practice are to continue to be the principal source of legal assistance to poor people, it would seem that some powerful barriers at present hindering access to the schemes, and to private practitioners in general, will have to be overcome. There is, first of all, a very limited knowledge of the existence of the various state schemes. In a survey conducted by the Commission of Inquiry into Poverty among low wage earners, only 54.4 per cent responded affirmatively when asked whether it were possible to obtain free or very cheap legal help or advice.[51] Very little publicity is given to the Law Society schemes, and next to no advertising, even though institutional advertisements are permitted. Most states schemes are centralized, or at most, have branch offices in major metropolitan areas. The Victorian Committee is located on the upper floor of a high rise building in the centre of Melbourne. One does not usually have to visit the office to apply, but many do. Assistance may be required from a lawyer to fill in a complicated written application before the form can even be considered by the committee. The solicitor to whom an approved applicant is referred to is likely to be located in the central business district – over 80 per cent of

Australian practitioners have offices within a 25-kilometre radius of the centre of the major cities.

Most of the offices of the Law Society schemes are open only during business hours,[52] as are most private practitioners', requiring the client to be absent from work for an interview. Often immediate legal assistance is necessary. While most schemes will permit an officer to supply an emergency certificate, there are sometimes delays in processing and approving applications. In New South Wales, over 25 per cent of the applications have been unprocessed after six weeks.

Limited range of services offered

The Law Society schemes are basically referral agencies. They are able to do little more than arrange for representation in appropriate instances by a private member of the profession. Matters such as organizing community legal education, or pressuring for substantive law reform, are well beyond the ambit of these schemes. There is a lack of practice of preventive law – such as negotiating standard form contracts, examining documents, or preparing social security claims – services which the private profession is capable of supplying to those with the ability to pay. While it is obvious that no clear cut division can be made between legal aid and legal advice, in general, advice is usually confined to matters involving contemplated litigation. Such advice as is available outside matters of litigation is usually "pure" advice – follow-up activities such as letters or telephone calls are less frequently offered.

Eligibility requirements

For most schemes both a test of legal merit and a means and needs test must be satisfied before any application is approved. Neither is without its problems. The usual merits requirement is expressed as "a reasonable ground for taking, defending, or being a party to proceedings". Its unsatisfactory nature lies in who should determine reasonableness and on what grounds. Should a single legal practitioner (or even a committee of practitioners) usurp the function of the court by determining the merits of a matter? What criteria should the committee use – likelihood of success, amount in controversy, importance to the potential litigant, or possibility of creating a new precedent? Should access to the court for those unable to pay full private fees depend upon an assessment made in the absence of argument by a lawyer who has fully researched and considered the matter? There may well be a precedent, legislation, or regulation, or even an absence of law on the subject which makes success unlikely. Yet a favourable decision would aid many similarly situated. Looking solely at "likelihood of success" will severely limit any creative law function which legal assistance could serve for the poor. The general lack of any class action legislation in Australia[53] means that only through individual, assisted cases can the common law develop remedies in the poverty area.

Applications are processed in bulk; there is little time to dwell on the merits of any single application. Unfortunately appeal from a decision rejecting the application exists in theory only. Legal practitioners make decisions to conserve limited funds in the absence of concerned laymen (such as welfare officers or social workers) or any articulated policy. Social reform, test cases, and structural changes to the cycle of poverty are unlikely to emerge from the Law Society schemes.

The means and needs tests applied by the state schemes may also serve to deny access to the courts in an arbitrary and unsatisfactory manner. A means test which imposes a "specific limit on the permissible resources of the potential client", such as in New South Wales, seldom takes account of inflation and may have the draconian effect of eliminating otherwise deserving potential litigants. Different cases incur different costs. Persons just above the cut-off point are deprived of access by the fortuity of possessing an additional asset or income. The means tests in Australia are drawn so far below average income, or even the poverty line, as to eliminate from eligibility all but those in the most dire circumstances.

The means test employed in other states is the flexible "unable to afford the normal cost of the service required". States which utilize this still require information regarding assets and income. Consistency of treatment is an obvious problem. The composition of the committee may change, and persons in similar circumstances may be treated unequally. Neither individuals nor private practitioners are able to determine eligibility for assistance with any certainty, and eligible persons may well be discouraged from applying.

Other comments

There are some limitations inherent in the use of a legal aid system which refers applicants to private practitioners. The lawyers who participate cannot concentrate upon the problems of the poor. In so far as these problems are different from those of the rest of the population, no expertise is generated.[54] The necessary network of contracts, such as those with the State Housing Commission or social welfare agencies, are not likely to develop. The Australian legal profession tends to be fragmented into numerous small firms or individual practitioners rather than concentrated into larger units. As a result, many legal practitioners cannot devote adequate time or resources to socially deprived clients without lessening the attention they give their own regular fee paying clientele. The poor, more often than others, are faced with emergency situations such as eviction, repossession, or loss of electricity, which demand an immediate response. A system which depends upon written application, decisions by committee and referral is irrelevant. These obstacles are further compounded by the fear and reluctance of the poor to turn to a private practitioner – a man of another socio-economic class. The result is a massive underuse of the legal system by the poor and a loss of access to justice.

Salaried legal services

There is no purely salaried legal service in Australia. Certainly the most widespread of the so-called salaried legal services in Australia is the ALAO, created and funded by the Commonwealth government, The present Commonwealth government, when in opposition, threatened to destroy the ALAO, and now expresses a strong preference for legal aid commissions funded, in part, through the central government but organized and operated by each individual state. For this reason the future of the ALAO is, at best, uncertain.

The ALAO was conceived in 1973, and by late 1974 had thirty offices in operation throughout Australia and another twenty-eight planned. With the chage in government, this growth was reversed. The ALAO now operates as a branch of the Attorney General's Department, as no legislation conferring upon it an independent statutory basis has ever been passed. The service is intended to aid "all persons experiencing problems arising under federal law" and "all persons for whom the Australian government has a special constitutional responsibility, regardless of the nature of the legal problem presented".

The present lack of political commitment to the ALAO, and the consequent halt in growth of its funding, stands in contrast to the very widespread publicity which attended its opening and the tremendous caseload which it built up. These changes have undoubtedly affected the ALAO adversely. Originally it was intended to be a storefront community organization ready to experiment in new forms of services. It was to address itself to the problems of the gaps in the existing system, the lack of assistance in divorce cases, and magistrates' courts, and "the bottomless pit of ever increasing legal aid".[55] The overwhelming caseload has resulted in most litigation being referred to private practitioners. The salaried lawyers themselves do no more than interview, advise, and refer if further action is required. Offices formerly planned for four or five full-time professional staff are run by one or two. Rather than the planned "drop-in-off-the-street" neighbourhood service, appointments are now needed and often can be granted only months ahead.

On March 8, 1976, new means guidelines took effect which severely limit eligibility for assistance. While the test remained "inability of the applicant to afford the cost of legal assistance in the particular case", the guideline interpreted "inability" as a forty dollar net weekly income. In calculating the net weekly income, deductions previously allowed such as food, clothing and half rent are no longer permitted.[56] Dependent allowances were lowered. No aid at all, except in case of hardship, is available for simple dissolution of marriage. Minimum levels of contribution by the assisted party are now set. A merits test based upon benefits that might accrue and likelihood of a favourable determination has been instituted. In short, it is becoming difficult to receive assistance from the ALAO.

Relationship between the ALAO and the existing legal profession were unhappy at best when the ALAO was opened. The private profession zealously guarded its reputation for independence, freedom from governmental control, and its autonomy in the legal field. The lack of any legislative basis for the ALAO and the lack of demarcation between its function and that of the Law Society schemes were equally damaging. As it became apparent that most of the litigation work was to be given to the private profession (who are paid 90 per cent of normal fees) and agreements were signed with each state co-ordinating responsibility for the provision of legal aid in defined areas, the hostility lessened. Today, the future of the ALAO is threatened much more by political and ideological preferences than by organized opposition from the private legal profession.

Aboriginal Legal Services

Perhaps the most successful of the so-called salaried legal services are the Aboriginal Legal Services. Originally a volunteer organization formed by

Aboriginals, practitioners and academics, it has become a government-funded (through the Department of Aboriginal Affairs) but wholly independent storefront organization. A series of independent offices in each state has opened, tied to each other only by similar aims and haphazard communication. Aboriginals have had cause to regard the received European law as a hostile instrument of repression and discrimination. Most of their contact has been with the police and criminal law. The ALS has succeeded in bringing to the Aboriginal community the notion that they too have rights and such rights can be enforced in Australian courts.

The ALS is much more than a scheme granting legal assistance; it has become a focal point for a wide range of activities – social, political and legal. The management and direction of the ALS is drawn almost exclusively from the Aboriginal community. Anyone who is considered by the community to be Aboriginal is eligible for the full range of assistance available. This is always free; no contribution is required. Field officers, usually Aboriginal and rarely legally trained, are available on a twenty-four hour per day basis, travelling to the remote areas in all states where Aboriginals are living, to answer emergency needs. Representation is arranged through referrals to the private profession, drawn from a roster of those willing to serve and be sympathetic to the ALS and the Aboriginal cause.

Suggestions arise sporadically that the ALS be amalgamated with other legal services such as the ALAO or brought within the newly projected state legal aid commissions. The ALS has always fiercely resisted any such move. Its separate identity and community base has enabled it to achieve a dimension of community legal awareness and education which, arguably, could not be replaced. An awareness that access to courts in civil matters can be achieved by Aboriginals is almost wholly due to the ALS approach and its further development should be encouraged.

Public Solicitor – New South Wales

Prior to the passage of the Legal Aid (Miscellaneous Provisions) Act 1974 (N.S.W.) the Public Solicitor, a salaried service, played an active role in the provision of legal assistance to the poor. That act, *inter alia*, presaged a movement that would turn over to the Law Society scheme responsibility for all legal aid in civil matters. Now, the Public Solicitor in New South Wales can give civil legal aid only for certain prescribed classes of proceedings, most of which are heard in Courts of Petty Sessions. No other state-salaried services provide legal aid in civil matters.

Other legal services

The Law Society schemes and ALAO are the comparatively well financed schemes that supply legal assistance throughout Australia. Those collected under the miscellaneous term "other legal services" offer, in the writer's opinion, the more innovative, more experimental (for Australia) approach and may still be influential in shaping the scope and means of delivery of legal services in Australia.

Voluntary legal services

A group of lawyers, students, social workers and residents concerned at "the evident lack of representation of people in the magistrates' courts and the general availability of the process of law to the people"[57] set up the Fitzroy Legal Service.[58] Their intention was to extend legal services to people in neighbourhood suburbs, to provide such service without charge, to develop a local awareness of legal rights, to practice "preventive law" and to provide legal education and foster community involvement. Space was donated within the town hall and immediately became a focal point for the local community. Much of the work was done on a purely voluntary basis, though later a commonwealth grant allowed expansion.

The Fitzroy Legal Service has a full time co-ordinator, a full time administrator, and a full time solicitor. The solicitor gives "clients" in need of representaiton a choice between referral to a private practitioner, or representation by a salaried solicitor specializing in what may be called Poverty Law. The co-ordinator has organized a Legal Resources Book which has been a commercial success, and is updated twice a year. It is intended to supply information, in an accessible form, in Poverty Law, for lawyers in legal services and private practice, as well as for social workers, citizens advice bureau workers, clergyman, youth workers and others who are confronted with similar problems. Other voluntary legal services have usually operated without full time personnel, have been open more restricted hours, and have confined their operation to dispensing advice, making telephone calls, drafting letters, filling in legal aid applications, and referring persons needing representation to members of the private profession.

The widespread acceptance and use of the service has caused a geographic limit to be placed on the clients eligible for assistance and the heavy caseload has reduced the service's ability to carry on some of its research and law reform aims. Today financial difficulties plague the service; the continued availability of full time staff is in doubt. The Fitzroy model of a volunteer neighbourhood legal centre has been followed throughout Australia, usually on a smaller scale. Services occupying town halls, ALAO offices, or rented premises often open one or two nights per week. Members of the legal profession have been very willing to donate their time and Law Societies and Bar Councils have co-operated by exempting these centres, and the volunteers, from rules on advertising and barrister/solicitor relationships.[59] Victoria, South Australia, and New South Wales have been noteworthy for law student involvement in the services; some students receive University Law School credit for their legal activities. In South Australia and Western Australia, volunteer solicitors give advice, write letters and act as a referral service for a fee of two dollars. The Western Australian scheme operates with sixty volunteers rostered for a half day service each month; each volunteer is required to attend a seminar on the operation of the scheme, and on relevant areas of law. Duty welfare officers participate in both the seminars and advice centres.

Chamber Magistrates

The Chamber Magistrates in New South Wales provide an interesting service not now offered in other states. Chamber Magistrates and Clerks of Petty Sessions, both court officials with some legal training, offer advice and referrals to those who seek assistance. The public at large may avail itself of the service, which is free. Interviews are conducted daily at morning and afternoon sessions lasting about two hours. Assistance may be given in preparing applications, giving advice, or referring people to appropriate bodies in matters including motor traffic violations, matrimonial and custody issues, damage and debt suits and the like. Since the courts are distributed throughout New South Wales, the service is available on a more widespread basis than other schemes. A survey[60] showed that Chamber Magistrates were the best known source of legal assistance in the state. Given the ease by which other states could transform already existing buildings and personnel with little expense, this scheme appears worthy of further study. The court officials are not fully trained legally and cannot offer the range of services or expertise that other legal assistance plans provide; used in conjunction with other plans, however, they comprise a very effective package.

Legal assistance is available from a multitude of other sources as well. Trade unions, welfare agencies, radio shows, newspaper columns, citizens' advice bureaux, bank migrant services,[61] credit unions, trade associations and the like offer referral services or advice on a range of topics. In the area of maintenance and affiliation, the South Australian Department of Community Welfare Officers interview, advise and, when necessary, supply representation. In New South Wales volunteer solicitors are appointed as honorary court solicitors and receive pay only from costs recouped from the losing unassisted party.

The future

Australia could justly regard itself as being genuinely concerned to ensure equality before the law, especially with regard to access to its courts. There is undeniably good will on the part of government and the legal profession alike to provide adequate services. Equally undeniably, there is a rather shallow financial commitment and a highly conservative professional attitude towards the scope and mechanism of delivery. The Law Society schemes are clearly centred on the single client, applying what some have described as the "band-aid" approach. Even those schemes intended to offer a wider approach have succumbed to overwhelming caseloads.

The immediate future of legal aid in Australia can be predicted with a fair degree of accuracy. The coalition Liberal–National Party government is dedicated to a co-ordinated state-by-state approach to legal aid, with each state setting up its own legal service commission which will be responsible for all legal services available within the state. Funding will be through grants from the Commonwealth government as well as from traditional sources. States with Liberal or coalition governments embrace the suggestion with more ardour than Labour state governments. Three states and one territory have already enacted legislation, while Tasmania and the Northern Territory are likely to create a commission soon. No state is unalterably opposed to the proposals. Those that advocate state commissions assert that all legal assistance will be co-ordinated, and unnecessary waste of limited funds through overlap will be eliminated. The state-by-state approach will enable local conditions and circumstances to be taken into account more easily. Both salaried and private lawyers may be included within the delivery system. Legal need studies could be commissioned to determine the placement of such neighbourhood offices as are envisaged. Any stigma of welfare or perceived inferiority of a salaried service is said to be minimized through this approach.

The most heated debate in Australia, at the moment, arises over the composition of the commissions. The Western Australian commission is composed of persons appointed by the state Attorney-General and the Law Society. In South Australia, nominations are made by both the Commonwealth and state Attorneys-General, the Law Society, and by the Council of Social Services. Strong arguments have been advanced that users of the services, welfare agencies, neighbourhood organizers and other concerned non-lawyers ought to participate in a meaningful way in the formulation of policy and in monitoring the operation of legal aid in their communities. The fear is expressed that experienced practitioners and officers of the Law Society, who less often deal with the poor, will place too much emphasis upon a continuing use of the private profession on a "fees for services rendered" basis and legal aid will continue to be available only to a few.

No studies have been conducted in Australia comparing the costs of models as against private practitioners, or assessing consumer satisfaction with the services presently offered. Neighbourhood law offices of the ALAO were located without any detailed examination of the needs of the communities; in some instances they replaced or competed with existing voluntary organizations.

It is even clearer what legal aid in Australia will *not* be in the foreseeable future. There are no realistic plans to approach legal aid as an instrument for improving the position of the poor in society not only by giving equal access to courts, but also by promoting social change through education, organization and law reform. There are no projects to organize test cases, to have a legal service act as a clearinghouse for strategies and research, or to lobby for legislative changes. The vocabulary of legal aid abroad is not yet part of the Australian idiom. Prepaid legal insurance, public interest groups, and group representation are practically unknown. A system where duty solicitors – that is, salaried persons or volunteers on a roster – are available daily at specified courts to advice, represent, or seek an adjournment for any litigant without counsel is not offered for civil matters. The use of paraprofessionals or interface personnel in legal services is in its infancy in Australia. In general, the provision of legal assistance is regarded as a service solely within the competence of fully trained legal practitioners, regardless of the particular assistance requested. Yet law students are found capable of conducting preliminary interviews in some schemes, and clerks of court and chamber magistrates[62] can give preliminary advice, refer and take applications for the Public Solicitor. Officers of the Department of Welfare[63] even supply representation in matters of maintenance and affiliation. Aboriginal field officers in remote areas are often forced to act as mini-legal aid schemes by themselves. The public could benefit by fuller involvement of paralegals in the provision of assistance. Welfare agencies now refer clients to the law schemes but do not participate in order to offer a "package service" to persons with both welfare and legal problems. Law students are not permitted to represent persons before courts, nor to participate in Law Society or government schemes. Interpreters are involved in legal aid only on call in specific instances. McKenzie men[64] or friends of the court are almost unknown in Australia.

Means of access other than legal aid

Any system of legal aid intended to assist an individual client to achieve equal access before the courts will eventually face the problem of limited resources. The "bottomless pit of legal aid" argument is well known, and cannot easily be overcome regardless of the delivery mechanism chosen. Developments other than the provision of legal assistance enabling the underprivileged to participate more fully in the legal process in Australia have significantly ameliorated the situation. It would be well beyond the scope of this paper to detail such developments, but they may be alluded to here.

Dispute-resolving tribunals, including those which give recourse against administrative decisions, apart from the ordinary courts, have achieved a prominent position. While some are merely courts by another name with the adversary system and professional panoply, others are more accessible. The small claims tribunals, for instance, often place limits or outright bars on the appearance of lawyers,[65] and may use a modified inquisitorial procedure. There are several other areas where de-legalization, or at least de-professionalization, of areas of civil law would remove the need for legal aid. The whole area of matrimonial causes has been simplified (though a role for advocates remains) through the creation of the Family Court of Australia.[66] Australia seriously considered a plan of earnings-related benefits for anyone suffering serious sickness or injury, however incurred. Determinations would have been made through administrative proceedings, with review by a judicial tribunal. This would have replaced the entire personal injury fault oriented system, including automobile accidents and industrial accidents, which occupies a majority of the civil courts' time. A Senate committee eventually recommended that the bill be withdrawn and reconsidered. It is no longer under active study.[67]

Some states have no-fault motor accident compensation boards[68] which minimize the necessity for lawyers, but even in these states a tort cause of action requiring proof of fault continues to be available in the ordinary courts.

Reform of the substantive law is another method of achieving legal equality. The Australian Law Reform Commission has the task of reporting on the review, simplification and modernization of the laws within the competence of the Australian Parliament. Each state and territory has at least one Law Reform Commission as well.[69]

To the extent that their efforts are directed to creating a change from a concern over the properties interests to an active protection of disadvantaged persons in the community and to the extent that such changes are accepted by the respective parliaments, Australia will have moved towards equal justice. Law reform commissions are by no means the only groups to recommend changes in legislation. Tenants' unions and environmentalists also play an active role in this regard.

Another approach has been the distribution of "do-it-yourself" kits which eliminate the need for a lawyer or for the courts. For example, a do-it-yourself conveyancing kit is available which, if properly used, might enable one to transfer ownership in property. Kits are also available for do-it-yourself divorce.

Conclusion

Recently legal assistance has opened the courts to many who were formerly deprived of participation in the legal process. A national Commission of Inquiry into Poverty has highlighted the deficiencies in this nation's legal system and the legal profession's approach to poor people. A climate for further sympathetic and effective development of law has been created. Both sides of the political spectrum accept the obligation to ensure that no person is denied access to the courts simply because of lack of means. Unfortunately, economic constraints and conflicting political ideologies have hampered progress. The present situation is unsatisfactory. It is not that Australia has not already done much to ensure that the underprivileged enjoy equality before the law; it is that it has the capacity to do so much more.

Notes and References

1. *Poverty in Australia*, First Main Report, April 1975, Professor Ronald J. Henderson, Chairman (A.P.G.S. 1975). The Second Main Report entitled, *Law and Poverty in Australia*, Professor Ronald Sackville, Commissioner (A.G.P.S. 1975) focused, *inter alia*, on legal services. The latter report was based upon several research studies arranged by the commission, some of which are referred to in this report.
2. *Poverty in Australia, supra*. on p. 14. Some caution should be exercised in relying upon the figure today as double figure annual inflation has been the norm since then.
3. See *infra* at p. 47.
4. See Cass and Sackville, *Legal Needs of the Poor* (A.G.P.S. 1975), esp. pp. 12–52.
5. R. Tomasic, *Australian Legal Aid: Policy Advisers and Governmental Initiatives* (Law Foundation of New South Wales, 1975), criticizes the methodology of the survey but agrees with the conclusions drawn.
6. J. Stubbs, *The Hidden People: Poverty in Australia* (Melbourne, Cheshire-Lansdowne, 1966), pp. 7–8.
7. *Law and Poverty in Australia*, p. 262. The survey figures are from J. W. Brown, R. Hirschfeld and D. Smith, *Aboriginals and Islanders in Brisbane* (Commission Research Report, A.G.P.S., Canberra, 1975), pp. 59ff.
8. R. G. Nettheim, editor, *Aborigines, Human Rights and the Law* (A.N.Z. Book Co., Sydney, 1974), pp. 64–5, 76–7.
9. See *infra*, pp. 62–3.
10. J. L. Martin, "Migration and Social Pluralism" in *How Many Australians? Immigration and Growth* (Angus & Robertson, Sydney, 1971), p. 108.
11. See note 4.
12. The implications for migrants of *Hartley* v. *Fuld* [1965] 2 All. E.R. 655, *Filios* v. *Morland* [1963] S.R. (N.S.W.) 331, and *Dairy Farmer's Co-op.* v. *Acquilina* [1963] 109 C.L.R. 458 is detailed in A. Jakubowicz and B. Buckley, *Migrants and the Legal System* (Commission Research Report A.G.P.S., Canberra, 1975), pp. 37–9.
13. *Territorial Justice in Australia* (N.S.W. Bureau of Crime Statistics and Research, T. Vinson, Director, 1974).
14. Abel-Smith, Zander and Brooke, *Legal Problems and the Citizen* (Heinemann, London, 1973), pp. 213–14 found as a result of a survey

they conducted that the number of law firms in the selected boroughs of London did not correspond with the proportion of the population which had used solicitors during the relevant period.

15. In a survey taken by Cass and Sackville, 70 per cent of those responding agreed that "lawyers are mainly interested in making money" and only 13 per cent agreed that "lawyers are champions of the poor". See *Legal Needs of the Poor*, pp. 82-3.
16. Most work on the relationship between representation and outcome has been undertaken in the criminal law area, see e.g. T. Vinson and R. Hormel, "Legal Representation and Outcome", 47 A.L.J., 132 (1973) which showed a clear association between legal representation and securing a less severe penalty.
17. The s. 81 phrase "for the purpose of the Commonwealth" has been construed both in *Attorney-General for Victoria (ex. rel. Dale)* v. *Commonwealth* [1945] 71 C.L.R. 237, known as the *Pharmaceutical-Benefits Case*, and more recently in *Victoria* v. *Commonwealth* [1975] 8 A.L.R. 277 known as the *A.A.P. Case.* See, for a more detailed explanation of the Constitutional issues, "Forum-Constitutional Challenge to the ALAO", 1 *Legal Service Bulletin*, 164 (1975).
18. See Constitution ss. 51(29), 51(26) 51(23A), 51(27) and 51(23) and (23A) respectively.
19. See Constitution ss. 51(22), 51(14), 51(23 and 23A), 51(2) and 51(20) respectively.
20. The South Australian Law Society, "Information for Guidance of Practitioners", (1972), p. 1. See generally *Legal Aid in Australia* (A.G.P.S. Canberra, 1975), pp. 35-6.
21. New South Wales: *Legal Practitioners (Legal Aid) Act 1970* and *Legal Aid (Miscellaneous Provisions) Act 1974.*
    Queensland: *Legal Assistance Act 1965-1974.*
    South Australia: *Legal Practitioner Act Amendment Act 1969.*
    Tasmania: *Legal Assistance Act 1962* and the Society's authorized *Legal Assistance Scheme 1974.*
    Victoria: *Legal Aid Act 1969.*
    Western Australia: Until July 1, 1977 – *Legal Contribution Trust Act 1967* and *Legal Assistance Rules 1971*. After July 1, 1977 – *Legal Aid Commission Act 1976.*
22. e.g. Queensland Act, s. 5.
23. e.g. Western Australia.
24. e.g. Queensland Act, s. 7(1) and Tasmanian Scheme, s.3.
25. Western Australian Act of 1967, s. 40(3).

26. See *Legal Aid in Australia*, p. 10.
27. Tasmania Act, s. 5.
28. Western Australia Act of 1967, s. 4.
29. South Australia Act, s. 24i(1).
30. e.g. in New South Wales, no representation is available for Petty Sessions, New South Wales Act 1970, s. 8(1).
31. e.g. Queensland Act, s. 19(2).
32. e.g. New South Wales Act 1970, s. 10(1).
33. e.g. South Australia Act, s. 24i(3)
34. See *infra*, p. 54.
35. The Western Australian scheme was replaced by the Legal Aid Commission Act 1976 and the Legal Aid Commission Amendment Act 1977. This commission commenced operation on April 17, 1978. See pp. 55-6 *infra* for further details.
36. Interview with Mr. L. C. Wood, Secretary of the Legal Aid Committee, May 7, 1974, as per *Legal Aid in Australia*, p. 63.
37. e.g. Queensland Act, s. 19(3).
38. E. Mathews and A. Oulton, *Legal Aid and Advice* (Butterworths, London, 1971), p. 124.
39. *Queensland Legal Assistance (General) Regulations 1966-1974*, 27(7).
40. e.g. Victoria Act, s. 8(1).
41. New South Wales Act s. 7. This mandatory contribution was removed for very low income earners previously eligible for aid under the Legal Assistance Act by a 1974 amendment, but it is retained for all applicants above that means level.
42. e.g. Victorian Act, s. 11(1), (4).
43. Western Australia: Legal Aid Commission Act 1976 (No. 143 of 1976), Legal Aid Commission Amendment Act 1977 (No. 60 of 1977); South Australia: Legal Services Commission Act 1977 (No. 25 of 1977; Queensland: Legal Aid Act 1978 (June 1978 – number unknown at time of writing); A.C.T.: Legal Aid Ordinance 1977 (No. 31 of 1977).
44. Legal Services Commission Act 1977, s. 10.
45. The professional bodies in Victoria – The Law Institute and Bar Council – have made their submissions which have, in turn, been criticized. See 50 *Law Institute Journal* (Vic.) 174 (1976) and J. Gardner, "Legal Aid at the Cross Roads", 2 *Legal Service Bulletin*, 52 (1976).
46. Commonwealth Legal Aid Commission Act 1977 (No. 80 of 1977).

47. See Victorian Yearbook 1975, pp. 867-9. Figure achieved by adding all civil cases heard in the Magistrate's Court, County Court and Supreme Court.
48. See *Legal Aid Committee Report 1974-1975,* 50 *Law Institute Journal* 43 (1976). The figures for the year 1975-76 are available but were not used, as they show a considerable decrease in applications approved pursuant to an agreement made with both the Commonwealth and Victorian governments substantially vacating the matrimonial field. See *Legal Aid Committee Report 1975-1976*, 50 *Law Institute Journal*, 465 (1976).
49. In 1975, one defalcation of a legal firm totalled over $6 million and two others approached $1 million each. Money in the trust fund, formerly used to finance legal aid, was diverted to reimburse clients who had deposited trust funds with solicitors. In Victoria, no money whatever from that source was available in 1975-76, and only an amendment to the relevant provision of the Legal Profession Practice Act 1958 (Vic.) was funding made available in 1977. The committee now receives a guaranteed annual payment of $500,000 from the Solicitor's Guaranteed Fund.
50. See 50 *Law Institute Journal*, 465, 466 (1976).
51. See *Legal Aid in Australia*, p. 33.
52. The South Australian offices are an exception. They open during the evening hours to give legal advice, though at that time they are staffed by volunteers.
53. This may soon be altered. The Australian Law Reform Commission has received a reference on February 1, 1977, entitled "Reference: Access to the Courts" which includes, *inter alia*, developing and reforming the law "upon the capacity and rights of persons to be heard in courts and proposals which have been made relating to class actions". The 36th Report of the Law Reform Commission of South Australia (1977) recommends that legislation be passed to facilitate class actions.
54. J. M. Fitzgerald, *Poverty and the Legal Profession in Victoria* (1975) conducted a survey asking, *inter alia*, what proportion of working time was spent on legal work of any sort for poor persons. The mean answer was 10 per cent, a result which Fitzgerald, on the basis of other data, asserts is probably exaggerated. See Fitzgerald, Ch. 4.
55. Speech by Senator L. K. Murphy, Q.C., from Parliamentary Debates, December 13, 1973.
56. The detailed ALAO guidelines may be found in 2 *Legal Service*

Bulletin 21 (1976). With inflation, and a failure to revise the means test upwards since 1976, a number of pensioners now receive wealthier benefits in amounts that disqualify them for ALAO assistance.

57. Submission made to the Australian Commission of Inquiry into Poverty by the Fitzroy Legal Service, p. 1.
58. Fitzroy is a working-class suburb close to the city of Melbourne, Victoria.
59. For example, the Solicitors (Professional Conduct and Practice) Rules (Vic.) made pursuant to the Legal Profession Practice Act (Vic.) provide in part that "A Solicitor shall not in the course of or in connection with his practice as a solicitor insert or cause or permit to be inserted on his behalf any advertisement in any newspaper or other publication . . .". Many of the voluntary Legal Services advertise the hours they are open and the services provided. The Law Institute has not raised any objection to such advertisements. The rules of Bar Council in jurisdictions with divided profession, require members of the Bar to take instruction only from solicitors, and not from lay clients. Yet the Bar Council has permitted its members to participate in voluntary legal services and advise lay persons without instructions from a solicitor.
60. See *Legal Needs of the Poor*, Ch. 11.
61. Many of the large trading banks have made available to migrants at no cost, full-time multi-lingual staff, who *inter alia* advise migrants on legal and commercial matters, and supply translations for legal documents.
62. See *infra*, p. 65.
63. See *infra*, p. 66.
64. A McKenzie man is a person who sits beside a litigant, prompts, gives advice and quietly assists. From *McKenzie* v. *McKenzie* [1970] 3 W.L.R. 472.
65. See e.g. *Small Claims Tribunal Act 1973* (Vic.) s. 30(3).
66. The Family Law Court was instituted under the *Family Law Act 1975* (Cth.).
67. The draft National Compensation Bill 1974 was contained in *Compensation and Rehabilitation in Australia* (A.G.P.S., Canberra, 1974). The Report of the Senate Standing Committee on Constitutional and Legal Affairs is contained in *Clauses of the National Compensation Bill 1974* (A.G.P.S., Canberra, 1975).
68. e.g. The Motor Accidents Board (Vic.) is created by the *Motor*

Accidents Act 1973 (Vic.), s. 5.

69. For a complete list of Australian Law Reform Agencies, and their current operations see *Reform 1976–1977.*

BERNHARD KÖNIG*

Austria

The settlement of private disputes is one of the essential state functions which forbid self-help. The domestication of the socio-political powers on the one hand and the refusal to permit self-help on the other are tantamount to depriving the individual of his civil rights unless he is also offered the appropriate channels to seek the protection of the state when his legal rights are infringed.[1] If the state is to fulfil this function satisfactorily, it is no longer sufficient merely to provide speedy and efficient procedures for the assertion of claims and the enforcement of legal judgments; what is required in addition to a formal guarantee of accessibility to the courts is the actual creation of this accessibility for all social groups: "The state, having recognized litigation as a proper instrument of legal protection, must ensure that this instrument is available to rich and poor alike."[2]

It can safely be said, however, that many citizens avoid "the path to the institutions of the law", either because they do not know their rights, or because these institutions are themselves alien to the people, or because they balk at the risk of high legal costs, which are usually hard to assess in advance even for those with legal training. For these reasons some people will waive their right to assert a material claim or will agree to a settlement out of court, which is often less advantageous than the court's judgment would have been. This phenomenon can be observed particularly among those social groups commonly labelled "lower class" or "lower-middle class".[3]

The flood of literature and learned comments on this problem and

*Translated by Dr. Christopher March. Paper published in German under title "Chancengleichheit im und vor dem Gerreichtstadt" which appeared in Osterreichisches Anwaltsblatt 1978, at pp. 55–62.

related questions, especially in the German Federal Republic,[4] shows how pressing the matter is and equally how complex the concept of "equality in and out of court" really is. This report presents a specifically Austrian view.

(a) Equality in court

Equality will not be achieved simply by applying, in the course of legal proceedings, those regulations that are designed to protect the interests of the underprivileged,[5] since the main obstacle to equality of access in the assertion of claims is the prospect of having to bear the costs of the proceedings, either temporarily or, in the event of an unfavourable judgment, finally.[6]

Zeiller[7] himself was one of the first to criticize the fact that "the costs of a case are often considerable and may entirely swallow up the disputed amount" and that they therefore "deter the aggrieved and underprivileged citizen from seeking redress through the just workings of the law." In Austria a system of legal aid[8] was therefore established for the purpose o of overcoming these obstacles to court access.

The predecessor of the present legal aid scheme was *Armenrecht* (legal aid for the poor), which Grünberg[9] called "a socio-political instrument for the immediate benefit of the lower classes", and although this *Armenrecht* was not explicitly formulated in the 1781 Code of Court Procedure (*Allgemeine Gerichtsordnung*), the tendency in Austrian legislation on civil proceedings to "make recourse to litigation as independent of material wealth as possible"[10] was reflected at that time in the "relatively small role played by sureties in legal proceedings in Austria" and soon led to explicit statutory provisions which formulated the state's obligation to disburse the costs of a case to poor parties, including both court fees and costs of representation. The chapter dated 1.11.1781,[11] section 8 stated:

> Such persons as provide credible evidence of their indigence, whether in the form of a document issued by the relevant authority or in any other form, demonstrating their lack of wealth and possessions beyond the minimum means of subsistence, shall be exempted from all charges, and the charges, in the case of a dispute between an indigent party and a wealthy one, shall be recorded only so that they can be charged to the latter, should he be sentenced to pay the costs of the case.

A decree issued in 1791[12] also made provision for the legal representation of the poor. Subsequent legislation defined "the poor" who were to be exempted from paying stamp duties, as "those persons whose income from their estate, wealth, pension, work or service is no greater than the standard daily wage in the said person's place of residence."[13] Beyond this objective[14] criterion, no further proof was required of the party's inability to pay the costs of litigation. It is perhaps worth mentioning that as an extension of the common law concept of *Armenrecht* the assisted party was only called upon to reimburse court fees and legal costs if the assisted action resulted in an improvement in his financial situation.[15]

Although *Armenrecht* was extensively improved by the Code of Civil Procedure (ZPO) in 1895, soon after its introduction further suggestions for reform[16] were voiced, and these have continued to receive support.[17]

More recent developments include a resolution approved by the upper chamber of the Austrian parliament on June 26, 1968 to the effect that "the conditions which are required to be fulfilled for the granting of legal aid under present legislation are no longer consonant with current social standards and expectations,"[18] as well as a complaint lodged by a Viennese lawyer with the European Commission on Human Rights[19] and with the Austrian Constitutional Court.[20] These developments paved the way for a redrafting of *Armenrecht* in 1973. Although the resulting Legal Aid Act (*Verfahrenshilfegesetz*)[21] by no means revolutionized traditional juridical thinking,[22] it certainly provided more than mere rewording,[23] and it represents a major step towards equality of access to the courts.[24]

This is evident from the fact that the Legal Aid Act enlarges the beneficiary group in comparison with the regulations hitherto in force. In the new Act (ZPO s. 63, para. 1), a person is entitled to free legal assistance if he is incapable of bearing the costs of proceedings without serious harm to his maintenance or that of those members of his family whom he supports; the sums needed for such maintenance are considered to be such amounts as will ensure a simple life style for the party and his dependent family. According to the explanatory notes accompanying the government bill on the Legal Aid Act, this "simple" life represents "an objective concept, based on a modest life style, which, however, also takes the relative needs of the individual party into consideration with regard to the means required to maintain the party's spiritual and physical well being and his earning power".[25]

Section 64, para. 1, sentence 1 in combination with s. 63, para. 1 of the ZPO also makes provision for a situation where an applicant for legal aid may be able to meet a part of the costs without endangering his basic maintenance (partial legal aid). Each certificate of eligibility therefore lists which of the benefits enumerated in s. 64, para. 1 of the ZPO have been approved and to what extent.[26]

The introduction of the Legal Aid Act in 1973 has reduced the mass of formalities previously involved in applying for legal assistance. Previously, a certificate of entitlement to legal aid for the poor (*Armenrechtszeugnis*) had to be issued by the local council of the applicant's place of residence[27] and sometimes had to be endorsed by the district authority. This certificate, together with an application for legal aid for the poor, was then submitted to the court of first instance. Under the present regulation, however (s. 66 of the ZPO), an applicant need simply present a "declaration of assets",[28] drawn up by the applicant himself no more than four weeks before submission of the application, as the basis for his written or oral application for legal aid.[29] Printed forms are available from the courts for both the applications and the declaration of assets.[30]

A further positive innovation, and one whose practical consequences should not be underestimated, is contained in s. 63, para. 2 of the ZPO.[31]

Prior to the Legal Aid Act of 1973 corporate bodies were only eligible for legal assistance if they fulfilled the requirements pertaining to natural persons, and if the funds necessary for the assertion of the claim could not be made available by the corporate bodies themselves or by the parties with an economic interest[32] in the litigation, and if a failure to take legal proceedings would be against the public interest. The formulation[33] and origins[34] of s. 63, para. 4 of the law prior to the Legal Aid Act, highly reminiscent of the legal philosophy and judicial opinions prevailing in Federal Germany, produced a degree of inequality in the treatment of natural persons and corporate bodies to the extent that the latter were practically excluded from all benefits of *Armenrecht.* Thus the small limited company was more or less deprived of its legal rights in cases of hardship. The new Legal Aid Act eliminated the public interest requirement which was discriminatory and thus incompatible with the constitutional guarantee of equality before the Law. It also extended the group of potential beneficiaries to include other parties *sui juris.*[36]

The Austrian legislation of the nineteenth century set aside the assisted party's obligation to reimburse the legal aid fund except where the "poor" party had gained assets as a result of the action.

Later, in the ZPO of 1895, the obligation to repay costs was abolished entirely;[37] hence Pollak's[38] fitting remark that the ZPO (1895) "offers total and not merely temporary exemption from the payment of costs".

In 1943,[39] however, s. 125, para. 1 of the German Code of Civil

Procedure was incorporated almost word for word in the Austrian ZPO, and this act of assimilation reintroduced the unrestricted obligation of the assisted party to reimburse the legal aid fund "as soon as capable of doing so without detriment to the basic maintenance of the assisted person and his family".

This obligation to reimburse was not subject to any time limit after the ruling of the court had become legally binding; it necessitated, however, the keeping of continuous records, which was an unworkable requirement. Finally a time limit on the obligation to reimburse was imposed by s. 71 of the SPO; now, the repayment of costs can no longer be prescribed after a period of three years after termination of proceedings.

On the other hand, the SPO brought no change to the unhappy requirement of a preliminary opinion on the merits of the case of the applicant, whether plaintiff or defendant. Under s. 63 of the ZPO, legal aid is to be granted to the beneficiary only if assertion or defence of the claim has some chance of success and does not appear to depend on an arbitrary decision.[40]

An examination of "the merits of the claim asserted by the applicant for legal assistance for the poor"[41] was not a requirement of the 1895 ZPO. The explanatory notes to the government bill concluded[42] that as a rule it was not possible to conduct a serious examination at the application stage and that any such examination that did take place would represent a prejudicial 'assessment of probability" of the expected outcome of the proceedings. "A decision on an application for legal assistance must usually be taken without the means of assessing the justness of the proceedings. Nor can one demand that the applicant party should make such means available to the court, since, before submitting an application for legal aid, the party would require the services of a legal adviser to provide the necessary instructions for assembling the requisite documents and information." Only with the assistance of a lawyer would it be possible "to clarify the situation to such an extent that a decision might be taken as to whether proceedings could be taken with some chance of success" or not. Thus only a lawyer could apply to be released from a case where the action appeared arbitrary or hopeless (Article XXXIII of the introductory act to the ZPO prior to the Legal Aid Act).[43] A consequence of these provisions was the phenomenon of "intimidatory proceedings"[44] initiated by parties who used "the protection of the legal aid system to sue arbitrarily for large amounts in order to force a settlement on the opposing party, who would fear the legal costs, all the more since he would have no hope of being reimbursed for his own costs by the insolvent plaintiff".[45] This phenomenon led to the introduction of a statute which made the granting of legal aid dependent on the condition that the intended assertion or defence of a claim must have some chance of success and may not appear to depend on an arbitrary decision.[46] This condition for the award of legal assistance was adopted unchanged in the Legal Aid Act.[47]

Little change[48] was also made to the provisions concerning legal representation for the poor. As long as "legal representation is compulsory or appears necessary by virtue of the difficulty of the case" (s. 64, para. 1, item 3 of the ZPO), the assisted party is entitled to be provided with the services of a lawyer free of charge.[49] The lawyer appointed to a case is nominated by the Austrian Bar Association,[50] and the remuneration, apart from any costs recovered from the opposing party,[51] is made in the form of a lump-sum payment from the legal aid fund to the Council of the Bar Association for the lawyers' pension, disability and survivors' fund.[52]

The Austrian solution to the important question of equality before the law does not represent the *ultima et optima ratio*. In addition to the recognition of the freedom of the legal profession, the provision of free choice of advocate is equally a principle of justice in the constitutional state.[53] This principle, which of course can only be realized in the case of the legal-aid lawyer if accompanied by a modification of the system of remuneration to take into account the level of service offered, will require consideration in the future.[54]

(b) Equality out of court

There are many people whose legal rights are forfeited because they are not aware that they possess such rights or because they do not know how to enforce them.[55] Yet rarely is this ignorance the fault of the people themselves. The necessity of regulating large areas of social life has resulted in a flood of legislation, the contents of which are for the most part entirely comprehensible only to the specialist; as a result, there is widespread ignorance of the law and a consequent dependence on the professional sources of expert legal advice.[56] The need for preventive legal services[57] is increasing.[58] Obviously the opportunities for meeting such needs can be expressed as a function of the individual's financial situation.

The foregoing discussion of the Austrian legal aid scheme does not extend to extra-judicial advice for low income groups. Such persons can obtain legal advice free of charge from an institution attached to the District Courts known as the *Audienzkanzlei*, which is staffed by practising and probationary judges. As far as advice and information are provided without necessarily leading to legal proceedings, this institution represents a service *praeter legem.*[59]

The *Audienzkanzlei* is supplemented by a free legal information service[60] offered by some[61] of the regional bar associations in Austria on one or more days per month; this service has been in operation since 1951 in Salzburg,[62] 1964 in Tyrol,[63] 1970 in Vienna, Lower Austria and Burgenland,[64] and 1972 in Upper Austria.[65] The service, originally intended for the indigent, requires no proof of the party's eligibility. The lawyers, who provide this service on a *rota* basis, offer preliminary information on the legal interpretation of the case presented as well as on the possible proceedings to be taken and the chances of enforcing any resulting claims.

There are numerous problems raised by this extra-judicial advisory service: for example, the need to progress from the preliminary information, which is given free of charge, to legal advice and legal representation, which are not; the problem of the lawyer on duty referring inquiries to his own practice; and the fear that lawyers might abuse this free service for advertising purposes, as well as the danger that the service would be used for unmeritorious claims. In spite of these problems, this institution represents a valuable social service which is not financed by the state or by the lump-sum remuneration from the legal aid fund. The attendance figures at the centres[66] show that this facility for obtaining free preliminary advice from the legal profession is attractive.

In addition to the above source of information, there are numerous institutions in Austria that offer specific legal advice. Various local authorities, chambers of commerce, employees' associations, and trade unions, as well as public and private interest groups offer legal advice services in the fields of law pertaining to their own spheres of activity and interests.[67] As a rule, access to these services is limited to the members of these bodies.

Occasionally there is criticism of the fact that in such organizations the legal advice is rarely dispensed by qualified members of the legal profession, the implication being that an unqualified adviser offers poor quality advice. Experience has shown, however, that these organizations have experienced staffs who provide absolutely correct and satisfactory advice and assistance in their individual fields of law. At all events, these institutions certainly serve to relieve the social pressure on lawyers to provide legal advice free of charge.[68]

On the other hand, where the party thus advised feels the need to assert or defend a claim in court, then, for reasons which have recently been explored by Haslinger,[69] "the fully qualified physician" is preferable to the "ambulance man". Thus, calls for a more open approach, perhaps in the way of a "consumer representative", represent *reformationes in peius*!

In summary, the Austrian combination of the legal aid system on the one hand and the legal advice services offered by the courts, lawyers, private organizations and interest groups on the other constitutes a fully acceptable and consumer-oriented formal guarantee of public access to the courts.[70] Admittedly, improvements are still possible and desirable. The socio-political "bandwagon" effect of "equality in and out of court", however, must not be permitted to lead to a list of demands that are doomed from the start because of the realities of the situation.

Notes and References

1. Fechner, Kostenrisiko und Rechtswegsperre – Steht der Rechtsweg offen?, *Deutsche Juristenzeitung* (*DJZ*) 1969, 349ff.
2. F. Klein, Zeit- und Geistesströmungen im Prozesse, a lecture printed in: Franz Klein, *Reden/Vorträge/Aufsätze/Briefe* (hrsg. von Friedlaender, 1927) I 131; also by the same author, Die Parteienvertretung im künftigen Processe, *Juristische Blätter* (*JBl*) 1893, 350: ". . . the pursuance of a legal right should not appear to depend on a company's funds".
3. On the subject of the admissibility of minority languages in Austrian courts as a solution to a barrier that has mainly political implications, namely the "language barrier", cf. Vilfan, *Die Österreichische Zivilprozessordnung von 1895 und der Gebrauch der slowenischen Sprache vor Gericht* (1970) 5ff.; Veiter, Minderheitensprachen in Österreich als Gerichtssprachen, in *Der Staatsbürger* 1976, Folge 16, 1f.; on specific aspects König, *Konformität, Aktenwidrigkeit und offenbare Gesetzwidrigkeit im zivilgerichtlichen Verfahren* (1975) 30, footnote 22. In general Bausinger, Sprachschranken vor Gericht, in: *Festschrift* (*FS*) K.-S. Kramer (1976) 12ff.
4. Cf. Baumgärtel, *Gleicher Zugang zum Recht für alle* (1976); by the same author, Chancengleichheit vor Gericht – Utopien und Möglichkeiten, in: *FS Lange* (1976) 943ff.; Knoppke – Wetzel, Rechtsfürsorge durch "private" Anwälte oder durch Anwälte in "öffentlichen" Rechtsfürsorgebüros, *DJZ* 1976, 145ff.; see also the reports presented by Grunsky and Trocker to the 51st Convention of German Jurists (DJT) (1976) on the subject: Empfehlen sich im Interesse einer

effektiven Rechtsverwirklichung für alle Bürger Änderungen des Systems des Kosten- und Gebührenrechts?, as well as the authors they quote. In view of the abundance of papers on this subject, it was not surprising that Baur should open his remarks at the 51st DJT with the comment that everything had already been said more than once; see also Baur, Kostenrecht – Armenrecht, *Neue Juristische Wochenschrift* (*NJW*) 1976, 1380.

5. These include sections 180ff., 204, 432, 434 of the ZPO. See the early critique of the Austrian ZPO by Menger, *Das bürgerliche Recht und die besitzlosen Volksklassen*[4] (1908), especially 36f. In this field the Austrian ZPO broke new ground; it contains "nothing of the easy-going quality of the Viennese, nothing of the notorious muddling of the Austrians, but rather one has the impression of something of *the sharp wind that will blow within the social state*" (Guttmann, Der österreichische Prozess und die deutsche Reform, *Rheinische Zeitschrift für Zivil- und Prozessrecht* (*RheinZ*) 1 [1909] 239; cf. the other references in König, *Konformität* 25f. footnote 3).
6. Cf. Waldner, *Die Lehre von den Processkosten nach österreichischem Process- und Privatrecht* (1883); Pollak, Die Zivilprozesskosten nach österreichischem Recht, in: *FS Wach* I (1913) 103ff.; and more recently Sellert, Die Akzessorietät von Kostentragung und Prozesserfolg. – Ein historisches Problem von aktueller Bedeutung, in: *FS Erler* ("Rechtsgeschichte als Kulturgeschichte", 1976), Elsener, Der "arme Mann" (pauper) im Prozessrecht der Grafen und Herzoge von Savoyen, in: *Tijdschrift voor Rechtsgeschiedenis* 1976, 93ff., Schuler, Die "armen Lüt" und das Gericht. Eine Strassburger Schrift über die Reform des geistlichen Gerichts, in: *Recht und Schrift im Mittelalter*, hrsg. von Classen(1977).
7. Grundsätze über die Haupteigenschaften einer Civil-Gerichtsordnung, in: *Jährlicher Beytrag zur Gesetzkunde und Rechtswissenschaft in den Österreichischen Erbstaaten* 3 (1808) 140.
8. Bundesgesetz vom 8.11.1973, mit dem das Einführungsgesetz zur Zivilprozessordnung, die Zivil prozessordnung, die Strafprozessordnung, das Jugendgerichtsgesetz, das Verwaltungsgerichtshofgesetz und das Allgemeine Verwaltungsverfahrensgesetz zur Regelung der Verfahrenshilfe geändert werden (Verfahrenshilfegesetz), *Österreichisches Bundesgesetzblatt* (*BGBl*) 1973, 569. – Interesting comparative aspects in Trocker, *Report, 51st DJT* (1976) B 62ff., and in Gottwald, Aremenrecht in Westeuropa und die Reform des deutschen Rechts, *Zeitschrift für Zivilprozess*) (*ZZP*) 89 (1976) 136ff. Cf. also König,

Igualdade de chance na sala de audiencias e fora dela – da sua situacao do ponto de vista austriaco, in: *Revista de processo* (São Paolo) 1977/78.

9. Der socialpolitische Gehalt der österreichischen Civilprocessgesetzgebung, *Österreichische Gerichtszeitung* (*GZ*), 1900, 67.
10. Menger, Die Lehre von den Streitparteien im österreichischen Civilprocess, Zeitschrift für das Privat- und öffentliche Recht der Gegenwart (*GrünhutsZ*) 7 (1880) 664.
11. *Justizgesetzsammlung* (*JGS*) 28.
12. Hofdekret vom 24.1.1791 *JGS* 106.
13. Hofkammer-Präsidial-Decret vom 26.7.1840 *JGS* 457, §1.
14. Menger, Lehre, *GrünhutsZ* 7 (1880) 667. For a detailed discussion of the earlier "Armenrecht" see Holzgethan, Über das Armenrecht der Parteien im österreichischen Civilprocesse nach älteren und neueren Gesetzen, Zeitschrift für österreichische Rechtsgelehrsamkeit und politische Gesetzkunde (*WagnersZ*) 1843 II 65ff.
15. Cf. Z 2 des Erlasses des Finanzministeriums vom 8.2.1853, über den Umfant des Armenrechts im streitigen Verfahren und über die Berichtigung der baren Auslagen, welche mit der Verhängung der Curatel über wahn- und blödsinnige oder mit der Anordnung der Fortdauer der Vormundschaft über volljährig gewordene vermögenslose Personen verbunden sind, österreichisches Reichsgesetzblatt (*RGBl*) 110; section 16 der Advocatenordnung 1868 (Gesetz vom 6.7.1868 *RGBl* 96).
16. Cf. Stössel, Zur Reform des Armenrechts, österr. *Anwaltszeitung* (*AnwZ*) 1932, 336f.; also Toth, Zur Reform des Armenrechts, *AnwZ* 1932, 438f., and Brassloff, *Reformen und Reformvorschläge auf dem Gebiete des Privatrechts und Zivilprozessrechts* (1936) 56ff.
17. Cf. the explanatory notes on the government bill for the Legal Aid Act, 846 of the Beilagen zu den stenographischen Protokollen des Nationalrates, 13. *Gesetzgebungsperiode* (3.7.1973) 8.
18. 266. Sitzung des Bundesrates der Republik Österreich", am 26.6.1968, stenographische Protokolle des Bundesrates 6821, 6826.
19. "Gussenbauer gegen Republik Österreich", Appl. Nr. 4897/71; Cf. Gussenbauer, Müssen wir Anwälte für den Staat ohne Entgelt arbeiten?, *Anwaltsblatt* (*AnwBl*) 1970, 302ff., "Ein Ombudsman für Österreich", *SWA-Studienarbeit* 1970, 19; "Rechtsschutzhilfe statt Armenrecht", *SWA-Rechtsgutachten* Nr. 47, 3; and also the references in Trocker, *Report, 51st DJT* (1976) B 62 footnote 180 and in the explanatory notes (footnote 17).

20. Decision of Verfassungsgerichtshof 19.12.1972, Kundmachung des Bundeskanzlers vom 9.1.1973 *BGBl* 42, und des Bundesministers für Justiz vom 8.1.1973 *BGBl* 43.
21. See footnote 8. Quotations from the ZPO without further designation are taken from the ZPO as defined in this Act.
22. Fechner, Kostenrisiko, *DJZ* 1969, 352, designates *Armenrecht* in general as a "relict of the 19th century".
23. The Legal Aid Act makes use of the term "Verfahrenshilfe" instead of the discriminatory word "Armenrecht", for who wants to be officially designated as "poor" ("arm") in an age in which "poor" is equated with "failure"?
24. Kininger, Der wirtschaftlich Schwache im österreichischen Zivilprozess, *Österreichische Juristenzeitung* (*ÖJZ*) 1976, 9ff., dismisses the Act as mere "marginal corrections"; diss. op. Baumgärtel, *Zugang* 183, and by the same author, Chancengleichheit vor Gericht durch Pflichtrechtsschutzversicherung oder Prozesshilfe?, *DJZ* 1975, 429, footnote 50 ("the Austrian legal aid scheme could serve as a model for reform measures in Germany").
25. Explanatory notes (footnote 17) 12.
26. §64 Abs 2 ZPO; but note the limitation imposed by §64 Abs 2 Satz 2, ZPO (on this point Fasching, Kommentar zu den Zivilprozessgesetzen, *Ergänzungsband* (1974) 26). The idea of a statutory provision for "partial legal assistance", a suggestion discussed much earlier in the court decree of 4.11. 1793 JGS 132, was reactivated for the ZPO in the debate on the 8th amendment to the Relief of the Courts Act (Gerichtsentlastungsgesetz) (Verordnung vom 26.7.1933, *BGBl* 346) in: "Begründung des Vortrags an den Ministerrat" (printed in: Hermann, *Achte Gerichtsentlastungsnovelle* [1933] 8). Trocker, *Report, 51st DJT* (1976) B 63f., considers it questionable whether partial legal aid "can provide a larger number of persons than hitherto with unrestricted access to the courts".
27. §65 Abs 2 und 3 ZPO (old version), in connection with the statutory order 23.5.1897, über das Armenrecht und die Ausfertigung und Bestätigung von Zeugnissen zur Erlangung des Armenrechts, *RGBl* 130.
28. Section 69 of the ZPO makes statutory provision for sanctions in the case of incorrect or incomplete entries in the declaration of assets.
29. For the competent courts see §65 ZPO.
30. See Erlass vom 5.11.1973, über die Auflassung der Formblätter ZPForm 3 und 4 (alt) und AussStrForm 66 und 67 sowie über die

Neuschaffung der Formblätter ZPForm 1, 2, 3 und 4 und über das Vorgehen bei der Ausfertigung und Zustellung des Formblattes ZPForm 4, *JABl* 14; Specimens of these forms are printed in Nowak, *Handbuch der Verfahrenshilfe* (1974) 133ff.

31. Similarly Trocker, *Report, 51st DJT* (1976) B 63 footnote 183.
32. For an interpretation of this concept see Fasching, *Kommentar Ergänzungsband* 11.
33. Cf. § 144 Abs 4 German ZPO.
34. § 63 Abs 4 ZPO (old version) was only introduced in Austria with the statutory order on the further simplification of the administration of civil procedure law (4. Vereinfachungsverordnung) vom 12.1.1943 deutsches *RGBl* I 7 (§ 9 Z 1).
35. Fechner, Kostenrisiko, *DJZ* 1969, 352; Däubler, Bürger ohne Rechtsschutz?, *Der Betriebs-Berater* (*BB*) 1969, 545; Isola, Schwierigkeiten beim Zugang zur Rechtspflege, in: *Recht und Politik* 1974, 67.
36. Explanatory notes (footnote 17) 12.
37. Admittedly, an obligation to reimburse continued to exist in cases where the certificate of eligibility was rescinded and legal assistance was subsequently withdrawn becasue the conditions for eligibility had not been met at the time of issue (§71 ZPO 1895).
38. System des Österreichischen Zivilprozessrechtes mit Einschluss des Exekutionsrechtes[2] (1932) 171.
39. 4. Vereinfachungsverordnung 1943 (footnote 34) § 9 Z 7.
40. Should the clearly arbitrary nature of a claim or its hopelessness become apparent after legal aid has already been granted, either an *ex nunc* declaration of extinction was issued (§68 Abs 1 ZPO) or the legal aid was withdrawn *ex tunc* (§68 Abs 2 ZPO). Fasching (*Kommentar* II (1962) 443) considers this the commonest case for the application of section 68 para. 2 of the ZPO.
41. Materialien zu den österreichischen Civilprocessgesetzen I (1897) 221.
42. Materialien I 221; cf. also 645.
43. The provisions of section 191, para. 5 of the 1930 rules of procedure (Verordnung vom 1.3.1930 *BGBl* 74) for courts of 1st and 2nd instance were (according to Pollak, *System* 179) illegal: "Legal aid for proceedings to be taken at a court of law shall be refused where the claim would be nonsuited by virtue of lack of competence of the court, exclusion of recourse to the court, the case being *sub judice*, or "res judicata."
44. Klein, Probevortrag an der Wiener Universität, printed in: Franz

Klein, *Reden/Vorträge/Aufsätze/Briefe* I 7; Grünhut, Der Strafrechtliche Schutz loyaler Prozessführung, *Schweizerische Zeitschrift für Strafrecht* 51 (1937) 44.

45. That at least is the opinion of "Begründung des Vortrages an den Ministerrat" zur 8. Gerichtsentlastungsnovelle (printed in Hermann, *Achte Gerichtsentlastungsnovelle* 7).
46. 8. *Gerichtsentlastungsnovelle* 1933, Art III Z 2.
47. Cf. Kininger, Der wirtschaftlich Schwache, *ÖJZ* 1976, 10.
48. But cf. §70 ZPO (old version).
49. Cf. the regulations on the provision of a lawyer in a case where the venue is not the place of residence of the assisted plaintiff or defendant, which does not meet the qualifications listed in the text (§64 Abs 1 Z 4 ZPO).
50. §67 ZPO, §45f. Rechtsanwaltsordnung (RAO).
51. §70 ZPO, §16 Abs 2 RAO.
52. §§16 Abs 3, 47ff. RAO. Vgl Trocker, *Report, 51st DJT* (1976) B 62 Anm 179.
58. From this point of view there has recently developed a questionable tendency in Austrian legal advice insurance policies, in which the insurance company reserves the right to nominate the lawyer of its choice instead of leaving free choice of advocate to the policyholder (see König, Rechtsschutz-Versicherung und freie Anwaltswahl, *ÖJZ* 1977, 387ff.; Orator, Richtlinie 33 a – Begründung und Bedeutung, *AnwBl* 1977, 164f., und Schuppich, Rechtsschutzversicherung und Konsumentenschutz, *AnwBl* 1977, 365f.).
54. Cf. Kininger, Der wirtschaftlich Schwache, *ÖJZ* 1976, 11f. and the proposals of the SWA-Rechtsgutachtens Nr. 47 (footnote 19) 26f.
55. Isolat, Schwierigkeiten, in: *Recht und Politik* 1974, 68.
56. Cf. Spitzer, Rechtsfürsorge und Rechtsanwaltschaft, *AnwZ* 1932, 409ff.; Schuschnigg, Rechtsfürsorge und Rechtsanwaltschaft, *AnwZ* 1932, 429f.; Weninger, Erste anwaltliche Auskunft, *AnwBl* 1971, 224f.
57. In particular on this point see e.g. Isola, Schwierigkeiten, in: *Recht und Politik* 1974, 68ff.; Röper, Grenzen behördlicher Rechtsberatung, *NJW* 1975, 1546ff.; Schoreit, Rechtsberatung Minderbemittelter durch öffentliche Rechtsauskunftsstellen oder durch Armenanwälte?, *Zeitschrift für Rechtspolitik* (*ZRP*) 1975, 62ff.; by the same author *Rechtsberatung unentgeltlich* (1974); by the same author Nulltarif bei der Rechtsberatung?, *Die öffentliche Verwaltung* (*DÖV*) 1975, 380ff.; Herbst, Die Rechtsberatung Minderbemittelter in der Praxis,

ZRP 1975, 219ff.; to the history Isermann, "Freie Rechtshilfe" und "Gemeinnützige Rechtsauskunftsstellen" vor 1933 in Deutschland und im Ausland, in: *Recht und Politik* 1975, 31ff.

58. Zeiller urged in 1806 (Nothwendigkeit eines bürgerlichen, einheimischen Privat-Rechts. Grundzüge zur Geschichte des Österreichischen Privat-Rechts. Eigenschaften eines bürgerlichen Gesetzbuches, in: Zeiller, *Jährlicher Beytrag zur Gesetzkunde und Rechtswissenschaft in den Österreichischen Erbstaaten* 1 (1806) 62): "If one wishes to lay down the principle that ignorance is no defence before the law, then it must be made possible for everyone to attain a knowledge of the law. The display or reading of a statute book in public places, or publication in pamphlet form would be an ineffectual conceit. A more fruitful suggestion would be to refer our youth and those sections of the population that are usually experienced in law . . . to the authorities and certified jurists, whom it shall behove to offer true advice that the aforesaid might act with discretion."
59. See Langer, Rechtsuchender und Richter in Österreich, *DJZ* 1977, 376ff.
60. In the case of the Bar Association for Vienna, Lower Austria and Burgenland it is known as "Erste anwaltliche Auskunft" (EaA).
61. In Styria, Carinthia and Vorarlberg the regional Bar Associations do not operate legal advice centres that provide legal information free of charge. Dr. Leo Kaltenbäck, President of the Styrian Bar Association, expressed the view of the Styrian Committee in a letter dated 2.12. 1976, *GZl.* 538/76: "The decision [not to establish a free legal information facility] was based primarily on the consideration that, beyond the statutory obligations to work within the legal aid scheme in accordance with the provisions of the ZPO and the Lawyers' Practice Rules, there is no justification for making further inroads into the principle of fee-earning services for the legal profession, all the more so as the profession must in principle be remunerated for its services if its members are to continue to be able to maintain themselves on them. The argument put forward by the Bar Association of Vienna, Lower Austria and Burgenland, namely that if lawyers do not offer the service other people will, was not accepted as valid by the General Assembly because, as experience has shown to date, these other people by no means possess the knowledge and training of the lawyers. A further significant factor was the observation that it is difficult to draw the line between preliminary advice offered free of charge by a lawyer and the case where the duty lawyer who provides

the information at the same time solicits business for his own practice; indeed it is difficult in general to draw the line between preliminary advice free of charge and thorough legal advice proper. A final important reason for the negative decision was the observation made by our older members in the Nazi period that such institutions tend to be highly popular with malcontents and people seeking to change the world." The President of the Bar Association for Carinthia, Dr. Armin Dietrich, wrote a letter dated 24.11.1976, *GZl.* 418/76: "The Assoiation's members have repeatedly expressed the view – the last time was on the occasion of the 1975 AGM – that the very generous state system of legal aid together with the audience days operated at the Austrian courts guarantee adequate protection under the law for the socially disadvantaged." Similarly, the President of the Vorarlberg Bar Association, Dr. Wilfried Konzett, stated in his letter of 16.12. 1976 "that the Vorarlberg Bar Association rejected the motion to introduce a free legal advice service".

62. In reply to my enquiry, the President of the Salzburg Bar Association Dr. Gustav Gressel, provided the following information in his letter of 29.11.1976, *RAK* 541/76: "Our legal advice centre is at present staffed on every first and third Tuesday of the month. With the exception of the President and lawyers over the age of 65, all our colleagues with a practice in Salzburg help to staff the centre on an alphabetical rota basis. When the centre was first opened the idea was to make free legal advice available only to those persons who qualified for assistance under the legal aid scheme. In fact, for many years now, we have offered our free information services to all-comers, i.e. an average of 400–450 persons per annum. It cannot be said that malcontents attend our centres constantly or particularly frequently. At the most such people appear twice and then stop coming when told that no assistance can be provided."

63. The President of the Tyrolean Bar Association, Dr. Ernst F. Mayr, gave the following account in his letter of 1.12.1976, *GZl.* 1516/76: "At the request of the Innsbruck District Court, the Tyrolean Bar Association took upon itself to provide gratuitous legal advice through its members on one afternoon per week. This decision was first taken by the Committee of the Tyrolean Bar Association before being confirmed by the general assembly on 30.3.1965. The service is operated every Tuesday in the Association's offices. In 1975, 237 persons made use of this advisory service, and a similar figure is expected for 1976. The system has certainly proved a success; the general public seems

to have a real need for such a service, although there are always some people who come time and time again with the same question."

64. On the basis of a decision taken by the Committee of the Bar Association for Vienna, Lower Austrian and Burgenland on 20.10.1970, an "Erste anwaltliche Auskunft" was instituted, initially in Vienna (now in Stockerau, too); the centre is staffed by lawyers working on a voluntary basis 98 lawyers having offered their services in June 1976 (cf. the reports in *AnwBl* 1970, 93, 100, 255, 311; *AnwBl* 1972, 75f.; *AnwBl*, 1977, 252). On 28.10.1975 the Committee of the Bar Association approved the following "Guide-lines for the 'Erste anwaltliche Auskunft' (EaA)": (a) The information service provided by lawyers in the EaA shall be free of charge. (b) The information offered shall be restricted to a legal opinion on the subject matter of the enquiry and an examination of the question whether the assistance of a lawyer is advisable. The time allocated to each enquiry shall not exceed ten minutes, if possible. (c) The Bar Association cannot be held responsible for information provided in the framework of the EaA. (d) The information provided in the EaA shall not be considered to constitute a brief to the lawyer offering the information. Therefore, the latter may, at his discretion, agree to represent any party to the dispute, unless there should appear to be the danger of a conflict of interests. (e) The duty lawyer shall reveal his name. In the EaA, however, the lawyer shall accept no brief or power of attorney. (f) Should the recommendation be made to consult a lawyer in his practice, it shall be pointed out that, outside the framework of the EaA, a fee must be paid for any such consultation. (g) The duty lawyer may provide an estimate of the probable legal costs. However, he is not permitted to examine the services rendered and fees charged by other colleagues. (Printed in *AnwBl* 1975, 491.) These guide-lines are based for the most part on a "Study on the Arrangements for an extension of the "erste anwaltliche Auskunft" of 20.8.1975, presented by the lawyer Dr. Heinz Barazon. In the last few years attendance figures for the EaA have shown a regular rise (1973: 1.779 informations; 1974; 2.372; 1975: 3.093; 1976 (to 23.10.): 4.093). – For the above information I am indebted to the President of the Bar Association for Vienna, Lower Austria and Burgenland, Dr. Walter Schuppich, and the lawyer Dr. Heinz Barazon, who were kind enough to discuss the matter with me in person.

65. From the Upper Austrian Bar Association I received the following information in a letter dated 24.11.1976, *GZl.* 560/76: "Since April 1,

1972 the Upper Austrian Bar Association has provided legal advice free of charge every Thursday. This legal assistance is given by a lawyer with the purpose of suggesting to those in need of advice how they might proceed in the defence or assertion of a claim. The advice is offered on a once-only basis and has purely informative character. The service is also open to persons who are not resident in Linz and also regardless of their financial status. From 1924 to 31.3.1972 lawyers of the Upper Austrian Bar Association provided free legal information to deprived persons at a legal information centre established in the Linz City Council offices. The present information office of the Bar Association is attended on average by 25 persons per week, making an annual average of about 700. Of these 700 persons, experience has shown 10% to be malcontents." For further information on the services offered by the "legal information centre established in the Linz City Council offices" cf. Spitzer, Rechtsfürsorge, *AnwZ* 1932, 413 footnote 5.

66. Cf. footnotes 60, 61, 62 and 63.
66. The Family Advice Promotion Act (Familienberatungsförderungsgesetz) (Bundesgesetz vom 23.1.1974 *BGBl* 80) shows that the legislature is paying particular attention to certain information centres. Under the terms of this law, the federal government is obliged to subsidize family advice services, including those of a legal nature, operated by the *Länder*, municipalities, other legal entites in public law and corporate bodies in private law (§ 2 Abs 1 Z 2 lit a leg. cit.). Examples of "information and complaints offices" are listed in Schönherr, Die Volksanwaltschaft realistisch betrachtet, *ÖJZ* 1976, 602f. – For a discussion of historical models in Austria see Spitzer, Rechtsfürsorge, *AnwZ* 1932, 410; Isermann, "Freie Rechtshilfe", in: *Recht und Politik* 1975, 37.
67. Thus Rehbinder, Die Kosten der Rechtsverfolgung als Zugangsbarriere der Rechtspflege, in: *Jahrbuch für Rechtssoziologie und Rechtstheorie* 4 (1976) 410.
68. Rechtsanwälte oder Verbrauchervertreter, *AnwBl* 1976, 439f.
70. Cf. Schönherr, Volksanwaltschaft, *ÖJZ* 1976, 566, who therefore criticizes attempts to impose on the ombudsman (at that time still in the debating stage) "an obligation to provide free legal information" as "unrealistic".

FREDERICK H. ZEMANS

Canada

Introduction

This paper will discuss some of the significant developments in legal aid and legal services in Canada during the last decade. Particular emphasis will be upon the delivery systems of the provinces of Ontario, Quebec and Saskatchewan and upon the experimental projects developed within each of these jurisdictions. These projects go beyond a juridical approach to provide the citizen with an opportunity to participate in the legal aid delivery system and in the administration of justice.

In reviewing legal aid in Canada, one becomes immediately conscious of its rapid growth during the last decade. The expenditure of public funds on legal aid throughout Canada, including the Northwest Territories, for the year 1976-77 was estimated to be in excess of $70,000,000.[1] Seven years ago the total expenditure of public funds on legal aid outside of Ontario was less than one million dollars.[2] At that time the first federal assistance was given in the form of grants by the Federal Department of National Health and Welfare to establish community clinics in four Canadian provinces.[3]

The contemporary history of Canadian legal services began in 1967 when the Ontario Legal Aid Plan, having obtained a substantial financial commitment from the Ontario government, became the first provincial plan to pay lawyers to handle both civil and criminal cases. This plan was an adaptation of the English "judicare" model with the private practitioner as the deliverer of legal services in both criminal and civil matters; it is governed and administered by the legal profession through the Law Society of Upper Canada. The Ontario model has become the flagship of legal aid plans in Canada and is Canada's oldest and most expensive provincial plan,[4] but its coverage has remained primarily limited to the resolution of criminal and domestic litigation. During the 1976–77 fiscal year, the cost of the Ontario plan amounted to slightly over 28 million dollars in a province with a population of approximately 8 million people.

The extremely rapid development of legal services in Canada during the past decade can be attributed to a growing consciousness of the need of the poor for greater access to the services of the legal profession. During the late 1960s, Canadian law schools – and more particularly their students – established legal aid clinics and assisted poverty and self-help groups which were responding to the social ferment of the period.[5] As well, low income communities and the legal profession were both pressing for government funding of legal aid and community clinics. Recent commitments of provincial and federal monies has meant that Canada currently exceeds by a wide margin the *per capita* expenditures on legal aid both in England and the United States.[6]

Recognition of the need for an effective legal aid system existed; the major issue was the model to be used. Again, Canada was torn between its two historical allies, England and the United States. By 1970, the ferment with respect to legal aid had permeated the law societies and provincial governments in Canada. Nova Scotia, Quebec and British Columbia assessed their limited legal aid services and pressed for substantial provincial government funding of previously voluntary schemes. The "Great Canadian Debate" on legal services was beginning.[7]

Stimulating the debate further, and, in the eyes of many lawyers, creating further tension, the Federal Department of National Health and Welfare funded the Dalhousie Clinic in Halifax, the Saskatoon Community Clinic in Saskatoon and the Point St. Charles Clinic in Montreal in 1971. All three of these clinics had close ties with law schools in their respective communities. As well, in March 1971, the same department gave a grant to Osgoode Hall Law School to create a community clinic in Toronto. The writer was the first director of this project, Parkdale Community Legal Services.

The fire was further fuelled in September 1971 by *The Legal Services Controversy: An Examination of the Evidence*, a study prepared for the National Council of Welfare by Larry Taman. The report compared the Ontario judicare and neighbourhood legal services delivery schemes and provoked practitioners and legal academics to choose sides in the impending struggle. Shortly thereafter, in October 1971, Edgar and Jean Cahn spoke at the First Canadian Conference on Poverty and Law in Ottawa.

They noted the growing controversy over the appropriate legal aid model in Canada and attempted to develop the "Canadian Compromise". They sought to defuse what they called "a new Holy War between the true believers of conflicting Orthodoxies".[8] Although sharply critical of judicare as a programme which "resists any form of accountability" and "which tends to become a full employment programme for lawyers rather than an instrument of justice for clients", they ultimately recommended that the distinctions between the United States and Canada should encourage Canada to develop its own unique delivery system; it should not "preclude experimental use of judicare to supplement neighbourhood legal services offices . . .".[9]

The battle lines were more clearly drawn when a sub-committee of the Law Society of Upper Canada published a report in late 1972 taking issue with the legal services model. The Community Legal Services Report[10] described community clinics as placing legal aid applicants in the position of "captive clientele" for full time lawyers employed in such clinics.[11] The report forcefully recommended the maximum use of the private bar as duty counsel on a part-time basis in any clinic facilities that might be established.[12] Concerned that staff lawyers would deliver inferior service, it recommended that there should not be a division within the profession.

Each of the Canadian provinces provides legal aid in unique and distinct ways. In the past decade, all ten Canadian provinces have been stimulated to review their provision of legal services to the underprivileged of their provinces and to develop unique adaptations of the judicare or neighbourhood legal service delivery models. All have established plans to provide some services in criminal cases. Only Prince Edward Island and New Brunswick lack an extensive legal aid scheme to provide services in civil matters as well. British Columbia, Manitoba, Quebec, Saskatchewan and Newfoundland have established bodies independent of the legal profession for administration of their plans. In the other provinces, legal aid remains under the control of the private Bar. The Osler Report on Legal Aid on Ontario in 1974[13] recommended that the control and administration of the legal aid plan should be vested in a statutory non-profit corporation named "Legal Aid Ontario" comprised of twenty persons of whom nine should be appointed by the Law Society of Upper Canada.[14] This recommendation was not adopted by the Ontario government.

Nova Scotia, Saskatchewan and Prince Edward Island have chosen community legal centres with staff lawyers to deliver legal services. Alberta,

New Brunswick and Newfoundland have followed Ontario's lead and chosen judicare while British Columbia, Manitoba and Quebec have developed mixed systems which reflect the Canadian compromise. Ontario and Alberta are subtly modifying their judicare schemes. Although both plans are still controlled and administered by the provincial law societies, community clinics are no longer deemed repugnant. Both Alberta and Ontario are experimenting with clinics in remote areas. The Ontario plan is funding over thirty autonomous clinics through a Clinical Funding Committee created in 1976. The Canadian debate continues but the tension has decreased as compromises are reached and the realities discovered. Although the citizen perspective in Canadian legal aid is in its embryonic stage, my detailed examination of legal aid in Quebec, Saskatchewan and Ontario reveals a gradual development of schemes responsible to the public.

As interpreted by the Canadian and British courts, sections 91 and 92 of the British North America Act have given the federal government exclusive legislative authority in matters of criminal law[15] while the provincial governments are responsible for the delivery of legal aid services by virtue of their exclusive jurisdiction over the administration of justice[16] and matters of property and civil rights.[17] Despite the primary responsibility of the provinces for the administration of legal aid, the federal government contributes to the costs of legal aid in criminal matters. In 1972, the federal government entered into an agreement with the provinces for cost sharing of legal aid services delivered in criminal matters.[18] The federal contribution was set at 90 per cent of the provincial expenditures to a maximum of $0.50 *per capita*. To benefit from this agreement, each province must provide legal aid services to any financially eligible person who is charged with an indictable offence or prosecuted under *The Extradition Act*.[19] *The Fugitive Offenders Act*[20] and in all Crown appeals in federal criminal cases..

During the last decade, the federal government has indicated that it wishes to increase its involvement in legal aid services. It initially became involved through the innovative demonstration programmes of the Department of National Health and Welfare and the Department of Justice. In 1975, the then federal Minister of Justice indicated that the federal government was seriously considering a more substantial presence in the area of legal aid by attempting to set minimum national standards for the availability of comprehensive legal services to the economic disadvantaged through cost sharing in the provincial legal aid programmes.[21]

Poor people compose approximately one quarter of Canada's population. Statistics Canada estimates that in 1973 17.2 per cent of all Canadian households were below the poverty line.[22] This is an absolute subsistence poverty line which is updated for changes in the cost of living. These figures must be compared with the relative poverty figures prepared by the Canadian Council on Social Development which estimates that in 1973 22.9 per cent of the Canadian population was below the poverty line. A third indicator of poverty is the Special Senate Committee on Poverty which states that in 1973 27.4 per cent of the Canadian population was living in poverty.[23]

A close scrutiny of the available data with respect to low income people in Canada indicates that in terms of basic food, shelter and clothing requirements, as determined by 1961 real living standards, the situation of the low income Canadian has improved; that is, fewer and fewer Canadians are going without these basics. In terms of possessing an adequate quantity of goods and services in relation to what the average Canadian possesses, however, the plight of low income Canadians has not improved; the real position of the poor has not increased relative to that of the average Canadian.[24] Unfortunately, the enormous increase of new wealth in Canada since 1946[25] has had little direct benefit for the poorest earners but, rather, has gone to raising the standard of living of the wealthy.[26]

Although Canada has developed a multitude of federal and provincial social welfare schemes, their impact on real poverty has been demonstrated to be minimal.[27] The creation of old age pensions, unemployment insurance, family allowance benefits and welfare payments tend to reduce the most acute aspects of poverty. The income and social security programmes created in the last two decades in Canada have prevented the inequality between the rich and the poor from worsening, however, they have not reduced inequality within Canadian society. The organized and articulate of the poor are demanding a citizen's or "civilian perspective" in Canadian legal aid as a result of their concerns with the Canadian income tax structure and social welfare programmes.

The following discussion will consider the specific legal aid schemes in three provinces: Quebec, Saskatchewan, and Ontario. These provinces have been chosen because they represent the three basic methods of delivering legal services to the poor. Quebec has chosen to implement a mixed judicare/staff scheme while Saskatchewan primarily uses staff lawyers in community law offices. Ontario retains the judicare system which delivers legal services through the private bar.

Quebec

It was not until 1972 that Quebec had any comprehensive legal aid system outside of the city of Montreal.[28] Prior to that time there had been limited availability of legal services in most areas of the province. In Montreal, the local Bar had set up a legal aid bureau operating in both the criminal and civil areas in 1956. The Legal Aid Bureau of the Bar of Montreal had a number of salaried lawyers acting as public defenders in criminal cases. On the civil side, the bureau referred cases to practising lawyers prepared to accept them on a gratuitous basis.[29] All Montreal lawyers were liable to be asked to take on such cases,[30] and it was considered their professional obligation to handle legal aid cases without remuneration. Most of the civil cases handled were matrimonial and the level of service was acknowledged to be quite low.[31]

In 1967, in an effort to assist in the establishment of a broader service, the Government of Quebec began to make increasingly larger annual grants.[32] During the year April 1, 1970, to March 31, 1971, more than 18,000 persons received, free of charge, the professional services of advocates through the Montreal Bureau.[33] With constantly increasing numbers of applications, the bureau staff of salaried lawyers was no longer able to meet caseload needs and, as a consequence, greater pressure was put on the voluntary services of advocates in private practice. In an attempt to create a more structured legal assistance plan, the Bar of the Province of Quebec and the provincial government signed an agreement in the summer of 1971[34] whereby the Bar agreed to provide legal assistance in criminal matters at a tariff of 60 per cent of the established fee schedule and free of charge in civil matters.

Quebec opened its first community clinics in the early 1970s.[35] These were influenced by, and to a great extent emulated, American neighbourhood legal service offices.[36] In March 1972, Bill 10, *The Legal Aid Act* of the Province of Quebec was introduced providing for the creation of a "Legal Services Commission", independent of both the government of Quebec and of the legal profession; composed of twelve persons[37] chosen because of their special knowledge and awareness of the legal problems of the underprivileged. Legal services were to be provided in each region of Quebec by local corporations[38] whose boards of directors were to have at least one-third local residents as well as one-third lawyers.[39] Clients' problems were to be handled by full-time lawyers and each local office was to have a director of legal services.[40] Between the provincial commission and the local corporations, there were to be regional corporations which had a limited advising and co-ordinating role. Community clients and the involvement of low income communities constituted the philosophical thrust of the 1972 draft legislation.

Bill 10 met with considerable opposition from the Quebec legal profession which felt that it was under pressure from the provincial government.[41] Only recently the government had implemented a new small claims court Act[42] which, in an attempt to provide more expeditious and less expensive resolution of smaller actions, had excluded lawyers from appearing in that court.[43] The provincial Bar passed a resolution requesting a judicare system for Quebec similar to the Ontario Legal Aid Plan, arguing that a judicare system provides for independence of the legal profession and for the right of the client to free choice of a lawyer.[44] A small group within the Quebec Bar supported the proposed legislation and was critical of the stance taken by the profession.[45] The General Council of the profession proposed a compromise solution which advocated freedom of choice to the poor client through a mixed legal aid system combining neighbourhood legal services with utilization of lawyers in private practice.

The Quebec government accepted some aspects of the compromise position and, although unwilling to divert the public funds necessary to create a judicare scheme, did make major concessions to the Bar by broadening the previously very limited category of cases in which referrals could be made to private practitioners. In addition, it upgraded the role of the regional corporations by de-emphasizing the local clinic as the basic unit for legal services. *The Legal Aid Act*[46] of the Province of Quebec received royal assent on July 8, 1972, and on August 23, 1973, members of the Legal Services Commission were appointed.

The Act provides for the commission to be responsible for ensuring the provision of legal aid to economically underprivileged persons; for establishing regional legal aid corporations; and for providing legal aid.[47] The commission is also responsible for developing information and research projects relevant to the legal problems of the poor.[48] Eleven regional corporations in various areas of Quebec have been charged with providing legal aid to their region by establishing legal aid bureaux in various parts of their territory. Board members of these corporations are appointed by the commission: one-third from the legal profession and one-third from the residents of the area served.[49] In addition, the regional corporations are to promote the establishment of committees, to advise the director of the bureaux on the needs of the economically disadvantaged of the area and, if necessary, make recommendations to the regional corporations.[50]

The Quebec *Legal Aid Act*[51] provides for continuation of community-based clinics in existence prior to the introduction of the Act and for the establishment of new clinics upon the recommendation of the regional corporation.[52] These clinics are to retain their community boards of directors and to be semi-autonomous. Unlike the bureaux, they do not fall under the direct jurisdiction of the regional corporations.[53] There were four clinics at the time that the *Legal Aid Act* was proclaimed. In 1974 there were five clinics.[54] By 1976 only two clinics remained and during the summer of 1977 funding of St. Louis Legal Services in Montreal was terminated by the commission. The entire concept of community clinics would seem to be in jeopardy in Quebec.[55] In a system which attempts to deliver legal services through a combination of staff lawyers, community clinics and the private Bar, loss of major clinic facilities endangers the quality, the quantity and the availability of community legal services. It is questionable whether or not staff lawyers or the private Bar are ready or even willing to fill the significant gap left by the loss of the clinics.

If a person wishes to obtain legal aid in Quebec, he must apply to a local bureau office. If he is financially and legally qualified, a legal aid certificate will be issued except if summary advice is given.[56] Legal aid is to be available to any "economically underprivileged" person.[57] The Act generously defines the areas in which he can obtain legal services.[58] The Quebec scheme makes legal aid a right and not a privilege and defines it as "every benefit granted . . . to an economically underprivileged person to facilitate access to the court, professional services of an advocate or a notary and necessary information concerning his rights and obligations."[59]

The Quebec plan provides for a compromise judicare-staff lawyer shceme and allows the client the right to a specific lawyer of his choice.[60] Although commentators[61] and administrators of the plan stress the absolute free choice of counsel[62] the most recent statistics reveal that 75 per cent of all cases were handled by staff lawyers through the bureaux. In contrast Legal Aid Manitoba, a more judicare-oriented mixed delivery system, handles approximately 75 per cent of its cases through lawyers in private practice.[63]

During the initial year of operation, the Quebec Commission determined that the cost per case handled by lawyers in private practice amounted to approximately $200 plus 10 per cent for administrative expenses. In contrast, cases handled by staff lawyers cost approximately one-half this amount.[64] It should be noted that the Quebec Act allows the commission the flexibility to designate that certain types of professional services must be rendered exclusively by staff lawyers.[65]

The Quebec Act provides some experimental and supplementary

services which attempt to deal with problems of the low-income community and to go beyond the specific problems presented by individual clients. The Act provides for services for groups, although regulations for such have stringent financial eligibility criteria.[66] Various community education projects have been undertaken and monies have been allocated by the commission for education and advertising.[67]

Within the first year of operation, the commission established a research and information department[68] at its Montreal offices. This department was established because the commission recognized that the plan provided services to approximately one-third of Quebec's population[69] and yet little research data was available on Quebec's low income population and its legal problems. The research division provides opinions in specific cases[70] and conducts staff development seminars for bureau lawyers. The dearth of Canadian legal resources in the areas of law practised and the bureaux' remoteness from adequate law libraries stimulated the research division to produce a loose-leaf resource manual of sociological and legal data relevant to low income citizens.

With a *per capita* expenditure of $4.20 for 1977–78 (as compared to Ontario at $3.64 and Saskatchewan at $3.43), Quebec has the highest per citizen investment in legal aid. Use of legal aid services is continually expanding; applications in 1976–77 increased 13.7 per cent of the previous year. The upper income limits of the financial eligibility requirements were increased in April 1978 so that the legal aid programme could keep pace with inflation. For example, a couple with two dependants can now earn $180 per week and still qualify for legal aid; previously, the cut-off point was $155 per week. Although this increase in the maximum acceptable income does not extend the provision of legal services to a new group, the mere fact of retaining services for the same group will cost the programme an additional $3,605,100 in 1978–79.[71]

As of March 31, 1977, legal aid offices were situated in one hundred Quebec cities, and there were 306 salaried staff lawyers, 438 support staff, and sixteen articling students or law students. Staff lawyers have an average of 5.1 years experience.[72]

The Commission des Services Juridiques has expressed only limited support for the training and use of paralegals. The Commission leaves the development of lay advocacy and paralegal programmes to each bureau and limits its involvement to assessment of projects and funding when budgets permit. Thus the 1977 report cites four instances of recent paralegal projects.

The Community Legal Centre of the Mauricie/Bois-Francs region, for example initiated a project to train representatives of citizens' groups to assist in social welfare and unemployment insurance matters. This project is to encourage clients to solve their own problems with some assistance from a community member.

The Community Legal Centre of the Northwest Region has attempted to facilitate access to legal aid among native peoples by hiring an Inuit on a part-time basis to assist advocates visiting the Poste-en-la-Baleine area. As well, in conjunction with the Grand Council of the Crees, the regional corporation hired and trained a court worker to become the liaison officer between legal aid advocates and the Cree reserves of Waswanipi and Fort George. The measure of success of this operation is indicated by a request from the Grand Council of the Crees to hire three additional court workers.

A survey made of former Quebec legal aid recipients[73] revealed some rather interesting data. While aid was given to approximately as many men as women, 90 per cent of the women aided sought help for civil problems, while 43 per cent of the men sought help in criminal matters. The average age of a legal aid recipient was 39.7 years. Most recipients were urban residents with little education and an average annual income of just over $7,000 for a family of three to four persons. Twenty per cent were single parents, and nearly all of these were female single parents. These statistics suggest that the Quebec plan has had little impact on the standard of living of legal aid recipients. The Sociology Section who conducted the survey concluded that the figures confirmed:

> . . . that legal aid clients are recruited amongst the economically deprived groups of society; not only are the clients economically weak when they just come to our Bureaus, but they still are one or two years later. This last statement, however, throws cold water on the hopes that the war on poverty could be won through legal aid.[74]

Despite the initiatives in poverty law research, community education and test case litigation, the Quebec scheme during its early years has not fought the poverty war battle that it had proclaimed but rather has emphasized a case-by-case approach to legal aid. The Quebec Legal Services Commission has not encouraged local participation in the newly created bureaux. The Legal Services Commission commenced a study of local citizen participation in the legal aid plan. Produced by Diane Deschamps, this report was entitled "Advisory Committees: Participation or Illusion"[75] and indicated that local citizens had very little say in the operation of the legal aid plan. Less than 25 per cent (six offices) of the legal aid bureaux in existence at the time the study was conducted had ever had an advisory committee, and only about 7 per cent were active. Most of the committee members enjoy a high socio-economic status and work in management as professionals or semi-professinals in social or health-oriented fields. The average annual income of members of advisory committees is $9,705.00 while the average income of clients was $7,134.36. Barely 52 per cent of the clients were employed while 41 per cent received a form of pension or social welfare.

Members of the advisory committees generally had little knowledge of the structure, financial state, or policies of the Legal Services Commission. It is interesting to note that, of the six active advisory committees, three are composed primarily of legal aid "beneficiaries" or persons who would be eligible for legal aid while the other three committees are primarily composed of representatives of local groups and local "elite". These committees have five to ten members who meet every second or third week. The most active are involved in the internal as well as the external operation of the Legal Aid Bureau. The major activity of active committees is the organization of special interest meetings to provide legal information to neighbourhood groups of tenants, divorcees and the elderly. Only two committees intervene regularly in the internal operation of the bureau and in hiring personnel.

Saskatchewan

In Saskatchewan, prior to 1967, all legal aid was provided on a voluntary basis, with the exception that the Attorney-General would arrange payment for the defence of serious criminal cases. The only way for an accused person in less serious offences to arrange for his defence was to find a lawyer willing to act without charge. By the mid-1960s, it was apparent that private practitioners could no longer handle the work on a charitable basis and, in 1967, after several years of negotiation between the provincial Attorney-General and the Law Society, the Saskatchewan Legal Aid Plan (Criminal Matters) was enacted.[76] The 1967 scheme was administered by the Law Society through local legal aid committees and relatively low fees were paid to lawyers by the provincial government. The plan worked most unsatisfactorily in rural areas due to the paucity of available lawyers with criminal expertise combined with an inadequate fee schedule that did not compensate for travelling time. In civil matters there was no legal aid and the only available assistance was the Needy

Person's Certificate under the Queen's Bench Rules of Court.[77] The certificate provided needy persons with an exemption from court costs and from liability for costs if he should lose.

One of the major provocations for change in Saskatchewan was the creation of the Saskatoon Legal Assistance Clinic in 1969. Originally, the clinic operated as a voluntary scheme run from a community centre and was staffed by volunteer lawyers, faculty of the College of Law, University of Saskatchewan, and by law students. The offices were open on a part-time basis and the law students, working under the supervision of the Bar and the faculty, were the primary deliverers of legal services.

In June 1971 the Saskatoon clinic was one of the four clinics in Canada which received demonstration grant funding from the Federal Department of Health and Welfare. At this time it was fundamentally reorganized and staff lawyers and paralegals were hired. Originally the clinic had been directed by a board composed of students and faculty of the College of Law, and three members of the Saskatoon Bar. After receiving the Health and Welfare grant, the clinic moved towards increasing community input and in 1972 a split control structure was initiated: the Legal Council of Directors had the President of the Saskatoon Bar Association as its chairman, a professor of law as its secretary, and two members of the Bar and three professors as directors; and a Citizens' Advisory Board was composed of representatives of community groups, clients, law students and members of the Legal Council of Directors. In 1973 these two boards were merged into one board consisting of two members of the Bar, two law professors, three law students, three middle-class community people (non-lawyers) and ten representatives of community groups.

Since 1971 the clinic has handled cases for citizens living in the Saskatoon area who cannot obtain legal services from any other resource. All types of civil cases are handled; the caseload is approximately 1,500 per year.[78] The clinic has undertaken a number of signifcant test cases in the welfare law area and initiated a Citizens' Commission on Family Law. The commission, composed of a magistrate, an unemployed member of the Citizens' Welfare Improvement Council, a United Church minister, a law professor and three members of community groups, encouaged other community groups to present briefs to the commission regarding the impact of the legal system on family life and provided counsel to assist groups in the preparation of briefs. Active in community education, the clinic has developed a number of radio and television programmes dealing with legal topics.

In the same year that legal aid legislation was passed in Quebec,[79] the

Saskatchewan Attorney-General appointed a committee to look at legal services in Saskatchewan.[80] Chaired by Dean Roger Carter of the University of Saskatchewan, Faculty of Law, the committee had wide terms of reference:

(a) To review the entire system of legal aid in order to determine the needs of legal aid for the 1970s;
(b) To examine and make recommendations as to the extent of the need for subsidized programmes of legal assistance;
(c) To uncover the causes of under-utilization of legal services by the poor, if the evidence suggests such under-utilization;
(d) To articulate pre-conditions for adequate programs such as criteria of eligibility, personnel requirements and related matters; and
(e) To compare the various systems of organization, delivery of legal aid services to those in need which are now used in other jurisdictions.[81]

The Saskatoon Legal Assistance Clinic presented a brief to the Saskatchewan Legal Aid Committee vigorously arguing that as a community law office it was actively engaged in fighting poverty.[82] The brief argued that the community, in contrast with the private law office, is a better foundation for legal aid programmes.[83]

The Final Report of the Saskatchewan Legal Aid Committee made a number of important recommendations and indicated an evolution in the sophistication of the discussion of legal services in Canada.[84] The report recommended:

(A) A legal aid scheme must, in its administrative operation, be divorced as completely as possible from any government department or agency. The Committee saw that the poor were skeptical and, on occasion, antagonistic towards government administrative structures. The Committee also felt that it was fundamental to the traditional role of the lawyer that he must be independent of any direct or indirect governmental or community pressure[85] and should not be prevented from pressing claims against a government department or agency controlling the legal aid plan. As well, a legal aid programme must be insulated against political pressures or patronage.
(B) Legal aid should be regarded as a matter of right, not charity.[86] This attitude could best be achieved by some degree of local community involvement (by poor persons and their organizations) in the establishment and operation of the legal aid plan.
(C) A legal aid scheme should be capable of acting as a vehicle for social change. The legal aid system, after recognizing common problems faced by poor persons, should permit the scheme to deal with these problems by lobbying at the appropriate levels of government or

before the appropriate government agency for changes in the laws.[87] The report stresses the need for educational efforts designed to familiarize the poor with their legal rights and obligations, and the fields of law which directly concern their daily lives.[88]

(D) A legal aid scheme must be comprehensive. The Committee stated that a scheme must provide legal services for any situation encountered by a poor person where it would be reasonable for him to receive the services of a lawyer. The Committee stated that "reasonable" is not to be judged by comparing the cash value of the legal services with the case value of the result. The criterion must be the seriousness of the case or problem to the particular individual. A legal aid scheme must not be limited to serving the poor person only when he has a "middle-class problem".

The committee stressed that the northern and remote areas of the province had special needs. In particular, the need for community involvement is greater in remote areas, particularly in the native communities. The committee recognized the fact that native people are generally hostile to existing government structures.[89] It concluded that the private bar or judicare schemes[90] could not provide the educational programmes, the handling of the "uneconomic case" or group approaches to poverty which the committee regarded as necessary and fundamental to legal services. The committee was concerned with the development of expertise on the legal problems of the poor which the private practitioner would not have the opportunity to develop in his daily practice. The committee therefore recommended the clinic approach with some involvement of the private bar.[91]

The Community Legal Services (Saskatchewan) Act, 1974,[92] enacted on May 10, 1974, is an attempt to implement the recommendations of the Saskatchewan Legal Aid Committee. It incorporated the principles of community education, community development, and social change, contained in the Carter Committee Report.[93] The Act creates an independent Community Legal Services Commission responsible for co-ordinating the development of legal aid throughout the province by funding local legal aid clinics, providing technical back-up facilities and, if necessary, providing direct legal aid services. The composition of the commission represented a first in Canadian legal aid programmes with its movement away from control by either the government or the legal profession.

The Commission consists of three members appointed by chairmen of local clinic boards from amongst their number; one member appointed by the provincial cabinet from members of the Law Society of Saskatchewan nominated for that purpose by the benchers of the Society; three members appointed by the cabinet representing the taxpayers of the province, another lawyer who is appointed by the Attorney-General of Canada and the person holding the office of Provincial Director. It is significant that the commission's composition recognizes the three elements of a legal aid system – the deliverers, the funders, and the recipients of the services. All three groups are equally represented, with the possibility that the non-lawyers could be a majority on the commission.

The Community Legal Services (Saskatchewan) Act, 1974[94] provides that legal services are to be delivered primarily by community law offices employing full-time staff lawyers. Area boards are to be incorporated to provide the services of the plan. Twelve boards have been elected from residents of the area who join the area legal aid society and each board has opened a community law office.[95] Each board is empowered to advise the area staff on the legal need of the area residents to establish committees to review financial refusals of eligibility, to negotiate area contracts with the Provincial Director, to establish information and counselling programmes, and to advertise the provision of legal services. To ensure that the boards are involved closely in the decision-making process, the Act abolished the position of area director which had been in the first draft of the legislation. The Saskatchewan plan represents a significant attempt to provide the consumer of legal aid with the power to effect the development of the structure and politics of the delivery system.

All civil cases with the exception of cases involving conflict of interest are handled by salaried lawyers working in clinics.[96] The plan offers a freedom of choice of counsel in respect of criminal matters coming under the *Criminal Code* or other federal statutes;[97] the choice is from staff lawyers and solicitors who choose to put their names on panels. A solicitor on a panel, however, has the right to decline his services. In all other cases the plan provides for a community legal services delivery system.

During its early years of operation, the Saskatchewan plan has developed as a predominantly staff lawyer delivery system with 86 per cent of the recipients served by staff lawyers and 14 per cent by private practitioners.[98] It is presently operating thirteen full-time offices on an annual budget of slightly over $3,000,000. The plan employs thirty-nine staff lawyers and twenty-three other professionals and paraprofessionals. With a population of just under one million[99] Saskatchewan has the third highest *per capita* expenditure on legal aid, of the Canadian provinces, at $3.43 per person.[100]

The area boards and local clinics have become involved in educational and preventative law programmes in the areas of housing, welfare law and landlord–tenant matters. In some areas, training programmes for the community have been offered and street workers and paraprofessionals employed.

All of the thirteen local area boards except the Northern Legal Services Office are controlled by the community. The Northern Legal Services Office is administered directly by the Saskatchewan Community Legal Services Commission.

Financial eligibility for the plan is determined by several alternative requirements. If a person receives all or part of his income through social assistance he is automatically eligible. If, however, his income is less than he would receive if he were receiving social assistance, or if paying for legal services would drastically reduce his income to such a point that he would be eligible for social assistance, a person is eligible for legal aid. The plan sets maximum income levels to determine if a person would be eligible for social assistance. These income levels are extremely low. For example, a couple with two children can have a maximum annual income of $7,993 ($153.71/week) in order to qualify for legal aid. This should be compared with $9,360/annum ($180/week) in Quebec.

Not quite half the cases handled by the plan are criminal matters: in 1976–77, 43.3 per cent were criminal, while 56.7 per cent were civil matters, 37.3 per cent of these being family matters (21 per cent of the total).

The plan has weathered internal difficulties. Lay-offs in 1977 led to job uncertainty and unionized staff considered the possibility of a strike. In addition, a dispute between the Saskatchewan Community Legal Services Commission and a district legal aid society arose when personnel problems caused the termination of services to prisoners in Prince Albert's three penal institutions. However, the Saskatchewan plan continues to develop and handle an effective delivery of legal services with a high degree of citizen input.

Ontario

Prior to 1951, Ontario did not have a statutory scheme, with most legal aid performed on an *ad hoc* basis by members of the Bar. The Attorney-General's Department provided financial assistance for legal aid services in a limited number of criminal cases. In capital offences, indigent accused were assisted by the Attorney-General's Department through the payment of nominal *per diem* fees to volunteer counsel.[101] Although there were no enabling provisions in the Rules of Practice, it was the custom of the Ontario Court of Appeal to consider the granting of leave to appeal in criminal cases on the basis of written requests from the prisoner as essentially *in forma pauperis.*[102]

It was common during this period for indigents to be tried without benefit of counsel. The so-called "dock brief" said to exist in England, involving the appointment of counsel then present in court to represent indigents did not exist to any great extent in Ontario.[103] The unrepresented accused was likely prejudiced to a greater extent by pre-trial occurrences, particularly in regard to questioning, statements, inducements to plead guilty or even attempts at plea bargaining, than at the trial, where developed jurisprudence allowed the judge to assist unrepresented defendants. There was, as well, no organized civil legal aid system in Ontario before 1951, although it was undoubtedly possible for a plaintiff to find a lawyer willing to take his case if it involved the prospect of sizeable damages.

Legal services in Ontario have developed in a manner similar to that of England. In October 1950 the British Labour government's *Legal Aid and Advice Act*, 1949,[104] received a third reading. The government had accepted the recommendations of the Rushcliffe Committee,[105] and had not "socialized the legal profession" but, rather, left the control of the new legal aid plan in the hands of the Law Society. Ontario's Law Society of Upper Canada had not been disinterested in the English developments and in 1948 had appointed its own committee which recommended that a scheme similar to that proposed by the Rushcliffe Report should be instituted in Ontario. The primary responsibility for organization of legal aid was to rest with the Law Society. The committee also stated that once the scheme was put into operation, a good case could be made for assistance from the province in the financing of the scheme.

The Ontario Legal Aid Plan was introduced in 1951 with the passing of *The Law Society Amendment Act (1951).*[106] The amendment simply enabled the Benchers of the Law Society to "establish a plan to provide legal aid to persons in need thereof, to be called 'The Ontario Legal Aid Plan' and for such purpose to make such regulations as are deemed appropriate".[107] The Ontario plan was different from the British plan in two respects. First, legal aid continued to be provided by volunteer lawyers as the profession remained unwilling to admit that it could not care for the legal needs of the poor without receiving a fee for service from the government. Only disbursements were paid and the funds to cover these and other administrative expenses came from the provincial government. Secondly, the financial eligibility requirements were much more stringent under the Ontario plan, restricting eligibility for the plan to the nearly destitute.[108] This was in marked contrast to the British effort to ascertain the amount an applicant actually had available to pay counsel with the proviso that expenses would only be defrayed out of "disposable" income.

The plan covered most civil cases,[109] but only indictable criminal matters, and was administered locally by the county and district law associations. Appeals were excluded in both civil and criminal cases except where, in the opinion of the Povincial Director, there appeared to have been a miscarraige of justice.

The voluntary plan went into effect throughout most of the province,[110] although relatively limited use was made of the scheme.[111] During the late 1950s it became apparent that the administrators of the plan were having difficulty finding enough volunteers to handle cases and that the profession was beginning to reconsider its position on the payment of lawyers from public funds for legal aid.[112] By 1963 it was obvious that the volunteer plan could not satisfy the existing need.[113]

In July 1963 a Joint Committee on Legal Aid was established to report on the existing plan and to make recommendations for the future. This committee was chaired by the Deputy Attorney-General and composed of senior and highly respected members of the profession.[114] After some pressure[115] the committee agreed to hold public hearings for parties thought to be interested.[116] Its terms of reference were to inquire into and report on the existing Ontario legal aid plan and to investigate and report on legal aid and public defender schemes in other jurisdictions.

The Report of the Joint Committee on Legal Aid[117] was tabled in the Ontario Legislature in April 1965. It recommended a comprehensive fee-for-services legal aid plan administered by the Law Society and subsidized by the provincial government. In October 1965 the Attorney-General requested the Law Society to appoint a committee to draft legislation to implement the report. This new committee drafted the *Legal Aid Act*[118] which was passed by the legislature on June 28, 1966, and made operational on March 19, 1967, when legal aid offices were opened in each county in the province and legal aid duty counsel appeared for the first time in the criminal courts. Ontario had acquired the most advanced legal aid scheme then existing in Canada.

The plan is administered through a rather elaborate system of administrative offices situated in forty-six areas which basically coincide with the counties and districts of Ontario. In each area there is an area director who is responsible for the operation of the plan within his area. Lawyers participating in the scheme receive remuneration on the basis of 75 per cent of a legal aid tariff.

An important advance in the new legislation was the creation of an Independent Advisory Committee to represent the general interests of the Bench, the Bar and the public – partial recognition that legal aid was a matter of public and not merely legal concern. The 1967 Ontario legislation: (a) abandoned the previous charity keynote of the earlier scheme; (b) recognized that lawyers handling legal aid cases were entitled to at least partial remuneration for professional services rendered under the plan; (c) recognized that indigents were deserving of more than charity service; (d) acknowledged that legal services were the responsibility of government and not only the legal profession.

One of the important innovations was the introduction of duty counsel in criminal matters – a concept that had originated in Scotland. In Ontario, duty counsel are assigned to every criminal court of first instance and to some juvenile and family courts. They are present in court to advise accused, on their first appearance, of their rights to plead guilty or not guilty, to apply for bail, or to ask for an adjournment. Duty counsel will also make submissions with respect to sentence where an accused pleads guilty.

The salient feature of the Ontario plan is that it provides legal services by the private Bar at no charge or at a reduced charge to those who qualify for services by virtue of the type of service required and by their financial position. Eligibility for legal services in criminal as well as civil matters has been determined legislatively by the government of Ontario and administratively by the Law Society of Upper Canada. This represents a marked departure from the system of the United Kingdom, where eligibility for legal services in criminal as well as civil matters has been determined legislatively by the government of Ontario and administratively by the Law Society of Upper Canada. This represents a marked departure from the system of the United Kingdom, where eligibility for assistance in criminal matters is determined by the courts rather than by the administrators of the plan and the respective law societies have little or no responsibility for administration on the criminal side. Reliance on the private Bar distinguishes Ontario from virtually all American states.

Financial eligibility is determined by the provincial Ministry of Community and Social Services. A major time delay results from the two to three weeks required to determine eligibility. The Ministry of Community and Social Services has devised an elaborate system of inquiries and *formulae* not available to the public.[119] The Osler Task Force on Legal Aid[120] recommended that the financial assessment procedure of the Ministry of Community and Social Services be terminated and a simplified assessment procedure be developed based on published tables of eligibility regularly made available to the public.[121] At the present time, each case is treated on its own merits. The basic criterion for evaluation is whether or not the applicant has any disposable income to pay for the services of a lawyer after he has met all his financial obligations according to his station in life. If determined to be financially eligible, the Area Director determines if he is legally eligible. Before a legal aid certificate can be issued in civil matters, a solicitor's opinion must be obtained.

Ontario legal aid was founded and continues on the assumption that the public can best be served by the private Bar. When an applicant has ultimately obtained a certificate, he may select a lawyer from either the civil or criminal panels and take his legal aid certificate to that lawyer. The certificate allegedly places the indigent client in the same position as a person of modest means.[122] Unfortunately, few low income citizens are familiar with a lawyer and most do not have ready access to members of the profession. The legal aid certificate requires the recipient to choose a professional who is often unknown and generally of a different economic station.

As in England, the Ontario Legal Aid Plan is administered and governed by the Law Society through its Legal Aid Committee. The ultimate authority still rests with the Benchers of the Law Society, although the Legal Aid Committee acts as a board of directors for the Ontario Legal Aid Plan.[123] The chairman of the Legal Aid Committee commented recently that:

> Lay participants in legal aid are essential and most helpful although we must guard against a deification of such participation for in my view, since we are dealing with dispensing of legal services this can be done effectively, in the main, by practising lawyers.[124]

At present, the Legal Aid Committee is composed of nineteen lawyers (thirteen of whom are Benchers), ten lay members and one law student. The ten lay members of the committee are primarily professionals working in related social welfare fields. Although some middle-class professionals may be necessary, the Legal Aid Committee's make-up demonstrates tacit agreement with the chairman's opinion that direct consumer participation is not a priority. The citizens being served by the plan are excluded from setting priorities as to the type and extent of service by the professionals who willingly assume responsibility for their problems.

In addition to the Provincial Legal Aid Committee, each area has an area committee which has a minimum membership of five persons, the majority of whom must be members of the Law Society. These committees are appointed by the Law Society and used primarily to determine whether applicants for certain cases can receive legal aid. In addition they hear appeals when the Area Director has refused to grant a certificate. Area committees have been utilized in an advisory capacity on a limited basis, but they are only in a position to request or recommend. They cannot implement those recommendations. The area committees have virtually no membership from the client community and are composed primarily of lawyers and social welfare workers.

With the exception of 1976-77, the Ontario Legal Aid Plan caseload has risen on a continuing basis; 1976-77 saw a slight decrease in the number of formal applications and in the number of certificates issued.[125] Criminal matters occupy approximately 50 per cent of legal aid given in Ontario; approximately 30 per cent of the cases are divorce and other domestic matters. The plan is clearly litigation-oriented. Every year a sizeable number of applicants are refused legal aid certificates on the grounds that their needs are outside the scope of the plan.[126] It is difficult to estimate how much greater the demand might be if the plan had neighbourhood and community offices and offered advice and representation in legal problems of the poor (i.e. social welfare and small claims).

The Ontario government responded to the rapidly rising cost of legal aid and the pressures for change by creating the Task Force on Legal Aid in December 1973. The task force was chaired by the Honourable Mr. Justice John H. Osler, and there were six other members. They were to "review" the plan "in depth" and "determine the parameters of the future direction and development to ensure that it has the capacity to meet its objectives in the years ahead".[127]

The Osler Committee was the first review of legal aid in Ontario which included non-lawyers. In the process the committee attempted to reflect a number of perspectives with a varied composition: a Supreme Court judge, two Benchers of the Law Society of Upper Canada (one of whom was vice-chairman of the Legal Aid Committee), a social worker, a journalist, a former chairman of the Ontario Human Rights Commission and a law professor. There was considerable interest in the work of the committee which received 285 written submissions and 105 oral submissions in the three months of hearings in ten different centres throughout the province.

The Osler Report is a thorough and comprehensive discussion of the

Ontario legal aid scheme. It is clearly a compromise document which attempted to balance the interests of the members of the committee and the competing arguments presented to it.

The Law Society is complimented, with certain reservations evident in the report:

> It is enough to say that our inquiries have led us to have nothing but admiration for the founders of the Ontario Plan. We find that it had been conscientiously and energetically administered by The Law Society and that, particularly in the more recent years, a degree of imagination has been brought to bear upon its administration. While it is a reasonably comprehensive Plan, it is not sufficiently comprehensive for today.[128]

The report made a number of important recommendations although its continuing attempt to reach a compromise deprives it of the clarity that we find in the Carter Report on Legal Aid in Saskatchewan. The report recommends that the control and administration of the legal aid plan should be vested in a statutory corporation. It was not expected by the legal profession that the committee would recommend the plan be taken from the Law Society. The rationale for the change is explained in the carefully worded language which is characteristic of the report:

> A number of briefs were delivered and submissions made to us representing that the position of The Law Society under the present scheme involves a conflict of interest. The public good must be the sole purpose of the Legal Aid Plan, whereas The Law Society is by statute the governing body of the legal profession and must be primarily concerned with its welfare. The term "conflict of interest" may not be one appropriate in the circumstances, and we state emphatically that no suggestion was made to us at any time that The Law Society or its Legal Aid Committee has in fact permitted such a conflict to develop. Nevertheless, it is impossible to perceive the direction of the Legal Aid Plan as being sufficiently singleminded if it is left in the hands of a Committee of The Law Society, reporting to Convocation, the governing body of that Society, both groups being composed overwhelmingly of lawyers.[129]

The proposed solution is that the legal aid plan should be vested in a statutory corporation with nine members of the board appointed by the Law Society and nine by the provincial Attorney-General. This is a most unwieldy and unsatisfactory a solution to the control issue. It does not create a partnership but a board which will be independent neither of the profession nor of the government. There is, as well, no recognition of the legitimate place of the consumer of legal aid on the board. The Saskatchewan model would have provided a more reasonable compromise of consumer, professional and government interests.

A significant criticism of the Ontario fee-for-services scheme is that it perpetuates a Victorian concept of charity in that the profession continues to assist the poor by contributing 25 per cent of the legal aid tariff, rather than accepting the premise that all citizens should have access to the legal system. Lawyers have been expected to receive only 75 per cent of their fee as part of their professional responsibility and because of the continuing reluctance of the Law Society to accept the concept of payment for legal aid. The Osler Task Force on Legal Aid recognized this problem:

> In our view the time has come for us to recognize that Legal Aid is an important right that must be available to those who need it. The existence of a charitable element is inconsistent with the principle of the Plan and compromises the dignity of the recipient. The legal profession of this province has made an enormous contribution of some $14,260,000.00 in the first 6½ years of the operation of the Plan and it is with some regret, but with no hesitation that we recommend the termination of the policy.[130]

The abolition of the 25 per cent mandatory contribution was recommended. In addition the task force recommended that the tariff should be reduced by 10 per cent to account for the fact that there are no bad debts. Although this recommendation was made in 1975, the 25 per cent contribution by legal aid lawyers has remained and inflation may make it difficult to remove.

Criticism of the Ontario plan[131] in the early 1970s originated with the student Legal Aid Societies, created pursuant to the Legal Aid Act Regulations[132] to handle referral for the Area Directors. These student societies created clinics to fill some of the more obvious gaps in the Ontario plan. Another source of pressure on the Ontario plan was the movement towards staff lawyers and community clinics in Manitoba, Quebec and Saskatchewan and within Ontario by the funding of Parkdale Community Legal Services.

Parkdale Community Legal Services was funded in 1971 and became the first legal services office in the midst of Ontario's judicare scheme. The crucial seed money came from the federal Department of National Health and Welfare, the Council for Legal Education for Professional Responsibility (a Ford Foundation subsidiary) and York University. Parkdale was initially staffed by law students working in the clinic for academic credit, an articling student, a social worker involved in community development, two secretaries, and the writer as both director of the legal services office and a professor of clinical training.[133]

From the outset the office involved the Parkdale community in the external and internal planning, development and administration. During the early years public meetings were held on a monthly basis to discuss and set policy. During 1973, a board was created which reflected the partnership between the Parkdale community, Osgoode Hall Law School, and the profession. The board has fourteen members of whom seven are elected by the community; two are members of the law school faculty; two are practising lawyers; one a law student; one a member of the office; and the director. The staff person has in recent years been a community legal worker who is active in the community, thus giving the community a majority on the board. The board is responsible for funding; hiring and firing personnel; community education; monitoring the quality of service and for setting the philosophy and policies of the office.

Ontario's legal aid programme has not been static; there have been important developments in several areas and various experiments with the provision of legal services. On April 1, 1977, there was a pilot project introduced which employed full time duty counsel in Toronto's provincial courts. Six lawyers were hired to advise defendants on pleas, requests for adjournments, applications for bail, and even sentencing in the event of a guilty plea. Although, the Law Society assured a concerned Bar, when the project was introduced, that it would not lead to the introduction of a public defender system in the province, Attorney-General Roy McMurtry announced one year later that the government intended to investigate the public defenders' offices as a supplement to legal aid.[134] Another development is the recent regulation[135] which permits a judge to be informed of the fact that a person has a legal aid certificate, or has made application for one.

Community law clinics have had a rapid growth in the province, even though Ontario remains dedicated to the judicare system. The Legal Aid Committee has expressed the concern that clinical lawyers do not have sufficient freedom to represent a client fully when challenging a government agency and that clinic files cannot be protected sufficiently to guarantee a client's right to privacy.[136] Nevertheless, the committee felt that clinics offer valuable services in the areas designated as "poverty law" – those areas of the law that concern welfare, unemployment insurance, workmen's compensation, landlord-tenant law, and similar areas. By

Regulation 160/76 the Clinical Funding Committee was established to fund Parkdale Community Legal Services and several other projects then in existence, and to make recommendations regarding the funding of "independent community based clinical delivery systems", defined by the regulations as "any method for the delivery of legal or para-legal services to the public other than by way of fee for service". This includes preventive law programmes and educational and training programmes that are calculated to reduce the cost of delivering legal services. The Law Society has retained control over the development of community clinics as it appoints two of the three members of the Clinical Funding Committee.

The number of clinics in Ontario has increased dramatically in the past few years. In late 1975 the Ontario Legal Aid Plan provided funding for seven clinics; by the 1976-77 fiscal year this had grown to twelve, and by 1977-78 to twenty-seven. As of April 1978 there were thirty-three clinics being funded, with the expectation that a further eight to ten clinics will receive funding during 1978-79. In 1975-76, $295,597 was through OLAP for community legal services groups; this amount grew to $915,112 in 1976-77 and to $1,643,076 in 1977-78.

Along with the growth in the number of clinics there has also been an increased specialization in the services performed. While over one-third of the clinics provide general "proverty law" assistance, others now specialize in one area such as workmen's compensation, environmental law, research and education, or correctional law. The majority are located in urban environments. Most are in Toronto and the others in urban areas serviced by a law school – Windsor, Ottawa, London, Kingston; or in close proximity to one – Oshawa, Hamilton. The Law Society has recognized the need for service in other areas and after prolonged discussions with area residents, announced in February 1978 the opening of a clinic in Thunder Bay to serve the northern native community. With initial funding of $37,000 from the Ontario Legal Aid Plan, the service will open an office in Thunder Bay and satellite offices in surrounding communities. The central office will be staffed by a lawyer, a paralegal, and support staff while the affiliated offices will be run by paralegals only.

The following is a description of some of the projects currently funded, many of which make extensive use of community legal workers.

Metro Tenants Legal Services, established in 1976 to aid tenants encountering problems with Ontario rent control legislation focuses almost exclusively on the needs and rights of tenant associations. This involves representation at rent review hearings and county court applications by tenants for the termination of tenancies, abatement of rent, and the return of security deposits. The clinic is presently staffed by four full-time paralegals and a lawyer who serves as duty counsel, reviews files, and supervises case preparation. The staff paralegals learn in on-the-job training programmes and from an instruction programme offered by Parkdale Community Legal Services.

Individual tenants with residential problems can receive assistance from Tenant Hot Line. Established initially as a telephone service the office now receives "walk-in" clients. The staff includes seven paralegals and one staff lawyer.

A more typical community clinic is Neighbourhood Legal Services which provides both summary advice and assistance as well as case service in the areas of welfare law, unemployment insurance, landlord and tenant matters, and housing standards. The clinic is staffed by two lawyers and six community legal workers of whom four are former clients of the office.

Injured Workers Consultants is a clinic that provides legal assistance to injured workers pursuing claims before the Workmen's Compensation Board and other administrative tribunals. Staffed entirely by community legal workers, the clinic places priority on hiring staff who can speak a second language since a large proportion of its clientele does not speak English. In the last nine months of 1977, for instance, of ninety-five new cases opened, only thirty-four were for English-speaking clients while thirty-two were Italian, ten Spanish, eight Greek, five French and one each were for members of the Chinese, German, Czechoslovakian and Yugoslavian communities.

In conjunction with these clinics, the legal aid plan also helps to fund a number of "Duty Counsel Clinics". These are not permanent clinics but rather are duty counsel who rotate to a number of specific locations and who give summary legal advice and take legal aid applications. These clinics are often associated with local social service agencies and operate out of neighbourhood centres, shopping centres, community colleges, hospitals and libraries.

Legal aid's progress in recent years has been both puzzling and heartening. The statistical data for 1976-77 and 1977-78 indicate a levelling off of demand for legal aid and a tightening up of the system with a rising number of refusals. Officials contacted at the legal aid offices could offer no explanation for either phenomenon.

Ontario has witnessed an increase in the volume of criminal legal aid from 47 per cent of the certificates of eligibility issued in the first two years of the plan's operation to 53.7 per cent and 54 per cent in the last two years.[137] Criminal costs have similarly risen from $1,444,926.00 in 1967-68 to $12,738,782.00 in the 1976-77 fiscal year when the Ontario Legal Aid Plan paid for 37,712 completed criminal cases.[138]

In face of the growing costs of criminal legal aid, and the allegations from some litigation counsel and judges with respect to the deterioration in the quality of defence work being offered by some lawyers under the legal aid plan, the Attorney-General of Ontario, R. Roy McMurtry, announced in April 1978[139] that his department was undertaking a study of the public defender system presently operating in Montreal and Washington, D.C. If Ontario adopted a public defender or staff lawyer system for criminal legal aid it would be initiated in Metropolitan Toronto. An accused person could lose the freedom of choice aspect of the present Ontario scheme and rather would be assigned a salaried defence lawyer for certain offences. The Attorney-General claims that "the rising cost of the legal aid plan is not in itself a factor"[140] in his decision to study the public defender system but is rather concerned as to whether the Ontario taxpayer is well served by legal aid expenditures.

There is no doubt that the over six million dollars expended on criminal legal aid for Metropolitan Toronto's criminal caseload, which is approximately 50 per cent of the cost of criminal legal aid in Ontario, catches the bureaucrat's attention. Despite the high cost of legal aid for York County (primarily Metropolitan Toronto) during 1976-77, 17,100 criminal cases received certificates for legal aid[141] as compared to 21,679 criminal cases receiving assistance in the city of Montreal.[142] The average cost for a criminal case in York County was $387.17 in contrast to $299.38 for the rest of Ontario.[143] There are no comparable figures available for Quebec where the vast majority of criminal cases in Montreal are handled by the public defender's office (18,057 out of 21,769 cases). Although there seems to be little doubt that the cost per case of the public defender scheme is much lower than that of the judicare system, we have not had an effective evaluation undertaken as yet of the strengths and weaknesses of each scheme. There are allegations made that the quality of defence services being supplied by some lawyers under the legal aid plan has been deteriorating, but there is little or no evidence to verify these allegations. If anything, the evidence is to the contrary.[144]

Although the Ontario Legal Aid Plan remains primarily litigation-oriented, an encouraging development has been the recognition by the administration and the Legal Aid Committee that community clinics and paralegals (community legal workers) have a vital role to play in the delivery of legal services. The emphasis, however, has been on establishing clinics in urban areas, thus leaving large parts of Ontario without such assistance. The Law Society's Legal Aid Committee is beginning to grapple with the role of community clinics and seems determined to confine clinics to a rather limited definition of "practising law for poor people". Ontario is *de facto* moving more and more towards a mixed delivery system combining the strengths of both judicare and community legal services. However, as long as the Law Society retains control over the administration of the plan, it would seem to be determined to keep the clinical approach subordinate to the fee-for-service concept of legal aid, which has been the hallmark of the Ontario Legal Aid Plan since its inception.

Conclusion

The evolution of legal assistance in contemporary society must be responsible to the political and social fabric of the nation or jurisdiction in which legal aid schemes are established. It is interesting to observe that developments in most Western countries bear remarkable similarities, beginning from the assumption that inequality with respect to access to justice is an outgrowth of the availability of legal services. Most schemes ignore the perhaps more relevant socio-economic distinctions between the traditional users of the justice system and the poor. It is apparent that the major Canadian developments during the last decade are basically adapted from the British judicare model and the American community law office. Both programmes are premised on the belief that the provision of legal services on a gratuitous basis will be the greatest assistance to low income citizens.

Despite heated debates and considerable rhetoric, the Canadian provincial schemes have much more in common than might seem immediately apparent. Most provinces have developed schemes using both staff lawyers and private practitioners with a varying mix of civil and criminal caseloads. The concept of the staff lawyer is still perceived as a threat to the traditional individualistic approach of the legal profession, and has generally been opposed by the organized Bar.

Legal services remain a low priority in both the budgets of the provinces and the federal government. The last decade witnessed a growth of commitment of public funds coincident with the period of high government spending and general economic buoyancy. As governments are defeated or change their budgetary priorities we have witnessed a cut-back or "holding-the-line attitude".

Canada requires a critical and reflective assessment of the development of legal aid at this time. The era of expanding budgets is ending; and the demand will be increasingly strong to examine both the cost effectiveness and the impact of legal aid expenditures in the civil and criminal areas. But the difficult question remains: who is to determine what is in the public interest and whether the private lawyer, the staff lawyer or the community legal worker is the most effective method of delivery of legal services? We need to have the provincial plans co-ordinate their record keeping and statistical information so that the legal researcher can compare the cost of legal aid in each province on a case-to-case basis; can compare the cost of the private practitioner with the public defender; and based on documented information make recommendations about the future of legal services.

Cost effectiveness is not a term to be used only by government evaluators, law professors or legal aid administrators. The effectiveness of legal services must be measured in terms of their impact on over one-quarter of Canada's population – of the clients of legal aid. It is essential, before new funds are expended, to ascertain what impact, if any, developments to date have had on the low income community and the institutions of bureaucracies that were created to serve them. Provincial law societies and governments have allegedly pressed for public funding of legal services in a variety of models in the belief that "access" would improve the lot of the poor person and perhaps alleviate, if not eradicate, the effect of poverty. It becomes apparent however that provincial governments are not prepared to invest sufficient amounts of public funds to provide legal counsel for the multitude of legal and social problems confronted by the low income citizen. Ultimately the role of the legal researcher will be to integrate statistical information regarding cost effectiveness, to compare the social and economic impact of various models of delivery of legal services and to recommend to government the best means of responding to the needs of the recipients of legal aid. The willingness of Canadian provincial and federal governments to respond to the changing perspectives of legal services may foster the development of legal aid schemes which allow the poor access both to legal services and ultimately to a substantial degree of social justice.

Notes and References

1. According to a brief on the Federal-Provincial Agreement concerning legal aid prepared by the provincial Attorneys-General for submission to the Minister of Justice in June 1977.
2. Expenditures on legal aid in Ontario during 1971 were approximately 12 million dollars. See the Annual Report of the Ontario Legal Aid Plan published by the Law Society of Upper Canada, 1972, at p. 21.
3. These four clinics were: Dalhousie Legal Aid Service in Halifax, N.S.; Community Legal Service, Inc., in Point St. Charles, Montreal, Que.; Parkdale Community Legal Services in Toronto, Ont.; and the Saskatoon Community Legal Assistance Society in Saskatoon, Sask.
4. According to an address by John D. Bowlby, Q.C., chairman of the Legal Aid Committee of the Law Society of Upper Canada at the First International Colloquium on Legal Aid and Legal Services held in London, England on October 25-8, 1976. But see Table 1, which indicates that on a *per capita* basis Quebec spends more on legal aid.
5. See Norm Lareson, unpublished paper, "History of Legal Aid in Manitoba" (1977). Changing professional role models were hastened by young and progressive faculty members in Canadian law schools and by radical professional groups such as the Law Union in Ontario. As more Canadian law students participated in American graduate programmes, the writings of Edgar and Jean Cahn, as well as Stephen Wexler began to have an impact.
6. It is difficult to get accurate comparative figures with respect to *per capita* expenditures on legal aid. The Canadian average is approximately $3.36 per person, as Table 1 demonstrates. I have been unable to obtain comparable figures for the United States for both civil and criminal representation in 1977, but some writers estimate the American expenditures on legal services to be approximately $1.25 per person. See Roland Penner, unpublished paper, "The Development of Community Legal Services in Canada" (August 1977), p. 146.
7. The "Great Canadian Debate" over whether community legal services or the Ontario Legal Aid Plan and judicare model should be adopted is a term which I attribute to Professor Roland Penner of the University of Manitoba Faculty of Law and a pioneer in Canadian legal aid

Table 1

Budgets, populations, *per capita* expenditures and coverages, per province, 1977–78

Province	Approved Budget	Population	*Per Capita* Expenditure
Alberta	$3,880,000	1,867,000	$2.08
B.C.	8,226,500	2,512,000	3.27
Manitoba	3,269,000	1,033,000	3.16
New Bruns.	775,000	694,000	1.12
Newfoundland	625,000	558,000	1.12
Nova Scotia	1,225,000	836,000	1.47
Ontario	30,522,200	8,394,000	3.64
P.E.I.	70,600	122,000	0.58
Quebec	26,366,900	6,285,000	4.20
Saskatchewan	3,239,470	945,000	3.43
Sub-total	78,199,670	23,246,000	3.36

8. *The Law and the Poor in Canada*, ed. Irwin Cotler and Herbert Marx (Montreal, 1977), pp. 44ff.
9. ibid., pp. 44ff.
10. The Community Legal Services Report was prepared by a subcommittee of the Law Society of Upper Canada Legal Aid Committee. The subcommittee was composed of Patrick S. Fitzgerald, Peter de C. Cory and Lyle S. Fairbairn.
11. The Community Legal Services Report, p. 7.
12. ibid., p. 31.
13. *The Report of the Task Force on Legal Aid*, published by the Ministry of the Attorney-General, 1974. The task force was chaired by the Hon. Mr. Justice John H. Osler.
14. See the summary of major recommendations in the report, Recommendations #1 & #2, p. 119.
15. Section 91(27) of the *British North America Act.*
16. Section 92(14) of the *British North America Act.*
17. Section 92(13) of the *British North America Act.*
18. See the 1972 federal-provincial agreements collected in Memorandum of Agreements Respecting Legal Aid in Matters Related to the Criminal Law, 1972.
19. *The Extradition Act*, R.S.C. 1970, c. E-21.

20. *The Fugitive Offenders Act*, R.S.C. 1970, c. F-32.
21. The Hon. Otto Lang, ex-Minister of Justice of Canada, "The Future of Legal Aid in Canada" (in *Access to Justice*, the Canadian Council on Social Development, 1975, at p. 78).
22. See David Ross, *Canadian Fact Book on Poverty* (Ottawa: the Canadian Council on Social Development, 1975) at p. 12. More recent figures published by Statistics Canada on the distribution of income among Canadians suggest that some three million Canadians live in poverty. See *Bearing the Burden, Sharing the Benefits. A Report by the National Council of Welfare on Taxation and the Distribution of Income*, 1978, at p. 1.
23. See *Poverty in Canada: Report of the Special Senate Subcommittee on Poverty* (Ottawa: Information Canada, 1971).
24. While the average Canadian earner had a purchasing power increase of $1,603 between 1946 and 1971 (in 1961 dollars), the top decile of earners received almost three times that amount ($4,576). In contrast, the bottom 50 per cent of earners had a net purchasing power increase of only $360, while the poorest decile lost an average of $126 per earner in the same period. Had the change been measured from 1951 to 1971, the results would have been more dramatic as the poorest decile has lost an average of $184 while the richest gained $4,840. See Leo J. Johnson, *Poverty and Wealth*, 1974, New Hoggtown Press, at pp. 6–7.
25. See note 24.
26. "The lowest-income twenty percent of Canadians receive barely 4% of the total national income. The highest-income twenty percent, in contrast, receive more than 40% – a share ten times as great. The injustice of such an unequal distribution of income is compounded by the fact that the relative shares have remained virtually unchanged over the quarter century that the government has been gathering such data. In 1951 the bottom fifth of Canadians received 4.4% of the national income and the top fifth got 42.8%. In 1976 the counterpart figures were 3.9% for the group at the bottom and 44.0% for those at the top.

    "While the respective proportions of total income have remained more or less constant, the income gap separating the richest and poorest twenty percent of Canadians has grown enormously over the past twenty-five years as a result of the multifold increase in national income. In 1951 the gap stood at $3,060 – adjusting for inflation, the equivalent in 1976 dollars of $6,900. By 1976 the difference between the richest and poorest fifths had increased to $18,000. In other words, the gap, expressed in dollars of equal value, had multiplied by over two and a half times" (*Bearing the Burden, Sharing the Benefits*, at p. 1).

27. See Johnson, *supra*, note 24.
28. Most writers date the initiation of legal aid in Quebec at 1951 when the Quebec Bar set up a legal assistance system. Little data is available with respect to this scheme other than that very limited services were provided. In civil matters there were *in forma pauperis* proceedings which allowed for the dispensation of court costs in a limited number of proceedings.
29. Considering the size of Montreal's population the service provided was minimal. As an example, in 1964 there were 3,000 applicants for legal aid but only 700 cases were court representations and 75 per cent of these were domestic disputes.
30. Although the Bar claimed that all lawyers were required to take legal aid cases, it is clear that a very small percentage of the profession provided this service except in cases where a contingency fee of 15 per cent of damages recovered was obtainable.
31. See Walter Merricks, "Quebec's New Plan", *The New Law Journal*, September 28, 1972, at p. 853.
32. *The Delivery of Legal Services in Canada*, Ian B. Cowie, Federal Department of Justice, Ottawa, 1974, at p. 37.
33. See Cowie, *supra* note 32, at pp. 37-8. More than 4,550 of these persons were assisted by approximately 1,550 advocates in private practice. The other cases were handled by salaried lawyers of the staff of the bureau.
34. The pressure to develop a more adequate legal aid system provoked the government and the Bar to enter into two successive agreements with respect to legal aid during the winter and summer of 1971.
35. The Point St. Charles clinic, the first clinic in Quebec, opened as a community-controlled clinic in 1969 and hired its first staff lawyer in 1970. In 1971 and 1972 legal aid clinics were opened in Quebec City and Sherbrooke.
36. Community Legal Services Inc. in Point St. Charles was stimulated by an article in the *Montreal Star* of August 1969 by Professor Herbert Marks, describing the Cambridge, Massachussets, community legal assistance office, "Law Graduates and their People-Awareness".
37. S. 12.
38. See ss. 31-50. The intention of Bill 10 was to create a neighbourhood

legal services scheme in Quebec similar to the American model established under the *Economic Opportunity Act*, 1964.

39. S. 35.
40. The Director of Legal Services was to be an advocate (s. 37).
41. Merricks, *supra*, note 31, at p. 854.
42. This act was "An Act to Promote Access to Justice". It was enacted June 29, 1971, and became Book 8 of the Code of Civil Procedure.
43. The Quebec government has also introduced a new professional code which the profession saw as detracting from its autonomy. See Merricks, "Quebec's New Plan", at p. 854.
44. Quebec lawyers argued that: "The freedom to choose the professional or the clinic from which one wishes to receive legal services answers the profound aspirations of a good number of the underprivileged. It would not be equitable to establish structures in the area of justice which tend to set up a justice for the poor and a justice for the rich." Similar arguments have been put forward by various representatives of the profession at the national and provincial level in Canada. See Canadian Bar Association, Legal Aid Liaison Committee Report, August 1972.
45. The Fédération des Avocates du Quebec (FAQ), comprising about one-fifth of all Quebec's lawyers argued that there is an essential conflict between the Bar's two roles of protector of the public interest in the administration of legal aid and by regulation of professional misconduct and as a lawyers' "trade union".
46. *The Legal Aid Act (Loi de l'aide juridique)*, S.Q. 1972, c. 14.
47. The commission is charged with the provision of legal aid to the underprivileged by virtue of s. 22(a) and with establishing legal aid corporations by s. 22(b).
48. The responsibility for information projects is contained in s. 22(f) and for research projects is contained in s. 22(g).
49. The composition of the board is given in s. 35; however, the final third of the board is not stipulated.
50. The advisory committees are to have a maximum of twelve members with area representation to promote the needs of local lower income residents. See *The Legal Aid Act* (1972), s. 32(a).
51. S.Q. 1972, c. 14.
52. S. 32(c).
53. The local corporations are dependent upon the regional corporation for their funding on an annual basis and therefore must meet the standards and priorities set by the corporation.

54. Cowie, *supra*, note 32, at p. 39. They had been established at Laval University at Point St. Charles, at the University of Sherbrooke, at St. Louis, Montreal and in Hull which is attached to the University of Ottawa.
55. The Legal Services Commission allegedly "ordered the closing of the office on very short notice and re-assigned two staff lawyers with lengthy experience in the community to other positions in the provincial scheme". Jim Stewart wrote in the July 9, 1977, *Montreal Star* that "the St. Louis office and others like it (the Point St. Charles legal clinic recently accused the government of trying to kill it through budget cuts) didn't harmonize too well with legal aid bureau's bureaucrats. They were based on ideas of citizen participation, popular services, community needs, and local decision-making".
56. During 1976-77 the Quebec plan operated eighty-eight full-time offices in seventy-four cities and towns and employed 295 staff lawyers, 404 support staff and forty-five articling students.
57. Economically underprivileged is defined in the Quebec Act as "any person who in the opinion of the commission or, as the case may be, of a legal aid corporation, lacks sufficient financial means to assert a right, obtain legal counsel or retain the services of an advocate or notary without depriving himself of the means of subsistence", according to the criteria established by regulation.
58. Examples of areas where legal aid is prohibited pursuant to Regulation 3.19 are defamation actions, an action for breach of promise by the plaintiff only, or the defence of a parking ticket.
59. S. 1(c).
60. The applicant is not presented with a list of generally unknown lawyers to select from as is the case in Ontario and other judicare provinces but rather the legal aid recipient must request the services of a specific lawyer. The applicant will obtain a staff lawyer unless he requests otherwise.
61. See Ian Cowie, *supra*, note 32. See also Rosalind Brooke, "Legal Services in Canada", 1977, 40 *Modern Law Review*, 533.
62. Legal Aid Services in Canada (1976), André Saint-Cyr (unpublished).
63. ibid. In 1975-76, 77.6 per cent of all recipients in Quebec were served by staff lawyers while only 22.4 per cent were served by private practitioners (see p. 36). In the same year only 25.7 per cent of all recipients in Manitoba were served by staff lawyers while 74.3 per cent were served by private practitioners. In Manitoba there are twenty-six salaried lawyers and ten articling students employed

full-time in neighbourhood clinics with 600 lawyers on legal aid panels.

64. R. M. Cooper, report on the Quebec Legal Aid System in *Toward Equal Justice: A Comparative Study of Legal Aid in Modern Societies*, 1975, at p. 617.
65. Section 52 of the *Legal Aid Act* states that the commission may provide in certain exceptional situations, taking into account the requirements of good management, that certain professional services for legal aid shall be exclusively rendered by advocates employed by a coproration.
66. These criteria seem to have been designed in fact to deter groups from seeking legal services. Regulation 3.11 requires that the names, addresses, occupations, assets and debts of *each* member of the group be given.
67. "Minute Juridique" was a legal information campaign in which 100 one-minute texts directed to the average citizen were prepared by legal specialists dealing with topical legal problems. These were broadcast over one year and the most popular eighteen were rewritten and presented on television by well-known artists for twenty-six weeks and repeated several times a week at prime viewing times. Over 500,000 copies of booklets containing the "Minute Juridique" scripts were distributed free in legal aid bureaux and credit unions.
68. The commission hired three lawyers, two sociologists, one librarian and three law graduates to staff the back-up centres.
69. Quebec has a population of 6,285,000 and it is estimated that approximately one-third of the population or 2,000,000 are eligible for legal aid.
70. During the first year of operation, 600 opinions were provided in specific cases submitted by staff lawyers.
71. See the article in the *Montreal Star*, April 17, 1978.
72. Fifth Annual Report, 1976–77.
73. ibid., pp. 20–1. This survey was conducted by the sociology section of the Expertise Education and Research Department. See the Fifth Annual Report for a discussion of its findings.
74. Fifth Annual Report, p. 24.
75. ibid., p. 104.
76. The intention of this agreement was to allow the Benchers of the Law Society to make rules for the establishment of a comprehensive legal aid plan. In fact, the scheme was only implemented on the criminal side.

77. The applicant had to be indigent and demonstrate that he had reasonable likelihood of success. The legal aid certificate was granted at the discretion of a committee of Benchers of the Law Society. Applications were received by local legal aid committees composed of volunteer lawyers who appointed counsel on a rotating basis.
78. Thirty-five per cent in family law, 21 per cent consumer law, 8 per cent landlord and tenant, 7 per cent welfare, and 9 per cent criminal.
79. May 1972.
80. The committee was chaired by Roger Carter, Q.C., Dean of the College of Law, University of Saskatchewan and had six other members including a provincial court judge and the Director of the Saskatoon Legal Assistance Clinic. Their report is referred to hereinafter as the Carter Committee Report.
81. Final report of the Saskatchewan Legal Aid Committee of 1973, terms of reference.
82. The brief indicates the community law office is not only engaged in fighting poverty but "in wresting from bureaucrats, landlords and law enforcement officers some basic rights of citizenry in this country".
83. The Saskatchewan Legal Aid Committee brief states that the committee had received materials indicating that community legal services model was a cheaper method of delivering legal services and suggests that "it is a happy coincidence that for once in our complicated society 'better' can also mean cheaper".
84. Final report of the Saskatchewan Legal Aid Committee, Chapter 7, General Conclusions.
85. If this is not the case then wittingly or otherwise, he may fail properly to represent the interests of his client.
86. The committee stressed that the legal aid system should encourage the client and the professionals working in the system to adopt this attitude.
87. Another approach suggested was a class action leading to a judicial solution to the problems faced by groups of poor persons.
88. The commission states that such programmes should equip poor persons to deal with their legal problems and in some cases to prevent problems from arising.
89. Final Report of the Saskatchewan Legal Aid Committee, Chapter 7, p. 7.
90. Here referring to the scheme in Ontario, or similar schemes.
91. The committee stated "the legal aid scheme which provides for some

reasonable degree of healthy professional competition between salaried and non-salaried professionals is . . . desirable. This system ensures that the quality of legal services available to poor persons is kept at a high level".

92. The Community Legal Services (Saskatchewan) Act, 1974, S.S. 1973-74, c. 11.
93. See note 80.
94. S.S. 1973-74, c. 11.
95. There is a clinic to serve Northern Saskatchewan which does not have an area board.
96. Cases involving a conflict of interests are referred to private practitioners.
97. See section 21.
98. The Carter Committee Report and its implementation is a Canadian version of American legal services with a limited degree of involvement of the private lawyer. The commitment of the government to adequate funding and to providing the citizen with input and the right to request preventative services provides Saskatchewan with unique opportunities.
99. 945,000.
100. See note 6 for a comparison with expenditures in other jurisdictions.
101. *Report of the Joint Committee on Legal Aid*, tabled in the Legislative Assembly, April 14, 1965, pp. 9-10. Hereinafter cited as R.J.C.L.A.
102. Disbursements in the preparation of appeals to the Ontario Court of Appeal and the Supreme Court of Canada in capital cases were also paid but no payment of counsel fees was provided for.
103. R.J.C.L.A., p. 10.
104. 12, 13 and 14 George VI C. 51 (U.K.).
105. The report of the Committee on Legal Aid and Legal Advice in England and Wales, 1945.
106. *The Law Society Amendment Act, 1951*, S.O. 1951, c. 45.
107. ibid.
108. In 1951, the plan was restricted to those persons whose annual earnings or other income was less than $1,700.
109. Matters specifically excluded from civil coverage included, *inter alia*, defamation, breach of promise of marriage, alienation of affection.
110. Between 1952 and 1963 legal aid or advice was given in only 41,420 civil and 13,465 criminal cases.
111. Report of the Task Force on Legal Aid, 1974, p. vii.

112. *Toronto Globe & Mail*, September 13, 1958.

113. Report of the Task Force on Legal Aid, 1974, p. vii. A series of critical articles appeared in Toronto newspapers. Ruth Worth, in an article in the *Toronto Globe & Mail*, remarked that "Legal Aid in Ontario is still a charity given to those who, in the discretion of the executive or local director of the Legal Aid Plan, are worthy of it". She was dismayed that the Law Society could regard $26,000 as an adequate budget with which to handle 7,000 cases. She stated that ". . . of 2,000 members of the Bar who practice in Metropolitan Toronto, only 100 give legal aid on a regular basis." See the *Globe & Mail*, February 8, 1963.

114. The committee was chaired by William B. Common and was composed of members of the Law Society of Upper Canada and members of the civil service of Ontario, appointed by the Attorney-General. It is interesting to note that no potential recipients were on the committee and the only non-lawyers were the Director of Welfare Allowances of the Department of Public Welfare and the Secretary of the Treasury Board.

115. The *Globe & Mail*, editorial, July 22, 1964.

116. The Committee travelled throughout the province and received ninety-six written submissions and eighty-nine oral submissions. All but eight of the oral submissions were made by lawyers.

117. Province of Ontario, Joint Committee on Legal Aid, Report (Toronto, 1965).

118. *The Legal Aid Act, 1966*, S.O. 1966, c. 80 [now R.S.O. 1970, c. 239].

119. In 1974, the Ministry had a separate branch numbering seventy-seven persons for the sole purpose of performing these assessments. The Osler Report estimated that the direct costs of legal aid assessments was approximately $784,000 for the year ending March 31, 1974.

120. See note 13.

121. Osler Report recommendations 60–2. See p. 126 of the report.

122. In 1976 the chairman of the Legal Aid Committee of the Law Society of Upper Canada stated that 67 per cent of the province's Bar is listed on the legal aid panel. It is not possible to determine how many of these lawyers actually take cases.

123. Changes to the composition of the Legal Aid Committee took place after the Task Force on Legal Aid in Ontario recommended that the control and administration of the Legal Aid Plan should be vested

in a statutory non-profit corporation.

124. Address by John D. Bowlby, Q.C., at the First International Colloquium on Legal Aid and Legal Services, London, England, October 1976.

125. In 1963, the last year for which data on the voluntary plan is available, the plan handled 11,956 cases. In the first year of operation of the new plan, in which lawyers were remunerated on a fee-for-services basis (1967-68), 38,860 certificates were issued and 67,204 persons were assisted by duty counsel – an increase of approximately 1,000 per cent over the voluntary plan. In 1975-76, 107,193 persons made formal application for legal aid, and 86,486 certificates were issued. In 1976-77, however, 103,177 persons made formal applications (a decrease of 1.4 per cent), and 76,649 certificates were granted (a decrease of 3.8 per cent). 1977-78 saw a slight increase only – 105,118 applications were made, and 76,730 certificates were granted. Both 1976-77 and 1977-78 have seen increases in the number of refusals as a percentage of applications. It is still too early to tell if the decreases in applications made and certificates granted (although there were slight increases in 1977-78, the figures are still not as high as they were in 1975-76) is significant; however, they may indicate a tightening of requirements for eligibility in face of ever increasing costs.

126. For several years the percentage of applications refused remained at about 28 per cent of applications. In 1976-77, however, the percentage of applications refused increased to 31 per cent, and in 1977-78 it increased to 32.8 per cent. Thus nearly one-third of those who actually apply for legal aid certificates are refused. Figures released by the plan for the first nine months of 1977-78 indicate that refusals were chiefly a result of failure to provide adequate financial information or failure to complete arrangements to repay the plan (resulting in 10,527 of the 25,997 refusals). Additional reasons were that the applicant was considered able to retain his own lawyer (6,037 refusals); or that the applicant did not face a prison term or loss of means of livelihood (3,207 refusals). In addition, 1,746 applicants withdrew their applications.

127. Order-in-Council, December 19, 1973.

128. *Report of the Task Force on Legal Aid*, p. 22.

129. Larry Taman, "Legal Aid in Ontario: More of the Same?", 22 *McGill Law Journal*, 369 at 377.

130. *Report of the Task Force on Legal Aid*, p. 22.

131. Larry Taman, in "Legal Aid in Ontario: More of the Same?", writes at p. 371: "It is said to be the most costly delivery model available, heavily biased in favour of litigation and against preventive services, largely incapable of the kind of outreach which is necessary to attack the unmet need for legal services, too diffused to husband limited resources by developing energy-saving strategies of test cases, and community education, and too inflexible to respond to the demands of changing circumstances."
132. O. Reg. 257/69 ss. 74-7.
133. Parkdale currently employs, in addition to the law students working there, four lawyers, two articling students, six community legal workers and six support staff.
134. See *Macleans Magazine*, June 12, 1978.
135. O. Reg. 536/76 s. 137. Apparently this is intended to prevent counsel from abusing the system and prolonging the trial so as to gain maximum fees.
136. *Law Society of Upper Canada Gazette*,Vol. 9, 1975, p. 257.
137. Law Society of Upper Canada, Ontario Legal Aid Plan, Annual Report, 1969, p. 17 and Annual Report, 1977, p. 27.
138. ibid., Annual Report, 1969, p. 19 and Annual Report, 1977, p. 28.
139. Maclean's, June 12, 1978.
140. R. Roy McMurtry, letter to the *Toronto Star*, June 5, 1978.
141. Law Society of Upper Canada, Ontario Legal Aid Plan, Annual Report, 1977, p. 27.
142. Commission des Services Juridiques, Fifth Annual Report, p. 34.
143. Law Society of Upper Canada, Ontario Legal Aid Plan, Annual Report, 1977, p. 28.
144. James L. Wilkins, *Legal Aid in the Criminal Courts* (Toronto, 1975), p. 136.

JEAN PRADEL

France

Abstract

The principle of legal aid has long been accepted in France, but its application has undergone a major transformation since the 1972 legislation. Until then, legal assistance was provided as a charitable gesture towards the poor; now it is considered a legal right. Professor Pradel describes three main features of the new system: its field of application, its procedure and its limitations and benefits. Legal aid can be requested by any French national who has a serious cause of action and who lacks financial resources (this is assessed by comparison with pre-established scales). Legal aid may be available for commercial, administrative or civil actions (penal matters are regulated by other provisions).

Aid may be awarded for any kind of legal procedure, for example, litigation, appeal, contract or execution. The request is ordinarily presented to the legal aid office which evaluates it and makes a decision as to the appropriateness and extent of need. An appeal procedure may be taken in case of refusal. There are also provisions for withdrawal in case of fraud. This procedure is fairly lengthy, and may take two to three months to be completed, but an emergency procedure may be used in proper cases. Professor Pradel discusses the limitations and benefits of this new legislation; among the limitations he points out the difficulties that may arise when the matter in issue "cannot be distinguished from the award of legal aid", for example, in cases of alimony where the determination of need for legal assistance may influence the final decision of the judge. Another limitation is the fact that legal aid is valid only for the particular instance for which it was requested and awarded. Among the benefits,

Professor Pradel mentions the availability of a lawyer for the legal aid recipient who is relieved of paying legal fees and costs. Lawyers and other legal personnel are remunerated according to a fixed scale, depending upon the nature and importance of the work involved. In conclusion, the author expresses satisfaction with the new system which protects the interests of all involved – a marked contrast with the pre-1972 situation.

On s'accordera aisément sur la nécessité de principe de l'aide judiciaire. N'est-il pas légitime en effet de dispenser de certains frais et honoraires tout usager du service public de la Justice qui se trouve totalement ou partiellement démuni de ressources suffisantes?

L'idée, fondée sur une considération de justice élémentaire, est si profonda qu'elle a presque toujours été retenue par le législateur. Déjà, dans l'Athènes antique, des avocats étaient désignés d'office pour les indigents. En France, du Livre de Justice et Plet à l'Edit de 1610 instituant un avocat des pauvres, le droit d'ancien régime est tout empli de ce souci de "faire droiture tant aux pauvres comme aux riches". Et si l'ordonnance de 1667 organise la justice sans se soucier d'assurer aux pauvres le libre accès aux juges, le durcissement sera de brève durée. Dès la loi des 16–24 août 1790, les pauvres retrouvent le libre accès au prétoire: soucieuse d'égalité, la Révolution se devait d'assurer autant celle des justiciables que celle des citoyens. Ce courant retrouvé allait s'épanouïr avec la Révolution de 1848: une révolution aidant l'autre, la loi du 22 janvier 1851 organisait l'assistance judiciaire. Retouché par les lois des 10 juillet 1901, 31 mars 1903 et 14 décembre 1907 ainsi que par les décrets des 22 décembre 1958 et 30 décembre 1960, le système allait être refondu par l'importante loi du 3 janvier 1972 toujours en vigueur, qui modifie l'esprit de l'institution et qui substitue en conséquence l'expression d'aide judiciaire à celle d'assistance judiciaire.[1]

Car si nulle discussion n'est permise sur le principe d'une aide, l'hésitation est en revanche possible sur la conception de celle-ci. On peut d'abord imaginer l'institution dans une optique charitable, non sociale. Dans ce système, l'organisme chargé de déterminer les bénéficiaires de la gratuité, appelé bureau, a toute latitude pour apprécier l'opportunité de l'admission sans être tenu par une fixation à l'avance des règles relatives au taux de revenus, et les auxiliaires de justice ne perçoivent aucune rétribution. Ainsi avait fait le législateur avant 1972, qui entendait venir au secours du pauvre ou plutôt de l'indigent comme l'on disait alors: dans la France des Misérables, le romantisme judiciaire faisait écho au romantisme littéraire d'un Lamartine ou d'une George Sand.

Face à cette première conception, on peut en concevoir une autre, faisant de l'aide judiciaire un droit de nature sociale affirmé sans ambiguité[2] et entraînant les conséquences inverses de celles que l'on vient d'indiquer. C'est le système de la loi de 1972, et qui pourrait d'ailleurs être renforcé par un système d'aide juridique. On rappelera que lors des travaux parlementaires de cette loi, on avait proposé d'instituer au siège de chaque tribunal de grande instance un service public de consultations juridiques assurées par les membres des barreaux, chaque consultation donnant lieu au versement d'un droit forfaitaire versé à des fonds d'aide judiciaire. Les auteurs de cette initiative entendaient ainsi compléter les dispositions du projet de loi sur l'aide judiciaire par l'institution d'une véritable aide juridique afin d'opérer un "rapprochement de la justice et du citoyen".[3] Inspiré des droits anglais et allemand, cet amendement fut repoussé. Il est permis de le regretter car les deux aides sont inséparables, l'application de la loi n'étant pas uniquement contentieuse.

La timidité relative du législateur de 1972 ne l'a pas empêché d'affirmer que l'aide judiciaire est bien un droit. Et ceci va inspirer une bonne part de sa réglementation. De cette institution dont on se bornera à décrire les principes directeurs,[4] on examinera le domaine, la procédure et les effets.

I – Le domaine de l'aide judiciaire

L'accès à la justice ne devant être freiné par aucune raison d'ordre matériel, notre droit conçoit l'aide judiciaire de manière large, qu'il s'agisse des personnes pouvant en bénéficier, des juridictions devant lesquelles elle s'applique ou des actes pour lesquels elle peut être demandée.

A) Dans son article 1er, la loi du 3 janvier 1972 dispose que "les personnes dont les ressources sont insuffisantes pour faire valoir leurs droits en justice peuvent bénéficier d'une aide judiciaire".

a) Par personnes, il faut entendre évidemment les personnes physiques de nationalité française. Et la loi de 1972, en son article 1 ajoute deux catégories de personnes. La première est constituée par "les étrangers ayant leur résidence habituelle en France". Le texte apporte ici un précision utile car jusqu'ici la loi était muette:[5] il traduit une extension de l'institution en réduisant à néant l'opinion doctrinale selon laquelle le bénéfice de l'aide judiciaire est un droit civil au sens de l'article 11 du Code civil, c'est-à-dire un droit ne pouvant être accordé aux étrangers que sous réserve de réciprocité.[6] La seconde catégorie ajoutée par la loi de

1972 est constituée par "les personnes morales à but non lucratif ayant leur siège en France", l'aide ne pouvant toutefois leur être accordée qu' "exceptionnellement".[7] Il s'agit en fait des personnes morales de droit privé dont la montée en droit judiciaire se retrouve en procédure pénale où de nombreuses lois récentes leur accordent le droit de se constituer partie civile.[8] Il a été jugé que la masse des créanciers d'un débiteur en règlement judiciaire ne saurait être considérée comme faisant partie du nombre des personnes morales à but non lucratif visées par la loi.[9]

Une seule limite a été posée à l'énumération des personnes: le candidat à l'aide judiciaire doit faire état d'une demande sérieuse. Selon l'article 3 de la loi de 1972, "l'aide judiciaire est accordée aussi bien au demandeur dont l'action n'apparaît pas manifestement irrecevable ou dénuée de fondement qu'au défendeur. En matière de cassation, l'aide judiciaire peut être refusée au demandeur si aucun moyen de cassation sérieux ne peut être relevé". L'appréciation du caractère manifestment irrecevable ne pose guère de difficultés et il faut féliciter le législateur d'avoir limité l'aide judiciaire en empêchant la naissance de procès trop téméraires. Plus délicate à mettre en œuvre est l'appréciation du bien-fondé de la demande en justice. Comme il est inconcevable que l'organe accordant l'aide judiciaire empiète sur la compétence de juge en exerçant à sa place un pouvoir juridictionnel, il apparaît que cet organe doive se borner à un examen *prima facie* de l'affaire, à une appréciation du "bon sens" de la demande.[10] On notera que cette condition ne concerne que le demandeur, non le défenseur pour lequel la nécessité d'une insuffisance de ressources suffit.

b) Cette dernière condition, commune au demandeur et au défenseur, peut avoir deux sens. Ou bien, l'on se contente d'une indigence, d'une insuffisance de ressources, appréciée de façon discrétionnaire par la bureau saisi de la demande, ou bien l'on établit des barèmes. Avec la loi de 1972, notre droit abandonne le premier système au profit du second.[11] Et poussant fort loin le second système, la loi nouvelle distingue entre une aide totale, une aide partielle et un refus, selon des tranches préétablies de revenus. Selon les articles 2 de la loi du 3 janvier 1972 modifiée par celle du 22 juin 1976, et 66 du décret du ler septembre 1972, modifié par celui du 15 octobre 1976, le demandeur à l'aide judiciaire totale doit justifier le fait que la moyenne mensuelle de ses ressources est inférieure à 1500 F. Le demandeur à l'aide judiciaire partielle doit justifier le fait que cette moyenne est inférieure:

1°) à 2500 F s'il s'agit d'une instance devant laquelle le recours à un avocat ou avoué est obligatoire;

2°) à 2000 F s'il s'agit d'une instance devant laquelle cette représentation n'est pas obligatoire.[12]

Deux moyens d'individualisation sont prévus: les plafonds sont affectés de correctifs pour charges de famille[13] et le bureau peut, à titre exceptionnel, accorder une aide à des personnes dont les ressources dépassent les taux légaux, mais qui sont "particulièrement dignes d'intérêt au regard de l'objet du litige ou des charges prévisibles du procès.[14]

Ce système pose toutefois une difficulté tenant à la détermination des ressources qui doivent être prises en considération. Selon l'article 15 al. 1 de la loi de 1972, "le bureau prend en considération les ressources de toute nature dont le demandeur a directement ou indirectement la jouissance ou la libre disposition, à l'exclusion des prestations familiales. Il peut avoir égard aux éléments extérieurs du train de vie". Mais que décider dans le cas particulier d'un bien non productif de revenus comme une maison? Comme l'article 15 décide qu'on doit tenir compte de l'existence de biens même non productifs de revenus, à l'exclusion des locaux constituant la résidence habituelle du demandeur et des biens qui ne pourraient être vendus ou donnés en gage sans entraîner un trouble grave pour l'intéressé, on en déduit que le fait d'être propriétaire d'un appartement, d'une maison ou plus généralement d'un bien nécessaire à la vie ou à la profession du demandeur ne fait pas obstacle à l'admission à l'aide judiciaire.[15] On s'est demandé également si les ressources du concubin de la personne sollicitant l'aide judiciaire pouvaient être prises en considération. Comme notre droit s'attache à la situation réelle du demandeur, il faut répondre par l'affirmative.[16]

C'est ce même désir de voir les bureaux "saisir" la situation réelle du candidat, qui a conduit la jurisprudence à décider que les avantages en nature et les ressources du conjoint peuvent être pris en considération même si le demandeur à l'aide judiciaire est marié sous le régime de la séparation de biens.[17]

Il faut enfin tenir compte, dans les ressources du requérant, du montant des pensions alimentaires dont il est créancier ou débiteur; il est à remarquer qu'une difficulté pratique demeure: celle de savoir si ces pensions sont effectivement payées.

B) Evident à l'égard des personnes, le libéralisme du législateur se marque également sur le plan des juridictions devant lesquelles l'aide judiciaire peut jouer. Selon l'article 4 de la loi de 1972, l'aide s'applique à "toute instance portée soit devant une juridiction relevant de l'ordre judiciaire, à l'exclusion des juridictions pénales, soit devant le Conseil d'Etat, les tribunaux administratifs ou le tribunal des conflits; toute action concernant une personne civilement responsable exercée devant les juridictions de jugement; toute action de partie civile devant les juridictions d'instruction et de jugement". Ce texte appelle deux remarques.

La première conduit à marquer le caractère extensif de ce passage. La loi de 1851, plusieurs fois remaniée, énumérait les juridictions devant lesquelles s'appliquait l'assistance judiciaire. C'est pourquoi le silence sur les tribunaux paritaires des baux ruraux ou sur les juridictions arbitrales était la cause de certaines hésitations. Celles-ci sont aujourd'hui levées puisque l'aide judiciaire est désoimais possible devant toutes les juridictions civiles, commerciales et administratives.[18]

La seconde remarque consiste en une précision. En excluant l'aide judiciaire devant les juridictions pénales, sauf pour les actions de partie civile, l'article 4 doit être compris à la lumière d'une distinction entre la personne poursuivie et la victime désireuse de se porter partie civile. Pour la première, le système de l'aide judiciaire est remplacé par celui de la désignation d'office d'un défenseur. On doit ici rappeler que lors de l'interrogation de première comparution, le juge d'instruction "donne avis à l'inculpé de son droit de choisir un conseil parmi les avocats inscrits au tableau de l'ôrdre et, dans le cas contraire, par le président du tribunal" (art. 114 al. 3 C. proc. pén.). Et devant la cour d'assises, "l'accusé est . . . invité à choisir un conseil pour l'assister dans sa défense. Si l'accuse ne choisit pas de conseil, le président ou son délégué lui en désigne un d'office" (art. 274 C. proc. pén.).[19] Or, la désignation d'office ne doit pas être confondue avec l'aide judiciaire: d'abord parce qu'elle est davantage une garantie des droits de la défense qu'une aide véritable; aussi parce qu'elle n'est pas liée aux ressources de la personne puisque rien d'interdirait théoriquement à une personne très fortunée de solliciter la désignation d'un avocat d'office.[20] Lorsqu'il s'agit au contraire de la victime désireuse de se constituer partie civile devant la juridiction d'instruction ou de jugement, on en revient au système de l'aide judiciaire; une exception à noter: le pouvoir en cassation sur intérêts exclusivement civils n'est pas englobé.

C) La conception large de l'aide judiciaire apparaît enfin dans le domaine des actes pour lesquels elle peut être réclamée. L'article 4 de la loi de 1972 prévoit l'aide "tant en matière gracieuse qu'en matière contentieuse" et pour "tout acte conservatoire, toute voie d'exécution, soit d'une décision de justice, soit d'un acte quelconque".

L'aide judiciaire est donc possible en premier lieu pour les litiges. Elle l'est d'abord pour tout litige, quelle qu'en soit la nature civile, commerciale ou administrative. Elle l'est également, soit pour tout le litige, soit pour une partie seulement de celui-ci puisqu'elle "peut être accordée pour tout ou partie de l'instance" (art. 1).[21] L'insuffisance des ressources peut en effet apparaître en cours d'instance. Elle l'est enfin pour une action en elle-même et non pour une action devant telle juridiction déterminée. Et ceci signifie deux choses: d'abord si la juridiction saisie d'un litige pour lequel l'aide judiciaire a été obtenue est incompétente, ce bénéfice subsiste devant la deuxième juridiction saisie (art. 5); ensuite, l'aide continue à s'appliquer en cas d'appel ou de pourvoi en cassation après avoir joué en première instance (art. 6). Toutefois, l'article 6 posant la règle du maintien de l'aide en faveur du plaideur qui a obtenu une décision qui lui profite (et qui est l'objet d'une voie de recours), on peut se demander si l'aide joue aussi en faveur du plaideur qui, après avoir obtenue l'aide, a perdu son procès en première instance et exerce une voie de recours. Il semble qu'en ce cas, l'aide judiciaire ne doive pas être automatique, tant en raison de la lettre de l'article 6 que de l'exigence d'une demande sérieuse (art. 3). Le plaideur débouté devra donc faire une nouvelle demande d'aide judiciaire.

En second lieu, l'aide judiciaire s'applique aux actes de juridiction gracieuse[29] et aux actes conservatoires. Elle peut donc être sollicitée pour une demande d'homologation ou d'autorisation (en matière de tutelle, d'adoption, de régime matrimoniaux, . . .) pour des inventaires, appositions de scellés, etc.

Enfin, les actes d'exécution sont susceptibles d'aide judiciaire. Celle-ci s'étend évidemment de plein droit aux actes d'exécution d'une décision pour laquelle l'aide avait été obtenue. Mais elle peut aussi être accordée sur demande spéciale pour tous actes d'exécution à opérer à la suite d'une décision qui aurait été obtenue sans aide judiciaire.

Le domaine de notre institution est donc considérable. Mais on sait que l'intérêt d'une institution se mesure également à ses possibilités de fonctionnement. Qu'en est-il au juste de l'aide judiciaire?

II – La procedure de l'aide judiciaire

La loi a confié le soin de statuer sur les demandes d'aide judiciaire à des organismes autonomes: les bureaux d'aide judiciaire.[23] Il aurait été concevable de confier cette mission à la juridiction saisie du litige, comme le font les droits allemand et suisse. Cette conception se heurte cependant à un obstacle chez nous: l'aide n'étant attribuée qui si la demande apparaît sérieuse, il était à craindre que le tribunal ne manifeste un préjugé favorable au demandeur auquel il en aurait accordé le bénéfice.

Cela étant, le décret d'application du 1er septembre 1972 prévoit deux procédures: l'une normale ou de droit commun et l'autre exceptionnelle, applicable en cas d'urgence, dite de l'admission provisoire. Une règle est cependant commune à ces deux voies: la décision d'admission à l'aide judiciaire est caduque si, dans l'année de sa notification, le juge n'a pas été saisi.[24]

A) Minutieusement réglementée, la procédure de droit commun commence par la rédaction d'une demande d'aide judiciaire,[25] écrite par le postulant, contenant des indications sur la nature du litige[26] et adressée au parquet de la juridiction dans le ressort de laquelle il demeure. A partir de là, la procédure se déroule en deux ou trois phases.

Tout d'abord, le parquet vérifie la régularité formelle de la demande. Il peut inviter le requérant, le cas echéant, à compléter le dossier et même à "recueillir tous renseignements qu'il estime utiles à l'information du bureau et . . . faire entendre le requérant:[27] ainsi au contrôle de la régularité formelle peut s'ajouter une instruction sur le bien fondé de la demande.

Le bureau est alors saisi du dossier par le parquet: c'est la deuxième phase. Si le bureau s'estime insuffisamment éclairé, il peut ordonner une instruction complémentaire. Dès qu'il est complètement instruit, il prend sa décision, statuant à la majorité des membres présents, la voix du président étant prépondérante en cas de partage. Dans sa décision, le bureau peut admettre la requête totalement ou partiellement, ou la rejeter. Dans les deux premiers cas, la décision doit indiquer la nature des procédures ou actes en vertu desquels l'aide est accordée. Dans le second, elle doit préciser en outre le montant de la contribution du bénéficiaire, et éventuellement, le montant des diverses échéances et les modalités de paiement. Enfin, dans le troisième, la décision doit indiquer les motifs du rejet: cette limitation de la motivation aux seules décisions de rejet n'est pas très heureuse puisque toute décision peut faire l'objet d'une modification.[28] Il a été jugé que le bureau qui motive sa décision par les mots "ressources suffisantes" et qui n'indique pas le montant des ressources, méconnaît les dispositions de l'article 38 du décret du 1er septembre 1972; en effet, une telle omission empêche de contrôler la conformité de la décision aux prescriptions légales.[29]

Une troisième phase peut en effet s'ajouter. Tout d'abord, on prévoit une possibilité de réformation de la décision par la voie d'une sorte d'appel porté devant le bureau supérieur.[30] Ce recours ne peut d'ailleurs émaner que du parquet, et non pas du bénéficiaire, pour qui le bénéfice de l'aide judiciaire ne constitue pas un droit, ni des membres des professions sur lesquels retombera la charge de l'aide. En outre, le procureur de la République ou le ministre de la Justice peuvent inviter le bureau à réviser la décision qui a été rendue: cette rétractation peut s'appliquer dès qu'une nouvelle délibération sur le montant ou les modalités de paiement apparaït "utile",[31] elle permet donc d'éviter dans certains cas le recourse, toujours assez lourd, au bureau supérieur. Enfin, les textes ont imaginé une possibilité de retrait du bénéfice de l'aide judiciaire: retrait obligatoire lorsque ce bénéfice "a été obtenu à la suite de déclarations ou au vu de pièces inexactes",[32] retrait facultatif "s'il survient au bénéficiaire pendant l'instance, ou l'accomplissement des actes, des ressources telles que si celles-ci avaient existé au jour de la demande d'aide judiciaire, la demande n'aurait pas été accueillie même partiellement.[33] Cette révision est confiée au bureau même qui avait statué. Elle donne lieu à une décision motivée qui peut faire l'objet d'un recours.

Malgré le voeu du législateur, cette procédure est donc assez lente. En pratique, un délai de deux à trois mois s'écoule entre la date de la demande au parquet et celle de la décision du bureau. D'où l'admission dans certains cas d'une procédure d'urgence, dite de l'admission provisoire.

B) Cette seconde procédure est beaucoup plus simple et donc plus rapide. Ce caractère apparaît à divers égards.

D'un côté, le formalisme de la demande est simplifié: en effet, l'admission provisoire est sollicitée "sans forme"[34] et la requête peut être adressée aussi bien au président du bureau ou de la juridiction qu'au procureur de la République (ou procureur général) alors qu'en droit commun seul ce dernier a compétence pour la recevoir. Et une demande n'est même pas toujours nécessaire puisque l'admission provisoire peut être prononcée d'office si l'intéressé a formé une demande ordinaire qui n'a pas encore fait l'objet d'une décision définitive.

De l'autre côté, le magistrat du parquet, s'il est saisi d'une demande d'admission provisoire ou d'office en cas d'urgence, transmet sans délai le dossier, avec son avis au président du bureau compétent pour prononcer l'admission provisoire.

Enfin, la notification à l'intéressé est faite immédiatement.

On notera cependant que l'admission provisoire n'est prévue qu'en cas d'extrême urgence. Et il a été jugé que cette urgence pouvait résulter notamment d'un délai. La procédure de l'admission provisoire est donc applicable si le jugement a été signifié (ce qui fait courir le délai) ou encore, s'il est sur le point d'être signifié.[35]

III – Les effets de l'aide judiciaire

On insiste volontiers sur les effets positifs de l'aide judiciaire au profit du bénéficiaire et des auxiliaires qui vont devoir l'assister. Il ne faut pas oublier cependant les effets négatifs qui marquent les limites de l'aide judiciaire quant au fond du litige.

A) Si la décision d'admission à l'aide judiciaire entraîne des conséquences sur les frais du procès, elle ne saurait en avoir d'autres. De manière plus précise, les effets négatifs de la décision sont au nombre de deux.

En premier lieu, quelle qu'ait été l'appréciation du bureau sur la valeur des droits invoqués en justice, cette appréciation ne lie en rien le juge quant à la question de fond. Selon l'article 44 du décret du 1er septembre 1972, "les décisions des bureaux ne peuvent être communiquées qu'au demandeur à l'aide judiciaire, à ses conseils au Ministère public et au garde des Sceaux, Ministre de la Justice" et "elles ne peuvent être ni produites, ni discutées en justice, à moins qu'elles ne soient intervenues à la suite d'agissements ayant donné lieu à des poursuites pénales". Parfaitement logique, la règle donne pourtant lieu à des difficultés lorsque le litige principal a un objet très proche de la demande d'aide judiciaire, par exemple lorsqu'il porte sur une demande d'aliments ou de provisions *ad litem*. Dans ces deux cas, il faudra bien apprécier l'insuffisance des ressources. Mais même là, l'appréciation portée par le bureau ne saurait lier le juge quant à la question de fond.[36]

Cette indépendance entre les deux procédures est d'ailleurs poussée fort loin puisque le dépôt d'une demande d'aide judiciaire n'interrompt pas les délais de prescription relatifs à l'action au fond[37] et ne proroge pas le délai d'appel.[38]

Second effet négatif, le bénéfice de l'aide judiciaire ne vaut que pour l'instance en vue de laquelle elle est demandée. Une limite est cependant admise à cette règle: l'aide reste acquise lorsque la juridiction du fond se déclare incompétente si l'affaire doit être portée devant une autre juridiction.

B) Plaideurs et praticiens s'intéressent cependant davantage aux effets positifs de l'aide judiciaire. Ceux-ci sont en effet particulièrement puissants.

D'une part, on désigne un avocat (ou un avoué, ou un huissier) au bénéficiaire de l'aide judiciaire. Dès l'admission, le secrétaire de la juridiction compétente au fond adresse une copie de la décision au bâtonnier ou au président de l'organisme professionnel concerné. Celui-ci désigne l'auxiliaire qui prêtera son concours au bénéficiaire de l'aide judiciaire. Ainsi, ce dernier ne choisit pas son avocat, la gratuité allant de pair avec l'absence de choix.[39] Il n'en irait autrement que si un avocat ou officier public ou ministériel prêtait déjà son concours au bénéficiaire de l'aide judiciaire avant son admission: des raisons pratiques imposent alors que l'homme de loi ayant déjà pris connaissance de l'affaire n'en soit pas déssaisi:

L'avocat peut-il refuser son ministère après avoir été désigné? Malgré le mutisme de la loi du 3 janvier 1972 et du décret du 1er septembre 1972, il faut répondre négativement. En effet, l'article 88 du décret du 9 juin 1972 sur le statut des avocats décide que les conseils sont tenus de déférer aux désignations et commissions d'office sauf pour un motif légitime d'excuse ou d'empêchement admis par l'autorité qui a procédé à la désignation ou à la commission.

D'autre part, et c'est le second effet positif, le bénéficiaire de l'aide judiciaire est dispensé de payer les honoraires et frais, c'est-à-dire "les droits de timbre et d'enregistrement et les taxes assimilées . . . les redevances de greffe, les honoraires et émoluments des avocats et officiers publics et ministériels, les honoraires afférents aux expertises ou constats, les taxes des témoins, les frais de transport des magistrats, des avocats, des officiers publics et ministériels et des experts".[40] Bien entendu, l'exoneration peut être totale ou partielle, cette dernière laissant "à son bénéficiaire la charge d'une contribution.[41] Inversement, si le bénéficiaire de l'aide judiciaire perdant son procès est condemné aux dépens, il est tenu de supporter la charge des frais effectivement engagés par son adversaire, c'est-à-dire les débours, droits et émoluments de l'avocat de celui-ci.[42]

Enfin, le troisième effet positif consiste dans un système original d'indemnisation des avocats et officiers ministériels ayant prêté leur concours au bénéficiaire. Il s'agit d'ailleurs moins d'une rémunération proprement dite que d'une contribution aux frais résultant du concours apporté aux assistés. Mais distinguons:

Dans le cas des huissiers et greffiers, il est prévu une "indemnité forfaitaire"[43] qui est déterminée par le décret d'application du 1er septembre 1972.[44]

Dans le cas des avocats et avoués, un système différent est prévu. S'il s'agit d'aide judiciaire totale, l'article 76 du décret du 1er septembre 1972 modifié par celui du 15 octobre 1976, décide que le bureau fixe l'indemnité en fonction de l'importance des tâches et dans des limites qu'il indique, ces limites variant selon la nature de l'affaire. Par exemple, en matière de loyers commerciaux ou d'expropriations, l'avocat touche entre

180 et 350 F; devant le tribunal administratif, l'indemnité est comprise entre 500 et 1000 F; devant le tribunal de grande instance, pour un divorce, elle varie également de 500 à 1000 F. En cas d'aide judiciaire partielle, l'article 77 du décret précité décide que les limites de l'indemnité versée au praticien "sont égales à la moitié, au quart ou au huitième de celles qui sont prévues à l'article précédent selon que la moyenne mensuelle des ressources du bénéficiaire de l'aide est comprise entre 1500 F et 1850 F, 1851 et 2150 F ou 2151 et 2500 F. Enfin, que l'aide soit totale ou partielle, l'indemnité est payée à l'auxiliaire de justice par le secrétaire de la juridiction près de laquelle est établi le bureau d'aide judiciaire qui a prononcé l'admission; et elle lui est versée après le prononcé du jugement sur le fond ou sur justification de l'achèvement de sa mission. Et il est bien certain que l'avocat a droit au paiement du montant total de l'indemnité qui lui a été accordée par le bureau, même si le litige a trouvé une solution avant que la procédure n'ait été conduit jusqu'à son terme: l'indemnité a un caractère forfaitaire.[45]

Apparement complexe, ce système d'indemnisation des auxiliaires de justice est en réalité assez satisfaisant si l'on songe qu'avant 1972, rien n'était prévu. Une indemnisation était du reste devenue d'autant plus nécessaire que "l'extension de l'aide judiciaire à de nouvelles catégories de plaideurs constituait pour leurs conseils une surcharge abusive si elle n'était compensée par le versement d'une indemnité".[46] Ce système donne donc aux auxiliaires de justice une satisfaction légitime.[47]

Tel se présente dans ses grandes lignes le systéme français de l'aide judiciaire. S'il est vrai que, comme toute institution, celle-ci ne vaut que par la qualité des praticiens chargés de l'appliquer, on doit convenir que l'outil permet de respecter les intérêts légitimes de toutes les personnes concernées par un procès et avant tout, ceux du plaideur de fortune modeste.

Notes and References

1. Et qui entraîne en même temps une augmentation du nombre des plaideurs aidés: 50,000 admissions avant 1972 contre environ 100,000 aujourd'hui. Du ler janvier au 31 décembre 1975, on a compté pour la métropole et les départments d'outre-mer 145,651 demandes, 80,976 admissions à l'aide totale, 13,661 admissions à l'aide partielle et 11,343 rejets. Troisième rapport annuel sur le fonctionnement de l'aide judiciaire en date du 10 mai 1976.

2. Voire promu au rang des garanties constitutionnelles en tant que conséquence du principe de l'égalité de tous devant la loi. Le problème s'est d'ailleurs posé sur ce terrain devant les cours constitutionnelles de plusieurs pays comme l'Italie ou l'Allemagne Fédérale, v. B. Oppetit, L'aide judiciaire, D.-1972, chronique p. 41, n° 4.
3. Rapport de Grailly au nom de la commission des lois de l'Assemblée Nationale, p. 17.
4. Sur la réglementation technique, on lira les études suivantes, Juris-classeur de Procédure civile, partie générale, fascicule 122, mars 1973, par J. Pradel, Répertoire Dalloz.
5. On distinguait selon que la question était ou non résolue par une convention internationale. Dans le premier cas, les difficultés se réduisaient à l'interprétation de cet acte. Dans le second, la pratique tandait à accorder l'assistance judiciaire aux étrangers dès lors qu'ils remplissaient les conditions exigées des Français eux-mêmes.
6. Et cette règle nouvelle s'accorde avec la disparition de la caution *judicatum solvi*.
7. Bur. sup. aide judiciaire. 27 octobre 1976, circulaire du Ministre de la Justice n° 77-1 du 25 janvier 1977, n° 47, rejetant la demande d'une association de lutte contre le proxénétisme, au motif que le décret d'application visé à l'article 31 de la loi de 1972, qui doit fixer "les modalités d'estimation des ressources des personnes morales" n'est pas encore paru.
8. R. Merle et A. Vitu, Traité de droit criminel, 2ème éd. 1974, II, n° 894. J. Pradel, Procédure pénale, 1976, n° 216.
9. Bur. sup. aide judiciaire 26 juin 1973, D-1973, 651, note 2, Laroche de Roussane, et 16 juin 1976, circulaire du Minstre de la Justice 77-1 du 25 janvier 1977, n° 44; add. F. Derrida, l'aide judiciaire dans les procédures de règlement judiciaire et de liquidation de biens, D-1974, chronique, p. 19.
10. Cette condition n'est pas nouvelle, v. circulaire du 23 octobre 1912. Bureau d'assistance judiciaire près la Cour d'Appel de Paris, 12 janvier 1912, S-1912, II, 121, circulaire du 11 février 1914. Même condition à l'étranger, v. J. Crespel, L'assistance judiciaire en droit comparé et projets de réforme, 1957, p. 155 et s.
11. Le système antérieur à 1972 était très critiquable, entraînant de graves inégalités selon les régions puisque les critères d'appréciation variaient beaucoup d'un bureau à l'autre.
12. On notera que pour l'appréciation des ressources, on prend en considération l'année antérieure à celle de la demande, ce qui peut

s'avérer injuste.

13. Art. 2 de la loi du 3 janvier 1972 et 65-68 du décret du 1er septembre 1972 modifié par décret du 15 octobre 1976.
14. Art. 16 de la loi du 3 janvier 1972.
15. Avant la loi de 1972, les bureaux avaient tendance à débouter les demandeurs qui, propriétaires d'un immeuble, étaient censés disposer de ressources suffisantes.
16. V. en ce sens travaux préparatoires, J.O. 11 décembre 1971, débats Ass. nat. p. 5553-54; note R. Laroche de Roussane au D-1975, 621 sous Bur. sup. aide judiciaire, 17 décembre 1974 et Bur. sup. aide judiciaire, 16 mars 1976, Circulaire du Ministre de la Justice 77-1 du 25 janvier 1977, n° 37. D'ailleurs, l'article 15 al. 3 de la loi de 1972 décide qu'il peut être tenu compte dans l'appréciation des ressources, de celles des personnes vivant habituellement au foyer du demandeur.
17. Bur. sup. aide judiciaire, 10 mars 1976, D-627, note P. Laroche de Roussane.
18. Seules échappent à l'aide judiciaire les juridictions professionnelles, mais l'hypothèse est presque d'école.
19. On notera une légère différence entre les deux situations, l'assistance d'un avocat pouvant être refusée dans le premier cas, non dans le second.
20. Cependant, devant le tribunal correctionnel, notre droit en revient au système de l'aide judiciaire. Selon l'article 29 de la loi du 22 janvier 1851, non abrégé, "les présidents des tribunaux correctionnels désigneront un défenseur d'office aux prévenus poursuivis à la requête du ministère public ou détenus provisoirement lorsqu'ils en feront la demande et que leur indigence sera constatée".
21. Cette disposition, introduite dans la loi par la voie d'un amendement d'origine parlementaire est susceptible de deux interprétations; l'aide pouvant être accordée soit pour certaines catégories de frais, les autres restant à la charge de l'intéressé, soit pour l'une des phases de la procédure à l'exclusion des autres. C'est cette deuxième interpretation qui est la bonne, v. en ce sens, travaux préparatoires, J.O. débats Sénat, 16-12-1971, p. 3132 et Bur. aide judiciaire, Colmar 09-10-1973, D-1974, Somm. 13. En pratique, l'aide judiciaire est accordée le plus souvent pour la totalité de l'instance v. Troisième rapport annuel sur le fonctionnement de l'aide judiciaire, 10 mai 1976, p. 7.
22. Bur. sup. aide judiciaire, 19 février 1974, circulaire du Ministre de la Justice 75-3 du 28 janvier 1975, n° 9, affirmant que l'aide judiciaire

s'étend au recours gracieux préalable.

23. Il est établi un bureau auprès de chaque tribunal de grande instance, cour d'appel et tribunal administratif. Egalement auprès de la Cour de cassation, du Conseil d'Etat, du Tribunal des conflits, enfin auprès de la Chancellerie où siège le bureau supérieur d'aide judiciaire. De formation collégiale, tout bureau comporte un président qui est magistrat et divers assesseurs (avocats, magistrats, représentatns du Ministre des Finances et du Ministre chafgé de l'aide sociale). V. art. 14 de la loi du 3 janvier 1972 et 1 à 17 du décret du 1er septembre 1972. On compte en tout 236 bureaux et sections de bureaux.
24. Art. 44-1 du décret du 1er septembre 1972, modifié par le décret du 15 octobre 1976.
25. Une "simple lettre" selon l'article 25 du décret du 1er septembre 1972.
26. A la demande, le requérant doit joindre des pièces justificatives: déclaration de ressources ou de situation fiscale et, s'il est salarié, attestation délivrée par l'employeur.
27. Art. 33 du décret du 1er septembre 1972.
28. Une fois rendue, la décision est notifiée à l'intéressé et, en cas d'admission, au service des Impôts.
29. Bur. sup. aide judiciaire, 14 décembre 1974, D-1975, 381, note P. Laroche de Roussane.
30. Les décisions des bureaux établis près les tribunaux de grande instance sont déférées au bureau établi près la Cour d'appel. Celles des bureaux établis près les Cours d'appel et de la Cour de cassation sont déférées au bureau supérieur siégeant à la Chancellerie. Enfin, les décisions des bureaux établis près les tribunaux administratifs sont déférés au bureau établi par le Conseil d'Etat.
31. Art. 43 du décret du 1er septembre 1972, modifié par le décret du 15 octobre 1976.
32. Art. 2 al. 1 de la loi du 3 janvier 1972.
33. Art. 29 al. 2 de la loi du 3 janvier 1972.
34. Art. 46 du décret du 1er septembre 1972.
35. Bur. sup. aide judiciaire, Lyon, 11 octobre 1972, D-1973, 374, note P. Laroche de Roussane.
36. Triv. civ. Strasbourg, 13 juin 1956, D-1956, p. 731.
37. Cass. civ. I, 20 février 1957, Bull. civ. I, n° 88, p. 74.
38. Cass. soc., 8 juin 1961, Bull. civ. IV, n° 610, p. 483, Cass. civ. II, 17 juillet 1975, D-1975, I.R. 201.
39. Les rapports entre l'avocat et le plaideur étant des rapports de con-

fiance, le second peut refuser le premier et se choisir un autre défenseur. Mais perd alors le bénéfice de la gratuité et devra régler ses honoraires à l'avocat qu'il a choisi, Cass. civ. 13 juillet 1908, S-1910, I, 22.

40. Art. 8 de la loi du 3 janvier 1972.
41. Art. 9 de la loi du 3 janvier 1972.
42. P. Laroche de Roussane, L'aide judiciaire, 1973, n° 76-77, Add. Trib. gr. inst. Chartres, ord. pr. 25 juillet 1974, D-1974, Somm. 113.
43. Art. 20 al. 2 de la bi du 3 janvier 1972.
44. L'article 81 prévoit pour les huissiers une indemnité de 20 F par exploit et de 44 F par procès verbal. L'article 82 relatif aux greffiers prévoit pour chaque instance 90 F pour les greffiers en chef de Cour d'appel ou de tribunal de grande instance et 65 F pour les greffiers d'insurance ou de tribunal de commerce. ces taux résultent d'un décret du 15 octobre 1976 ayant modifié celui de 1er septembre 1972.
45. Art. 19 de la loi du 3 janvier 1972 et 86 du décret du 1er septembre 1972, combinés, circulaire du Ministre de la Justice du 14 février 1977.
46. Exposé des motifs de la loi du 3 janvier 1972, p. 5.
47. Complétée pour l'assisté par une exonération des frais de justice, sauf que le bénéficiaire condamné aux dépens supporte les frais exposés par son adversaire ayant gangé le procès. On notera cependant qu'aucune rémunération n'est prévue au cas de commission d'office. Il est d'ailleurs question d'abandonner ce système injuste.

GOTTFRIED BAUMGARTEL*

Germany

I

Equality of opportunity for access to the court is not guaranteed in the Federal Republic of Germany, either for the economically underprivileged minorities or for a large part of the middle class. This is due in part to a dramatic increase in lawyers' and court fees. "Guest workers" are underprivileged in so far as the language barrier operates especially to their disadvantage.

Inequality of opportunity for legal protection is a result of three factors: language (the inability of those with little education to express themselves effectively); lack of information about the availability of legal aid (discussed in section II of this paper); and a cost barrier, which affects a large part of the middle class, who do not qualify for legal aid under the present financial requirements. A person who engages in a legal action must, if the action goes through two instances, expect the following costs for lawyers and court fees (excluding witness fees and expert witness fees): for a dispute of 3,000 DM, 2822 DM; for a dispute of 5,000 DM, 4267 DM; for a dispute of 10,000 DM, 7668 DM; and for a dispute of 26,000 DM, 14,193 DM. In actions for a dispute over 3,000 DM, within the competence of the provincial court, a lawyer is required. A small estate dispute can lead to costs high enough to endanger the economic existence of a middle-class family.

The language barrier is an important factor in any discussion of access to the legal system in the Federal Republic of Germany. The wording of

*Translated by Dr. Paula Bauer Weiss, Toronto, Canada. Previously published in *Hernon im Humane Justiz*, ed. Peger Gilles.

statutes is complex, presumably in the interests of accuracy and certainty: the terminology may be easily comprehended by professionals, but is foreign to nearly all laymen, however well-educated. This leads to the hesitancy of lay persons in legal matters. If the middle class experience difficulties, the problems are greater for less-educated persons. This problem cannot be reduced by resorting to a more colloquial construction of statutory language, because this would necessarily lead to an even greater number of ambiguous clauses.

A legalistic language can be overcome only by intensive effort on the part of legislative draftsmen. The chief responsibility in overcoming this problem lies with the lawyer, who must serve as an interpreter between the citizen and the court. A study conducted in the Federal Republic of Germany showed that, in the eyes of the public, the skill of the lawyer had a significant impact on the success of the proceedings. Ninety-five per cent of the 1100 people questioned said that "it is important to the success of an action if one has a good lawyer". The lawyer functions as an interpreter not only in judicial areas but also out of court. Timely legal advice can keep a citizen who is not familiar with the law, but who is convinced of the merits of his position, from initiating an unnecessary action.

The judges also play an important role in overcoming the language barrier. Civil actions could be simplified considerably if the courts were to adhere strictly to the principle of oral proceedings, as the rules of practice provide, and were to move away from the written proceedings, which are very common in practice and which are incomprehensible to the layman. With respect to encouraging the use of oral proceedings the Stuttgart model is ideal. The amendment of December 1976 has led to main proceedings based on the Stuttgart model, effective July 1, 1977.[1] In the future, civil proceedings shall be carried out in a well prepared "main appearance" at which the parties are present.

These efforts of all the legal persons (lawyers, judges) involved in the proceedings should be supported by the legislature with accompanying measures. This means that in all cases where repeal or relaxation of the requirement of counsel is considered, as has been suggested in the Federal Republic of Germany, it must be remembered that the removal of the lawyer as interpreter precludes the possibility of overcoming the language barrier. The assistance of a lawyer in the proceedings should be encouraged rather than eliminated.

An increase in legal education programmes in intermediate and high schools would de-mystify legal proceedings and principles for many people.

In addition, there should also be more widespread dissemination of information through adult educational classes and radio and television publicity in order to increase the understanding of the law at all levels of the population. Such efforts could be geared to the background of the particular segment of the population they are aimed at.

The cost barrier has two aspects. There are those cases in which the economically stronger parties exploit the high cost risk in order to bring an opponent to his knees. The other, more important, group of cases is those medium- or high-value actions which present such a cost risk for most citizens that under some circumstances the economic existence of a family is threatened.

The cases of the first type can easily be remedied by legislative measures. For example, patent law and the unfair competition law provide that the value of the dispute can be lowered by the court in favour of the poorer party. Consumer associations should be given standing to proceed against more powerful economic entities, such as large corporations. There also exists legislation class actions in the statute on general business provisions which came into force on April 1, 1977.

Cases of the second type present a different problem. Access to the court depends entirely upon the financial situation of the individual citizen. The cost barrier is apparent in a comparison of the costs of actions with the average income of the citizen. The monthly income of a four-person middle income household was about 2,200 DM net in 1975, and the monthly income of a four-person higher income household was about 3,800 DM net. If these figures are compared with the cost risk figures it becomes clear that even middle-income people risk a considerable part of their yearly income if they become involved in an action of even a medium value.

Numerous proposals have been made to meet this situation such as the abolition of court fees and partial assumption of costs by the state, the introduction of compulsory legal insurance, relaxing the requirement of counsel, and the abolition of the duty to repay costs. All these suggestions appear to be impractical, as I have discussed elsewhere (Gleicher Zugang zum Recht für Alle, Prozessrechtliche Abhandlungen, Heft 43, Carl Heymanns Verlag, Cologne, 1976, pp. 113ff.), for fundamental reasons, and not solely in response to the present poor economic situation of the state. [Translator's note: Professor Baumgärtel's criticisms of these suggestions which appear in the work "Gleicher Zugang zum Recht für Alle" are as follows. The abolition of the tariff makes lawyers dependent upon political forces for payment; it is subsidized by taxation; and it would lead to too many actions being brought. Similarly, a partial state payment would also be subsidized by taxation and would permit unmeritorious actions being pursued. Compulsory legal insurance would lead to the institution of a preliminary hearing to decide whether or not an action is meritorious, adding still another stage; it would make lawyers dependent upon insurance agencies for payment and it would also lead to the undesirable result of having the proceedings run by the insurance company. Relaxing the requirement of counsel is undesirable because a citizen's interests are better protected with a lawyer than without a lawyer. Abolishing the duty to repay costs would lead to uncertainty and there is no proof that it would actually help the situation.] The only way to introduce equal access to the courts is by means of a thorough reform of legal aid.

A legal rights commission, instituted by the Minister of Justice, developed a proposed model of cost assistance which is meant to replace the discriminatory legal aid. In contrast to the current legal aid regulations, the range of eligibility is extended into the middle class. Full costs are granted up to a specified net income cut-off point. Included, as before, are the temporary waiver of court fees as well as the corresponding appointment of a lawyer for the temporary gratuitous representation of the client. The income cut-off point is about twice the welfare cut-off point. Parties with greater income must make monthly payments for the costs; but up to a maximum income (which according to these proposals is about 5,000 DM for a single person, net) they receive scaled aid.

This model, however, has disadvantages. First, it retains the low payments to the legal aid lawyer. If one wants to do away with the distinction between legal aid and private clients, then the appointed lawyer must also receive full fees. Only such a system guarantees free choice of a lawyer. Another disadvantage lies in the basic retention of the duty of the unsuccessful legal aid recipient to repay the costs. This regulation will prevent many from instituting actions, since one cannot tell in advance whether an action will be successful. In my opinion, it would be consistent to waive the duty to repay costs, for at least the poor classes who receive full legal aid, and allow the state treasury to make up the costs. The middle class can protect itself from costs by purchasing private legal insurance.

II

When considering the question of what means exist to increase the availability of legal aid, one must distinguish between the need for out-of-court legal aid and the mechanics of that aid. The legal advisory system which exists in the Federal Republic of Germany provides out-of-court legal advice for a large part of society. In governmental matters, every citizen, regardless of his income and means, has a right to information from government officials. In larger cities central advisory centres have been set up. These centres handle citizen complaints and inquiries, and serve as information centres for guest workers. The finance offices are required to give legal advice on tax questions to every taxpayer.

Since the end of the nineteenth century free legal aid has been given by the area bar associations. In 1973, sixty-four out of a total of 170 existing local bar associations gave free advice to middle income citizens. Eligibility is largely determined on the basis of the legal aid scales, which correspond roughly to the welfare scale. Even a notary gives free advice under these provisions. In addition, legal aid is available through the *Sozialamt* [social office] (according to s. 8 of the Social Welfare Statute) in matters that are social/legal in nature. Private bodies such as artisans' groups, trade unions and tenants' associations advise their members. Thus, there is already in existence a comprehensive legal advisory system and hence is no need to provide free out-of-court legal aid to every citizen, irrespective of his income. A true need for free out-of-court legal advice exists only for the economically deprived segments of society. These people are doubly disadvantaged: they lack the means to pay a lawyer, and because of their inarticulateness they are especially intimidated by legal proceedings.

To ensure equality of access, the legal aid available to poor people must be of the same quality and include the same services as are available to people of means. Legal aid must not be restricted to legal advice and the preparation of simple documents, but must also include out-of-court attempts to settle disputes and actions. Further, it must offer individual out-of-court representation similar to that available to the rich. It would be a disadvantage for the poorer classes if they were provided only with a neutral mediator.

For the dissemination of legal advice and the carrying out of out-of-court business advice in legal matters, the lawyer alone provides services. The lawyer has an advantage over the government jurist and the judge in that he can represent the citizen against the state without a conflict of interests. As a rule, the lawyer possesses good communication skills and is able to overcome a client's inarticulateness; it would be useful if the bar, where necessary, would work closely with social workers in order to ensure effective communication between client and lawyer. Private welfare organizations do not provide legal advice to people of moderate means. They see their duty as giving social advice – for example, advising the elderly, giving advice on matrimonial matters, advising drug addicts, and so on (compare section III below).

Legal advice given by free lawyers has existed on a voluntary basis since the beginning of this century. It is not granted in all judicial districts. There is no law requiring that out-of-court legal aid be provided for those of moderate means, although aid is available for the severely economically disadvantaged. Such aid is not the duty of the lawyer. In individual provinces (for example, Bavaria and the Saarland) experimental state-organized free legal advisory systems for those of moderate means are available through lawyers in their offices or through legal advisory centres (compare in general Baumgärtel, "Gleicher Zugang zum Recht für alle", 1976, pp. 43ff.). Lawyers receive a reduced fee for their work. Experiments such as these are useful for the eventual development of legislation providing out-of-court legal aid to equalize opportunity of access to justice.

Public legal advisory centres have existed for some time in Hamburg, Lübeck, Berlin, and, recently, in Bremen. In these centres, legal advice is given by government jurists, active or retired judges, state lawyers, legal administrators, and lawyers. This does not include out-of-court business advice or individual representation against an opponent. The advisor is in the position of a neutral mediator. In Berlin, legal advice is given by staff lawyers. Public advisory centres exist on an experimental basis in other provinces (for example, in Hesse and Rheinland-Pfalz).

The lawyer's model has an advantage over these two organizational forms. The free lawyer represents the interests of the individual citizen. This is especially significant if the lawyer must represent his client against the state. The organizational forms are governed by the structures of the respective provinces. Thus, Nordrhein-Westphalia, a province of broad flat expanses, needs a widely scattered net of advisory centres; it is most efficient if legal advice is given in the existing lawyers' offices. Central advisory centres would be more suitable for areas with large cities. Such a system would allow free choice of a lawyer and so permit optimum equality of opportunity.

In order to encourage a collaboration between the legal profession and social workers of various agencies it would be sensible to arrange for the social agency to administer means tests and to allocate certificates of entitlement for legal aid. The social agency would also serve the necessary function of providing non-threatening initial contact, thus alleviating much of the mistrust of the legal profession. This preliminary stage would also have a certain preventive utility, since the agency can, according to s. 8 of the social welfare statute, make referrals to other appropriate groups and centres.

III

Legal aid and social assistance advice can be distinguished according to their objects. While in legal advice (for example, in rental, inheritance, and family matters) the legal adviser stands in the foreground, in social matters (for example, advising the elderly, giving matrimonial advice, and advising drug addicts), psychological and medical questions, among others, play a decisive role. Both areas are fundamentally separable, even in an organizational sense. There are, of course, cases in which both elements appear to be equally strong; for example, in advising guest workers and battered wives. In these mixed cases legal questions as well as social questions appear. It is a question of where the point of emphasis lies. Of course there are human problems and motivations that enter every legal matter and which overlap in the social area. For example, in planning the estate of a family man, questions about provisions for various family members often arise. However, advising in a testamentary matter is not social work; legal advice remains in the foreground.

Advising of those of moderate means on legal matters which have substantial social aspects, such as matrimonial disputes, can best be handled by collaboration between the legal aid adviser and the social worker.

IV

There is undoubtedly a close link between the structure of legal aid and the entire concept of the administration of justice. Because they are connected, legal aid in out-of-court matters should be provided by lawyers. They possess greater experience in handling actions than do the government jurists active in public advisory centres, and the lawyers are aware of the possibility of an action from the beginning.

An Act to simplify civil proceedings of small value came into force on July 1, 1977. To guarantee a speedier process in matters involving up to

500 DM a special written procedure has been introduced (s. 128 III of the Rules of Procedure). In addition, family courts have been created by the first matrimonial reform statute; all family matters, including divorce proceedings, are dealt with at these courts.

In order to give the court a better explanation of the socio-economic background of a dispute, the simplification amendment in s. 278 introduced the so-called "main limitation time", which provides that the parties appearing in the matter are to be heard personally. The court must arrange the personal appearance of both parties within a specified time (s. 141).

Note

1. The so-called "Stuttgarter Modell" is a special type to handle the civil procedure. Its main characteristic is the concentration of the oral proceedings in one well-prepared "main appearance". The amendment of December, 1976 has adopted this model which has been practically realized before by the civil courts in Stuttgart.

   All persons involved in the civil procedure should work together to achieve an equal access to the courts.

   Accompanying measures are for instance an intensified and more broadly extended law education in schools.

   Finanzämter are authorities which are charged with the administration of all kinds of taxes.

MARTIN PARTINGTON

*Great Britain**

Introduction

From very early days, English legal history has contained spirited statements to the effect that justice demands that assistance should be given to the poor to obtain their legal rights. *Magna Carta*, for example, stated:

> To no one will we sell, to no one will we refuse or delay, right or justice.

More specifically, a Statute of Henry VII, 1495, stated:

> . . . [The] Justices . . . shall assign to the same poor person or persons counsel by their discretions, which shall give their counsel, nothing taking for the same; . . . and likewise the Justices shall appoint attorney and attorneys for the same poor person or persons . . .[1]

However, there has always been a considerable gap between sentiment and reality in the actual provision of legal services for the poor in England.[2] Despite increasing concern with this issue in the twentieth century, there are still many people in Britain who argue that this gap has not been bridged. This paper reviews some of these arguments and offers a summary of the main features of current pressures for reform.

*This is an extensively re-written version of the paper prepared for the conference, *Towards Justice with a Human Face*, held in Ghent, Belgium, in September 1977.

1. Statutory provision of legal aid in the U.K.

Since British legal aid legislation has been used as a model for a number of legal aid or "judicare" schemes in countries around the world, it will be helpful, first of all, to provide an account of the existing statutory framework. In fact, there are three quite different types of legal aid which are the subject of separate statutory provisions.

(i) Criminal legal aid

Legal aid for representation of defendants in criminal cases is run by the criminal courts themselves, under the general supervision of the Home Office. A kind of criminal legal aid scheme began as early as 1903, under the *Poor Prisoners' Defence Act.* But help was only available to prisoners who disclosed their defences. When the Court of Criminal Appeal was established in 1907, the judges ordered that no prisoner should come before that court without legal aid. However, no changes were made regarding legal aid for the trial itself. Not until the *Poor Prisoners' Defence Act, 1930* was the disclosure of defence rule dropped; in the same year legal aid was made available for summary trial and committal proceedings in the magistrates' courts. Despite changes in the rules, however, many courts exercised their new powers only sparingly.[3]

Criminal legal aid provision was formalized still further under the *Criminal Justice Act, 1967*,[4] passed after a review of criminal legal aid provision by a departmental committee, chaired by Lord Widgery, was published in 1966.[5] This committee tried to establish criteria for the uniform granting of legal aid in criminal cases.[6] However, these criteria were not embodied in statute. The *Legal Aid Act, 1974* now provides that criminal legal aid shall be ordered "where it appears to the court desirable to do so in the interests of justice";[7] further, legal aid should not be granted "unless it appears to the court that his means are such that [the defendant] requires assistance in meeting the costs. . . ."[8]

For the most serious criminal cases, which are triable in the Crown Court, legal aid is now granted on a very extensive basis. For example, in 1976, 96 per cent of defendants who appeared in those courts received legal aid.[9] (The granting of legal aid for summary trials in magistrates courts is rather more uneven and remains a cause for concern.[10]) The rather vague "means test" is not strictly administered. And, although under the legislation, the criminal courts do have power to make a legally aided defendant pay a contribution towards his costs,[11] this rarely happens.[12]

(ii) Civil legal aid[13]

The Civil Legal Aid scheme began in 1950 after the *Legal Aid and Advice Act, 1949* had been passed. This, in turn, was based on the recommendations of the Rushcliffe Committee which reported in 1945.[14] (This Act may also be seen as just one facet of the welfare state legislation enacted by the post-World War II Labour government.) The legislation provided for the creation of a three-tiered scheme: the provision of legal advice; the provision of legal assistance short of litigation; and the provision of legal representation in cases involving litigation. However, the first two parts of the scheme never worked adequately due to delays in implementation, and inadequate government funding[15] and have now been replaced by legal advice and assistance (which is discussed below). This section will therefore concentrate on civil legal aid in the narrow sense of legal aid for representation in civil litigation.

Civil legal aid is administered in a much more rigorous way than criminal legal aid. Applicants for civil legal aid have to satisfy two major tests: (a) a means-test; and (b) a "merits" test.

(a) The means test is administered by special legal aid offices of the Supplementary Benefits Commission (SBC).[16] Applicants have to show that both their "disposable" income and "disposable" capital fall below certain limits.[17] This will determine either whether they get legal aid entirely free or whether they will be entitled to legal aid on payment of a contribution.[18] There is no appeal from decisions of the SBC on its assessment of applicants' resources, but it will in practice always review its decision if an applicant (or his/her solicitor) complains.

(b) The merits test is also provided for in the legislation,[19] and states that an applicant must both show he has "reasonable grounds for taking, defending or being a party" to proceedings, and that it should not be "unreasonable that he should receive [legal aid] in the particular circumstances of the case". This test is administered in the first instance by a local legal aid committee, and appeals may be taken to an area legal aid committee.[20] These certifying committees are composed entirely of practising lawyers (barristers or solicitors).

The first part of the test is designed to show that the applicant has a valid case in law on the evidence available. (The applicant has to provide a fairly full statement of his case on the application form.) One consequence of this is that litigation on doubtful points of law is unlikely when the prospects of success are slight.[21] The second part is designed to prevent legal aid going to a claimant where, for instance, the gains of victory are likely to be very small compared with the expense of taking the proceedings. This has the effect of preventing, for example, small claims being pursued under legal aid.

If the applicant for legal aid is successful in winning his case,[22] a charge is imposed on any damages recovered, whereby all the costs paid out by the Legal Aid Fund are recovered before the applicant gets anything.[23] If the applicant loses, he may be required to pay the costs of the winning side, but the practice is to limit this liability to the amount of the contribution (if any) that the unsuccessful applicant was required to pay under the legal aid scheme. There are also provisions for the payment of costs out of public funds to successful unassisted litigants who have won against legally aided clients and who would otherwise be unable to recover their costs.[24]

Legal aid is theoretically available for most kinds of action in the High Court, though in practice the vast majority of civil cases which are legally-aided are matrimonial and personal injuries cases. Legal aid is not, however, available for most tribunals: cases before the Lands Tribunal[25] and the Employment Appeal Tribunal[26] are the two main exceptions. But the vast range of social security tribunals, rent tribunals and Rent Assessment Committees are not included within the scope of the legal aid scheme.

(iii) Legal advice and assistance

As remarked above, the provisions of the *Legal Aid and Advice Act, 1949* dealing with legal advice and legal assistance short of litigation did not work well. Thus in 1968 the Law Society produced plans for a more comprehensive legal advice and assistance scheme. After considerable modification in the light of criticisms from, among others, the Society of Labour Lawyers,[27] a revised scheme was proposed which was the basis for legislation enacted in 1972.[28] The basic principle of legal advice and assistance (also called the "green form scheme", or "the £25 scheme") is that a solicitor should be able to provide up to £25 of legal advice and assistance[29] on any legal question to clients who fall below "disposable" capital and income limits[30] either for no charge or on payment of a fixed contribution by the client.

The initial means test is here administered by the solicitor in person. If the cost of the advice and assistance will be more than £25 (a cost-limit which has not been altered since the original 1968 proposal and whose value has thus been heavily eroded by inflation), the solicitor may obtain authorization from a local legal aid secretary to spend up to a higher amount.[31]

The potential scope of this part of the legal aid scheme is very wide indeed, covering, for example, criminal matters, social security and housing matters, as well as personal injuries and matrimonial matters. Any advice and assistance may be provided short of actual representation in litigation which, as we have seen, is covered by criminal or civil legal aid. The width of the scheme was designed, at least in part, to meet objections that private lawyers were not able, for financial reasons, to get involved in the kinds of question that most directly affect the majority of people in the country (i.e., questions relating to various types of social legislation operating within the welfare state). However, this official attempt to persuade lawyers to give advice and assistance outside their traditional areas of expertise does not appear to be working well in practice; the majority of legal advice and assistance applications are still to do with matrimonial problems.[32]

2. Demands for improvements in the provision of legal services

Despite the statutory provision of a range of legal aid and advice facilities, there has developed over the last ten years increasing pressure for substantial improvements in the provision of legal services. In this section we look at some of the factors that have led to these demands for improvements.

The most important factor was the "rediscovery of poverty" in Britain.[33] After World War II, the creation by the then Labour government of a very broad system of National Insurance[34] was thought to have eliminated the worst problems of poverty in Britain. For many years this complacent view was accepted. However, in 1962, Professors Abel-Smith and Townsend conducted research that revealed that a considerable number of families, where the breadwinner was in full-time employment, were taking home pay at the end of each week which was less than the amounts laid down by the state for basic subsistence.[35]

This work effectively started a much broader debate which covers such topics as: (a) the problems of low pay; (b) the adequacy of state benefits for those who are out of work; (c) the effectiveness (or otherwise) of providing benefits by using means tests; (d) the adequacy of family allowances for children; (e) provision of benefits for the elderly; (f) provision of benefits for the disabled; and so on.

In addition to these essentially financial issues, concern also developed again over the condition of Britain's housing and the failure of successive British governments to eradicate slum dwellings and provide decent living accommodation for all families.

These concerns were marked by a great increase in pressure group activity;[36] a number of responses from government;[37] and considerable academic endeavour.[38] This is not the place to go into a full discussion of the present debate on poverty. Suffice to say that from the mid-1960s poverty has been an issue which has once again clearly become the subject of public debate.[39]

A second factor was that a number of people in Britain also became aware of similar developments in other countries, in particular the so-called War on Poverty that was initiated in the U.S.A. As is well known, an integral feature of this "war" was the massive increase in the use of legal services as part of the strategy for attempting to win increased rights for the poor and underprivileged in that country. In this climate of opinion, it was not surprising that a number of lawyers in the U.K. began to think about the possible relationship between poverty, law and the legal system.[40]

At a theoretical level, this is a very complex issue, to which this paper cannot begin to do justice. A number of important questions may be briefly identified. For example: how far does the actual body of law represent the legitimate interests of different groups in society? Has a correct balance in the law been struck? Or does the law merely represent the interests of the ruling class? Such questions have not yet been adequately analysed, at least by lawyers in Britain. There tends to be an assumption that British law is more or less "even-handed" (i.e., well-balanced). But of course such an assumption begs the question. It is a common, and, it is submitted, valid, criticism of lawyers (particularly by sociologists) that they fail to examine what the power bases are on which much English law is founded.[41] For example, it is assumed by many lawyers (and this is reflected in much legislation on, say, town planning, urban renewal, and housing) that the property rights of owners of land should be protected, or, if they cannot be protected, the owners should be compensated, often generously, for their "loss of rights". But the same lawyers do not ask why the owners of land are said to have "rights" in the first place. It may ultimately be that the failure to raise these issues will mean that the provision of better legal services will not really achieve anything very substantial for the poor and underprivileged in British society.

Notwithstanding these theoretical questions, but rather basing their work on the assumption that British justice is even-handed, lawyers have come to a second group of problems which we may describe as "technical issues" in the sense that they raise questions about the technical problems of getting ordinary people to lawyers; getting legal help to those who are thought to need it; getting legal procedures to operate in a cheap and flexible way; and so on. It is on these questions that effort in recent years has largely been concentrated by lawyers, and to which this paper devotes its prime focus of attention.

Apart from the discussions leading to the enactment of the *Legal Advice and Assistance Act* in 1972,[42] a number of specific developments have occurred which may be seen as related to a more general demand for improvements in the provision of legal services:

(i) "Justice for All", 1968[43]

This was the first major report to arouse debate on the question of legal services. In it, the Society of Labour Lawyers[44] analysed the workings of the *Legal Aid Act, 1949*, noted some of its successes, and, more importantly, its failures, and came up with a number of suggestions for reform.[45] The most radical of these ideas, drawn from American experience, was that the services of a local legal centre should be made available without a means test to people living in poor neighbourhoods.

(ii) Neighbourhood law centres

A small number (twenty-five or so) of neighbourhood law centres has been established since 1971. They employ salaried solicitors and aim to provide a comprehensive legal service to members of the communities in which they are situated (usually poor areas of cities – most of them are in London). The range of work they can do is subject to arrangements that the solicitors have entered into with the Law Society under which they agree not to do certain categories of work; in particular, buying and selling houses and handling matrimonial issues. This effectively ensures that they do not drain away from local private practitioners work that is both profitable and in which such practitioners have considerable expertise. Some law centres are also specifically moving away from providing legal services for individuals, to giving legal services for groups existing within the community in which they operate.

(iii) Legal advice centres and other sources of information and advice

In addition to the above there has been an enormous increase in the numbers of centres providing legal advice. Legal advice centres,[46] other information and advice centres,[47] housing aid centres,[48] and consumer advice centres have all been created in great numbers in many places around the U.K. But their establishment is not part of any overall plan, depending rather on local initiative.

(iv) Duty solicitor schemes

In a number of towns, solicitors have organized voluntary rotas to ensure that all people appearing on criminal charges, who have no legal representation, are in fact represented.[49]

(v) Legal Action Group

This new pressure group was formed in 1972 to campaign specifically for improvements in legal services and legal procedures. Through its *Bulletin*[50] it also provides a unique service in providing source materials on "welfare law" – broadly defined – in Britain.

(vi) Other pressure groups

A number of anti-poverty and related pressure groups now employ lawyers to provide advice and to launch test-case litigation in the courts, in particular, the Child Poverty Action Group, SHELTER (a charitable housing organization), and the National Council for Civil Liberties.

(vii) Research and education

The Nuffield Foundation has funded a number of research projects into aspects of "unmet legal need".[51] Further, the Institute of Judicial Administration, Birmingham University, has produced two reports on topics in this field.[52] Increasing interest is being taken in British law schools in developing courses in welfare law, urban legal problems and similarly related areas.[53]

All these developments may be seen as manifestations of a widespread, though certainly not unanimous, feeling that the legal aid scheme, relying on the use of solicitors in private practice, was not proving itself an adequate mechanism for getting legal help to all who needed it. Although the government responded in limited ways to the kinds of pressure outlined above,[54] it was not prepared to put forward a more comprehensive policy. However, in 1976 it did appoint a Royal Commission on Legal Services that might make proposals for the future development of legal services in Britain. This commission will not report until 1979, so it is not yet possible to discuss or even predict its conclusions. What is possible is to identify more specific criticisms of the legal aid scheme which have been revealed as a result of the initiatives outlined above, and to note some of the main proposals for reform that have been made in the light of such analysis.

3. Present defects in legal aid

Such defects may be divided into two categories: remediable defects and structural defects.

(a) Remediable defects

Remediable defects are those which, with more government money and comparatively little alteration of the statutory framework, might be easily remedied. They include the following:

(i) the means-test limits are too low;[55]
(ii) the contribution levels are too high;
(iii) the statutory charge on damages awarded is crippling, particularly for those who wish to bring small claims;
(iv) the "merits" test is too restricted and leads to inconsistencies in the granting of legal aid;
(v) levels of remuneration for lawyers are too low, especially for legal advice and assistance short of litigation;
(vi) costs for the successful opponents of legally aided litigants are not awarded frequently enough;
(vii) there is no legal aid for representation before most tribunals;
(viii) there can be practical difficulties in applying for legal aid; the forms to be completed are long and complex; and there are unnecessary delays;
(ix) criminal legal aid is granted too haphazardly;
(x) the administration of legal aid (split between the Law Society, the Supplementary Benefits Commission, the courts and solicitors,

with policy developments in the care of the Lord Chancellor's office and criminal legal aid with the Home Office) is confusing and irrational. Further, this means that there is no clear ministerial responsibility for the scheme.

(b) Structural defects

Even if all the defects just listed were eradicated, however, the problem remains of whether the legal aid scheme would even then be able to provide an effective legal service for all members of the community. It may help to state some of the structural defects which are argued to exist:

(i) Location of solicitors
The siting of solicitors' firms in most towns is totally inimicable to the development of comprehensive legal services since they are predominantly situated in city centres and are far from conveniently placed.[56]

(ii) Psychological barriers
Abel-Smith, Brooke and Zander discovered that many people, almost as a matter of principle, refuse to go to solicitors. They simply would not conceive of so doing.[57] Many more do not go for fear of the expense.

(iii) Ignorance of legal rights
Many people do not understand the law or how it might help them. They may not even appreciate that they have problems which could be classified as "legal".[58]

(iv) Education and background of lawyers
Many lawyers just do not understand the problems of the poor in Britain, or how the law might be used to protect them. Further, most legal education is not designed to develop insight into these matters.

(v) Community issues
It is often argued that existing legal education and practice encourages lawyers too much to see their cases as battles between individuals and to ignore wider implications. One of the important contributions of the law centres (see above) is that they have sought ways to see some of the problems that come to them not merely as individual problems but also as community problems. This is a perspective on their work which the private practitioners do not have.[59]

(vi) Control of legal services

Stemming from the above points there is also a frequently stated view that legal services would be more comprehensively developed if responsibility were taken away from the Law Society and placed in the hands of a more independent agency.

4. Proposals for reform

Proposals for reform tend to depend on the extent to which the defects outlined above are acknowledged as valid. For example, Seton Pollock[60] has argued that most problems would be overcome if government money were to be provided to enable the full Rushcliffe scheme to come into effect.[61] His view, a not unnatural one for someone employed by the Law Society, is that, given sufficient resources, the private legal practitioner can extend his areas of expertise and thus provide a complete legal service to the community. More radical critics argue that it is not just a question of the provision of more finance. What is needed as well are new styles of legal practice geared specifically to needs and demands articulated within working-class communities and not restricted to those which the private legal practitioner is prepared to provide.

This final section cannot hope to detail all the reform proposals that have been put forward, since the range and scope of such proposals is many and varied. However, a summary of some of the key reform proposals will be useful, not only for the purposes of this paper, but also as a yardstick by which to judge the actual reforms proposed by the Royal Commission when they appear.[62]

In relation to the remediable defects, there is now widespread acceptance of the idea that many details of the legal aid scheme need to be improved. An influential source of detailed suggestions on these issues is now the Lord Chancellor's Advisory Committee. Through their working party on the financial provisions relating to legal aid, they have strongly recommended (for example) the raising of the various means test levels; a relaxation of the contribution conditions, together with the suggestion of no contribution at all in certain categories of litigation; an increase to £45 in the amount of work that can be done under the legal advice and assistance scheme and, in addition, the abolition of the sharp distinction between advice/assistance and representation so that straightforward cases could be completed more speedily; the more flexible administration of the legal aid charge. Many of the groups campaigning for change would broadly endorse these suggestions.[63]

Another general proposal is that legal aid should now be made available for representation before tribunals. A major objector to this suggestion is the highly influential Trades Union Congress which has been very hostile and is still very sceptical of this suggestion. This seems to be in part because it fears that if legal aid is available to all before tribunals, this will deprive Trade Unions of one of their main advantages, i.e. the provision for their members of free legal assistance. But in addition, the T.U.C. sees trade union strength lying in collective action, and fears that encouragement of individual cases, particularly before industrial tribunals, may weaken union bargaining power.

On remedies for the defects classified as structural, there is less consensus. However, the following four topics are being widely discussed:

(i) Extensions of law centres

The evidence of law centres' work, revealed in their annual reports, suggests that whatever else may happen, these centres must be continued and increased in numbers. It is clear that they are performing services and engaging in types of legal work which are quite beyond the scope and experience of the private practising solicitor. For example, they have developed expertise in areas such as social security and housing law, juvenile crime, protection of battered wives; they have launched public education programmes; they have taken up community legal issues, such as planning and public health matters.

At present, the law centre movement is under considerable financial stress and one may expect steps to be taken to try to ensure that their worst financial crises are solved.

(ii) Non-means tested legal services

A theme which underlies much of the foregoing, which is also beginning to be developed, is that attempts should be made to define a range of basic legal rights for the assertion of which legal services should be made available as of right, without means test. These would relate to such matters as the right to a home, or a job, or a basic income. This idea, if adopted, would much more clearly recognize legal services to be a branch of social services provision than has hitherto been the case.

The important point here is that many of the legal rights which Parliament has created in its welfare state legislation are too often going unused by default as people, through ignorance or fear, fail to exercise those rights. Parliament already authorizes considerable expenditure on law enforcement (e.g. the police, trading standards officers, environmental health officers, etc.). It should also provide legal assistance where that is clearly needed. The Rushcliffe Report was based on a view of legal services developed before the massive increase in these publicly granted rights; thus proposals simply to improve legal aid to meet Rushcliffe's criteria will not suffice. The social and legal context within which legal services now have to be placed has altered in important ways since that report.[64]

This is, however, a controversial suggestion, since other commentators regard it as desirable that people should be required to pay at least somethings for pursuing any legal rights, unless they are in very poor circumstances.

(iii) Constitutional changes

Even more controversial are suggestions that there should be major constitutional changes in the bodies responsible for organizing legal aid. Two specific suggestions have been put forward, each with a number of variations. First, a Ministry of Justice should be created to provide a single, identifiable source of governmental responsibility for the administration of justice. This would bring a welcome rationalization to the current divisions of authority between the Home Office and Lord Chancellor's Office. Furthermore, if (as some have suggested) the minister should be in the elected House of Commons, rather than in the non-elected House of Lords (as happens at present with the Lord Chancellor), this could improve public accountability for the administration of justice, including questions relating to the provision of legal services to the poor.

A second idea, which also comes in a number of forms, is for a new Legal Services Commission, possibly to take over the administration of the existing legal aid schemes, certainly to be responsible for the development of a more comprehensive national network of publicly-funded legal services operating throughout the country. One advantage of this proposal is that no longer would the Law Society be seen to be so directly involved in the provision of legal services. This has, from time to time, caused the suggestion to be made that the Law Society uses its position only to advance policy suggestions that will most favour the private practitioner. Not unnaturally, the Law Society denies this claim, and the present Lord Chancellor (Lord Elwyn Jones) on a number of occasions has rejected the viability and suitability of this proposal. But this does not remove the possibility of conflicts of interest arising between what the public interest needs and what solicitors (and barristers) need which might be resolved against the public interest.

A modification of the idea is that after the present Royal Commission on Legal Services has finished its work, there should be created in its stead a Standing Committee on Legal Services, responsible for overall advice on legal services, including the implementation of the recommendations of the Royal Commission. It does not at present seem likely that any more far-reaching proposals for legal services commissions, such as have been found acceptable in other countries, will prove acceptable in the U.K.[65]

(iv) Lay involvement in legal services provision

A suggestion that is gaining increasingly widespread support is that there should be much greater participation by ordinary members of the public in the running of legal aid in particular and legal services in general. In Manchester, for example, an experimental Legal Services Committee has been formed by the Law Society with lay representation on it. Of course, the value of lay representation depends both on the quantity and quality of lay members. There is always the danger of lay representation becoming a public relations exercise.

In addition there are increasing calls for more lay participation in the legal process with simpler procedures and different types of court structure (e.g., small claims courts, family courts, housing courts) to encourage people to take advantage of their legal rights by using their own skills. There are a number of obvious problems in deciding how far these suggestions may be taken, but this might prove to be an alternative method for providing at least certain kinds of legal service.[66]

5. Conclusion

In the foregoing pages we have looked at the British legal aid scheme; looked at some of the pressures for reform; identified a number of defects with legal services provision for the poor; and discussed a range of suggested reforms. It is clear that similar discussions are going on in many countries throughout the world; this book and the conference from which it sprang are evidence of that. Perhaps now, more than ever before, there exist opportunities for the successful cross-fertilization of ideas, and it is to be hoped that these papers will contribute to this process.

But we should not forget that concentration on questions of procedural justice, which this paper has for the most part addressed, may divert attention from questions of substantive justice. While it may be important to improve legal services to the poor, we should also be asking how we may eradicate poverty itself from our society.

Notes and References

1. Cited in *Justice and Reform*, by Earl Johnson Jr. (Russell Sage Foundation, 1974), p. 3.
2. The best short review is to be found in B. Abel-Smith and R. Stevens, *Lawyers and the Courts* (Heinemann, 1967), chs. 6 and 12. Also see their *In Search of Justice* (Allen Lane, 1968).
3. For further detail see Abel-Smith and Stevens (1967), op. cit.; also *Legal Services for All*, Fabian Tract No. 454 (1978), p. 3.
4. The provisions have now been consolidated into the *Legal Aid Act, 1974*, Part II. A full account of Criminal Legal Aid is in Harris and Rickard, *Legal Aid and Advice* (1975).
5. Cmnd. 2934.
6. They were (a) that the charge is a grave one which may result in the accused losing his liberty or suffering serious damage to his reputation; (b) that the charge raises a substantial question of law; (c) that the accused cannot follow the proceedings because of inadequate knowledge of English, mental illness, etc.; (d) that the nature of the defence involves tracing and interviewing witnesses or expert cross-examination; (e) that legal representation is desirable in the interest of someone other than the accused. (The criteria are set out in full in Cmnd. 2934, para. 180.)
7. *Legal Aid Act, 1974*, s. 29(1).
8. ibid., s. 29(2).
9. *Criminal Statistics, 1976*, Cmnd. 6909, Table 24(c).
10. See, for example, evidence of the National Council for Civil Liberties to the Royal Commission on Legal Services.
11. *Legal Aid Act, 1974*, s. 32.
12. See, e.g., B. Cooke, "A View of the Contribution Aspect of the Criminal Legal Aid Scheme" (1970), *Criminal Law Review*, p. 485; and M. Zander, "Legal Aid Contribution Orders" (1976), *New Law Journal* (January 1), p. 4. In 1976, contributions totalling £1.1 m. were ordered to be paid, as against £32.8 m. expended on criminal

legal aid (*Criminal Statistics, 1976*, op. cit., p. 357); but no figures relating to sums actually recovered are available.

13. The most detailed account is in Matthews and Oulton, *Legal Aid and Advice* (1971 and 1975, supplement).
14. *Report of the Committee on Legal Aid and Advice in England and Wales* (1945), Cmd. 6641.
15. A general account of the expansion of legal aid facilities is in Abel-Smith and Stevens, *Lawyers and the Courts* (1967), ch. 12.
16. Formerly the National Assistance Board. The SBC was established in 1966 by the Ministry of Social Security Act 1966; it now functions under the Supplementary Benefits Act, 1976. The prime function of the SBC is to administer basic income maintenance payments to all those over 16 who are not in full-time work, and who fall below the officially-defined poverty line. The means testing for legal aid applications is a subsidiary function imposed on the SBC.
17. See *Legal Aid Act, 1974*, s. 6 (as amended). "Disposable" income and capital are defined in detail by the Legal Aid (Assessment of Resources) Regulations 1960 (as amended), made under *Legal Aid Act, 1974*, s. 11.
18. *Legal Aid Act, 1974*, s. 9(1).
19. Now *Legal Aid Act, 1974*, s. 7(5).
20. These committees are not appointed by the government, but are technically committees of the Law Society, the private body which represents the solicitor's side of the legal profession, and which, under legal aid legislation, has been given the task of administering the legal aid scheme. See Abel-Smith and Stevens, op. cit., p. 148, for comment on the history of this decision.
21. See Seton Pollock, *Legal Aid: The First 25 Years* (1975), p. 40; Zander, *Legal Services for the Community* (1978), p. 33.
22. And because of the filtering processes just described, the vast majority of litigants on legal aid do win their cases. In 1976-77, 90 per cent of assisted persons were successful or settled their cases prior to hearing. *27th Annual Report of the Law Society* (H.C. 172/1977-78), p. 30.
23. *Legal Aid Act, 1974*, s. 9(6).
24. *Legal Aid Act, 1974*, ss. 13 and 14. There is often criticism that these provisions do not operate as well as they were intended to.
25. Which deals with a range of complex issues relating to valuation of property, assessment of compensation for compulsory purchase, etc.
26. Which hears appeals from Industrial Tribunals on issues such as unfair dismissal, redundancy, discrimination in employment. Legal

aid is not available for cases before the Industrial Tribunals themselves.

27. *Justice for All* (Fabian Society, 1968).
28. Now *Legal Aid Act, 1974*, Part I, ss. 1-5.
29. e.g. making telephone calls, drafting documents, and very frequently, putting in a claim for full legal aid.
30. The means-test rules (*Legal Aid Act, 1974*, s. 3 (as amended)) are different from those in the main legal aid scheme.
31. In matrimonial cases there is now a blanket authorization given to provide up to £40 worth of legal advice and assistance.
32. Applications under the legal advice and assistance scheme are not, of course, the sole indication of the involvement of lawyers in ordinary people's problems; a vast amount of free legal advice is given on a voluntary basis in legal advice centres, citizens advice bureaux, etc., spread throughout the country: see Legal Action Group's *Directory of Legal Advice Centres.*
33. The seminal work is B. Abel-Smith and P. Townsend, *The Poor and the Poorest* (Bell, 1965).
34. Based on the report by Sir William Beveridge, *Social Insurance and Allied Services* (H.M.S.O., 1942, Cmd. 6404).
35. Then called the "National Assistance Scale Rates"; since 1966, the "Supplementary Benefits Scale Rates".
36. Among the most influential are: Child Poverty Action Group; SHELTER, the Campaign for the Homesless; Help the Aged; Disablement Income Group.
37. Such as the programme of Community Development Projects; the Urban Aid Programme; the establishment of Educational Priority Areas.
38. There is an increasing literature from all branches of the social sciences, in particular economics, sociology and social administration on the extent and nature of poverty in Britain.
39. Although the subject of public debate amongst intellectuals, liberal academics, radical political groups, by some government departments and some politicians, it is perhaps not too cynical to state that poverty has not become an issue of national public concern. Even today not many votes can be obtained by campaigning for a radical attack on the problems of poverty.
40. An influential description of the U.S. Neighbourhood Law Office was by Zander in *Justice for All* (Fabian Society, 1968), Appendix. For a critique of the rise in such interest, see now Bankowski and Mungham,

Images of Law (1976). There has now developed an increasing scepticism of the law for the poor movement in the U.S.A.; see Scheingold, *The Politics of Rights* (1974); Cloward and Piven, *Poor People's Movements* (1978).

41. See, e.g., the essay by P. Morris, in Morris, White and Lewis, *Social Needs and Legal Action* (1973); also the very critical paper, *Limits of the Law*, a report by the Community Development Project (1977).
42. Noted above in section 1.
43. Fabian Research Series 273 (Fabian Society, December 1968). See also Society of Conservative Lawyers, *Rough Justice* (1968).
44. Its members are all lawyers who are also members of the British Labour Party.
45. Not all their criticisms were new. Even the Law Society, the body responsible for administering civil legal aid, had drawn attention to a number of defects since the inception of the scheme in 1950.
46. See Legal Action Group Report: "Legal Advice Centres – An Explosion?" (1972); and *Law Society Gazette*, July 28, 1974, p. 727. In fact free legal advice is not a new phenomenon, considerable facilities having existed and developed since the 1890s. What may be different now is that people are coming to see such centres as means to an end (a more comprehensive legal service) rather than an end in itself. (See M. Partington, *Recent Developments in Legal Services to the Poor: Some Reflections on Experience in Coventry*, 1975.)
47. See the researches by Rosalind Brooke in *Information and Advice Centres* (Bell, 1972) and in *Legal Problems and the Citizen* (with B. Abel-Smith and M. Zander) (1973). For valuable information on trade union legal services, see Lewis and Latta, *British Journal of Industrial Relations*, Vol. XII, No. 1; and R. Brooke (ed.), *Advice Services in Welfare Rights* (Fabian Society, 1977).
48. See Harloe, *Housing Aid Centres* (Centre for Environmental Studies, 1977).
49. Reviewed by S. Hillyard, *Law Society Gazette*, June 3, 1975; *Legal Action Group Bulletin* (1974), pp. 207-10. An experimental scheme for civil cases has also begun in Bristol.
50. Available from LAG, 28a Highgate Road, London NW5 1NS. (Cf. the American *Clearing House Poverty Law Review*).
51. See now Byles and Morris, *Unmet Need* (1977).
52. See Borrie and Varcoe, *Legal Aid in Criminal Proceedings* (1973); Lee Bridges *et al.*, *Legal Services in Birmingham* (1975). This latter report is very important in demonstrating how hard it is for private

practitioners to do legal aid work, yet remain financially solvent.

53. Some of these developments are reviewed in M. Partington, "Teaching Welfare Law: Report of a Symposium" (1974, *Law Teacher*). See too Partington and Jowell (eds.) *Welfare Law and Policy* (1979).
54. In particular, the Lord Chancellor's Department and the Lord Chancellor's Advisory Committee on Legal Aid and Advice have become much more active in planning the provision of legal services.
55. This is now recognized on all sides as a serious problem. C. Glasser has estimated that whereas in 1964, 64 per cent of households with children were potentially eligible for legal aid, by 1974, the figure had declined to 23 per cent. Although this trend has been arrested by the annual up-rating of the means test limits that has occurred since 1974, there has been no overall reversal of the trend. (*26th Annual Report on Legal Aid*, 1975–76 (H.C. 12/1976–77), pp. 79–80.)
56. See K. Foster, "The Location of Solicitors" (1973) 36 *Modern Law Review*, pp. 153ff. See too, *Legal Services in Birmingham*, op. cit.
57. *Legal Problems and the Citizen*, op. cit.
58. See again Abel-Smith *et al.*, *Legal Problems and the Citizen*. Also M. Zander, "The Unused Rent Acts", *New Society*, September 12, 1968.
59. These and other points are discussed also in *Legal Services for All* (1978, Fabian Society); and *Legal Services: A Blueprint for the Future* (1977, Legal Action Group).
60. He was for many years the Secretary for Legal Aid to the Law Society.
61. See his *Legal Aid: The First 25 Years*, p. 2.
62. A far more comprehensive exercise on these lines has now been carried out by Professor Zander in his *Legal Services for the Community* (1978).
63. See, e.g., the author's *Legal Aid Means-Tests: Time for Re-appraisal?* (Child Poverty Action Group, 1978); evidence of the Legal Action Group and Society of Labour Lawyers (above note 59).
64. Again the Legal Action Group and the Society of Labour Lawyers develop these points most fully.
65. For further discussion of these ideas see Zander, *Legal Services for the Community*, ch. 8.
66. The Legal Action Group held a conference on Lay Participation in the Legal System in January, 1978; a report, *Life Without Lawyers*, is available from LAG (above, note 50).

VINCENZO VIGORITI

Italy

I. Legal aid models in general

This paper examines the means by which the Italian legal system seeks to alleviate one of the consequences of poverty: the impossibility of the poor obtaining legal assistance. It will be restricted to the study of the means by which the Italian legal system seeks to assure the poor that which the system fully assures the wealthy – legal advice out of court and legal aid and assistance in court.

The experiences of Western nations with legal services to the poor seems to indicate that these services are delivered essentially according to three models.

The first is the charity model, which developed in the medieval period when European nations were going through the process of political unification. The idea of legal aid as charity postulated that the poor were not entitled as a matter of right to any kind of legal assistance. The lawyers were thought to be morally obligated to assist the poor without remuneration. In the nineteenth century, most legal systems, under the pressure of the concepts of natural justice enhanced and refined by the eighteenth century philosophers and affirmed by the American and French Revolutions tended to combine the idea of legal aid as a matter of charity with the idea that poor people have a right to legal aid. What was due under charity became due under the law. The actual difference, however, was very small, and the poor made few gains: the implementation of the right still depended on the charitable efforts of the lawyers. The moral obligation of the lawyer to represent the poor became merely an honorific duty. The combination of law and charity by which the nineteenth-century nations attempted to handle the legal aid issue proved to be completely ineffective.

The second model is based on the political right of access to courts which was affirmed in the nineteenth century, and was formally granted to all individuals. It is an obligation of legal systems to provide access to courts even for the poor through an appropriate scheme of assistance. The Italian legal system accepts this view of legal aid in theory, but has failed to enact adequate legislation to realize it.

The new approach emerging in Italy "is marked by certain common themes: legal aid is a right to be protected by force of law; this protection requires affirmative state action and this state action must provide protection which is not merely formal, but actual and effective".[1] Although there are many ways to implement this right, most legal systems which conform to this second model seem to have chosen a state-compensated, private attorney solution.

The third model is also based on the supposition that individuals have a right to legal assistance, but it views legal aid more as a welfare right than as an individual right of each citizen to assistance. According to this view, legal aid involves:

> the establishment of a concrete governmental program, funded to the limit that political and budgetary constraints will allow and staffed with experts trained in social welfare administration. The end of this approach is to attack and ameliorate . . . [undesirable] social . . . conditions [by means of] the rational allocation of limited resources. . . . By attacking broad social conditions . . . it promotes effective economy and social equality.[2]

Although these three models are part of the historical experience of legal aid, they represent only a framework and their importance must not be exaggerated. Experience shows that the attitudes of the private bar, the force and organization of political and social institutions impede planning and exercise a decisive influence on legislative choices.

II. Barriers which affect access to courts

Before discussing some of the barriers affecting access to courts, the groups and the classes needing legal assistance in Italy must be identified. These include the unemployed, the under-employed, the employed with low incomes (who will generally be socially unintegrated, uneducated, or unskilled). Economic criteria, however, must be applied with caution. Experience shows that civil litigation may be a heavy economic burden even for the members of middle income classes. The more advanced legal aid systems are expressing concern as to the delivery of legal services to middle income citizens.

Civil procedure is marred by many barriers to access to justice for the poor. The Italian civil procedure is much more complicated and formalistic than is necessary. Judges, lawyers and scholars not only preserve the complexity and formalism, but they also augment it by creating formalities and using terminology incomprehensible to the layman. In large part this is due to the monopoly of the legal profession over the judicial process, a monopoly which has contributed to the separation of the procedure itself from the social context in which it is placed. This is not a particularly serious barrier to access to justice for the poor, however. No matter how much the complexity and formalism are reduced, procedure will always be complicated and this will always be a nearly insurmountable barrier for any citizen, and particularly for the poor. A similar procedure would still not allow the poor to defend themselves and thus avoid recourse to legal assistance. Self-representation cannot be considered a real alternative to legal aid: rather it is an instrument of the elite, and it presupposes independence and education, characteristics which are uncommon among the poor. Moreover, the Italian legal system appears reluctant to extend the extremely limited cases in which self-representation is permitted.

The organized bar is not the only body which discourages the client from appearing on his own behalf. The Constitutional Court has refused to declare unconstitutional Article 82 of the code of civil procedure which requires that parties be represented in court by counsel. Further, the government has recently proposed a reform of the court system and procedure before certain courts which would not permit self-representation except in the few cases provided for by the present law.

The poor are not educated and lack information about their legal rights and about the community legal services that are available. This is a more significant barrier to access to the courts. Because of lack of education, the poor generally are dependent and not assertive, and they are unable to protect their interests. Nevertheless, the Italian legal system considers an individual to be fully responsible for recognizing his problems, bringing them to the attention of the proper officials, and deciding how to proceed once legal aid is granted. Lack of education is merely an unfortunate trait of the poor – it does not prevent their being given the full responsibility of recognition and pursuit of their rights.

Lack of information about the availability of legal services produces similar results. In many cases, the lack of information is a result of a lack of publicity about services the legal system offers to the poor. In Italy, legal assistance should be given gratuitously by members of the bar, but it would be unrealistic to expect individual attorneys or even the organized bar to publish and distribute information about their obligation. In addition, the Italian canon of professional ethics prohibits solicitation of clients or incitement to litigation, which presents a further obstacle to the publicizing of the availability of services. An additional difficulty is that the commissions that are charged with the examination of the applications and the assignment of private attorneys to the poor are located in downtown court houses which are often remote from potential users. People who live and work in poor neighbourhoods are seldom, if ever, informed of the few opportunities that the system offers. Thus the poor do not usually seek legal assistance until they are sued because of the fear that accompanies legal problems and because of their lack of information. Then, due to the urgency of the situation, proper information on the availability of legal services is even more difficult to obtain.

The cost and delay of civil proceedings are serious obstacles to access to courts. This topic has not yet been adequately considered in Italy. Economists have commented that "there exist no official inquiries nor private studies which might give some idea of the reality of the situation."[3] It is extremely difficult to obtain data useful for our purposes. With the exception of the few available statistics, what follows is the result of a series of interviews which the author personally conducted with lawyers and judges practising in Florence and in other parts of Italy.

In general, the costs of a proceeding fall under two headings: court fees and costs of the proceeding itself.

The court fees are set at the beginning of every judicial year by the President of the Court of Appeal for each district; they remain the same for any type of action before the same judicial body, and they are relatively modest. These costs differ little from one district to another.

The court costs were a few thousand lire in 1963. Currently, in the district of the Court of Appeal of Florence, they were 8,500 lire ($10 U.S.) for the *pretura* (lower ordinary court of first instance); 18,000 lire ($22 U.S.) before the tribunal (higher ordinary court of first instance): and 23,000 lire ($28 U.S.) before the Court of Appeal. Stamp fees for complaint and summons and their service are additional.

The costs of the proceedings, from the beginning of the case to the execution of the judgment, are much higher than the court costs. Total costs vary widely from case to case as they depend on diverse factors such as the subject matter of the action, its value, and its length. In my interviews I found that such costs are difficult to ascertain accurately because of the unwillingness of the parties and their counsel to disclose them.

Article 90 of the Code of Civil Procedure states that each party must initially bear his own expenses. In addition, the losing party is generally obliged to reimburse his adversary's expenses, including counsel fees.

Procedural costs may include any of the following:

1. Judicial expenses, those costs pertaining to the direct intervention by the court. For example, such costs would cover notification made to the opposing party or to a witness, or official stamped paper for records. These costs are not high; notification by a tribunal costs less than 1,000 lire ($1.10 U.S.), and official stamped paper costs 700 lire ($0.90 U.S.) for four pages. However, the law prescribes the payment of special fees for the filing, exchange and photocopying of the acts of the proceeding, and these fees can be very substantial.
2. Witness and expert testimony. Witnesses are paid 700 lire ($0.90 U.S.) per day; if they do not reside within the jurisdiction of the court in question, they are allowed travel expenses, according to the Royal Decree of May 3, 1923, No. 1043. In practice, witnesses always forego this symbolic reimbursement which, they would only receive after a delay of many months.

   Expert testimony is relatively costly. Of course, it depends on the expert and the nature of his opinion. In the most prevalent type of case – that involving a medical visit for the verification of traffic accident injuries – the average cost is less than 70,000 lire ($62.00 U.S.): this sum is greater if the witness' expertise is highly specialized or if the verification requires numerous visits, analyses and tests. The expenses may be much greater for other types of expert testimony, such as for the authentication of a painting or for appraising an asset.
3. Counsel fees. These are by far the most important costs. In Italy, as in other European countries, there is no contingency fee system, despite the fact that Article 5, paragraph 3 of the Ministerial Decree of May 5, 1973 (regarding lawyers' fees for civil and criminal cases and for general counselling) provides that for the assessment of lawyers' fees a client's judgment award, even if not monetary, may be taken into account. There is an official fee schedule which sets forth in detail minimum and maximum counsel fees.
4. Fee for registration of the judgment. This fee depends on the amount in

controversy and the subject matter of the action. It is not required for the registration of a judgment deciding a labour dispute, and it amounts to a few thousand lire for property or family disputes. The fee is higher for contract disputes, and is significantly greater for inheritance disputes. Where a judgment of one and a half million lire ($1,652 U.S.) is awarded, the fee may amount to as much as 12,000 lire ($15 U.S.) for property disputes and 40,000 lire ($47 U.S.) for contract disputes.

The absence of recent studies on the costs of an action makes it particularly difficult to determine the ratio between costs and the amount in dispute. This is especially true for disputes involving small or modest claims, those in which poor people are more likely to be involved. For small claims, the only existing data do not go beyond 1963. At that time, the *pretore* had jurisdiction over disputes whose value was not more than 250,000 lire ($295 U.S.), and the tribunal had jurisdiction over disputes with a greater value. Sample costs were as follows:

For disputes which involved less than 100,000 lire ($118 U.S.), the average cost was 160.67 per cent. Costs amounted to 153.6 per cent when the action involved real property rights (*diritti reali*), 170.2 per cent for contract disputes, and 223.5 per cent for other types of disputes. For disputes involving less than one million lire ($1,178 U.S.) the average cost was between 51.5 and 60.9 per cent.

For disputes involving more than one million lire, heard before the tribunal, the average costs fell to 8.4 per cent.

There is some reduction of costs for disputes involving a large amount, but the degree to which this occurs denotes a clear bias against small claims. This situation has not changed since 1963, however; because of the inflation which has afflicted Italy, the amount of money for which an individual would be willing to go to court is now seldom less than 100,000 lire ($118 U.S.).

Exact data are not available for family disputes, divorce proceedings, and questions of civil status, in which the poor are often involved. From interviews with judges and lawyers, however, it appears that the average costs of divorce or separation proceedings amount to approximately 300,000 lire ($354 U.S.) for an uncomplicated proceeding involving no problems of child custody, alimony or child support, or the necessity of taking extensive testimony; otherwise the costs tend to increase.

In civil actions, the costs are slightly less, approximately 200,000 lire ($240 U.S.). It should be noted that if the proceeding is initiated by the *pubblico ministero* (similar to the U.S. district attorney), the state assumes the cost.

Specific fees and costs in Italian civil proceedings, apart from actions for very small claims, are not more expensive than civil proceedings in other countries. But their extreme length means that the costs accumulate to such an extent that low income people are at a major disadvantage in attempting to bring or defend an action.

In 1963 an average civil case of first instance lasted for 16 months in *pretura* and over 2 years in the tribunal. In 1970, a civil case lasted more than 18 months in *pretura* and about 30 months in the tribunal. By 1973 the situation had not improved at all. An analysis of the data for 1973 shows that the cases of first instance in the *pretura* lasted an average of one year, those in the tribunal of first instance lasted 2½ years, and those in the Court of Appeal of second instance lasted over two years. Statistics for 1974 and 1975 are not yet available; there is reason to hope for only a little improvement.

There are many reasons for delays, ranging from the influence of old and inadequate procedural laws, to the lack of services, to the chronic shortage of court personnel. Moreover, the situation is exacerbated by the low judicial caseloads, not only as compared to an optimal theoretical figure but also as compared with a theoretical normal figure.

The length of a proceeding increases costs so greatly that where feasible even rich parties prefer arbitration. Though it may at first appear more expensive than ordinary procedure, arbitration, because it is quicker, is in the end less costly. Only by reducing the length of proceedings will it be possible to reduce their costs appreciably.

III. Legal services available to the poor in Italy

The Italian legal system not only recognizes a legally protected right of the poor to legal aid, but also accords that right constitutional status in order to ensure universal access to courts. Article 24, paragraphs 1 and 2 of the Italian Constitution require that every individual be given an opportunity to present his claims and arguments at every stage of any judicial proceeding, without restrictions which would make the exercise of the constitutional right difficult or impossible. Towards this end, the courts, especially the Constitutional Court, have in their judgments been carving out a series of specific guarantees, implicit in the constitutional provision, which come into play at various points during a case and are designed to protect the right of access. Article 24 of the Constitution is being moulded according to the requirements of the various types of proceedings and assumes a different scope and content in each phase; the guarantees thus developing are all directed towards a common goal – the establishment and protection of the right of access to courts.

The third paragraph of the same article seeks to give meaning to the guarantees contained in the first two paragraphs and explicitly requires that "poor persons shall, by appropriate institutions, be assured the means to plead and to defend themselves before any judicial jurisdiction". This rule affirms the principle of equal protection of the laws established by Article 3 of the Italian Constitution. The Italian legal system, following the second model discussed above, considers legal aid to be a legally protected right of each person; the focus is on the individual rather than on poverty itself.

At present, in Italy, there are no public legal offices, either national or local, to which the poor can turn to obtain legal assistance or representation in court. This is an unfortunate consequence of the reforms which took place around the middle of the last century, and which abolished a system of legal assistance based on a network of public offices and instituted the present system of appointed lawyers.

At the time of the unification of Italy, there existed in the Kingdom of Piedmont a public office, the *Avvocatura dei Poveri*, whose duties and powers in defence of the poor, even if not very broad, were significant. This institution was extended in 1859 throughout the new kingdom, but was discontinued in 1865, primarily because of lack of funds.

The re-establishment of these public legal assistance offices was proposed unsuccessfully several times at the beginning of this century by prominent socialist lawyers who were convinced that the reform of legal aid would provide an opportunity to launch more pervasive reforms.

Three of these reform proposals are noteworthy: two were presented by representative Gallini in 1902 and 1905, and the third was presented by the minister and socialist representative Gallo in 1906.

The first project proposed the return of the office of the *Avvocatura dei poveri*, with divisions throughout the country attached to the tribunals; the members would have been taken from the offices of the public prosecutor and paid directly by the state. The second project also proposed the return to the *Avvocatura dei poveri*; the members, however, would have been lawyers, appointed by the king on the nomination of the bar association and salaried by the state. These offices would have been responsible not only for the representation of the poor in court, but would have provided out-of-court assistance as well. The third project, presented in 1906, anticipated the introduction of a mixed system of legal assistance which is the basis of present-day proposals of reform. This project sought to combine a system of legal assistance offices with the already operative system of legal aid granted by lawyers appointed on a case-by-case basis. The offices, composed of members of the judiciary and of the bar, would have been charged with the task of advising those who applied for legal assistance, and, if necessary, helping them to obtain evidence to sustain their cases. This proposal, however, depended too much on the voluntary co-operation of the members of the bar, failed to provide adequate compensaiton for the attorneys, and relied primarily on the good will of charitable institutions.

All these proposals were rejected. Thus, even before World War I, the ideal of creating public offices of legal assistance for the poor, an idea in line with the Italian tradition of legal aid, appeared to have been set aside.

The Italian legal system still tries to fulfil the constitutional obligation established in Article 24(3) by means of the Royal Decree of December 30, 1923, no. 3282. This statute declares legal aid to be an honorific duty of the members of the bar; attorneys must act for the poor if asked to do so, but will receive no fees unless their client succeeds and costs are recovered from the losing party. There is no provision for remuneration by the state. An application must be made to the proper commission; the applicants have to meet the criterion of poverty and face strict assessment of their chances of success.

There exists a considerable literature concerning legal aid in Italy and no purpose is served by repetition. I will limit myself to saying that this law is anachronistic and inconsistent theoretically. It makes the implementation of a legally and constitutionally protected right to effective access to courts dependent on the charitable efforts of the members of the bar, according to a model that even nineteenth century scholars considered untenable. Also, on the practical level, the law has been totally inadequate in responding to the legal needs of the poor. There are far too few applications for legal aid; the percentage of the cases in which legal aid has been granted is ridiculously low, less than 0.5 per cent of the cases initiated before ordinary civil courts. It is also clear that when, as is current practice in Italy, the lawyer reluctantly tenders his services as a charitable or professional obligation, he will tend to be passive to a fault. In spite of this, the Italian Constitutional Court, on two separate occasions, refused to declare this law unconstitutional.

The court recognizes that it is possible *de lege ferenda*, and from a point of legislative policy, to hope for a different and better system for the defence of the poor, but it adds that the inadequacy does not imply the unconstitutionality of the existing means for providing aid. "To consider, in theory, such means", said the court, "as insufficient, or of minimal efficiency, with respect to the scope expressed in the Constitution, is not to say that they are unconstitutional, and to deprive thereby the poor of even that assistance which they now have."[4] That court was considered liberal and progressive in comparison with the present court; it is clear, then, that the only hope of reform of the law of 1923 lies with the legislature.

The second instrument with which the Italian legal system seeks to guarantee access to courts to the poor is the law of August 11, 1973, No. 533, which radically changed the procedural rules for practical determination of employment benefits such as workmen's compensation, pensions, and health insurance. This law continues to provide legal aid using the appointed private attorney system but differs from the law in that applications for legal aid must be addressed to the judge of the case and not to a separate administrative commission; and it established that the fee of the attorney assigned to the party be paid by the state pursuant to the professional fee schedules (Articles 10-16).

This important innovation represents the first step towards the abolition of the charitable model of legal aid in Italy; it is the first instance of concrete affirmative state action implementing the right to legal aid. Too much enthusiasm, however, would be premature. Four years after the enactment of law No. 533, the provisions on legal aid have been applied in very few cases. This trend is not likely to change. There are probably two reasons for this. The first is that only those whose annual income is not in excess of two million lire ($356 U.S.) are eligible for legal aid (Article 11). This figure is very low and automatically excludes a significant number of recipients. The second reason is that the labour unions, which guarantee legal services to their members, desire to control the demand for legal assistance and therefore tend to discourage recourse to state legal aid.

Another contribution to legal assistance of the poor is offered by private religious, charitable and social organizations. Religious and charitable organizations do not, however, assume a particularly significant role. There are a few religious institutions that offer legal assistance to the needy, but this is always an occasional and secondary service and is available only to certain groups. These institutions do not have permanent legal aid offices, and their legal services are funded only to the extent of their budgetary priority, which is usually very low. Notwithstanding its size and power, the Catholic Church does not appear to be very willing to help the poor with their legal problems.

Private organizations interested in legal aid problems are insurance companies, unions and party organizations. "Prepaid legal services" are offered by several insurance companies which, in return for a fixed, relatively small fee paid over a period of time, guarantee representation and assistance, either by staff lawyers or private lawyers, up to a negotiated limit of legal expenses. This insurance scheme is, for the most part, used in connection with automobile accidents and is not significant. It is unlikely that the poor are aware of the existence of these plans; and even if they were, it is likely that they would be intimidated by the complex insurance contracts.

Since premiums must be paid to maintain coverage, the prepaid legal services system is used only by moderate income people who feel that there is some possibility of their being involved in legal controversies. Certainly, such a programme is not relevant to the needs of the hard-core poor who are unable to pay even the minimal fees.

Labour unions and political parties also try to fill the gaps left by the inadequate state legal aid system. Most of these organizations have established legal assistance offices that advise the poor, and, if necessary, represent them in court. A few unions have located offices in the poor sections of larger cities, to attempt to overcome the lack of information about the availability of legal services. Besides those offices, or as an alternative to them, the unions also retain private attorneys to assist and represent the workers. The workers' cases and their chances for success are assessed; if accepted, they receive full assistance. If the action succeeds, the private attorneys have to share part of their earnings with the unions.

The services offered by the unions are in large part a response to the demand for assistance that the state legal aid system would have to meet.

Of course, there are some negative aspects to the trade union schemes. First, legal services are only part of a range of benefits offered to members, and are not the main concern of the unions. Secondly, although the membership of unions in Italy is open to anyone without significant restrictions, it is clear that legal services are an organizational tool, and that only union members are eligible to receive them. Finally, the unions are fully aware of the political power flowing from their ability to organize an efficient system of legal assistance. They do not favour the proposals of reform of state legal aid which would eventually endanger their dominance in the area.

IV. Final remarks: a proposal

Prospects for reform of the state legal aid system in Italy are not promising. A proposal adopting the state-compensated private lawyer solution approved by the senate in 1973 appears totally neglected today.

State legal aid simply does not exist in Italy, and where the only services to the poor come from private organizations, there have been no proposals or social movements in favour of a change. A situation that in other countries would certainly stimulate legislative attention and be a ground for agitation and passionate debate among lawyers and sociologists appears to be tolerated with indifference. Those who still insist on discussing it are heard, if at all, with polite disinterest.

It is difficult to identify the reasons for this. One reason might be that legal scholars are totally unconcerned with the problems of civil justice and continue to discuss neutral topics, thus avoiding these issues with social implications. Another might be the indifferent and even hostile attitude of the Bar which is more interested in maintaining its rapport with the unions than in contributing to serious reform. A third reason might be the economic crisis which affects Italy and makes it unrealistic to think that the government will fund a legal aid programme. In addition, the poor are dispersed, disorganized, and unaware of their rights, thus they cannot agitate for legal aid. Or perhaps their indifference is due instead to an awareness that access to courts would be a small gain, given the present state of justice in Italy.

Nevertheless, in spite of the negative impact of all these factors and notwithstanding that it now appears unrealistic to speak of a legal aid programme, it seems impossible that the Italian system can continue to neglect the legal needs of the poor much longer. For this reason, I will try to indicate at least some guidelines to possible reform.

First, legal assistance to the poor is not an ideologically neutral question, and it cannot be addressed as a simple organizational problem. In essence, legal aid implies effective participation of the people in the political, economic and social organization of the country (Article 3 of the Constitution). Legal aid is a reform within the system, which undoubtedly aims to change it, perhaps radically, but does not presuppose its destruction. Making the right of access to courts effective for the poor can be a means of drawing the socially unintegrated classes into the legal process.

It has been suggested that the poor can relate more easily to the judiciary than to the legislature or the administration. By means of this relationship, that is, through justice, persons can be involved in social processes from which they had been excluded. This would allow us to go beyond the old guarantees of procedural due process and move towards a goal of justice for all which now appears tremendously far off and abstract.

To be successful, a reform must operate within the framework that considers legal assistance as a legally protected individual right, a right essential to the right of access to courts formally guaranteed to every individual. Of course legal aid must also be palced within the wider framework of the struggle against poverty and must be considered in a welfare perspective. But the Italian Constitution and other laws emphasize the individual aspects of this right.

The experiences of other jurisdictions, especially Sweden and Quebec, and the older Italian legal aid tradition indicate that a reform should combine a state-compensated private attorney system with a system of public offices staffed with salaried attorneys. Problems of co-ordination, financing, eligibility rules, and problems in the relationship between client and attorney would have to be considered. Some resistance and some criticism would certainly arise against the creation of public offices of legal assistance. The establishment of new public offices would undoubtedly be opposed, given the present state of the Italian bureaucratic machinery. The organized Bar, which fears state control of the profession through the institution of public offices staffed with salaried attorneys or state control of the choice and management of cases, is likely to criticize such a reform.

Nevertheless, a system of legal assistance based on a network of public offices integrated with a system of appointed private attorneys has many advantages. First, the existence of these offices can be adequately publicized without violating canons of ethics; secondly, recourse to the offices is much easier and more informal than recourse to private attorneys, and the admission procedure could be rapid and simple; third, besides representation in court, these offices could provide the poor with out-of-court assistance; fourth, a network of offices would utilize the funds available much better than would a state system based on the state-compensated private attorney. It would also permit the start of a policy of assistance not limited to the legal problem of poverty, a policy which would be adequately adapted by the offices to the needs of the different zones of the country. The presence of public offices would be a factor of uniting and organizing the poorer classes, and thus a factor of the promotion of a wider social reform.

1. Cappelletti, Gordley, and Johnson, *Towards Equal Justice: A Comparative Study of Legal Aid in Modern Societies*, p. 79.
2. Cappelletti, Gordley, and Johnson, *Towards Equal Justice: A Comparative Study of Legal Aid in Modern Societies*, p. 109.
3. C. Castellano, C. Pace, G. Palomba, C. Raspini, *L'efficienza della giustizia italiana e i suoi effetti economico-sociali* 9 and 53 (Bari, Laterza, 2a ed., 1970); *see* F. Forte and P. G. Bondonio, *Costi e benefici della giustizia italiana* 5 and 7 (Bari, Laterza, 1970): "an economic study of justice has not even been sketched out". These authors then attempt to elaborate their own economic theory on the costs and benefits of justice (*see* especially *id*. at 119-35), but conclude that "the classical instruments of cost-benefit analysis are, as far as we can tell at present, only partly applicable to the analysis of the administration of justice." *Id.* at 146; *see id.* at 140–46. *See also* L. Tomasini, *Sulla convenienza economica della lite giudiziaria, Riv. Intern. Scienze Econ. e Comm.* 390 (1969).
4. Const. Court. Judg. of Dec. 22, 1964 no. 114, 9 *Giurisprudenza Costituzionale* 1163, 1175 (1964); Const. Court, Judg. of March 3, 1972 no. 41, 95 *Fori It.* I, 1182, 1183 (1972) (dictum); Const. Court. Judg. of June 16, 1970, no. 97, 93 *Foro It.* I, 1848 (1970); Denti, *Processo civile e giustizia sociale*; *Il processo cum alienaziene*; Cappelletti, Gordley, and Johnson, *Towards Equal Justice: A comparative Study of Legal Aid in Modern Societies*, 70; L. P. Comoglio, *La garanzia costituzionale dell'azione e il processo civile* 323 (Padova, Cedam, 1970).

TAKESHI KOJIMA

Japan

I. Growing needs of legal aid

In Japanese society, as urbanization and industrialization proceed, the traditional methods of social control are becoming less effective. With family structure and community life gradually becoming disorganized, dispute settlement through conciliation and mediation has come to be increasingly difficult. There are clear indications that more people, especially in larger cities, tend to seek the settlement of disputes in accordance with legal standards. It is expected that in the future courts will play a more extensive role in resolving disputes.

Among others, the flood of personal injury cases resulting from traffic accidents, the explosive emergence of mass litigation caused by environmental pollution, and the phenomenal increase of medical malpractice, drug injury, etc. have caused the public to get involved in litigation. Today, litigation is no longer the affluent's luxury, but the ordinary citizen's necessity. That is to say, not only the rich but also the middle class and the poor have to face battles in court. This is why an increasing number of people have become aware of the importance of a day in court.

The need for legal services is evident in and out of court. Substantive law and procedural law are constantly changing and proliferating. Litigation is extremely complex and even mysterious to untrained laymen. There are vast unmet needs for representation by lawyers especially among people of moderate means. More lawyers have come to realize the need for the development of legal aid and assistance in litigation.

In view of this situation, we should pay more attention to the plight of people of moderate means in the legal process. The nineteenth century, it is said, was a century of production. In contrast, the twentieth century will be a century of distribution: an age in which for the first time the products of industry will be distributed widely among those who need them. However, the legal profession has, unfortunately, been primarily concerned with the improvement of the quality of legal services rather than a more equitable and even distribution of those services. This is the case in Japan, where the size of the legal profession is small. There are a little more than ten thousand practising attorneys throughout the country. Competition in the bar examination is extremely keen; roughly speaking, only 500 out of 30,000 applicants pass the examination annually. The expansion of the legal profession seems to be necessary for realizing the ideal of universal access to justice. The democratic principle of equality before the law will be hollow unless the legal services of lawyers are available for all.

The responsibility of the bar is heavy indeed, and it is by no means easy to discharge. A mere quantitative expansion of legal services is not enough. We have to explore more effective methods of making these services available to those who need them. In the modern times of mass production and mass marketing, infringement of legal right takes the form of mass phenomena. For example, large segments of society suffer from fraudulent sales schemes. To deal with widespread injuries we have to establish a comprehensive system for universal delivery of justice. Since the first step to justice begins with legal consultation, it is of vital importance that a lawyer's services are available for all.

II. The right to counsel

The right to counsel together with notice and hearing before a legally competent and impartial tribunal constitutes the basic elements of due process of law. A fair trial is simply impossible without the expertise of a lawyer. In light of the fundamental fairness doctrine, there can be no justification for maintaining a dichotomy of criminal procedure and civil procedure. However, as the situation now stands, there is a striking contrast between civil and criminal processes in Japan.

In criminal process, the right to assigned counsel has already been established. The Japanese Constitution Article 37(3) provides: "At all times the accused shall have the assistance of competent counsel who shall, if the accused is unable to secure the same by his own efforts, be assigned to his use by the State." The representation by counsel in trials is made compulsory in a case involving capital punishment, life imprisonment or imprisonment of more than three years (Criminal Procedure Code Article 289).

There are a variety of methods of providing legal services for the needy by either an individual lawyer or a legal aid organisation. Public methods are also of two types: assigned counsel or the public defender. The system of assigned counsel has been adopted for Japanese criminal procedure. The courts appoint lawyers in private practice on a rotating basis. Assignments are frequent, so that in almost half of all criminal cases an accused is defended by an assigned counsel. The system has recently been under attack. The quality of representation is said to be inadequate in many cases, since compensation of the assigned counsel is insufficient and some of the assigned counsel handle their cases without much devotion. One of the inherent weaknesses of the system of assigned counsel is that the panel of counsel is so wide that in larger cities, each lawyer is assigned only a few cases each year and has little chance of developing expertise in criminal matters.

On the other hand, in civil litigation, the legal right to counsel is still in a formative stage. It is the overwhelming opinion that neither the due process clause nor the equal protection clause furnish a basis for the legal right to have counsel provided. However, if reality is to be given to the ideals of the Constitution and social justice, it is essential that at least the moral right is recognized beyond the technical legal right. In this writer's opinion, both legal aid and assistance in civil litigation should be considered as a constitutional mandate, but this view is not shared by most commentators. In any event, legal assistance to the indigent should not be regarded as a mere charity, but as a right. There remains much to be done if the ideals of the Constitution are to be realized.

In civil litigation the indigent must surmount at least three financial barriers: cost, the expense of a lawyer's services and miscellenaous expenses incidental to litigation.

Potential litigants may lose their day in court if they cannot afford to pay the fees to launch a suit. Assistance in litigation is designed to remedy this situation and to attempt to make the courts more accessible. The Civil Procedure Code Article 118 provides: "The court may, on the application of a party who has no means to defray the costs of the suit, grant assistance in litigation, but only when there is some prospect of winning the case." According to Article 120, assistance in litigation has the following effects: temporary release from the payment of the costs of the suit; temporary release from the payment of the fees of the marshal and expenses for execution of his duty; temporary release from the payment of fees and expenses of the counsel whom the court has ordered to attend the party; and release from the liability to furnish security for the costs of the suit. It is worth noting that the attendance of counsel is ordered quite infrequently. This is so because the court may order counsel's attendance only when it prohibits the oral argument of parties who are unable to deliver such argument as may be necessary for the elucidation of the action (Article 135). Assistance in civil litigation concerns itself mainly with mitigating the indigent's plight in relation to the costs of the suit. Recently, some courts have granted assistance in litigation in almost every case where the litigants are represented by legal aid attorneys. This method of assistance is increasingly popular, even though its effects are rather limited. The trend is clearly visible in recent statistics which indicate that the number of cases in which assistance was granted in litigation has risen to 669 in 1967 from about 53 per annum in the 1930s. The use of this type of assistance remains very low (i.e. less than 1 per cent in 1977).

The indigent may get into court, but he may be helpless becasue he cannot afford a lawyer. Legal aid is designed to remedy this situation. A lawyer performs a vital role especially in civil procedure based on the adversary system. This report focuses on the structure and operation of legal aid in Japan.

III The eligibility standards for legal aid

Legal aid work has been provided mainly by the Japan Legal Aid Association. However, it should be mentioned that there are legal counselling services of very limited scale by private organizations such as law school and volunteer groups. The Association has 50 branch offices throughout the country, each of them located in the office of a local bar association. The Legal Aid Association is of comparatively recent origin. It was established in January 1952. The statistics in Table 1 indicate the number of people served by the Association.

In view of its importance the screening process needs some explanation. A client applies to the nearest branch office for legal aid. Upon receipt of an application, the screening committee within the Legal Aid Association decides whether to accept or to refuse the application on the basis of its examination of the merits of the case and of the financial status of the client. This committee is called the Legal Aid Examination Committee (Horitsuhujo-shinsa-Iinkai) and consists of members of the local bar

Table 1

Year	Legal Advice	Aid Granted
1952	195	49
1955	468	46
1960	827	314
1965	3012	1375
1970	5967	2417
1975	8536	2169
1976	9240	2207
1977	8872	2556

association, judges, officials of the Ministry of Justice, and men of knowledge and experience. The committee employs a part-time attorney (Shokutaku-bengoshi) specifically commissioned to examine the legal aspects of the case. He submits his report to the committee for the purpose of making the screening more efficient. In the course of interviewing an applicant the attorney generally gives the applicant legal advice. The status of the attorney differs between large cities and other areas. In large cities an attorney is employed on a full-time basis while in smaller centres attorneys are employed to screen applicants on a case-by-case basis.

An application may be rejected in any of the following situations: (i) if the case concerned is not worthy of receiving legal aid from the viewpoint of justice and law; (ii) if the client cannot prove the grounds why he needs legal aid; (iii) if the case concerned is required to be handled at a remote place, or if professional knowledge which is very special or difficult to obtain is necessary. As a matter of fact, small claims cases are often rejected because of the imbalance between the amount of the claim and the attorney's fees to be repaid to the Association after the litigation ends.

The committee, in granting legal aid, determines the expected amount of expenses of the case to be assisted (court costs, lawyer's retainer and other expenses). In practice the attorney's retainer has been set at around seventy thousand yen ($370) regardless of the value of interest at stake. Roughly 10 or 20 per cent of the retainer has to be donated to the Association. After the completion of the case, the Association determines the amount of the lawyer's fees and the portion of the expenses which is to be reimbursed by the client to the Association.

It is the Association's policy that the merit test as well as the means test must be applied. Legal aid may be granted out of sympathy in the expectation of a possible settlement, in a case in which the prospect of winning is dim. In other words, the prospect of a favourable settlement or conciliation would be enough. Even so, only about 2 or 3 per cent of the cases assisted have failed in the court. The result of legal aid litigation in 1977 is as follows: cases won – 24 per cent; settlements – 52 per cent; out-of-court settlements – 3 per cent; cases lost – 2 per cent; other – 15 per cent.

In contrast, the means test is controversial. The Japan Legal Aid Association Constitution Article 5 provides that one of its objectives is "to give aid regarding legal disputes to those who are without means". With an increasing social demand in mind, the Legal Aid Association has apparently been inclined to include the lower middle class in the legal aid scheme, in addition to the indigent living at the public charge.

According to the guildelines adopted in 1978, a client is financially eligible when the following requirements are met.

Table 2

The Maximum Income of an Eligible Client

Size of family	*Monthly Income*
1 (person)	110,000 or less (yen)
2	150,000 or less
3	170,000 or less
4	190,000 or less
5	230,000 or less

The statistics as of 1977 indicate that the means test is rather strictly applied in practice as only 20.3 per cent have an annual income of 600,000 yen or more; while 57.1 per cent of recipients are public charges.

Developments in the context of assistance in litigation have had a great impact on legal aid. In a mass injuries case caused by environmental pollution resulting from mining, the court held that several plaintiffs having an annual income of as much as one and a half million yen were entitled to assistance in litigation (*Mitsui-kinzoku-kogyo K.K.* v. *Yoshida et al.*, 629 Hanreijiho 22 Nagoya App. Ct., February 8, 1971). Furthermore, assistance in litigation was recently granted to a victim of a drug injury case whose income amounted to three million yen annually. In some mass tort cases, the screening committee has granted legal aid to a client with an annual income of approximately two million yen.

A small part of the middle class have been covered by the legal aid scheme. Eligibility standards are flexible and individual adjustments are made in exceptional cases, in which litigation expenses, medical bills and living expenses are unusually large in serious personal injury cases involving complex issues (e.g. drug injury cases).

It is advisable to explain why only 40 per cent of the applications for legal aid are accepted. For example, in Tokyo where an applicant is interviewed by the Association's part-time staff lawyers, many of the applicants are satisfied with the legal advice given during the interview and withdraw their applications. Thus, cases actually rejected by the screening committee are about 10 per cent.

Upon the acceptance of an application, the Legal Aid Association appoints a lawyer on the recommendation of local bar associations and pays him a retainer and expenses on behalf of the client assisted. The lawyer proceeds to take the necessary legal steps, beginning with the filing of a complaint. When the case comes to an end, the client assisted is requested, unless excused, to repay in a lump sum or by instalments, all or part of the money which the Legal Aid Association has paid on his behalf. The client usually has to repay immediately out of his recovery.

The legal aid fund has gradually expanded, and cases assisted have increased accordingly. Nevertheless, the present fund is far from adequate, as compared with the United States or Canada.

IV. Social impacts of legal aid

The nature of cases assisted is of special significance in evaluating the social impacts of the Association's activities. Policy considerations behind the eligibility standards are reflected in the statistics in Table 3. Some of the features illustrated by these statistics are worth mentioning. First, legal aid is limited to civil cases only. An extensive system of assigned counsel has been established as a separate entity to meet the constitutional requirements. Secondly tort cases constitute the greatest portion of all cases handled. The percentage of tort cases would increase if we took into account provisional attachments and dispositions incidental to those cases. Aid is usually given to plaintiffs in most of these cases. This makes a striking contrast with the situation in the United States, where damage cases are rejected whenever a contingent fee arrangement is possible. Thirdly, divorce cases were slightly more than 10 per cent in 1970. This

Table 3

The Nature of Assisted Cases

Kinds of Cases	*1965*	*1970*	*1977*
Monetary claim – traffic accidents	556	946	206
Monetary claim – other torts	225	532	515
Monetary claim – consolations	43	40	71
Monetary claim – sales	21	8	13
Monetary claim – debts	8	7	2
Monetary claim – rent	34	34	42
Monetary claim – loans	15	30	143
Monetary claim – others	20	59	73
Total	922	1656	1065
Real estate – registration	29	55	88
Real estate – declaration of title	16	23	24
Real estate – evictions	103	73	91
Real estate – others	11	49	38
Total	159	200	241
Family matters – divorce	133	274	651
Family matters – paternity	44	78	67
Family matters – inheritance, alimony	27	16	51
Family matters – other	27	37	52
Total	231	405	821
Other	63	156	429

also contrasted with the familiar pattern in the United States. The difference may be explained partly by the fact that the divorce rate is much lower and that divorce by consent is possible in Japan. However, the situation is changing rapidly. In 1977, family cases had shown a phenomenal increase and constituted 32 per cent of the total cases, mainly because of divorce cases. Fourthly, more than 80 per cent of the assisted clients are plaintiffs. This is closely related with the high rate of reimbursement. Fifthly, the striking decrease in auto accident cases is impressive. The change can be explained by several factors: lower accident rates, enhanced predictability of litigation results and fairly reliable assessment of damage by para-legals.

There are two methods of making legal services available to the people of moderate means. One is the "judicare" system and the other the "staff-lawyer system". Under the former system, a client who is granted financial aid goes to a private attorney of his own choice, so that most private attorneys participate in legal aid activities on rotating basis. One of its merits is to enjoy a broad support from members of the bar for legal aid. Under the latter system, a staff attorney who works on full-time basis, renders legal services to a client, so that legal aid activities are put in the hands of a small segment of the bar. One of its advantages is that staff-attorneys are able to develop an expertise in poverty law and problems peculiar to low income persons and to perform their duty efficiently.

We have adopted the judicare system in Japan. Under our system most lawyers are participating in legal aid activities. Private attorneys play a principal role, while law teachers and students' participation is negligible. Outside the legal aid activities under the Association's sponsorship, there are very small groups of voluntary teachers and students who are providing needed services to the poor. The situation here contrasts markedly with the one in the United States, where a number of law students perform a vital role in serving the poor under the supervision of staff-attorneys or teachers. This may be due to the differences in the legal aid policy as well as in legal education.

In order to meet the growing and ever-changing demands for legal services in the present-day society, we ought to re-examine our traditional system of legal aid. First, due attention should be paid to legal reform through test case litigation as well as individual services to a client. Secondly, comprehensive services have to be rendered to meet the real needs of people having closely-related multi-faceted problems in modern society. Thirdly, preventive services are most needed to avoid legal risks in advance. In view of the greater roles of legal aid in the future, it is desirable for us to establish a mixed system, which combines the broad support of private attorneys with the strength of staff attorneys. In this respect, legal advice by a part-time staff attorney in large cities may well be a sign of coming mixed system. It is most urgent for Japan to reassess its present litigation-oriented policy.

V. Free legal advice and assistance to settlement negotiation

One of the brighter aspects of legal aid is the successful implementation of a new circuit-rider scheme, namely "free legal advice by a travelling lawyer".

In 1974 the Legal Aid Association started free legal advice which was given at each branch office. In 1975, 11,538 citizens received advice. However, there is an imbalance yet to be corrected in the delivery of legal services. There is a heavy concentration of lawyers in larger cities, so that people in rural and remote areas often have difficulty in finding their own attorney. To remedy this deplorable situation, the Association launched free legal advice by a travelling lawyer in 1975. 708 voluntary lawyers participated and advised clients in 230 locations throughout Japan. Forty-nine million yen were appropriated in 1975 and about 2,500 people received legal advice. Thirty-four per cent of the advice given was for problems involving immovable property; 27 per cent for family matters, and 8 per cent for automobile accidents.

The scheme has proved to be highly successful in making legal services accessible to disadvantaged people. More people have come to be aware of the existence of legal aid, and after receiving free legal advice, some people apply for legal aid.

In 1977, attorneys of the regular legal advice scheme have handled 15,150 cases on 2,803 occasions, and the circuit-rider attorneys rendered advice to 2,970 clients on 287 occasions. The provision of legal assistance for settlement negotiation is under consideration. Even if cases are settled without court involvement, a just solution can be brought about speedily and inexpensively by the assistance of lawyers.

Table 4
Legal Advice Cases (1977)

	Regular Scheme	*Circuit-Rider Scheme*
Auto accident	8.2 (%)	5.3 (%)
Money claims	25.9	34.2
Real Estate	27.7	34.4
Family matters	26.0	26.3
Other	12.2	18.8
	100.0%	100.0%

VI. Financing of legal aid

Substantial funds are necessary to maintain legal aid activities. Voluntary contributions by public-spirited citizens and voluntary services by lawyers are valuable, but they are not sufficient to secure for every citizen effective access to justice. Voluntary contributions are often unreliable and lack continuity.

In present-day society, the government should finance the operation of legal aid to meet the growing needs of the indigent. Japan is no exception. Legal aid activities are administered by the independent corporation, but subsidies from the government are the most important financial source.

Although the traditional cry against socialism which governmental subsidies might raise, no longer has any forceful appeal to the public, there is still anxiety that an independent legal profession may be jeopardized by governmental control through allocation and regulation of subsidies. However, as the situation now stands, the danger of governmental interference seems to be slight, since the power of administering legal aid programmes resides mainly in members of the bar. The legal aid Board of Directors is composed of sixty-five members, and sixty-three of them are lawyers appointed on the recommendation of local bar associations on the basis of one out of every one hundred and fifty members. As well all the legal aid counsellors are lawyers.

There might be some apprehension that public officials would interfere in legal aid work, if the Legal Aid Association attempts to bring about law reform through test case litigation. The Constitution of the Legal Aid Association Article 15 provides that the expenses of the association shall be covered by subsidies, contributions project revenues, interest and other revenues (Tables 5 and 6). The item of reimbursement from assisted clients

Table 5
Revenue for Legal Aid in the Fiscal Year 1977

Subsidies from the Ministry of Justice	64,000,000 (yen)
Reimbursement from Assisted Clients	231,509,895
Contributions from Foundations	49,000,000
Debt	14,830,000

Table 6
Expenditures for Legal Aid in the Fiscal Year 1977

Legal Costs	48,302,732 (yen)
Retainer Fees	125,910,000
Success Fees	77,834,000
Security for temporary remedy	52,610,000
Legal Advice	49,000,000

may need some explanation. This furnishes a key to understanding the situation where the Association has been able to grant aid to more than 2,000 cases per annum, in spite of the insufficient subsidies from the government.

According to the present guidelines, when a case has been completed, a client is requested to reimburse in a lump sum or by instalments all or part of the money which the Legal Aid Association has paid on his behalf. There are, of course, some exceptions to this rule. A client might be excused from reimbursement, when he has lost the case, when he has recovered no money because he was a defendant or because his was a declaratory judgment case, or when the money recovered is indispensable for his living, education or medical treatment. Presently, 10 per cent of the clients assisted, including unsuccessful clients (who amount to about 2 per cent), are excused from reimbursement. In the past the number released from reimbursement amounted to as much as 25 per cent. But since the rise of negligence cases resulting from traffic accidents in which most of the clients assisted are plaintiffs, the reimbursement rate has increased. The self-supporting aspect of Japanese legal aid activities is significant.

As the number of legal aid cases has increased, administrative costs of the Association have continued to rise. In recognition that effective measures should be taken to remedy the grave financial difficulties confronting us, a special committee has been appointed to make an intensive inquiry into this matter.

Our traditional policy is that the bar should be responsible for the administration of legal aid and support it financially. As legal aid expands quantitatively, the bar's financial burden becomes heavier. It may be said that the bar is confronted with a choice of maintaining its traditional policy or having the government assume the burden.

Recently the Japanese Bar Association has decided to assume the responsibility for raising funds. In 1976 the Bar Association launched a fund-raising drive. Its goal is 1,500 million yen: 100 million yen from the Japanese Bar Association, 1,400 million yen from companies and individuals (lawyers and citizens). If the campaign is successful, about 95 million yen is expected annually.

As of 1975, administrative costs (screening committee expenses, salary for employees, etc.) amount to about 240 million yen. 80 million yen are borne by the Japanese Bar Association; 98 million yen by lawyers who participated in legal aid activities; 18 million yen are local governments' contributions.

If equal justice means access to the services of a lawyer in the broadest sense, not only representation in the courts but also assistance in attempting to reform the law, it is desirable that a qualitative improvement as well as a quantitative increase of legal services available to the poor be brought about. A solid financial foundation has to be built up in order to achieve the broader purpose of restoring the indigent's confidence in justice and ultimately eliminating poverty as such.

VII. The future of legal aid

The law and legal institutions change as social conditions change. They must change if they are to preserve, much less advance, the political and social values from which they derive their purpose and their life. Legal aid is no exception. The canons of decency and fairness which express the notions of justice must develop in response to the changes in society. The ideal of due process grows richer in its content in a more civilized society.

Recently the Japanese Supreme Court has declared by an overwhelming majority that a speedy trial is one of the essentials of due process (*Shotetsu Boku et al.* v. *Japan* (Takada-jiken), 287 Hanrei-Times 165 (Sup. Ct., G.B., December 20, 1972)). This is a hopeful indication that the Supreme Court has decided to make a citizen's day in court more meaningful.

We should not be satisfied with the progress that has been made so far. The ideal of equal justice under the law demands a sustained and many-sided effort. The objectives of legal aid are expanding from services for the poor to services for the middle class, from criminal process to civil process, and from representaion in court to preventive services.

If we fail to meet the challenges of the times, we shall soon be in grave trouble, and the days of democracy would be limited. Legal aid in Japan is at the crossroads. To build up a viable system responsive to social needs, we have to sharpen our sense of direction and make sound choices in the reform of legal aid.

SANG HYUN SONG

Korea

I. Laws and practices of legal aid in Korea

"Underprivileged", in the Korean context, refers to the economically deprived classes rather than to racial or religious minorities. Although the Korean standard of living has been rising recently, poverty has not been eliminated. The majority of farmers, fishermen, and factory workers remain poor, although most are literate, as a result of the compulsory six-year education system.

Various types of legal aid schemes have been instituted in Korea since 1953. A few law schools initiated a legal education-oriented legal aid programme, mainly to provide legal counselling. Organized labour has its own legal services scheme for union members, but, for political and economic reasons, it does not function very effectively. The Korean Bar Association has established a standing committee for legal aid; practising attorneys take cases on a rotating basis.* However, this scheme is limited in its coverage. Probably the two most active and effective legal aid programmes are the Korea Legal Aid Center for Family Relations, a private institution established and run by Madame Lee Tai Young, and the Korean

*The *Korea Times* dated July 30, 1978 reports: "The Korean Bar Association yesterday worked out a set of regulations specifying the criteria for people to benefit from legal aid projects the association would carry out beginning October 1. According to the regulations which have yet to be made public, the poor receiving government welfare subsidies and those who cannot afford legal counselling fees will benefit from the project. However, the regulations limit the legal help only to cases related to the payment of overdue wages, industrial disasters and traffic accidents. The Association said all the people to be covered by the legal aid projects would have all the legal struggle expenses financed by the Association."

Legal Aid Association, created by the Ministry of Justice in 1972. This paper deals mainly with the achievements of the latter government programme.

When a nation has an insufficient number of medical doctors, the health of its people is endangered. Similarly, the scarcity of judges, lawyers and prosecutors in a country poses a threat to citizens' rights.

The population of the Republic of Korea is approaching 35 million; yet there were only 540 judges, 390 prosecutors and 809 lawyers in the country as of December 31, 1976. This is a ratio of one judge for every 65,000 people, one public prosecutor for every 85,000 people and one attorney for every 43,000 people. Korea has no fewer crimes and civil disputes than do other advanced countries. Therefore, the scarcity of judges, lawyers, and public prosecutors naturally means enormous workloads and unavailability of legal aid to the general public. There is no likelihood that the number of judges and prosecutors will be drastically increased in the near future; the number of seats is fixed by statute and only those who pass[1] the rigid national judicial examination can fill them. Out of some 6000 applicants, about 100 pass the test every year. From these are recruited new judges and prosecutors. Those who pass the national judicial examination are admitted to the Legal Training Institute for a two-year course, which includes 15 months of practice in courts. However, not all graduates of the institute are given positions as judges or prosecutors. Last year, only fifteen were assigned as judges and ten as public prosecutors; the rest entered military service as law officers or began practising law. If the statutory limit of the number of judges and public prosecutors is not increased, more of those who pass the annual judicial examinations will have to choose to practise law. Until now, it has been unusual for young lawyers who pass the national judicial examination to start their careers by practising law; usually they first serve as judges or prosecutors while they are still in their twenties, and start practising law at advanced ages – a complete reversal of the practice in many Western countries. This tradition in Korea is largely a result of money problems; only young law graduates are content with the salaries of judges and prosecutors, which are much lower than income from law practice.

Although all Korean citizens are equal before the law, not all social classes have the same access to the law. The scarcity of lawyers also deprives many people of legal aid. The cost of retaining a lawyer is comparatively high in Korea,[2] but the lack of access to legal aid is not entirely related to money problems. Because there are few lawyers available, their social status and mystique are exaggerated. People with low incomes and little legal knowledge are shy of seeking help from lawyers who seem to belong to a different stratum of society. It is left to the government to develop social welfare programmes aimed at increasing the availability of legal aid.

There has long been a system of state-appointed defence counsel in criminal proceedings. However, the reluctant attitude in the performance as counsel on the part of the appointed lawyers (mainly because of low compensation) has reduced the effect of this system. Recently, nearly a dozen lawyers were subjected to public censure for their failure to appeal for their poor clients because of their indifference to the clients' needs.

In July 1972 a government-authorized legal aid organization was established, the aims of which are to provide equal protection under the law and render legal aid to every underprivileged person who, because of poverty or illiteracy could not obtain adequate legal remedies. The Korean Legal Aid Association (KLAA), comprising officials of the justice ministry, lawyers, law professors and a national assemblyman, has rendered assistance to underprivileged people in 5,253 cases, which involved 1.8 billion won ($3,600,000 U.S.). The KLAA has 42 district and branch offices throughout the nation, providing fairly wide geographical coverage.

A branch office or a district office takes legal aid applications, investigates the matters, provides legal counselling, and supervises the handling of legal aid provided for cases within its jurisdiction. All applications filed with these offices are sent to the Central Legal Aid Committee or the District Legal Aid Committee for consideration.[3]

The central committee consists of seven members and the district committees of five members; they are appointed by the President from among judges, prosecutors, practising attorneys and law professors. The committees approve the application, determine strategy and the applicable criteria for granting legal aid. A district committee has the power to approve applications for legal aid when the amount involved is one million won or less ($2,000 U.S.); this amount has been reported to be raised to 3 million won ($6,000 U.S.) during 1978. The approval of the central committee is required after deliberation by the district committee, where the amount involved is higher than one million won. Applicants who are not approved by the district committee may appeal once to the central committee.. An appeal must be made within 14 days after the service of the notice of refusal of the case from the district committee.

According to the regulations of the Korea Legal Aid Association, persons in one of the following categories are elibible to receive legal aid: (1) a person with no taxable income; (2) a farmer who pays less than 500 won in farm tax; (3) the surviving family of a disabled or deceased former policeman or veteran as defined by the Military Support and Compensation Law; (4) a person unable to obtain legal assistance because of old age or mental or physical disability; (5) a person who has lost his income as a result of flood, drought, fire or any other such disaster; (6) a civil servant whose rank is under fifth grade in the government hierarchy, a noncommissioned officer, or a soldier; (7) an employee or a factory worker whose monthly income is less than 50,000 won ($100 U.S.); (8) a daily labourer; (9) a person who does not own a house; (10) a person other than those listed above who is considered to be unable to take appropriate steps to seek legal assistance by himself, in view of his living standard, his need of legal assistance and other circumstances.

Those who can establish that they fall under one of these categories must file the appropriate forms with either the district office or a branch office. If the client makes an oral application the office fills out the necessary forms for him. The applications are sent to the district committee for consideration.

The district committee, after investigating the application and the economic situation of the client, decides whether to approve the application, the costs of action deemed necessary, and the conditions of the aid.[4] The committee reports its decisions to the director of the district office, who notifies the client.

The district committee may reject the case if it falls under one of the following categories: (1) if the case is considered unworthy of receiving legal aid in consideration of justice and law; (2) if a client fails to prove his need; (3) if the state or an administrative agency will become a defendant; or (4) other cases which are considered inappropriate for legal aid.

While deliberating on the application, the district committee may demand the personal appearance of the client whenever it is deemed necessary to hear his statement and conduct the investigation. The director of the district office, upon receiving the notice of the decision of the committee to grant legal aid, should designate an attorney to handle the case from among the legal aid lawyers who are appointed subject to the approval of the Minister of Justice. After an attorney has been appointed, the director of the district office, the attorney and the client are required to enter into a legal aid contract setting out the cost of the aciton, the legal aid conditions and other matters.[5] The amount of the attorney's fee is determined in accordance with the regulations in lawsuits against the state[6] (March 2, 1968, Order of the Ministry of Justice). The attorney must follow the legal aid provisions set out in the Civil Procedure Law: he must submit copies of the complaint, answer and the interim report to the district office or the branch office; and he must submit a report on the status of the case upon request of the president or director of a district office. He may ask the office for an increase in payment if it becomes necessary. The district committee may cease to render legal aid services upon the recommendation of the appointed attorney; if the client becomes ineligible for legal aid; or if the situation changes and the need for legal aid no longer exists. The appointed attorney may be dismissed by the director of the district office after consultation with the district committee if the attorney is regarded as unsuitable for the job; if he is dismissed, the director of the office withdraws all or part of the money paid to him.

When a case is concluded, the attorney must submit a copy of the judgment or a certified copy of the settlement to the district office immediately; the director of the office then forwards it to the district committee. The district committee then determines the expenses paid on behalf of the client and whether and to what extent the client has to refund them,[7] and reports to the director of the district office. The director notifies the client and the attorney that the client is required to reimburse the committee. Waiver or reduction of the refund may be allowed. The district committee may by motion or *ex officio* allow the client to pay the fee in instalments or waive the fee totally or in part, depending on the client's financial situation, the outcome of the case, if no money is received by the client from the adversary, or if the money received is less than the sum to be refunded. In such a case the district committee obtains the approval of the central committee through the director of the district office and, in cases of waiver, it also requires the approval of the Minister of Justice.

The procedures for legal aid can be summarized as follows: (1) the client files an application for legal aid with a district office; (2) the director of the district office takes up the case with the district committee; (3) the district committee decides whether to grant legal aid: (i) the district committee makes the final decision for cases of one million won or less, (ii) cases of over one million won need the decision of the district committee and also approval by the central committee; (4) the director of a district office appoints an attorney following the decision of the committee; (5) the director of a district office, the attorney and the client enter into a legal aid contract; (6) the attorney carries out the case in accordance with the terms of the contract; (7) when the case is completed, the district committee determines all the fees paid on behalf of the client and notifies the client and the attorney; (8) a client must refund the fee as requested by the district committee; (9) if the circumstances dictate, a waiver of the refund payment may be granted on application of the client by the central committee with the approval of the Minister of Justice.

During the past four years, the KLAA received 6,638 applications for legal aid; 1,385 (20.9 per cent) were rejected. Among the cases which received legal aid, 2,946 (76.8 per cent) were settled out of court, and 891 cases (23.2 per cent) were litigated. 1,101 cases are still pending in the courts. 1,203 cases (24.4 per cent) were tort actions seeking damage awards; 897 cases (18.2 per cent) were actions for wages and retirement grants. The remainder of the cases involved private loans (807, or 16.3 per cent), traffic accidents (667, or 13.5 per cent) and alimony (252, or 5.1 per cent).

Some 63 per cent of the persons visiting the association seeking legal aid had only a primary school education; 35 per cent had completed high school, and only 2 per cent had graduated from college. However, their opponents showed quite different backgrounds: 20 per cent had a college education and 50.7 per cent had graduated high school. Association statistics also revealed that 41.2 per cent of those who sought legal aid were low-income earners, and 16.1 per cent did not own their own homes. 13.9 per cent were wage earners, 12.6 per cent were salaried workers, and 5.5 per cent were farmers.

II. Assessment of the Korean programme

As the statistics show, the legal aid association in Korea has been well used by low-income people over the past four years. However, the criteria for granting legal aid are strict, since the association is short of funds. Thus, the likelihood of an applicant's success in court is an important factor in the decision to grant or refuse legal aid. The applicants must show that they stand a good chance of winning their suit. Obviously, it is not always easy for a client to do so. Compared to Japan and the Western countries, Korea is still at an early stage in the development of an effective legal aid scheme. The KLAA is virtually unknown to many people; clients visit the association only after first wandering into police stations and lawyers' offices.

The barriers to access to justice in Korea are litigation costs, illiteracy (to some extent), complexity in both civil procedure and legal aid procedure, delays in the courts and lack of information about the availability of legal services.

No legal aid programme in Korea has ever been motivated by religious feelings or as a liberal social cause. Mme Lee's programme was started as a voluntary part of her own law practice; the KLAA is a public legal office attached to and run by the prosecution office, supported by the central government. The legal aid programme of the Korean government views legal aid as an individual right of access to the courts. The programme has been patterned after the early stages of its Japanese counterpart in many repects; many of the charitable features and formalistic aspects have been removed, and what remains is a modern programme heavily committed to an essentially juridical approach. This approach is evidenced by the fact that legal aid is statutorily guaranteed by the Korean Code of Civil Procedure, as are other elements concerning procedural fairness; its administration is the responsibility of the Ministry of Justice. The programme is aimed at uniformity and impartiality in the decisions of the district committees on financial eligibility and prospects of success. The basic goal of the programme is to put the poor in the same position as those with means; this goal is reflected in the manner in which the eligibility standards are defined. The system places a great emphasis on the individual responsibilities of the applicant for aid. He must first recognize that he has a legal problem – this is not an easy task for a poor person whose life is closely affected by a tangled skein of welfare state legislation. The Korean programme provides him with almost no assistance in identifying his legal problem.

Because the standards of the programme, the kind of aid it provides, and its administrative structure emphasize uniformity and individual rights and responsibilities, the programme suffers from certain inherent shortcomings. It limits efficiency and impedes any attempt to deal with problems that transcend individual interests and capacities. It is unthinkable at the moment in Korea that the programme will finance test cases to change the law affecting the poor, or further any effort at legislative reform. The Korean programme is based on the traditional approach of individual rights. The prevailing attitude of both the legal profession and the government in Korea seems to be that legal aid is exclusively linked to the traditional right of individual access to the courts. Very few realize or admit that it is also linked to the struggle against poverty and hence to such social rights as the right to an adequate diet, to decent housing, and to medical care. Unlike the Legal Services Program of the U.S. Office of

Economic Opportunity (superseded in 1974 by the National Legal Services Corporation), the Korean programme was not designed as a part of a co-ordinated attack on poverty as a social condition. Both the political establishment of Korea and the legal profession refuse to recognize legal aid as a welfare right. The fact that it was not the bar but the government that initiated the legal aid programme, shows how insensitive the legal profession is to the problems of the poor. The next step of the Korean programme should be to have the organized bar take over the whole scheme and make it possible for the Ministry of Justice to withdraw, so that the Bar Association could fill a role similar to that of the Law Society in England.

The trend towards utilizing public interest lawyers has yet to emerge in Korea. Group legal services, which are required to make a welfare-right approach to legal assistance effective, are rarely demanded. Very few lawyers argue environmental or consumer actions. This perhaps indicates the conservative attitude of the Korean legal profession; and the whole climate seems to be unsuited to producing a crusader.

The goal of the Korean Civil Procedure Law and the legal aid scheme is to secure the just, fair, speedy and inexpensive determination of every action. Korea has yet to take a long time to realize the wider goals that the American legal aid scheme tries to reach.

Notes and References

1. Anybody can apply for the national judicial exam. If successful they have to take two-year course for judicial training, after which they become full-pledged lawyers eligible for the bench or the bar, or the public prosecutor's office.
2. According to the Attorney's Compensation Schedule set up by the two Seoul Bar Associations, which takes effect on July 1, 1978, the initial retaining fee for a civil litigation of $2,000 U.S. is about $300 as a maximum and the same amount for reward for winning the case. Some attorneys, mainly dealing with foreign investors, on average charge $60 U.S. an hour. When you see a doctor for a shot and medicine, their charge ranges $7–10 U.S. A bale of rice (80 kg.), on which Korean people mainly live, costs about $60 U.S.
3. As indicated in the next paragraph, it is the value of the subject matter that makes the jurisdictional difference. If the value of the subject matter of the application exceeds one million won, such application

should be decided by the District Committee, subject to approval of the Central Committee. If the value does not exceed one million won, the district committee has the final authority to determine the fate of the application. Thus the Central Committee must approve the action before the district office can proceed, provided that the amount involved exceeds one million won.

4. The conditions of the aid would be, for instance, which attorney will be selected to help the applicant from among the lawyers on the rolls, or what would be incorporated into the legal aid agreement between the selected attorney and the applicant, or whether such things as an injunction or preliminary attachment are necessary.
5. I refer to matters on how to proceed with the action, or how much authority the legal aid attorney is given; provision that the attorney is not allowed to receive any money or compensation in other form from the client; or provision that false representation in the application on the part of the applicant would constitute a cause for unilateral termination of legal aid by the district office.
6. There is an ordinance regulating lawsuits against the state that exists in the form of an order of the Ministry of Justice.
7. If the client wins the case, the district office collects from the recovery with no interest the legal cost, attorney's retainer, reward for winning the case and other expenses actually spent for the case. If, however, the client loses, no refund is demanded.

SANTIAGO ONATE LABORDE*

Mexico

Unlike Mexican criminal procedure, the evolution of civil procedure during the nineteenth century was quite slow and devoid of any profound transformations. Civil procedure substantially reflected the Spanish system (which was directly related to Central European common procedure)[1] prevailing in Mexico at the time of independence.

Civil procedure in Mexico is still archaic. The judge has a primarily passive role and the parties have active roles concerning the object of the trial. Hence, the procedure is not an effective means of settling social conflicts.

Excessive formalism, a high degree of centralization within the administration of justice, and the existence of a majority class largely subservient to a feudal regime (such as the system of "peonage") bar the poor from the judicial process. Given the political upheavals which shook the country during that period, however, civil law was by no means a priority. Unequal treatment in civil matters was relatively unimportant when compared to the problems that the developing proletariat had been suffering.

The liberal Ponciano Arriaga drafted an enlightened "statement of reasons" for his bill creating the office of "Attorney for the Poor". In the statement Arriaga emphasized how "the most numerous class" of the population suffered continued difficulties and abuse at the hands of the authorities and the upper classes. Such evils arose "from not having been fortunate enough to inherit property or to acquire an education"; on the poor fall "not only the weight and rigor of the laws, but also, and more terribly, the arbitrariness and injustice of many authorities and of many public officials". Arriaga rejected the alternatives of leaving the state directly in charge of protecting these powerless classes or of leaving their

*Translated by José Hernon Rima, Toronto, Canada, 1978.

defence to the philanthropic spirit of the lawyers, whom he described as "robed vultures who feed themselves on money, insensible animals in whose hearts the suffering voice of a poor man finds no echo"; the thought of a judge who assists the weaker party seems utopian as well because, he says, "the ears of some judges can only be pierced by one sound . . . a metallic one". He proposed an original institution – "the Attorney for the Poor", paid by the public treasury, but given complete independence. Unfortunately, this first Mexican attempt to guarantee access to justice[2] failed, and no comparable scheme has yet been implemented.

During the mid-nineteenth century, the most serious obstacles to civil justice were the cost of defence services and of counsel, judicial corruption, an aggregation of problems within the judicial system (which will not be analysed in detail here) and, above all, the material standards of wide segments of the population which remained separated from civil justice.

The 1857 Constitution provided numerous guarantees. It offered a solid base for the operation of an independent judiciary and affirmed the right of access to justice clearly and explicitly.[3]

However, political disturbances during this period seriously affected the administration of justice. The situation worsened after 1876; under the regime of Porfirio Diaz the judiciary lost its dignity when confronted by the power of the executive and became a simple instrument of the latter.

At the beginning of the twentieth century there arose revolutionary ideas which would crystallize in the years between 1910 to 1917. During this time, civil trials were blatantly repressive.[4] Collective agreements were considered to be mere contracts of *do ut facias*, and their interpretation and enforcement were left to the civil courts which, together with the penal tribunals in charge of punishing strikes and workers' associations, clashed violently with the rising workers. At the same time, growing industrialization generated serious housing problems; the scarcity of living quarters produced abuses by landlords, who were supported by the judiciary. The reaction of the oppressed classes was not directed towards obtaining substantive or procedural legal reforms, but rather towards a violent transformation of the social order through a revolutionary movement. The law, in general, and civil trials in particular, were undoubtedly contributing factors to the revolution.

Between 1821 (when the War of Independence ended almost three centuries of Spanish domination) and 1917 (when the Revolution triumphed) there were several laws passed relating to civil litigation.

When the revolution began, civil litigation was regulated by the Code promulgated in 1884. An "oral" procedure was available for the settlement of small claims: its efficacy was diminished by the fact that the parties controlled the course of the proceeding and by the discretionary powers of the judge.[5]

At the dawn of the revolution, the capitalist perspective of the dictatorial regime of Porfirio Diaz had transformed the 1857 Constitution and the spirit of the reform into a dead letter. The free access to justice, defended by Zarco in the constituent assembly, and the abolition of the feudal tenures obtained with the reform were but vain illusions by 1903.

The peasantry and the proletariat were outside the ambit of the administration of justice according to Flores Magon, outstanding representative of the working masses, "obscure within the society, but shining in the epics of a nation."[6] Popular discontent with deficient administration of justice was among the causes leading the people to fight the dictatorship. Carranza recognized this in his address to the Constituent Assembly of 1917.[7]

The Constitution Assembly of 1915-17, following the guidelines of the Constitution of 1857, included access to justice among its guarantees. The preliminary debates record the unanimous approval given to Article 17 as well as diatribes against the concept of civil litigation.[8]

The criticisms of the civil justice system voiced during this Assembly were substantially the same as those made in 1857. Lawyers were mere collectors for the rich households and severe regulation of the profession was demanded; there were some who argued that justice must be dispensed by lawyers, and that lay judges should be appointed. Neither of these suggestions was adopted. When worker representatives tried to create a new regulatory labour relations scheme, they mounted an attack against the class character of the civil litigation system and its inability to solve labour-management conflicts. Workers maintained that courts were ineffective in settling labour disputes becuase they did not seek to reconcile opposing interests in a conflict, but only applied laws drafted by jurists of whom the workers were tired because of their work against public liberties. Employers, said H. Victoria, were very skilled because they had lawyers running their businesses, they had the priests who counsel the workers to accept their fate and do their duty, they had the bureaucrats, and finally, they had the legal functionaries who traffic in the misery of the people.

Eventually, this conflict resulted in the creation of Boards of Conciliation and Arbitration which were given exclusive jurisdiction to investigate labour-management disputes; specialization was abandoned for the sake of social justice. The Boards are tripartite tribunals composed of employers, employees and government representatives.[9]

Thus, the Constituent Assembly of 1916-17 tried to provide easier access to justice for the working classes in the area of labour relations. Civil justice, on the other hand, remained almost unchanged, burdened with the defects which had existed since colonial days. For the Assembly, civil litigation had no political dimension, and it was not considered necessary to deal with the matter at the constitutional level.

It might have been expected that, after the revolution, civil laws and procedures would have changed. However, new procedural forms were not enacted until the 1930s in conjunction with the consolidation of the new regime, which gave Mexico the character of a modern legal state, and with it the codification of the substantive civil law.[10]

From 1917 on, there was a general tendency to "depoliticize" the judiciary, leaving the most blatantly political aspects of the process in the hands of the executive or in those of the rising bourgeoisie. These tendencies, particularly that connected with the executive power, have persisted to the present time.

Contemporary civil litigation has evolved with discouraging slowness particularly guarantees of access to justice. Little attention has been given to this problem by legislators or by judges.

In 1940, it was proposed to establish a mechanism which insured, within the local ambit, access to civil justice for economically deprived people. A public defender model was adopted,[11] but within highly bureaucratized parameters.[12]

The concept of "orality" was another attempt to insure better access to justice for the less privileged; and to simplify litigation. "Orality" in Mexico, despite recent reforms,[13] continues to be an idea far removed from reality. Litigation continues to be perceived by the working classes, and by wide sections of the middle class, as an "alienating"[14] experience.

The office of "justice of the peace," established for the settlement of small claims, operated within the parameters inherited from Spanish legislation; today, however, it has been transformed (as will be shown) into a debt-collection mechanism, or an enforcer for slum landlords.

Before going into a more detailed analysis of contemporary access to justice, it is important to note that the evolution of civil procedure in Mexico does not give evidence of a great deal of interest in guaranteeing the prompt and efficient settlement of litigation involving the underprivileged. The Constituent Assembly of 1917, which deprived the civil judges of jurisdiction in labour matters, but that did not solve the general problem of the underprivileged, nor did it modify the structure of civil litigation. Only during the last decade has the emergence in Mexico of the typical problems of a capitalist society brought about the development of a mechanism for dispute settlement. This development, as will be shown later, tends to remove certain kinds of dispute resolution from the judicial domain – for example, areas such as consumer's rights and the environment.

Access to justice in contemporary Mexico: positive legislation

At the present time, Article 17 of the Political Constitution of the United States of Mexico (February 5, 1917) establishes the basic guidelines for access to justice.

Article 17 states that:

> Nobody can be imprisoned for debts of a purely civil character. No person can avail himself of self-help to do justice or can use violence to maintain his rights. Courts should administer justice within the time periods and the terms prescribed by law; their services will be free: therefore court costs are forbidden.

With the exception of the first sentence,[15] the section contains the essential elements of the constitutional structure of the right to legal protection.

The Constitution reserves coercive powers for the state, thus withdrawing them from private hands.[16] This prohibition resulted from the fact that in 1916 (as in 1856) the landowners were "owners of land and masters of men", serving as judges in all litigation in which they became involved. Once self-help is excluded as a means of settling disputes, the state has the duty to resolve litigation through the legal system. This governmental duty is related to the prescription in Article 14 of the very same Constitution, to the effect that only through a trial conducted in front of previously established tribunals may an individual be deprived of his life, liberty, property, possessions or rights.

I have previously examined how both guarantees delineate a right to the legal system, while simultaneously establishing an objective limit to the ambit of all types of powers and authorities. In one aspect, the possibility of settling disputes through the intervention of state organs is guaranteed; in another aspect, the interested party is assured of the possibility of bringing an action in these organs with the purpose of settling a dispute through procedure, and in accordance with rules set out by that very same procedure.

The Constituent Assembly of 1916-17 also attempted to establish that justice would be administered "within the time periods and the terms prescribed by law", and that it should be "free". The first phrase constitutes, literally, a directive to the legislative power to enact procedural legislation in such a way as to avoid the unnecessary prolongation of trials. Hence, a duty is imposed upon the individual legislator, that, if not complied with, may theoretically generate an unconstitutional defect. Regrettably, this precept has not been followed to the letter by the legislative power nor has it been developed juridically.

Concerning the gratuitous nature of justice and the prohibition of court costs, it should be noted that such a rule (as expounded in the debates on the 1856-57 Constituent Assembly which generated it), tends to forbid the parties from paying judicial employees directly[17] thus dispensing with an almost absolute barrier to the economically underprivileged sectors. Hence, this gratuitousness constitutes a civil guarantee, as it leaves the total cost of judicial administration to the public treasury. A direct consequence of it is the absence in our system of tariffs, stamped paper, etc.[18]

The Constitution does not provide, however, that the parties should not incur any disbursements due to the judicial settlement of disputes. Disbursements are classified under two heads: court costs and client costs. Court costs are the amounts directed by the judge to be paid by one of the parties, to discourage unnecessary or frivolous actions and to reimburse those who have had to litigate in order to exercise their rights. Client costs are the amounts contributed by each of the parties in order to be able to participate in the trial, which include the professional fees of lawyers, expert witnesses, etc.[19]

The Constitution of 1917 affirms the right of "access to justice" in wide enough terms so as to allow its development to reach the point of socialization of litigation. There is no assured access to justice *tout court*, but to the judicial guarantees enjoyed by the courts. Most important, the Constituent Assembly recognized the need to design low-cost, expeditious and accessible litigation for the majority of the people of the country.[20] But this constitutional directive has not been followed. Procedural lawmakers have not complied with the duties assigned to them by the Assembly, particularly in the area of civil litigation.

The codification of civil procedure produced during the 1930s[21] is closer to the nineteenth-century concept of the process as a private matter between the parties, than it is to the possibilities for socialization of litigation opened by the Constituent Assembly. It must be recognized that the constitutional guarantee is merely an ideal.

In the 1932 Code of Civil Procedure of the Federal District, access to justice *per se* was scarcely considered. The nucleus of the procedural system is "the cause of action" regulated according to substantive criteria of Roman origin. The opening section of the Code states that the exercise of the "action" requires the existence of a right, the violation of a right, the repudiation of an obligation, or the need to declare, preserve or constitute a right, the capacity of the acting party and the interest to plead it. Already in 1930, however, the Supreme Court of Mexico, inspired by the doctrine of A. Rocco, had accepted the validity of the abstract theories; even today the process is seen as a mechanism for adjudication rather than as a means of dispute settlement.[22]

Procedural simplicity is essential if citizens from all social strata are to be afforded equal access to justice. Mexican civil litigation procedure, because it was conceived from an individual litigant's perspective (satisfaction of the claims of the parties above any other consideration), is far from simple. It continues to operate with marked formalism and within a highly bureaucratic structure which provides little help for the common man to understand and to participate in the judicial process without profound disorientation.

With the exception of actions before the justice of the peace (which will be referred to later), regular civil litigation is a legal process, that is, one whose judgments are totally based on the norms of codified law. This situation, combined with the principle of *ignorantia juris non excusat*[23] and with the complexities of substantive law, results in representation at trial by professional lawyers paid by the parties, thus creating a situation in which the rich and the poor have unequal access to justice. This is no obstacle to the simultaneous existence, in theory, of the principle of "freedom of self-defence".[24]

In order to attain a procedural equalization, regardless of the parties social or economic disparities, the classical solution, following the model of the Austrian *Zivilprozessordnungen*, is to give the judge wide procedural and directive powers through which at least "end-process" equality is assured. To that end, the Mexican legislation offers what has been properly characterized by Alcala Zamora as an apparent paradox:[25] our Code, faithful to the liberalism it champions, lacks any chapter or section dealing specifically with the judge and his powers; it does, however, contain a great deal of references to the powers of the judge throughout. These references are more of a quantitative than qualitative nature, because they are combined with clearly dispositive provisions[26] and with several hypotheses in which the agreement obtained between the parties determines the outcome of the process.[27] The District Civil Code of 1928, where the socializing tendency was more evident and had a greater effect than in the procedural law,[28] foresees the possibility that the judge, "taking into account the apparent intellectual backwardness of some individuals, their lack of contact with means of communication or their miserable economic situation, will be able, if the Ministry approves, to exempt them from the sanctions incurred in the violation of a law which they ignored, or if possible, to give them a term in which to comply, insofar as the law does not directly affect the public interest".

Another device which can be used to guarantee procedural equality is the regulation of court costs. An order to pay costs can be decreed, according to the District Code, when and in the opinion of the judge, recklessness or bad faith are present or when such an order is prescribed by law. Thus, good faith between the parties rather than egalitarianism is being protected. Moreover, the judge has no power to fix the amount of costs: this is left to the party in whose favour costs have been declared. Thus, although the objective or *chiovendian* system of costs, as practised at the Federal level, has not been adopted, there is no real possibility of using costs as an equalizing factor (as occurs in the system of contingent fees) or even as a deterrent to excessive litigation. Moreover, the regulation of this area is very deficient and gives rise to numerous disputes related to the execution of orders to pay costs. If it is considered that costs are generally anticipated by the party originating the dispute, a late or complex execution may negate the effects of the indemnity or compensation.

The desire of the legislature to realize the ideal of constitutionally guaranteed free access is evidenced in the structure of the court, of the justice of the peace. The procedure follows, generally, the Latin tradition of providing a simplified way to settle small claims. The Code has given this procedure characteristics of orality, quickness and immediacy. The judge must encourage the parties to settle amicably, and, if his admonition is not heeded, sentence will be based upon the known truth, without need to follow rules concerning the weighing of evidence, but in accordance with the judge's conscience. In cases involving very small amounts it is necessary that justice be made accessible to people with limited economic resources;[29] but, it must be remembered that a good legislative technique alone (such as that of the Mexican Code) is not sufficient; the men charged with the administration of justice must also abide by the norm.

Another institution intended to provide access to justice to the economically underprivileged is the public defender's office. It was created a few years after the enactment of the Code, but its organization and practices have prevented the achievement of this goal. The public defender's office is a bureaucratic organization which has never been consistently structured. The assignment of lawyers is made through administrative appointment rather than through competition, thus removing the guarantee of good counsel. Low salaries encourage the practice of some defenders of charging fees to their clients, in spite of the fact that the service is supposed to be free.

The selection criteria for entitlement to the services of a public defender are entirely discretionary. The statutes set income limits, and the criterion of *fumus boni iuris* reigns in practice.[30]

From the end of the 1940s, theoreticians had been concerned with the defects of civil litigation,[31] but the legislature was not. Important reforms were not enacted until more than thirty years after the Code first went into effect[32] and it was not until the 1960s when the problem of access to justice became more relevant, that a constitent attempt at judicial and procedural reform was made so as to achieve "prompt and expeditious justice".[33] But these incomplete reforms have accomplished little change and have not provided integrated solutions to such problems as costs and delays.

The first important procedural reform at the district level was effected in 1966. It was directed, in a lukewarm fashion, towards shortening the length of trials. A defendant's replies and rejoinders in writing were abolished; they were examples of the most absurd formalism, which, besides being repetitious, complicated procedures without offering any advantage. The reform also improved the regulation of the length of procedures and increased the amount of procedural fines. To reinforce the protection of the weak, the new law made mandatory the participation of the Public Ministry in issues referring to family matters.

Unsatisfied with partial reforms resulting from the modifications of the Civil Code and the judiciary, the Legislature attempted a comprehensive reform of civil litigation in March 1973. In the statement of reasons given by the Chief of the Executive to the Senate in the last months of 1972 he stated that "it is sought to substantially transform the actual systems to dispense justice with a sense of celerity and precision" so as to achieve "a judicial system based in clear and expeditious proceedings, so as to make possible the fast and objective application of positive law, which Mexican society has been demanding". In order to do that, "an essentially oral procedure" was proposed as a model for ordinary trials, in which the submission of evidence would be limited to one hearing. The chapter relating to appeals was modified in order to make procedures less complicated, and some rules related to executory process and foreclosures disappeared. Finally, a heading relating to family disputes was added "on the basis that all problems related to the family are of public order".[34]

The reform bill was widely discussed in legal circles and there was some opposition to the rather timid attempt at "orality" which was advanced; the Legislature accepted some critics' suggestions and left the bill substantially unchanged, despite some inconsistencies.

Despite the policy declarations contained in the statement of reasons and the approval of the bill, the reform has not resulted in the radical, effective changes which were expected. In the text of section 55 of the new Procedural Code, power was given to the judges to exhort the parties to "voluntarily arrive at a settlement". Since this was a licence, rather than a duty, imposed on the judge, its use is discretionary so it cannot be said that there is now a conciliatory procedural phase such as exists in labour matters, for example. This deterrent to excessive litigation which supposedly culminates in a mechanism which expedites the satisfaction of grievances and the settlement of disputes, without the dimunition of justice has had nominal impact due to the lack of judicial mediation.

The oral system proposed by the Legislature faces an almost insurmountable obstacle in section 87 of the same Code, according to which "sentences must be given within an eight-day period from the date of notice that the court is ready to give sentence." That is, sentences are not pronounced in the hearing (paradoxically named "evidence, pleadings and sentencing") thus slowing down the process by breaking the continuity between discussion and decision which characterized the oral system. According to the rules existing prior to the 1973 reform, sentencing occurred in the same hearing, or at least the decision on the litigation subject to further amplification; hence, it can be said that, far from being innovative, section 87 was a partial retreat.

Family disputes have been treated differently from other civil litigation. The reform movement of family procedure began in 1966 and culminated in the judicial reform of February 24, 1971, in which family courts were created, and in the reform of the Code of Procedure in 1973, when specific procedures for the settlement of family disputes were introduced.

The new procedure has a marked public orientation in which the judge plays a more active role. Among the important provisions are those which allow the judge to intervene officially in matters affecting the family

(s. 941), the parties to appear personally (s. 943), the absence of formalities, the wide role given to the participation of legal counsellors and experts, and pronouncement of sentence at the same hearing where evidence is given and arguments are made (s. 949).

The regulation of family disputes, and the small claims procedures are the most advanced areas of the district code of civil procedure; there is no doubt that this is the correct model to follow, providing that some technical shortcomings existing in both areas can be avoided.

The major faults of Mexican civil litigation are that the system is continually plagued by a lack of judges and of judicial personnel; the deficiency of the system of judicial appointements; that judgeship is not a career; and the low salaries of judges and their subordinates.

Despite all this, the last decade has witnessed several reforms of the judicial organization of the districts. First, the new Organic Law of the Courts of common jurisdiction was prolcaimed in 1968. This reorganizational law cannot be considered anything but a copy of the preceding statute; with reason, it has been described by Alcala-Zamora a Castillo as a model of how not to legislate. Important changes to the law of 1968 were made in 1971, when the family courts were created, and in 1975, when a territorial integration of the Federal District into one judicial district was effected. The 1975 reform also increased the jurisdiction of the justices of the peace to amounts up to five thousand pesos (the previous limit was one thousand), and established at least one justice of the peace on each one of the political divisions of the Federal District in an attempt to at least make justice geographically accessible to the masses.

Two further legislative acts also modified access to justice during the 1960s, even though only one of them has a direct influence upon civil litigation. The first was the creation, in 1971, of the Court of Administrative Law of the Federal District, to provide the citizens of the capital of the Republic a quick and efficient method of solving disputes between themselves and the local administration.[35] This tribunal has been characterized by its speed and the simplicity of its processes, and has provided easy access for the common citizen, thus protecting him from abuses of the administrative authorities.

The second innovation is the controversial Federal Law of Consumer Protection of December 18, 1975. The consumer's problems are approached as a unique sector of commercial law, one with a "public and social" character. Several of the regulations modify the contractual rules of the Civil Code, of 1928, and introduce the notion of the "consumer" to the Mexican judicial system.[36] The law establishes the Federal Consumer

Agency, a decentralized body of social service, with powers of enforcement, legal status and autonomous budget, to protect and promote the rights and interests of the consumer (s. 57).

The prerogatives granted to the Agency are numerous. The Agency is given powers to "represent consumers before competent authorities, when in the opinion of the Agency" ". . . the problem would affect collective interests" (s. 59, iii); secondly, it can "represent the interests of consumers before any type of administrative authority, by launching actions, motions or procedures to protect consumers' interests" (s. 59, i); Thirdly, it may "denounce" monopolistic practices and price, quality and other produce violations (s. 59, vi and vii); and finally, it should, as a conciliatory vehicle, "settle the differences between producers and consumers, serving as a friendly mediator", and in complaints against merchants, industrialists, providers of services, governmental agencies, decentralized agencies and other state institutions, it should serve as an arbitrator (s. 59, viii).

The Agency is given powers as complainant in front of the administrative organs of civil justice as well as of administrative tribunals. S. 59 (iii) introduces a new concept into Mexican civil procedure. Prior to 1976 the representation of the public interest in civil litigation was generally assigned to the Public Ministry, a body technically incompetent to carry out such functions. This new concept closely resembles the "konsumentombudsman" created in Sweden in 1970.

The Mexican legislature's decision to create the agency resulted from a clear political choice. Intervention in civil procedures involving consumers had been minimal.[37] due to the inherent difficulties with the process. To provide out-of-court solutions, and to insure that legitimate individual rights were not systematically violated by producers and merchants, the state decided to create an administrative body as the representative of the "under-privileged". The solution represents a break with the classic liberal scheme where the state plays a neutral role in commercial activities which are ruled by the principles of free competition and freedom of contract. This approach, giving standing to individuals, either in isolation or in *ad hoc* associations has not prospered because of the nonexistence of independent consumer organizations[38] and the limited development of a public interest law.

Although the Federal Consumer Agency was given the opportunity to intervene directly in the civil process, this has not happened during 1976-77.[39] Its mediation role has been substantial. During 1976-77, the Agency settled 60,000 cases (valued at one billion pesos), or half the number of all civil litigation cases dealt with by the trial courts in 1972 (the last year for which statistics are available).

The conciliation procedure followed by the Agency is very simple and is based on orality and speed. The conciliation agreements can be simply executed by ordinary jurisdiction and there is a limited right of appeal. The Agency has been an effective arbitrator (s. 59, viii, *in fine*), in respect of disputes between citizens and public services such as the electricity and telephone services. Rarely do parties decide to take their dispute with these public authorities to the ordinary tribunals.

Access to justice in contemporary Mexico: socio-legal approach

From colonial times in Mexico, judicial rules have been accepted but not obeyed. The 1957 Constitutional guarantees of access to civil justice were never implemented. It is of little significance to discuss the various legislative attempts to provide access to justice, unless a parallel investigation is undertaken to ascertain the impact of these measures. To that end, I have designed and conducted three opinion surveys; and have relied on judicial statistics as far as possible.[40]

Two major areas are examined: the legal assistance available to poor people, and the workings of the justices of the peace. This inquiry is limited to the district level.

The Federal District, where the capital of the Republic is located, is the main political centre; the district contains more than 18 per cent of the country's population, and many industrial, financial, commercial and bureaucratic activites are concentrated there. Most civil litigation takes place in the Federal District.

There are a total of 102 trial judges with jurisdiction on civil matters *latu sensu*,[41] a ratio of approximately 90,000 people per judge.[42] A little more than 100,000 civil matters per year are initiated at the trial level, which does not represent a very high index of litigation.

Following the model applied by Zander in his study of British justice, it is useful to examine the kinds of civil litigation dealt with by the competent tribunals.[43] Judicial statistics reveal that of the civil litigation concluded at trial, 59 per cent of the cases are of a litigious nature, 25 per cent belong to "voluntary jurisdiction" and the remainder are inheritance, succession and bankruptcy trials included under the "other" headings.

Of those cases dealing with litigation *per se*, 72 per cent are debtor-creditor actions, usually involving consumer credit instruments. Five per cent are related to dispossession and eviction, 4 per cent involve contractual disputes, and 2 per cent are actions for possession and replevin.

Prior to the introduction of family courts, the civil trial courts dealt with divorces and other family disputes. These matters comprised 7 per cent of all litigious matters resolved at trial by the civil courts. The creation of twenty-three family courts has been accompanied by a considerable increase in the number of cases. This increase does not necessarily represent an increase in litigation but rather demonstrates the existence of a problem of access to justice which is only now being met. As well, the less formal proceedings of the new family courts have led to a great reduction in the length of actions.[44]

These statistics made it easy to appreciate how the courts' function of protecting rights means, in reality, enforcing debts or proprietary obligations. Statistics for 1972 reveal that 97 per cent of these cases dealt with amounts exceeding one thousand pesos;[45] 60 per cent were resolved at trials lasting less than one year; 2.5 per cent of the trials lasted less than one month, 8 per cent of the trials continued for more than two years. It is interesting that almost 39 per cent have been concluded in other than the normal manner, that is, by judgment, so that the duration increases considerably when only the cases in which the judge has settled the litigation are considered. The length of trials, when compared with that of countries such as Austria or Germany is alarming.

Forty-five per cent of the national total of actions for eviction were originated in the Federal District; of these 88 per cent of the trials lasted less than a year, and only 12 per cent lasted longer than a year. On the average, these actions are the shortest. In eviction cases, where there is generally a class conflict, 60 per cent were terminated by judgment. The statistics of the district did not record one instance in which the court had found for the defendant.

Who goes to court? In my survey of 250 people with income below five thousand pesos per month (equivalent to $227 U.S.), only 2 per cent had initiated civil actions during the preceding year; all these actions involved family matters, usually divorce. Six per cent had been defendants, usually in eviction actions. If the data are measured against the index of civil litigation in the Federal District (11.2 per thousand inhabitants), it seems that poor people are plaintiffs in a percentage close to the mean, but appear as defendants on a scale quite above the mean.[46] The survey revealed that 37 per cent of the people interviewed had had no involvement with the courts during 1976; of those who did have a legal problem, 41 per cent of their cases related to labour relations, 32 per cent were criminal actions and only 22 per cent were civil actions.

Thirty-six per cent of these civil conflicts were brought to court, while the remainder were settled extra-judicially. Of that 36 per cent, only 40 per cent of the parties used the services of a lawyer; of those who did not, 12 per cent said that the legal profession inspired mistrust, and 43 per cent said they had no money to pay the fees. Of those who were represented by a lawyer at trial, 14 per cent said that his services were useless; 78 per cent felt that the fees payable were not reasonable. None of those who had had no legal assistance won his case.[47] Thus, where the poor are involved, the majority of their disputes do not reach court.

In those cases in which the people concerned did not resort to legal action, cases of "unmet need for justice", several tendencies appear. High costs of litigation deter people from using the courts. In Mexico there is a formal fee scale,[48] which has little application in reality. According to s. 223 of the Organic Law of Tribunals of the jurisdiction of the district, the scale is a supplementary source; fees are determined by mutual agreement between the client and the lawyer (s. 2606 and subsequent of the Civil Code); also, the fees set out in the Code are outdated. Interviews with fifty lawyers revealed that none of them had applied the tariff; they said that they considered the amount in litigation, the difficulty of the case, and the social level of the client when setting their fees. Seventy per cent of the lawyers surveyed said that they did not customarily take cases involving amounts under ten thousand pesos ($454), except for regular clients, or unless the client consented to pay the lawyer a high percentage (about 35 per cent) of the proceeds of the case. This seems to confirm the general hypothesis that the proportionate cost of justice varies inversely to the amount in litigation, thus further limiting access to justice for poor people.

Many people interviewed said that they did not use lawyers because they did not trust them. In a recent study, it was observed that over 75 per cent of the Mexican urban poor believe there is only justice for the rich and very few considered that judges could dispense justice.

In the preceding section we mentioned that one of the techniques used by the Legislature to guarantee access to justice for economically weak is the public defender. The majority of poor people are ignorant of this institution, or think that it only operates in criminal cases.[49] To illustrate its lack of effectiveness, it is enough to state that in 1972, there were fourteen civil public defenders for a population of almost eight million.

Beginning in June of 1973, the authorities of the Department for the Federal District initiated an assistance programme to alleviate the problem of access to justice for the underprivileged. Instead of attempting to reform the Office of the Public Defender, free legal offices were created, located in each of the administrative subdivisions of the Federal District. There are sixteen of these offices functioning today as part of the programme for restructuring social services.

These free legal offices are co-ordinated through a central headquarters which serves as liaison between each office and the authorities of the Department for the Federal District. There is a consultant in each office responsible for its performance. Each office uses a variable number of law students who have completed more than two-thirds of their professional studies; these students act as legal counsellors and consultants for one year, working four hours a day. The students receive no salary and cannot accept any fees.

The counsellors in the legal offices have three functions: they give legal advice, they defend at trial and they serve as mediators. At the end of three years of service they had given assistance in 46,611 instances – 26,678 consultations, 5,090 mediations and 14,843 judicial appearances. Almost 80 per cent of the cases were civil actions.

I interviewed several persons who had been assisted by the free legal offices, and received very favourable opinions. The trust that the offices have earned is manifested in the increasing number of people who go to them asking the staff to serve as mediators or friendly arbiters. The office consultants feel that this reaction is due to the traditional slowness and harshness of the court system and the lack of trust in judges.

The structure and function of the office of the justice of the peace should also be analysed. In order to understand its processes, I undertook a detailed examination of the activities of four of the thirty-six tribunals operating in the Federal District; I interviewed judges and secretaries in the civil division.

Far from being authentic tribunals for poor people, the courts of the peace function largely as collection agencies and enforcers of eviction actions. Although all the judges interviewed said that they preferred to deal personally with the parties rather than with their lawyers, they acknowledged that a lawyer was present in almost 80 per cent of the cases. They pointed out that lawyers were an obstacle to the judges' obligation to attempt to effect a conciliation between the parties; they also said that in most cases dealing with housing problems the landlord is accompanied by a lawyer, while the tenant undertakes his own representation; this generates a *de facto* inequality which the judges find hard to eliminate.

Orality works fairly well in the courts of the justices of the peace. In the courts examined, 60 per cent of the cases were concluded in under two months (nearly 70 per cent of those through conciliation), 20 per cent in between three and five months, and only 5 per cent in over one year. Often it is impossible to pronounce judgment in the same hearing ususally because a large amount of documentary evidence is presented.

The judges seldom base their judgments on "equity" (although they have a statutory right to do so). The judges interviewed declared that they understood that power to mean the possibility of tempering the rigours of the civil code.

In the survey of low income citizens it was found that, among those people who had been exposed to both the ordinary courts and the justices of the peace, 76 per cent preferred the latter, while only 2 per cent preferred the ordinary courts.

Summary

In this brief survey I have reviewed the legislative structure of access to justice, and investigated the social aspects of the issue. The concept of access to justice for the underprivileged is a recent creation within the science of judicial process, but its enshrinement at the political level nevertheless has a long tradition in Mexico. However, the goals have been reduced to projected norms that the Legislature has failed to develop and that the judiciary has not wanted or has not been able to expand.

The judicial process resembles, at least theoretically, the settlement of social conflicts. In civil litigation, there are three different interests: the private interests of the litigants themselves who seek to protect their rights through the judicial mechanism; the public interest which requires a guarantee of objective justice as well as the settlement of litigation through the exercise of the powers of the state; and the political or social interest, derived from the ideology of the state which the administration of justice in general and the judicial process in particular, possess. Historically, each of these interests has been served differently by the judicial process. It is clear, on the one hand that the greater or lesser weight exerted by these interests on the structure and performance of the process ultimately depend on the way in which social relations are articulated at a specific time and place. The structure of Mexican civil procedure remained static for almost 100 years while the country experienced profound social and economic changes. There was little development in the area of access to justice by the underprivileged. The barriers to justice which were criticized in 1857, in the revolutionary period, were attacked again in

1917; nevertheless, they still exist today. The evolution of this sector of the Mexican legal system has been minimal. Generally speaking, civil litigation continues to be directed towards the satisfaction of the private interests of the parties and is structured around a principle of disposition (*Dispositionsmaxime*), with the purpose of allowing wide participation by the parties in the resoltuion of the case (*Verhandlungsmaxime*). This results in an organic whole in which, for the sake of formal equality and neutrality or passivity on the judge's part, the unequal conditions prevailing in the social structure are left unchanged, very often with detriment to the very purpose of objective law.

Also relevant is the fact that civil litigation has concerned itself with the same kinds of disputes for decades, despite the social and economic evolution which has produced a greater number of new types of disputes. These new types of conflict arising from economic development have not been resolved through civil litigation. In Mexico, as in many other capitalist countries, a relatively smaller number of the major problems of modern society are coming before the law courts.

Problems such as the unjust enrichment of commercial entities at the expense of consumers are practically impossible to litigate; the small amount of damages *uti singulus*, coupled with the slowness and costs of the process generate what Novoa has labelled the civilly defenceless consumers.

Litigation also arises from the lack of planned industrialization and the urban sprawl which characterize contemporary Mexican society (creating grave problems for the environment and in patterns of land tenure), which cannot be solved through the ordinary civil trial. On the contrary, legislation[50] and practice are generating settlement processes that are not litigation oriented.

Thus, Mexican law shows a clear tendency to limit the types of litigation amenable to settlement through civil trials. The revolution took away the jurisdiction of the courts over labour-management disputes and over all kinds of agrarian matters; subsequently, it has been necessary to create a specific process to deal with the settlement of family disputes, as well as to establish an administrative body in charge of protecting consumer rights; problems related to environmental control are also dealt with by administrative action.

All this seems to indicate that, little by little, civil litigation is losing its importance and its functions are being reduced. The system has become a bastion of liberal capitalism, where all social relations are looked at under the prism of contract or liberty, as if the conditions that precipitated the birth of the Napoleonic Code, if not the Justinian Code, had indeed remained unchanged. In my opinion, there are two causes of this profound disconnection between society and civil procedure. First, there are the external factors; secondly, there are a number of structural elements which help to consolidate the problem.

It is important to observe, when considering the external factors, that civil litigation has never been and is not now a priority in Mexico. At the political level, the main issues are not related to civil litigation; if there is talk about problems with the administration of justice, it is directed to the workings of the Supreme Court, to criminal justice, or to the agrarian and labour relations processes. The disfunctions of the civil courts rarely trigger a political controversy; the administration of civil justice is not a high-priority issue.[51] This situation results from the training of the members of the judiciary as well as the ineffectiveness of judicial guarnatees, which subordinate the judicial power to the dictates of the Executive or to the economic power of the litigants.

Internal structural factors which permit the disconnection between civil justice and the society at large include the lack of social remedies within the Mexican civil process. Due to the very narrow limits on the area of legal standing, and to the rigidity of the principles belonging to the *ultra partes* application of judicial decisions, it has been impossible to include such remedies as the class action of Anglo-Saxon law. In addition, the participation of lawyers is an obstacle to settlement and leads to a trial process where authentic social solutions are subordinated.

We have already mentioned that the civil process is not amenable to solving the problems of the masses; it is equally true that even the typical objective of protection of individual rights is not served by contemporary Mexican civil justice, due to the costs and delays of the system. The civil process is not an effective mechanism for settlement of the typical disputes of modern society; as a result, we are left with "solutions" such as a return to self-help remedies, or with situations which find litigants either helpless or forced to deal with arbitration and settlement schemes which have fewer state controls than does the judicial process.

Which groups are most seriously affected by the system's shortcomings? These may vary, depending on whether we consider their socio-economic status or the kind of dispute to be resolved. The non-Spanish speaking Indians (2.5 per cent of Mexico's population) and illiterate Mexicans (23.7 per cent) are considered to be "underprivileged". Both groups, for economic and cultural reasons, are alienated from a formal, written civil justice system.[52] The low income, working-class citizen cannot use the civil process effectively; nor can individuals seeking protection in situations involving small amounts of money. Most of these inequalities are of economic origin, with the possible exception of the Indian communities where cultural values seem to be an important factor. For the most part, however, access to justice is definitely a class problem.[53]

The Mexican legal profession (unlike that in Great Britain, for instance) has been unwilling to attempt new methods allowing for a greater scope to the activities of civil litigation, in order to fill the needs of the underprivileged.[54] It seems that the lawyers and their traditional clients (commercial firms, banking institutions, construction companies, landlords and the wealthy) find the present situation quite convenient. Also, there have been very few attempts at the doctrinal level to find solutions to the problem of access to justice.

Perhaps the moment has arrived to demand from the doctrine, and from the legislature, what was asked by Euripides from the rulers: "Give us not subtleties, but what the city wants."

Notes and References

1. The principal source of Mexican procedure during the nineteenth century is Spanish law.
2. During the operation of the Spanish laws as well as of legislation exclusively dealing with the Indians, there were numerous norms and institutions which tried to guarantee fair justice to the Indians. Among them, the most important is the appointment of special attorneys and prosecutors to defend Indian interests.
3. The Constitution of 1857 dealt in greater depth than that of 1917 with problems such as access to justice, and in general with the guarantees which should be given to the judiciary.
4. Repressive in the sense that whenever there was a conflict between classes on a litigation, courts tended to favour those economically or politically powerful. This was especially clear in labour matters.
5. Within the code of civil procedure of 1848, three procedures are regulated: ordinary trials, summary trials (which include labour disputes) and verbal trials. In all three types there is the presence of formalism and the dispositive power of the parties over both the object of the dispute and the proceedings.
6. R. Flores Magon, "La Constitucion ha muerto" in *El dijo del Ahuizote* of February 8, 1903.

7. In his Inaugural Address in which his project for a constitution was presented, Carraza said: "there would assuredly be, not surprise, but amazement, even for those souls not too worried or insensitive to human suffering, if they were to know all the absues that the judicial authorities could not or did not want to stop", V. Carranza, "Declaratoria" in *Diario de los Debates del Congreso Constituyente*, Queretaro, December 1, 1916, Vol. I, No. 13, pp. 260ff.
8. In reviewing the Debate Record we have been unable to find any favourable comment concerning the system of civil litigation; the attitude of some judges is approved, but the system itself only deserved the most bitter condemnations.
9. This situation is obtained thanks to the eminently oral, informal and equitable character of labour justice.
10. Effected in 1928.
11. Regulation of May 7, 1940. There exists today, in matters of federal civil litigation, the office created in 1922, as well as several others in the labour, agrarian, criminal and administrative conflicts areas.
12. It is important to point out that its functions are limited to representation of clients, and do not comprise legal advice. Hence, even assuming that representation were successful, legal counsel and advice still would not be offered.
13. The law which reforms the Code of Civil Procedure for the Federal District, dated February 26, 1973.
14. In a survey we conducted directed to four different segments of the population, we obtained the following answers to the question: In case you had a legal problem, would you go to court:

	Students %	*Workers* %	*Merchants* %	*Professionals* %
(a) quite naturally?	0	0	32	61
(b) with certain fear?	14	4	18	14
(c) with distaste?	21	16	29	19
(d) with disgust?	65	80	21	6

Fifty persons were interviewed within each group: 48 per cent of them had had previous contacts with the judicial system.

15. The abolition of jail for debts of a civil nature is usually interpreted as a sign of humanism and as a characteristic of modern civil litigation. There are other interpretations, however: for example, Stalev, commenting on the 1879 reform of the Russian Code of Civil Procedure, maintains that prison as punishment for debt has a clear feudal nature,

and that, therefore, its abolition reflects the need to incorporate the processal system to the workings of capitalism (Z. Stalev, "The civil procedure in the European socialist states members of CMEA", unpublished, Sofia, 1975, p. 8). Despite the correct interpretation of Stalev, there is the curious case of England where prison for debts existed even until 1970 when the Administration of Justice Act abolished such practice so severely condemned by Charles Dickens one century before (see R. M. Jackson, *The Machinery of Justice in England*, Cambridge, 1972, pp. 99-100).

16. Self-help remedies allowed, by the civil law, with the previous approval of the court, are the execution of chattel and real mortgages by the creditor.
17. That is why the delegates maintained that the guarantee of free justice would be dead letter until the judicial functionaries were adequately paid by the state.
18. A direct ancestor of such norm is found in the Proclamation of Miguel Hidalgo made on December 6, 1810, in which slavery is abolished and, together with it, stamped paper for court actions. It is clear that the Constituent Assembly of 1857 speaks of "court costs" improperly as the fees of the judge, which up to then had been paid by the parties themselves.
19. The "mordida" appears as a persistent shortcoming in the Mexican system; that is, the illegal donation of money to judicial functionaries for them to either fulfil their duty within a reasonable time or to do it without hesitation. The Supreme Court has decided to consider "court costs" all fees and expenditure which can be proven and justified.
20. Furthermore, such guarantee has been sanctioned by Article 10 of the United Nations Declaration on Human Rights approved by the United Nations General Assembly in 1948.
21. There is in our country a superfluous "procedural federalism" which gives rise to thirty-two different codes. However, such diversity is apparent. In reality, as has been demonstrated by Alcala-Zamora, there are eight "families" of codes, the most important being the one to which the District Code of 1932 belongs.
22. The fundamental difference between both procedural models resides in the understanding of the object of the process. If it is considered as being litigation (as maintained by Carnelutti and Alcala-Zamora), there is no difficulty in making settlement the essential end of the process. On the other hand, if the object of the process is the satis-

faction of the parties or the subjective material law which is sought to be protected, then it is natural and logical to think of the process as a mechanism to ascribe rights and obligations more than to solve social conflict. It seems to us that the first approach more easily allows for the active intervention of the judge in the proceedings, and even for his actions as an instrument of procedural "equalization". However, it must be recognized that the theory which sees the satisfaction of the parties as the object of litigation (we are referring to the German doctrine of *Streigegenstand*), can be constructed in a way as to perfectly allow for the discretionary powers of the judge; this clearly appears to be the case in the study of O. Jaudernig, *Verhandlungsmaxime, Inquisitionsmaxime uns Streigegenstadt*, Tubingen, 1967, as a function of the distinction between self-limiting (*Selbstaggegrenzte*) and non-limiting through rulings (pp. 5–20) and even admitting the "richterliche Fragepflicht zur Aufklarung" such as it is contemplated in paragraph 182 of the Austrian ZPO.

23. Our Civil Code of 1928 tried to temper the principle when it stated on s. 21 that "the judges, taking into account the marked intellectual backwardness of certain individuals . . . are entitled to exempt them from the penalties which they have incurred due to a breach of the law they ignored, with the consent of the Public Ministry". In practice, this article is minimally applied.
24. There is no doubt that the principle of self-defence can be conceived as a double-edged sword. On the one hand, within an oral process in which immediacy must exist, the personal presence of the parties is very convenient (thus, for example, J. Bentham, *The Works of J. Bentham*, ed. Bowring, Vol. VIII, p. 599, where it is affirmed that a good judge must allow everybody to be heard directly, "and first of all those who are most likely to know about it, that is the Parties"; and M. Cappelletti, *La testimonianza della parte nel systema dell'oralita*, Milano, 1962, *passim*). The problem arises when one party goes accompanied by counsel and the other doesn't. In such cases, the dialogue between lawyer and judge is more fluid than that between the judge and the litigant, simply by virtue of professional "deformation". See, for example, Justice (a report by), *Litigants in person*, London, 1971.
25. Alcala-Zamora y N. Castillo, *El papel del juez en la direccion del proceso civil mexicano*, in "derecho Procesal Mexicano", op. cit., I, pp. 366ff., 371–4.
26. Norms which mostly refer to the mode of execution and which are

left to the discretion of the winning party.

27. That is, matters pertaining to the *Verhandlungsmaxime*, comprising cases such as ordinary trials in commercial matters, the enormous amount of litigation which could be submitted to arbitration, the freedom which exists in matter of evictions, etc.
28. See the preamble of the Code in which it is stated that the governing principle is to "harmonize the individual interests with the social ones, thus correcting the excesses of individualism". Nevertheless, as is maintained by Novoa Monreal in his brilliant essay *El derecho como obstaculo al cambio social*, Mexico, 1975, "a close scrutiny of the text demonstrated that the purpose was not accomplished and that the Code maintains, in general, the same plan, contents, institutions and forms of a traditional nature, with only some isolated modifications" (pp. 19-20).
29. Litigation of small claims usually involves confrontation between parties from different social classes (T. G. Ison, "Small Claims" in 35 *Modern Law Review* (1972, pp. 18ff.). On the other hand, the term "small claim" is only appropriate as a description of the amount in litigation, of the material value of the action; this does not mean, however, that the judicial settlement be easy from a legal viewpoint, or that the matter be of small importance for the individual or group of individuals involved. Lastly, litigations on small claims are of singular importance because they are an indirect means of protecting the salaries of the working classes.
30. The regulations of the Office of the Public Defender for courts of equity in the Federal District (*Official Gazette* of 29/4/1940) states, in the relevant sections that the defenders "will represent both plaintiffs and defendants in civil matters that cannot afford a lawyer" (Art. 1), these people would be "preferably workers or peasants without resources" (Art. 18), finally Article 19 determines that, once the person asking for help has related the details of his case and it looks as if he has enough means to pay for particular counsel, help cannot be automatically denied. Thus the final determination has a discretionary nature. As pointed out before, the Mexican Bar provided services of both representation and advice but it recently discontinued both due to economic reasons. Salient defects of the public defenders system are: the non-existence of an adequate system of appointments, the low number of public defenders, its highly centralized and bureaucratic structure, the discretionary character in which its services are given or denied, and finally, the lack of professional competence of

the defenders. Thee have been several attempts by the Autonomous National Unviersity of Mexico to structure offices to provide free legal services. None of them has achieved fruition mainly due to political reasons. Today, the Department of the Federal District has established Free Legal Offices staffed by students from the legal faculties of the city, and they seem to be working. Some labour unions give their members some legal aid services, but most of the time they only intervene in labour matters.

31. The Code Draft of 1948 is noteworthy.
32. Decree of December 30, 1966, effective 21/1/67.
33. Decree of December 23, 1969 (effective 17/1/1970), decree of March 10, 1971 (effective 24/3/71), decree of February 26, 1973 (effective 14/3/73), and decree of December 10, 1975.
34. Statement of reasons for the reform bill to the code of civil procedure, presented by the Chief of the Executive, Mexico, 1972.
35. Law of the Court of Administrative Justice of the Federal District of 1971(effective 17/3/71); amended by decree of 20/1/73.
36. The concept is not beyond reproach but has served to demonstrate the legislative recognition of a new type of subject. The law defines consumer as "he who contracts for the use or enjoyment of goods or the provision of services" (Art. 3), without establishing any distinction between physical and legal persons.
37. As in other countries, ordinary civil trials and even the "justice of the peace", were inaccessible to the consumer injured by commercial practices. It was even ridiculous to attempt settlement in court for amounts so low that the proceeds of the trial would scarcely cover the costs of the same. On the other hand, there is a staggering amount of consumer cases which require complex expert evidence of a scientific nature which can only be obtained at high cost. Finally, the formalism which dominated the 1932 Code (Art. 74 and 283), except in the area of "justice of the peace" (Art. 41 of the special heading) made the access to consumers without legal counsel even more difficult. When a problem related to consumer matters involved large industrial entities on both sides, they preferred to "escape from the state justice" (according to the expression by M. Cappelletti, *Parere iconoclastico . . .*, op. cit., p. 116) and submit their differences to private arbitration; on the other hand, when underprivileged parties confront a commercial entity, they must abandon the possibility of protection offered by objective law and must accept the demands and arbitrariness of their counterpart with the resulting denial of justice by the

state. The justice of the peace did not fulfil the need for consumer protection either, because it is based in a mere simplification of the ordinary procedure in which the assumption of equality between the parties continues to prevail (on the subject, see the proposals concerning "minor justice" made by V. Denti, *Problemi di riforma*, op. cit., p. 289). The Mexican legislature has preferred to leave the settlement of consumer problems outside the realm of the judicial process. To have selected an administrative body has great drawbacks, even of a constitutional character; as Barrera Graf points out (op. cit., pp. 195-6) the functions of a procedural character given to it do not properly belong to a "decentralized body" such as the Federal Consumer Agency. We do not believe the motive for this preference of administrative over judicial means by the Mexican legislature has been related to the negative influence that the American "small claims courts" have had in this matter: the courts, through the years, have become a type of "debt collecting agencies" (for an illustration, see Note, "Small Claims Courts as Collection Agencies", in *Stanford Law Review* (1952), p. 237). Rather, this choice must be interpreted in relation to the paternalist approach which characterized not a few of the pseudo "socializing" measures of the past regime. State mediation between consumers and producers has been preferred so as to avoid greater conflict even at the risk of generating decisions based in a political contest between producers and government, rather than in the application of the law. Finally, the deficient regulations regarding the procedural aspects of the laws of consumer protection (mainly those dealing with the length of time allowed for settlement) have extended the period between the presentation of the complaint and the meeting for settlement, which in practice does not exceed ten days when large companies are not involved, to months when they are. Then, the company involved simply declares that it does not wish to submit to the arbitration of the Agency. The law does not contemplate compulsory arbitration, because it could be declared unconstitutional (concerning this issue, compulsory arbitration of small claims was declared unconstitutional in the United States. See M. Rosenberg and R. Shubin, "Trial by Lawyer: Compulsory Arbitration of Small Claims in Pennsylvania", in *Harvard Law Review* (1961) pp. 448ff.). From a strictly constitutional stance, the Agency for consumer defence does not seem to have a solid basis for applying coercive measures of an economic nature to the parties, so as to assure a more efficient performance of its functions: this would be difficult to accomplish given the conventional nature of the settlement process. Hence, the efficacy of the Agency as an arbitrative body fundamentally depends on the will of the parties: this is not necessarily bad as proven, for example, by the experiments undertaken on small claims courts in Manchester and Westminster, England (see *The Consumer Council, Justice out of Reach. A case for S.C.C.*, London, 1970).

38. The determining causes of this situation are of a political nature; in a country lacking authentic political parties, where very often dissident opinions are repressed and in which the state closely controls the media, it is difficult to have pressure groups independent from the economically or the politically powerful.

39. Within Mexican civil trials, the prevailing criteria concerning standing as well as the effects of *res judicata* prevent the appearance of the "class actions" of the Anglo-Saxon law, or of the "collective actions" which have begun to appear in some nations of Continental Europe. Standing is not specifically regulated in the Code of 1932, but the norms related to "actions and objections" generate a typically "privatist" scheme, within which the right to ask for judicial protection is limited to those entitled to claim a right at trial (Arts. 1 and 2), thus closing the doors for the judicial protection of rights and interests not belonging to a particular individual but to the community or to a group. Respecting *res judicata*, our code is faithful to the tradition of fixing the limit of the judgment to the parties to the action, thus preventing that the so-called actions for the protection of collective interests have the effects which properly should belong to them. See, as a mere illustration, A. Homburger, "Private Suits in the Public Interest in the U.S.A.", in *Buffalo Law Review* (1974), 23, pp. 343ff.; "Developments in the Law of Class Actions", in *Harvard Law Review* (1976), 89, pp. 1319-644: this paper constitutes one of the most complete treatments of the topic. Concerning the Continental European Law, see V. Denti, "La azione a tutela di interessi colletivi", in *Rivista di diritto processuale* (1974), p. 1.

40. The surveys conducted were directed towards obtaining data of the parties (applied to 250 people of small resources) as well as to participants in the judicial system (fifty lawyers with more than five years in the profession, four "justices of the peace" and six clerks of the court). Concerning statistical data, we regret not having any after 1972 when the General Bureau of Statistics ceased publishing it; we were told that "nobody was interested in the information", which is quite picturesque as well as significant. Consequently, all post-1972

compiled with enormous difficulty and can only be considered as interim indicators.

41. Distributed as follows: forty-three ordinary judges of the Civil Trial Courts, twenty-three family judges and thirty-six justices of the peace of mixed tribunals.
42. In the period comprised between 1964 and 1977 the number of trial judges in civil matters increased by 100 per cent, while the population increased approximately by 75 per cent. The litigiousness index was stable; however, the length of trials experienced a notable increase. From this it can be inferred that the problem of delays cannot be solved by simply increasing the number of judges, but rather, by reforming the procedural structures and by better utilizing human resources. The latter has been attempted with good results in our highest court in which administrative reform begins to benefit the parties to the trial.
43. See M. Zander, *Cases and Materials on the English Legal System*, London, 1973, pp. 1–45.
44. According to judicial statistics of 1972, 65 per cent of contested divorces had a duration of more than one year, 12 per cent between twelve and twenty-four months and fifteen per cent less than one year because of an abnormal conclusion. Today, according to data obtained in an informal sampling of records of six family courts conducted by us, close to 35 per cent are settled in less than three months (45 per cent of those via judgment) and only 11 per cent surpass one year.
45. Amount which, at the time, equalled eighty US dollars and constituted the limit assigned to "justices of the peace". It also represented the equivalent of a month's salary, according to the minimum wage scales prevailing at the time.
46. A sample comprising actions brought in three different tribunals on two different bi-weekly periods produced the following data on the "users" of justice: in commercial executory processes, 72 per cent of the parties turned out to be banking institutions or finance companies; in eviction actions 16 per cent were real estate companies. The remainder were individuals. The judicial system is more accessible to commercial institutions than individuals because they hire lawyers to judicially collect debts and who are paid through a flat monthly fee and a percentage (generally low) of trial proceeds. This system is attractive for some professionals because it allows for generally fixed income received for work which requires little effort and imagination,

that is, routine. However, the continuing increases in the duration of trials have compelled lawyers to attempt out-of-court settlement, and only to initiate legal action if negotiations fail.

47. Several among them recognized that they had not sought legal counsel because, beforehand, they knew they had no defence, and preferred that trial be followed in default (69 per cent of the cases). Those who took some steps were generally advised by a friend.
48. Organic Law of the Courts of Equity of the Federal District of 1968, Arts. 222–315.
49. Even in criminal matters public defenders are quite deficient.
50. Among the various norms and regulations on the matter which have been issued in our country, one characteristic stands out in the great majority of them a right of "popular action" is given in case of ecological imbalances (air pollution, noise pollution, industrial waste, etc.). The terminology cannot be more inappropriate: there is not properly an "action" because there is no judicial body to *prima facie* deal with such disputes: there are only administrative organs (Secretaries or Under-secretaries of State) in charge of such events. Hence, at the outmost, one could speak of a "public notice". The workings of these institutions have left much to be desired during the recent past. When there was outrageous pollution in Santa Clara, State of Mexico, where chrome industrial waste put in jeopardy the lives of many people and caused the death of others, the authorities limited themselves to issue recommendations rather than apply the law to the guilty companies.
51. During the last ten years, the percentage of the budget applied to the administration of justice has remained stable at close to 0.3 per cent.
52. Concerning the Indian communities it does not seem appropriate to label them as "underprivileged". The enormous cultural differences existing between them and the rest of the population would result in grave harm to the Indians if subjected to the state justice. Only those who think that the judicial process such as practised today is something natural, eternal and immutable, can maintain that it is a privilege for every individual, regardless of his culture or ideology. Several Indian communities of our country have their own systems for settling disputes which are highly effective and are based on popular participation. The process has as its essential objective to settle litigation in the quickest and simplest fashion. The system, however, does not lack guarantees and is not based on ordeal; on the contrary, mediation and friendly arrangements prevail. See, on the matter,

L. Nader, "Choices in legal procedure: Shia moslem and Mexican Zapotec", in *American Anthropologist* (1967), pp. 394ff. "To make the balance: conflict resolution among Mexican Zapotec", in *Law in culture and society*, Chicago, 1969; L. Nader and D. Metzger, "Conflict resolution in two Mexican communities", in *American Anthropologist* (1965), pp. 584ff.; J. F. Collier, *Law and Social Change in Zinacantan*, Stanford, 1973, *passim.* A difference from what occurred during the Spanish colonial period, when some of the indigenous legal customs were respected, or from what occurs in some modern African nations, no attention has been given in Mexico to this type of procedure or to this type of dispute settlement. Concerning the possibilities of integrating such systems, see the important study of R. A. Bush, "Modern Roles for Customary Justice: Integration of Civil Procedure in African Courts" in 26 *Stanford Law Review* (1974), pp. 1123ff. Concerning the socio-economic underpinnings of the non-procedural modes of settlement, see W. L. F. Felstiner, "Influences of Social Organization on Dispute Processing", in 9 *Law and Society* (1974), pp. 63ff., and T. Eckhoff, "The mediator, the judge and the administrator in conflict resolution" in 10 *Acta Sociologica* (1966), pp. 158ff.

53. Given this characteristic of economic discrimination which we think we have demonstrated with solid reasoning, Mexican civil trials in general and the access to justice in particular contravene the dictates of the Constitution itself and of the Universal Declaration of Human Rights which forbid all discrimination or unequal treatment based on wealth, race, colour, etc. (see Abu Rannat, op. cit., note 81), as well as those of the Inter American Convention on Human Rights (the San José de Costa Rica Pact, 1969). This last agreement, which has not been ratified by Mexico, contains two articles (8 and 25) which delineate the right of access to impartial, prompt and effective justice. The Inter American Commission on Human Rights and the Inter American Court on Human Rights are created for the protection of rights. Standing in the court belong exclusively to the States (Art. 61, identical to Art. 44 of the Rome Treaty), while standing in the Commission, a body with quasi-judicial functions, follows the wider criterion of Art. 25 of the European Treaty, with which, theoretically, the possibility of an international control of access to justice in the signatory countries is opened (see Art. 25).
54. See, Justice (a report), *Going to Law*, London, 1974.

ROBERT BOMAN*

Scandinavia

1. Sweden

The *new* Swedish Procedural Code, which came into force in 1948 and is still in operation (although slightly modified), was mainly induced by a desire to create the best possible conditions for ensuring a result at trial corresponding to the true facts of the case. In civil actions, of course, the investigation of the court is limited by the claims, concessions, pleadings and admissions of the parties, in accordance with their private law rights of disposition. But within this framework provision is made for the court's assessment of evidence, which has become quite unrestricted now that the remnants of the rigid theory of cogency have been abolished. All evidence is heard or submitted to the court on a single occasion, at the trial, and the final judgment results from this hearing. Witnesses are examined by the parties or their representatives, and usually not by the court. The trial is oral, and adjournments are to be avoided as far as possible. This requires that proceedings be carefully prepared prior to the trial, and that the pre-trial proceedings be in most instances oral and take place before a judge.

The legislators have created an excellent procedure. Its costs, however, have proved to be a serious drawback. The legislators evidently felt that, under the new procedure, parties would be able to continue to conduct trials without authorized representatives. In practice, however, parties usually retained lawyers. Contributing to this was a strong Western influence which convinced many judges that their predominant duty was to observe and to record, not to direct the parties in conducting their

*Translated by Dr. Paula Baum Weiss, Toronto, Canada.

proceedings. Legal fees became higher and higher as a result of the general rise in the standard of living and creeping inflation. The collective costs of the parties in the action – costs which, according to the main rule, are to be borne by the unsuccessful party alone – could amount to a considerable sum. If the value of the subject matter of the dispute was slight, costs would frequently exceed the value of the litigation. The risk of being saddled with costs resulted in parties not daring to undertake proceedings in other than simple matters where they could choose the summary written documentary trial or the hortatory procedure. This gave debtors a trump card and did not strengthen the "repayment ethic". The risk of costs also weighed heavily in matters involving moderate amounts, especially when an appeal could be expected. Of course there was the statutory benefit of free legal proceedings: this advantage, however, was open only to those who were worst off economically. It was often said that only the poor and the rich could afford to litigate.

While various proposals to reform state-provided legal aid were considered, an insurance company introduced litigation insurance, which was quickly picked up by its competitors. Litigation insurance is for the most part not a separate type of insurance and cannot as a rule be purchased separately, but forms a block with other types of insurance such as home insurance (covering loss by fire, theft etc.) and cottage, motor vehicle, and business insurance. In each case the extent of the protection is limited in different ways. The litigation insurance that is connected to home insurance is valid for actions of the insured in his capacity as a private citizen (with the exception of, for example, divorce). The insurance is not valid for actions concerning the occupation of the insured, his real property, or motor vehicles. In criminal matters the insurance is valid in principle for the defence of a person accused of a crime of negligence, but only when there is no gross negligence. The insurance covers the individual costs of the insured with the exception of his personal costs for the court appearance and the wages lost because of it. If the insured qualifies for legal aid, he is required to seek it, and the insurance company will pay no compensation in respect of costs that the legal aid pays. In addition, the insurance company does not pay the costs which the insured has incurred through his own negligent conduct of the proceedings. There is an uninsured *excess* of 200 Swedish crowns. A feature of great importance is the fact that the insurance covers the duty to pay the costs of one's opponent, if costs are awarded against the insured. On the other hand, the costs of execution of the judgment are not covered. The maximum responsibility of the company is set at a total of 40,000 Swedish crowns.

The legislature has attacked the problem of high litigation costs in two ways. First, by the Small Claims Procedure Act of 1974, a simplified procedure was created for civil actions where the value of the subject-matter in dispute does not exceed an index-tied figure, which currently (1978) is 5,900 Swedish crowns. In this procedure several key trial principles are waived. The parties are supposed to conduct these actions without a representative (for which reason any attorneys' fees are not as a rule recoverable), and judges have an extensive duty of directing the proceedings so as to bring out the relevant matters. Litigation insurance is valid even in these actions, and an insured party can therefore recover the attorney's fees from the insurance company, apart from the uninsured excess. Secondly, the Legal Aid Act of 1972 (which came into force on July 1, 1973) replaced the earlier Free Legal Proceedings Act of 1919. Through the Legal Aid Act, the state contribution to litigation costs was increased considerably and, at the same time, a new administrative framework was introduced.

The background of the reorganization was as follows. Legal aid, as administered through the earlier Free Legal Proceedings Act (which, as the name indicates, dealt only with litigation costs), was as a rule administered by the courts. Besides this, there was a municipal legal aid plan, organized by the county councils, with a state contribution to costs. Two types of legal aid schemes developed. One was the Legal Aid Institute, which provided legal aid to persons of small means in litigation as well as out-of-court matters, i.e. essentially to the same category of persons as was defined in the Free Legal Proceedings Act. In practice, however, the category was often somewhat extended and the number of Legal Aid Institutes were relatively few. The second form of legal aid was that the County Councils entered into agreements with lawyers in the county to provide legal aid for those without means, in which case the costs were borne by the County Council. This scheme provided only out-of-court costs.

With the introduction of the Legal Aid Act, in 1973, the Legal Aid Institutes were reorganized into public law offices and their number was nearly doubled. These public law offices are state agencies, but special rules apply concerning their operations. The statute which normally governs administrative agencies in Sweden (the Administration Act of 1971), is only applicable to the purely administrative matters within the public law. Legal work is to be carried out in accordance with the professional conduct rules, and legal aid lawyers remain under the professional supervision of the Swedish Bar Association. The officials of the offices have a duty to preserve the confidentiality of that which is entrusted to them or that which they have learned in connection with their activities. Contrary to the principle otherwise applicable in the Swedish administration, viz. that all documents and papers are open for public inspection, the general public has no access to the documents of the public law offices. Generally, it is intended that matters should be dealt with in the same way as would be the case in a private law firm.

The public law offices have no monopoly on legal aid according to the Legal Aid Act. If the requirements for legal aid are fulfilled, such aid is also available to those who wish to use a private lawyer. But it is the duty of the public law offices to undertake matters in which the client is entitled to legal aid; therefore, unlike private lawyers, they cannot refuse eligible clients. On the other hand, the public law offices can, if time permits, accept non-legal-aid cases, preferably from private citizens, estates of deceased persons, and non-profit associations, which do not qualify for legal aid.

The Swedish concept is for the public law offices and private law firms to compete on equal conditions. Where the client is entitled to legal aid this is essentially the case. But public law offices which handle non-legal-aid matters can still be distinguished from private law firms in that public law offices use the legal aid tariff for all matters (if a tariff exists for the particular type of advice given), while private law firms need use the legal aid tariff only when legal aid is given.

The superior administrative authorities consist of six legal aid boards, one for each Court of Appeal district. Among other things, these boards decide whether to grant, and determine the extent of, legal aid for the applicant, appoint counsel, determine their compensation in those cases where it is not incumbent on the court to do so, and settle finally the question of costs when the matter has been brought to a conclusion. The legal aid boards consist of five members; the presiding member must have had experience as a judge, and two members must be lawyers, one from a public law office and the other a private practitioner. Resolutions can normally be passed, however, by the presiding member and the two non-lawyer members. The lawyer-members are generally only required to participate in matters of principle or of special significance. Routine decisions can be delegated to the officials attached to the board.

On the national level the National Swedish Courts Administration (*Domstolsverket*) functions as the central administrative authority. It issues detailed rules and regulations with respect to representation and tariffs, oversees representation, and functions as an appeal board. In appellate matters the *Domstolsverket* is the highest instance.

Forms of legal aid

Legal aid appears in four forms: (1) as general legal aid; (2) as legal aid to suspected persons in criminal proceedings; (3) as legal aid by an official assistant; and (4) as the giving of legal advice. Categories 2 and 3 are exclusive within their scope, and general legal aid (category 1) cannot extend into these areas. When a suspect in a criminal action, for example, cannot obtain legal aid under category 2, he also cannot receive general legal aid. Category 4 can be combined with each of the other three forms.

Legal aid by means of an official assistant refers to administrative matters (especially detention), but in certain cases it is also concerned with the carrying out of punishments. When a person is subjected to any such administrative action and needs counsel to protect his rights, an official assistant is to be appointed for him. In the examination of need, special attention is paid to whether there are conflicting statements, or if the facts are unclear in other respects. The examination of need is not directed to the economic situation of the client. The fee of counsel is set by the legal aid board and paid by the state. (This form of legal aid will not be considered further in this report.)

General legal aid

General legal aid is available in legal matters which do not fall into the other three categories. The provisions concern in-court as well as out-of-court legal aid.

Who is eligible for general legal aid?

This form of legal aid is available to natural persons. As far as legal persons are concerned, only estates of deceased persons can be considered.

General legal aid presupposes need. The test of need is only partially economic. In certain situations general legal aid is not available. The economic test is tied to the concept of a "basic amount" which also appears in the National Insurance Act of 1962. The amount is not fixed by the statute, but is set by the government every month, a measure of practical significance in times of inflation. The chief rule in the legal aid legislation is that general legal aid can be given to those whose yearly income does not exceed a sum which corresponds to eight times the basic amount for October in the year preceding the application. The size of the relevant basic amount is presently (1978) 11,800 Swedish crowns. A single applicant can accordingly not receive general legal aid if his yearly income exceeds 94,400 crowns. For every person to whose support the applicant contributes significantly, half the basic amount is added. An applicant who supports, for example a spouse and one child can thus have a maximum income of 106,200 crowns in order to qualify for general legal aid. No one who earns more than 129,800 crowns a year is eligible for general legal aid, and a person who earns this amount is eligible only if he supports at least six persons. There is, however, a modification in that more significant assets or debts bring about an "off-setting"; allowances are made by either adding or subtracting a reasonable amount to or from the figure representing the yearly income. The National Courts Administration has given rules for computing yearly income in these cases.

The applicant must pay a part of the costs himself, in accordance with his means. This part is called the cost contribution, and it is set – with one exception – by the legal aid board. The rules concerning the contribution to costs in ss. 12 and 13 of the Legal Aid Act are rather complicated, and only a few examples will be given here. The lowest contribution is at present 90 Swedish crowns and is paid by a single person with a maximum yearly income of 37,300 crowns, and by an applicant supporting a spouse and two children with a maximum yearly income of 55,000 crowns. A single person already at this income level makes a contribution to costs of 980 crowns. At a yearly income level of 94,400 crowns, which is the maximum a single person can earn in order to be eligible for general legal aid, he must make a cost contribution of 9,040 crowns, while the corresponding contribution for an applicant with a spouse and two children amounts to 2,550 crowns. If instead the latter earns 104,300 crowns per year, his contribution amounts to 5,140 crowns. Also, when it is a question of the size of the contribution, greater assets or debts are considered in the form of a credit or debit to the yearly income. If there are special reasons for doing so, the cost contribution may be reduced or completely waived. If the actual costs in the matter are less than the cost contribution, the balance is, of course, returned to the applicant.

A test of economic need is set for the estates of deceased persons as well, but with no fixed sum, either as a prerequisite for receiving general legal aid, or for the computation of the cost contribution. Instead, a more general examination of need is made, which is based on the amount of the estate and the economic situation of the heirs. It seems probable that more specific rules will be developed.

As to the non-economic test of need, which must also be satisfied, the annotated edition of the statute makes reference to s. 8 of the Legal Aid Act and further states that need should be assessed in relation to the benefits which can arise out of the granting of general legal aid.

Pursuant to s. 8, general legal aid is usually withheld when the applicant is a tradesman and the matter has some connection to his trade. Exceptions, however, can be made if there are special grounds. The term "tradesman" refers not only to the owners of a business and to craftsmen, but also to farmers, fishermen, and owners of rental housing. The annotated edition seems to assume that only tradesmen who are in an equivalent position to those people who have a low income can be considered for general legal aid, and one receives the impression that the upper yearly income limit is 30,000 crowns. The purpose of the limitation is unclear; there appear to be no significant reasons why a farmer with a yearly income of 50,000 crowns who is involved in a dispute about a purchased tractor should not be able to receive general legal aid, if a hired labourer in the same income class can receive such aid in a dispute about an auto purchase. Perhaps one reason is that the farmer's costs are considered a business expense and can be deducted from his income when computing costs.

If a person who has a legal claim is ineligible for general legal aid (or can get legal aid only by making a substantial cost contribution), he cannot gain an advantage by assigning the claim to another person who is in a worse economic position. If there is reason to believe that such motives were behind the assignment, general legal aid will not be given.

A person who has no justifiable reason for pursuing a matter is not eligible for general legal aid. The *travaus préparatoires* to the statute lists a few such situations: (1) the claim is clearly unfounded according to the law currently in force; (2) the evidentiary situation is such that the success of the applicant's claim is very improbable; (3) the opposing party has no means, and it is not expected that he will have any; (4) the claim is insignificant in relation to the costs.

With respect to the last point, it should be noted that when the value of the dispute does not exceed the index-tied sum mentioned above (5,900 crowns in 1978),* the dispute is to be litigated under the Small Claims Procedure Act. Under this system costs are lower. It is considered that the

*"Basic amount" is defined at pages 247–8.

party can handle the matter himself in these cases, after being advised, and that it could not have been the intention of the statute that he receive general legal aid. Also, other simple matters such as listing the assets of estates, registrations of land and of mortgages, and tax returns are excluded. Not even advice is given in these situations.

General legal aid is usually limited to disputes which are tried or handled in Sweden, and the applicant must, as a rule, be resident here.

The extent of general legal aid

The most significant advantage of general legal aid is the right to counsel. Counsel may be a lawyer or associate in a public law office or private law firm, or another suitable person. There is no statutory requirement of legal education, but a person other than a lawyer would seldom be appointed as counsel in court proceedings. One exception might be the appointment of an official of a tenants' association (without a legal education) as counsel in a tenancy dispute. According to the *travaux préparatoires* of the statute, it is of great potential advantage that non-lawyers can be considered as counsel, at least in disputes in more specialized areas. Further, general legal aid covers the costs of proof before the court and in arbitration proceedings (but not compensation for the aribtrator) along with other assorted costs. Section 9 of the legislation deals with this matter. In certain situations (for example, in the context of a motion for provisional attachment of property or eviction), the applicant must give security. The usual form of this security is the guarantee of a third party. The legal aid board can intervene and give the required security.

General legal aid does not, on the other hand, cover the costs which the applicant may be required to pay to the successful party, if he loses in a court of general jurisdiction. The costs in defeat must be borne by the applicant himself if he has no litigation insurance. The applicant is not reimbursed for such costs as he himself has brought about by conducting the proceedings negligently. When the applicant is successful, the opponent is usually liable to repay the entire legal aid costs, including the applicant's cost contribution. If the opponent is unable to pay the entire costs, or if he has been ordered to pay only a portion (for example, because the applicant is only partially successful), the costs of the state are paid first; only then will the applicant be compensated in respect of the cost contribution. If the applicant is not awarded any costs except those covered by legal aid, the opponent pays nothing to him. Payment is made instead to the state, which repays the applicant his cost contribution so far as it is covered by the sum paid by the opponent.

General legal aid for an action does not include costs of execution of the judgment. General legal aid can be obtained in execution proceedings, but this is a new matter and the applicant must pay a further cost contribution, which is seldom worthwhile.

The forms of general legal aid

General legal aid can be given with or without a decision of the legal aid board. An advocate (attorney) or an associate in a public law office or a private law firm can make a decision concerning general legal aid without the authorization of the legal aid board. The applicant bears the cost himself for general legal aid in this form and it can be contemplated only as far as the cost contribution of the applicant is adequate to cover the costs. The expression "legal aid" is therefore somewhat misleading. There is some justification for it in that counsel fees and the costs of proof are to be calculated according to the same rules which prevail when the state pays the costs after a decision of the board. This means that the costs can be held down through the use of official scales and limitations; for example, as regards the payment of witnesses.

General legal aid with the approval of the legal aid board presupposes a written application with details about the proposed litigation, the value of the dispute, and the economic situation of the applicant. The applicant must confirm the economic data under oath; any falsification of information is punishable. The applicant need bring no proof of the economic data, but the legal aid office can on its own initiative seek confirmation itself.

If the requirements for eligibility are satisfied, the legal aid board approves the application, appoints counsel if necessary, and stipulates the cost contribution of the applicant. It is possible that the applicant has already received legal aid without the approval of the legal aid board (see above). The applicant is then not required to pay a further-cost contribution, but an additional payment can become necessary if the legal aid board stipulates a higher cost contribution than the lawyer has specified. Counsel now has the right to receive compensation from public funds for the work performed on the matter even during the time when legal aid was given without the approval of the legal aid board. The applicant can consider as a cost contribution any amount that he has paid to the counsel or in respect of any other compensatable costs during this time. The cost contribution is always to be paid to the counsel and is used initially to pay his fee. If it turns out that the fee is lower than the cost contribution, counsel is responsible for paying the balance to the state. Only if no counsel is appointed is the cost contribution paid to the legal aid board. Moreover, counsel not only has the right to consider the cost contribution as his fee, but he is required to subtract the amount from his bill for reimbursement from public funds to the extent that the contribution is not used to pay other costs and disbursements. This means that counsel has a personal interest in seeing that the cost contribution is actually paid, and payment in advance is probably demanded in most cases. This does not mean, however, that the applicant is forced to pay the entire cost contribution at the beginning. On the contrary, the statute presupposes that payment can be made by instalments, as and when money previously paid in is exhausted.

The size of the counsel fee is fixed by the court in proceedings before courts of general jurisdiction; in the majority of other cases it is set by the legal aid board. In proceedings and matters before administrative tribunals or agencies, there is to a certain extent a double examination, since the decision-making body is asked to comment on the cost bill of counsel to guide the legal aid board. It is assumed in the *travaux préparatoires* of the statute that the fee is to be set according to tariffs based on the type of proceedings. The costs of the proof before courts of general jurisdiction are also set by the court, which must use the more restrictive rules which operate when the costs are paid or advanced by the state.

A recipient of legal aid can, under certain circumstances, be deprived of that aid. The situations are specified in s. 34 of the Act. In the case where the applicant succeeds, a monetary award can result in the loss of general legal aid or an increase in the cost contribution. Under s. 15 the cost contribution can be raised if the economic situation of the applicant is materially altered. This requirement of a material change is lacking in s. 34(5). According to the annotated edition of the statute, even a moderate change in the applicant's economic situation can lead to a loss of legal aid. If legal aid is lost, the applicant must undertake responsibility for costs. A judgment in favour of the applicant will not improve his economic position unless the opponent is solvent, but if he is, there is reason to believe that he can also afford to pay the costs that are awarded against him as unsuccessful party.

Advising

Advice is given by an advocate or an associate in a public law office or a private law firm. The approval of the legal aid board is not required. Advice may be given in situations such as the drafting of simple documents for a fee which at present (1978) is fixed at 90 Swedish crowns, paid by the applicant, for a conference of 20-25 minutes. The fee can be lowered or waived if there are special reasons for doing so – for example if the applicant has no income or only receives a pension under the National Insurance scheme.

Legal advice, unlike general legal aid, is not limited to certain categories of applicants. But, in conformity with general legal aid, certain common situations are excepted (such as listing the assets of descendants' estates, registrations of title to land and of mortgages, and tax returns). If the advice given leads to the applicant receiving general legal aid, the fee for the advice is included in the legal aid costs, and the applicant can apply the fee to his cost contribution.

A proposal for reform of the Legal Aid Act was announced in 1977 (SOU 1977:49). The main feature of the proposals was the simplification of administration by decreasing the work of the Legal Aid Boards and increasing the authority of the lawyers who initially interview legal aid applicants. Lawyers would be given the authority to determine whether legal aid should be granted in divorces and other family law matters as well as in any case where the time spent will not exceed six hours. The proposals also recommended that the financial rules should be simplified and that the time allowed for giving legal advice without the approval of the legal aid board should be extended to one hour. If the reforms are adopted it is anticipated that the work of the legal aid boards will decrease to such an extent that their number could be reduced to three for the entire country. It is interesting to note that the Swedish Attorney-General, who was the chairman of the committee which prepared the proposals, wrote a minority report urging the adoption of an even more simplified system according to which the decisions to grant legal aid and the extent of remuneration for counsel would generally be made by the authority responsible for determining the dispute or other matter in which the legal aid applicant is involved. This proposal would reduce the number of legal aid boards to only one or two for the entire country. The minority proposals received the unqualified support of the General Secretary of the Swedish Bar Association, who was attached to the committee as an expert. New legislation is expected in the spring of 1979, but it is an open question as to which proposals will be accepted by the Swedish government and Parliament.

2. Denmark

Danish law distinguishes between legal aid and "free process". Free process concerns the costs of an action, while legal aid refers in principle to aid out of court. Danish law has had free process rules for more than 150 years.

Legal aid is regulated by a proclamation of December 19, 1969, and includes (according to s. 3) the following benefits:

1. Advice (including the drafting of applications)
   - (a) in questions relating to the law of persons, family law and succession law (with certain exceptions);
   - (b) in questions regarding damages in tort;
   - (c) in insurance questions;
   - (d) concerning the sale of goods not related to the occupation of the applicant;
   - (e) concerning occupational tenancies; and
   - (f) in questions of employment which concern workers, assistants and functionaries.
2. Drafting an application for free process.
3. Drawing up the statement of claim in matters that are mentioned in 1 above as well as in other civil proceedings at the court of first instance when the value of the dispute does not exceed 2,000 Danish crowns.
4. Drawing up the documents for appealing against the decision of any administrative agency.

Legal aid can be refused when the claim of the applicant appears obviously unfounded or unreasonable, or when enforcing the claim would violate professional ethics.

Legal aid is provided by practising lawyers, though not by all. First, lawyers in the Copenhagen area are excepted. Since 1885 an originally fully private (but now state-supported) legal aid organization has existed in that city.* Secondly, only those lawyers permitted to represent parties who have been granted free process (which requires approval by the Justice Minister) may, in principle, provide legal aid; these, in fact,

**Studentersamfundets Retshjælp for Ubemidlede* (The Students' Union Legal Aid Centre for the Indigent). There are also other legal aid centres in the Copenhagen area as well as in other areas of the country.

are required to do so. But any other lawyer may inform the judge in the court area where the lawyer has his office that he is willing to provide legal aid. He thereby becomes entitled and compelled to give such aid. Legal aid need not be given personally by the lawyer; assistance by an employee in the lawyer's office is also permissible if additional action is not necessary.

Natural persons whose taxable income does not exceed 25,000 Danish crowns (with an additional 3,000 crowns for each child under 18 supported by the applicant) and whose taxable assets do not exceed 100,000 crowns, and who do not possess liquid assets (for example cash, bank deposits, easily converted securities) of a value of 20,000 crowns or more, are entitled to legal aid (s. 2). If the applicant is married and the spouses cohabit and are taxed jointly, then the taxable income and assets of the husband only are relevant. If the wife is taxed separately, the incomes of both spouses are summed up. The applicant must give the lawyer full data concerning his economic situation, and the municipality must certify in writing the accuracy of the data on taxable income and assets. In exceptional cases the judge can waive the requirements in s. 2; for example, if the income of the applicant has materially decreased since the preceding year. The legal aid organization in Copenhagen uses approximately the same rules, modified somewhat to the advantage of the applicant.

The basic fee of the lawyer is 80 crowns. However, the fee is doubled if the legal aid encompasses one of the measures named in s. 3 (1) as well as one of those in s. 3 (2)-3 (4). The applicant pays 25 per cent of the fee, the state treasury the remainder. Nothing seems to prohibit the lawyer from demanding the applicant's share in advance.

The *free process* is regulated by the Procedural Code (*Retsplejeloven*, "RPL") along with a special proclamation of December 19, 1969 (No. 562), and relates only to court proceedings, not to proceedings before administrative bodies. Benefits include:

1. No court and execution fees;
2. Free representation by a lawyer;
3. Payment by state funds of the necessary costs of testimonial proof, views and other measures for the investigation and clarification of the matter (according to the case law, costs incurred because of the questioning of parties before the court can be recovered in certain cases); and
4. No requirement of giving security in certain cases concerning the distribution of descendants' estates, etc.

Costs incurred because of number 3 above can be recovered by the applicant even if they arose before the application for free process was approved. The benefits need not encompass all costs, but can be limited to certain ones. For example, the benefit of representation can be refused if the matter is so simple that the party can himself conduct the proceedings. The limitation can also be employed if the economic situation of the applicant is so good that he can, in fairness, be responsible for a part of the costs himself.

If the applicant has been successful at trial, and his opponent launches an appeal, the applicant's costs will be covered on appeal, too. However, if an unsuccessful applicant launches an appeal, he must reapply for free process at the appeal level. If the applicant obtains a judgment capable of execution, execution costs are covered (with the exception of certain auction costs). The applicant's death will not extinguish the free process benefits.

The benefits of free process do not as a rule include the applicant's responsibility for costs *vis-à-vis* the successful opponent. There are, however, two exceptions. First, for the benefit of the applicant, when his economic situation and the character of the matter suggest that he ought to be fully or partially relieved of responsibility for costs *vis-à-vis* the opposing party, the court may make an order to that effect, and the opposing party then receives a corresponding payment from the state treasury. Secondly, for the benefit of the opposing party, if the applicant has no means to pay the costs awarded against him and there are special reasons, the court may order that those costs be paid by the state, in which case the state takes over the opponent's claim for costs against the applicant.

If the opposing party loses the action and costs are to be awarded against him, he must pay them to the state treasury. The opponent is not only to repay the disbursements of the state treasury, but also the estimated amount of court fees lost by the state. Further, the opponent must pay such costs of the applicant as the free process system does not cover according to the division of costs between the state treasury and the applicant which is fixed by the court. When the applicant's opponent loses the action but costs are not awarded against him, the court, by virtue of s. 335, can impose upon the applicant the duty to repay fully or partially the disbursements of the state treasury, if there are grounds for this. An example of such grounds would occur when the applicant has received a significant economic advantage as a result of the judgment. (The same rule holds when the applicant has given false information in order to be granted free process, or when the circumstances change so that he no longer fulfils the requirements for eligibility and it is considered that the applicant rather than the state should have the disadvantage thereof. In such cases the granting of the free process can be revoked and the effect of the decision to grant is thereby terminated.) It appears that the rule in s. 335 also can be used preventively, so that the court can impose upon the applicant the duty to pay the costs of evidence whose value appears dubious.

The regional government is responsible for making the decision to grant the free process at first instance. In cases where free process is not automatically available on appeal, or if the application is submitted only after the decision in a court of first instance, the application is to be made to the Justice Minister. The court, however, decides which lawyer is to appear for the applicant; it can choose from those lawyers who have been approved by the Justice Minister to act as counsel in matters involving free process.

According to RPL s. 330 a person who has a proper reason to go to trial and who cannot pay the costs associated with the proceedings without significant deprivation is entitled to free process. As far as the first condition is concerned, it is apparent that it is necessary that the applicant must be likely to succeed. The requirement, however, according to a statement of the Justice Minister, is not to be taken too far. Free process may be approved even when the outcome may be doubtful, in so far as one can accept that the applicant would have pursued the matter if he had had means of his own to do so. This is significant especially with respect to questions of the law of persons and of family law, as well as proceedings for compensation on account of serious disability. In practice it is customary not to grant free process in defamation actions or in pure collection proceedings.

The second condition is also not to be taken strictly literally. In a proclamation with practice directions of December 19, 1969 (No. 563), it was said by way of introduction that free process is to be granted after an assessment of the economic means of the particular applicant for carrying the action through. But the more detailed regulations prove to be generous. When the provisions came into force it was estimated, for example, that approximately 85 per cent of the population over 18 years were eligible. Free process as a rule is not to be granted if the applicant does not fulfil the economic requirements of membership in a recognized sickness fund. These requirements are: in the Copenhagen area, a maximum taxable income (for people with dependants) of 61,000 crowns, with and additional 7,940 crowns for every dependent child; and for people with no dependants, a maximum income of 45,800 crowns. The amounts are lower for the rest of the country: for a person with dependants, 53,600 crowns with corresponding additions, and for those without dependants, 40,200 crowns. Further, as a rule, free process is not to be granted when the applicant has assets which exceed 25,000 crowns liquid or 200,000 crowns collected. If the assets do not reach such amounts, they can still prevent granting of free process, but then there is an equitable determination where the income of the applicant, along with the size and placement of the assets, is assessed, especially if they are tied up in land or in business.* If the applicant cohabits with his spouse, the assets are detemined collectively. Even if the applicant has income or assets which exceed the limits set for granting free process, a decision to grant it is not wholly excluded. If the applicant has a very special need for help or if the costs will be exceptionally high, free process may be granted. If applications are made by several people suing or defending jointly, it will be determined if they can pay the costs collectively. If the applicant is under 18, the income of the parents is normally considered as well. In the same way as in legal aid, the applicant must provide an official verification of his taxable income and assets, and such other financial information as may be requested.

Finally, the Justice Minister can approve free process if there are special reasons for doing so, even if the requirements of s. 330 are not met. This is done in a small number of cases, and then usually for legal persons, especially foundations, associations, bankrupts' estates and estates of deceased persons.

The tariffs payable for lawyers' fees are not determined by the state, but the court stipulates the fee in each particular case. The tariffs of the Bar Association seem to be directive.

Litigation insurance was introduced in Denmark at a fairly late stage, following the Swedish example. As in Sweden, the insurance is included as part of other types of insurance (for example home or motor vehicle insurance). The most common variety is coupled with family insurance and covers the disputes of the insured as a private person. An insured who is eligible for free process is, however, according to the terms of the policy,

*In practice the scheme is not always so generous as the general statements imply. Krag-Jespersen mentions as an example the case of a pensioner who was denied free process. She had an income of 13,000 crowns, and assets valued at 50,000 crowns, of which 15,000 crowns were in bank deposits and the remainder in the form of bills of sale.

required to apply for it. If free process is granted, the insurance covers only the responsibility for costs *vis-à-vis* the opponent. If free process is refused on the ground that there is no proper cause for the proceedings, the insurance cannot be used. The insurance accordingly becomes fully effective only if free process is excluded on economic grounds. But even then certain costs and certain types of proceedings are excluded; for example, pure collection proceedings covering clear debts with the insured as defendant.

3. Finland

As in Denmark, Finland distinguishes between public legal aid and free process. Two laws passed in 1973 are presently in force.

The Act on public provision of legal aid

According to this statute, public legal aid is a municipal matter, although a state contribution is paid for actual operating costs. This contribution is paid out in accordance with a classification of the municipalities into ten classes on the basis of their financial strength, and varies from 50 per cent to 95 per cent of the costs. A municipality in a weak economic position can receive additional support.

A municipality is apparently not required to provide legal aid. The statute states only that the municipality *can* do this. If it does, a special legal aid bureau is to be set up with one or more positions for public legal counsel. The holder of such a position is to have passed law examinations and must have experience at the bar or on the bench. He must observe the rules of professional conduct of the bar and is subject to the professional supervision of the Bar Association. He is not permitted to carry on a private practice along with the post or to occupy another permanent paid position if it would interfere with his tasks as counsel.

Legal aid operations are under the supervision of a municipal legal aid committee, which in turn is supervised by the Justice Ministry. One member of the committee must be a lawyer, if there is one in the municipality. The legal aid bureaux across the country assist each other in return for the payment of their costs.

The statute does not regulate the extent of legal aid, nor does it contain restrictions on the categories of eligibile matters. The statute speaks only of necessary legal aid "in legal matters". It is not restricted to out-of-court matters. Public legal aid will not be given if pursuing the matter obviously would be a misuse of justice, if the matter has obviously slight significance for the applicant, or if his rights arose because of an assignment and it appears that the assignment was made in order to qualify for legal aid. In addition, the class of persons eligible for public legal aid is not extensively regulated. The class is described generally as natural persons who in respect of their income, means, duty to provide for dependants, and other circumstances influencing their economic situation are not without difficulty, in a position to get experienced aid themselves. Foreigners are not excluded.

The municipality can decide that their official employed as public legal counsel may, for a fee, also assist persons not entitled to public legal aid, provided that this facilitates the establishment of a public legal aid system in the municipality, or if it is difficult in a particular locality to obtain the assistance of a lawyer in private practice, as long as the additional services do not have a detrimental effect on general legal aid operations.

The application for public legal aid is made either orally or in writing to counsel at the legal aid bureau. On request the applicant must present evidence of his economic position, but counsel can and must on his own initiative make any necessary further investigations. Counsel decides himself whether to give legal aid. This can be given wholly without charge or for a partial payment by an applicant who has the means to contribute to the fee. If partial payment is made, the decision to grant legal aid should state not only how large a part of the costs but also the maximum amount that the applicant can be required to pay. If counsel wholly dismisses the application for public legal aid or grants aid in return for a partial payment, then the matter, at the request of the applicant, is to be submitted to the municipal legal aid committee for decision. If interim measures are needed to safeguard the rights of the applicant, counsel must deal with them on request.

If the applicant's opponent has come to the legal aid bureau earlier and an official there is assisting him or has assisted him, the applicant cannot be given public legal aid in the same bureau. He will instead be referred to a lawyer in private practice or to the legal aid bureau of a neighbouring municipality. If he is entitled to public legal aid, and the lawyer or bureau that assisted him receives no repayment of the costs from state funds, then the home municipality of the applicant is responsible for the costs. The same procedure will be followed if the legal aid bureau cannot give legal aid because of a case overload; the special nature of the matter; the applicant's lack of confidence in counsel, or if the applicant requests a transfer for a good reason.

If public legal aid is granted, but it later appears that any of the prerequisites was lacking or no longer exists, counsel is to decide whether or not legal aid is to cease. At the request of the applicant, such a decision may be submitted to the legal aid committee for examination. If it decides to terminate legal aid (or if it finally rejects an application after legal aid measures have been taken), the committee must at the same time decide that the applicant is to repay, fully or partially, the costs which have arisen, unless this is considered unreasonable. If legal aid is given for partial payment, counsel determines the amount that the applicant is to pay within the limits that were set earlier and the time in which repayment is to be made. (If the duty to repay now appears to be unfair, it can be altered or waived.) If the time limit is not complied with, the legal aid committee must request the provincial government to make arrangements for requiring the recipient to pay. If the sum obviously cannot be collected, no such request need be made.

The Free Process Act

This law, which replaced a 1955 statute, deals with free process in civil and penal matters before courts of general jurisdiction, water tribunals and land tribunals; matters belonging to the *jurisdictio voluntaria* (matters of an administrative nature – such as registrations – dealt with by the courts on application, usually by one party) where free process is necessary because of the nature of the matter and in order to provide legal protection for the applicant; and in matters concerning the reopening of proceedings in such actions and matters. The law also covers cases dealt with in administrative courts and courts-martial. With respect to the *jurisdictio voluntaria*, the wording of the statute implies that free process is normally not to be granted, either generally or in particular types of matters, unless it is necessary because of special circumstances as, for example, in a matter of great significance for the applicant. In general, free process is not approved if the matter is minor or if the applicant's rights arise from assignment and it appears that the assignment was made in order to obtain a grant of free process.

The benefits of free process are regulated in the statute. The applicant is relieved of court charges: mainly stamp duties on certain documents and fees on documents issued by the court, and charges for announcements in the official gazette. One important benefit is the exemption from the payment of the fee and the expenses of counsel appointed under the statutue. In addition there are benefits in relation to evidence; a witness called by the applicant will be compensated out of public funds, and the costs of other evidence adduced by the applicant and necessary for the clarification of the matter will be similarly compensated. If the applicant is required for evidentiary purposes to make a personal appearance before the court, the costs of his appearance are paid by the state. A special statute regulates the costs of the evidence and lays down certain limits on the amounts payable where public funds are to be charged. For "waste of time" – the principal item of which is loss of wages – the witness will be granted a maximum of 80 Finnish marks a day in cases where compensation is paid out of public funds.

The benefits further include exemption from execution fees and from the duty to advance execution costs. In general, all necessary execution costs are paid by the state if they cannot be obtained from the opposing party. Only one attempt at execution will be paid under the scheme, however, if the judgment debt has not then been satisfied in full on account of the impecuniosity of the debtor, a renewed execution attempt does not form part of the benefits of free process.

Nor does the scheme cover the applicant's liability for costs in relation to a successful opponent. The applicant must accordingly pay these costs himself, if he has means to do so. If the opposing party is unsuccessful and costs are awarded against him, he must replace the disbursements of the state for the action, but not its loss of court fees. If, considering the economic situation of the opponent, this seems unfair, the duty to repay can be modified or waived.

The applicant is to be provided with counsel when he himself cannot adequately protect his rights and interests in the action. The applicant need not make a special application for counsel, but the court can make an appointment on its own initiative. Counsel should preferably be a lawyer, but anyone who is entitled under the general law to represent others in court can also be considered. Before someone is appointed as counsel he should be consulted, but a lawyer or legally qualified person who commonly practises before the court can be appointed without his consent. If the applicant has suggested a competent person, this person should be appointed if it does not notably increase costs or if special reasons do not demand otherwise. If the applicant need not appear before the court in person, counsel can appear as trial representative. Counsel can, for good reasons, temporarily place another competent person in his place. Moreover, several counsel can be appointed if the significance of the matter requires it.

Counsel has the right to a reasonable fee for his work and any waste of time, along with the repayment of necessary expenses according to an itemized bill of costs, unless such a bill is considered superfluous. It may be so considered in simple cases, where counsel merely requests a fee. The opposing party has the right to see the bill, for the statute states that he has a right to be heard on it, if this can be done without difficulty. The amounts of the fee and reimbursement are determined by the court which in particular is to consider the quality of the work. There are, however, many simple actions of a routine character which usually leave no room for consideration of the quality of the work, but where a standard fee is paid. For actions which last a particularly long time, counsel can collect the fee every six months, or even for smaller periods of time, if he can show good reasons. If there are special circumstances, counsel can also collect advance payments to cover any costs amounting to large sums. If counsel is at the same time public legal counsel within the meaning of the Act on Public Provision of Legal Aid, the payment of costs which are awarded against the unsuccessful opponent shall be directed to be made to the municipality concerned in the proper proportion with reference to the fee of public legal counsel and the disbursements of the legal aid bureau.

The range of those entitled to free process is described as vaguely as in the Act on Public Provision of Legal Aid, and basically by the same terms. Thus a person is eligible for free process if, considering his income, means, dependants, and other circumstances which affect his economic situation he is not in a position to meet the court costs without difficulty. Apparently no strict guidelines have been worked out in practice, but it was normal – and perhaps still is – for every case to be determined separately. It is therefore impossible for an outside observer to describe more accurately the range of those entitled to aid. Mention may be made of one case where, in determining whether a minor was eligible for the free legal process, the economic situation of the parents was not considered, since they were not parties to the action and had no personal interest to protect in it.

Just as with public legal aid, free process will be partially approved if the applicant can reasonably pay a part of the expense himself. In the formal approval, the maximum amount the applicant will be required to repay the state is stipulated.* The loss suffered by the state in court fees is not a state disbursement.

The request for free process is submitted to the court which handles the matter or where the action can be brought by law. The request can be made before the action is brought, and free process can also be approved at that stage. Alternatively, the request can be made and examined at any time while the action is pending until the decision on the principal issue becomes final and non-appealable. The court rules on the question of free process. If the court is not in session, the presiding judge can approve the request temporarily until the court can rule on the matter. If the request is made only after the decision of the court on the principal issue is delivered but before the time limit for appeal has run out (or, if the applicant is the respondent, before the time for delivery of the respondent's notice has run out) the presiding judge in the lower court can grant the request temporarily until the appellate court has the opportunity to examine it.

Free process can be approved retroactively. In such a case the decision should stipulate which measures already undertaken are covered by the free process. The appointment of counsel cannot be made retroactively, but he can receive payment for his work from the time of the commencement of the free process to the time of his appointment as counsel. A person who is entitled to free process covering disbursements and costs already made can, as a rule, receive a corresponding advance from the state.

The application for free process is made in writing, but can also be presented orally if this is done at a hearing. The applicant must include a declaration in writing concerning his economic situation, verified by an administrative agency in his home municipality. The requirement of verification can be waived if the declaration appears to be accurate. If the principal issue is not yet before the court, the applicant must further present a statement of claim or, if he is the defendant, a written statement from which the cause of action may be inferred.

The rules that govern the withdrawal of the approval of free process and the duty to repay arising out of it correspond to those which operate in respect of the termination of the decision to grant public legal aid, except that a public prosecutor can make an application for the termination of free process. Whether the court can order that free process cease because the applicant has received significant benefits from the judgment

*The requirement that the applicant's part of the costs (for example 1/3), is to be stipulated has been abolished in the amendments of January 1977, apparently to dispose of one of the two limitations on the duty of the applicant to repay.

is not known from available material. The case is, however, covered by the wording of the statute.*

The final judgment states precisely the duty of the applicant to repay where there has been a partial grant of free process; repayment cannot exceed the maximum amount stipulated. Here, however, the disbursements of the state for the payment of witnesses called by the applicant whose testimony was obviously unnecessary is not included. The applicant can always be made responsible for paying such costs, unless it would be unreasonable to order payment. Furthermore, the duty of the applicant to pay, which only becomes a reality if costs are not awarded against the opposing party, can be softened if it appears to be unjust in the light of his present economic situation.

The decision to grant free process without a duty to repay cannot be appealed, nor can the appointment of counsel. Otherwise the decisions are subject to appeal, including a decision not to grant free process, to grant it only with the duty to repay or to terminate the free process, and decisions concerning the fee and reimbursement of counsel. Decisions of the kind in question, if taken in the course of the proceedings, may be appealed separately by means of the form of appeal known as *besvär*. Appeals against a decision given in conjunction with the judgment are made in the same way as appeals against the judgment, that is (in civil cases) by using the form of appeal known as *vad*. A public prosecutor can appeal even if he has not been a party to the proceedings.

Litigation insurance is also available in Finland. (See the discussion of litigation insurance in Sweden and Denmark above.)

4. Norway

Norway has old traditions with respect to legal aid, but the rules operating today appear to be the least liberal in Scandinavia. In 1976 a proposal for new rules was submitted by a state committee. Since the law will

*In my opinion – and this applies also to Danish and Swedish law – a further prerequisite should be laid down with respect to the duty to repay – namely that the opposing party be capable of paying the amount of the judgment. If the recipient of legal aid is not paid by his opponent, he does not benefit unjustly from the aid. But such a prerequisite is bound to cause the court difficulties. In Sweden the court usually has no information at the trial about the extent of the opposing party's solvency.

probably be substantially altered in the near future, the report on the present law will be rather summary, and the main points of the proposal will be given.

The current law

Consultation

The Norwegian law presently in force distinguishes out-of-court advising in legal matters (free legal advice, *fritt rettsråd*) from the free process (*fri sakførsel*). Advising was earlier organized in various ways by several larger municipalities. Recently, advising operations have been regulated by the Justice Ministry, and earlier regulations seem everywhere to have been replaced (except for the legal aid bureau in Oslo). Half the costs of free advice are borne by the state and half by the province.

Advising is usually done by lawyers, but in Oslo and in the province of Akershus it is handled only by the Oslo legal aid bureau. Provincial authorization is required for a lawyer to give legal aid for compensation by the community. For authorization it is required that the lawyer abide by the fee tariffs and the general conditions which govern the legal aid operation.

"Free legal advice" means gratuitous advice and direction, in out-of-court legal questions. A dispute need not be involved; the applicant can, for example, request free advice on eligibility for social benefits. The distinction between out-of-court questions and those that are handled in a lawsuit is not clear. Arbitration proceedings are seen as being out-of-court proceedings, and the applicant can consequently receive legal aid in the form of free advice. However, a more comprehensive mandate to represent applicants at arbitration proceedings should require the availability of free process for these proceedings.

Free advice is granted by the lawyer himself if it is only a question of a single consultation; otherwise the provincial government must give its approval. It is felt that a lawyer should not *refuse* a request for free advice on economic grounds but should direct the applicant to the provincial government since the latter has the power to dispense with financial conditions. If free advice is granted, the provincial government sets the lawyer's fee after the task has been completed. The fee encompasses normal office expenses, but for other expenses the lawyers can receive special compensation.

Single applicants who have a maximum income of 21,000 Norwegian crowns are entitled to free advice. For married applicants the income limit is 26,300 crowns but this sum refers to the joint income of the couple, except in divorce matters and other exceptional cases, where it appears natural not to consider the income of the other spouse. If the applicant supports one or more children under 16, the income limit is raised by 5,300 crowns. In order to get free advice the applicant may not possess assets that exceed 40,000 crowns or liquid assets worth more than 15,000 crowns. The same provisions apply to aliens living in Norway as apply to Norwegians.

By way of exception, the provincial government can grant free advice despite the fact that the income and assets limits are exceeded. For this, special grounds are required, for example, that the applicant, on account of some disability, will incur unusually heavy costs.

It is a further condition of free legal advice that it is necessary and reasonable for the applicant to receive the assistance of a qualified lawyer. A refusal on this basis is rare.

The applicant is to pay a fee of 50 crowns himself, but this can be waived by the provincial government, which apparently happens routinely in many areas.

Free process

Free process can be obtained for a dispute that is handled by a Norwegian court. The allowance includes the fees of the lawyer, and also the payment of court fees and certain costs in connection with the trial of the case. The responsibility for the costs of the proceedings which can be awarded against the applicant is not covered. Moreover, granting of the free process is only valid in the court to which the application refers. A new application must be made for costs on appeal or for costs for taking evidence at another court.

The free process is primarily granted by the Justice Ministry. The requirements for receiving the allowance are that the applicant cannot pay the costs himself, or that it is difficult for him to do so; that his case appears capable of being litigated; and that it appears fair that he be granted free process. No strict financial limits are set, but the decision is made on the basis of income, assets, debts, the burden of providing for dependants, and how heavily the applicant would be burdened by an acton. The economic situation of the spouse is taken into consideration in making the decision, as is the economic situation of the parents, if the applicant is a child.

In certain types of proceedings, the practice is more liberal, especially cases in whose outcome the state has an interest, for example, disputes over the boundaries of property; trials involving a public agency; trials where the applicant is facing a strong opponent; and trials of precedent-setting significance. The need for free process at first instance is considered to be less in tenancy matters and execution matters, and the practice is therefore more strict. The practice is also strict when the applicant can deduct the court costs as a business expense for taxation purposes.

The requirement that the matter be litigable means that there must be a reasonable probability that the applicant will win the dispute. Since this is difficult to determine on the basis of the particulars submitted by the applicant and obtained from the opposing party, the Ministry, it seems, seldom refuses requests on the basis that the matter is not litigable. It can happen that both the applicant and the opponent have a litigable claim.

Finally, as regards the requirement of fairness, the Ministry appears reluctant to grant free process in family and neighbour disputes or tenancy matters, if it appears that the applicant himself bears the responsibility for the origin of the dispute, or if he will not accept a fair offer of a settlement.

The allowance can be limited to a relief from court costs. When a lawyer is appointed as counsel, however, he is under a duty at trial to demand costs for the community from the opponent. The fee of the lawyer is paid according to a tariff.

In certain family matters, especially divorces, support, custody and affiliation proceedings, the court must give an indigent party the benefits of free counsel. It appears that the courts are somewhat more generous than the Ministry in this respect. Legal aid which is received from the legal aid bureau in Oslo can also include counsel at trial.

Litigation insurance was introduced in Norway in 1970. It is, just as in Sweden, sold with other types of insurance, for example, fire or home insurances. An insured who is likely to get free process is under a duty to apply for it. There is an uninsured excess which the insured must pay himself. The insurance, however, covers the responsibility for costs *vis-à-vis* the opposing party.

The proposal for a statute on free legal aid

Legal aid can take the form of free advice, free process, or waiver of court fees. It is intended that the aid be given by lawyers in private practice, but the statute foresees that state law offices could be set up. Lawyers as a rule will be required to give legal aid. The costs of legal aid, according to the statute, will be paid by the state.

Free advice

The distinction between free advice and free process is specified without making material changes in the law. Free advice is granted by the provincial government, but a lawyer can also grant it if it takes a maximum of five working hours.

A natural person residing in Norway is eligible for free advice. Foreigners are not excluded. Corporations, associations, foundations or unorganized groups will be eligible only under special circumstances.

The statute sets economic cut-off levels and, just as in Sweden, they are related to the "basic amount" of the social welfare legislation. The basic amount as of 1975/76, which was adopted by the Committee is 11,000 Norwegian crowns.

A person without dependants can receive free advice if his yearly income does not exceed six times the basic amount. The committee has also made a stricter alternative proposal, namely that the limit be set at four times the basic amount. If the applicant is supporting one or two children under 16 years, half the basic amount is added, and for three or more children, a full basic amount. The assets of the applicant may not exceed ten times the basic amount, and the part of the assets that consists of bank deposits and other liquid means must be less than 3½ times the basic amount. In the case of married people who have a common household and assets, their income and assets are accumulated, but the limit of income is raised to 7½ (alternatively 5½) times the basic amount. The income and assets of several persons may also be considered together if they have a common interest in the proceedings.

It is presumed that the applicant pays a certain part of the costs himself. The committee found the Swedish system too complicated and proposed a simpler variation which is not, however, intended to be recorded in the text of the statute. The applicants are divided into categories of single and married, and each of these categories is divided into three sub-categories, according to whether there are no children, one or two children, or more than two children. The contribution of the applicant to costs varies from 50 to 1,000 crowns in twelve income classes. At an income level of 60,000 crowns, a single person without children pays 700 crowns and, if he has one or two children, or more than two children,

500 or 300 crowns respectively. Married people with the same income pay 200 crowns if there are no children, 100 crowns if there are one or two chldren, and 50 crowns if there are three or more children. In the alternative proposal of the committee with lower cut-off levels it is proposed that the applicant pay only a set fee of 50 crowns or 100 crowns, regardless of income.

The provincial government can approve the granting of free advice, even if the income and asset limits have been exceeded, if this seems fair on account of special circumstances. The provincial government can also release the applicant from the payment of his part of the costs. A general condition for eligibility for free advice is that the aid be necessary and that it be fair that the applicant receive aid. Here no change in the present law is intended.

Free process

Legal aid in proceedings before Norwegian courts will be given either in the form of free process or as a waiver of court fees. The benefits are to be granted either by the court or – as a rule – by the Justice Ministry.

The benefits of the free process include full or partial costs for the assistance of a lawyer, reimbursement of the applicant's own costs occasioned by the proceedings, and court fees. In exceptional cases the responsibility of the applicant for costs *vis-à-vis* the opposing party as well as the fee of a private expert witness may be covered. If the applicant is successful and costs are awarded against the opposing party, the latter will be required to pay the expenses of the state for the legal aid. If the proceedings end in a settlement, the opposing party can be released from responsibility for costs, if this is justified for special reasons. In doubtful cases, the court can refer the question of the opposing party's responsibility for costs to the Justice Ministry.

The waiver of court costs as a separate benefit is determined according to the same rules as govern the free process.

The court may grant free process in family proceedings, tenancy matters, and proceedings for recovery of damages in personal injury matters, if the applicant has a yearly income of not more than four times the basic amount, and otherwise fulfils the economic conditions for free advice. In the alternative proposal, the limit of four times the basic amount is deleted. Otherwise, as conditions for granting free process it is proposed only that the court find that it is not unnecessary that the applicant receive legal aid in the matter, and that the legal aid does not appear to be unfair. That the matter be capable of being litigated is not set as another condition because the court should not take position on the outcome in advance.

Otherwise free process is approved by the Justice Ministry, which also examines applications in doubtful situations. For the hearing of the Ministry, only generally formulated rules are set out. It must appear just that the applicant receive legal aid. The applicant's ability to pay for the proceedings, his chances of success, the type of matter, and its significance, if any, in point of principle are to be considered. No change in relation to the present law is intended in the conditions for the granting of legal aid. If free process is approved, counsel is appointed by the court, which should accede to any desire of the applicant for a particular person. The court also determines the lawyer's fee. In general, the applicant can be charged with fully or partially repaying the legal aid expenses of the state, if his economic position has materially improved as a consequence of the legal aid. The Ministry may in exceptional circumstances grant legal aid in cases which fall outside the statute.

EDMUND WENGEREK*

Socialist Countries: Eastern Europe

I

The word "underprivileged" can signify either underprivileged or disadvantaged; neither designation appears in socialist law and jurisprudence. Only the Polish law of civil procedure makes a distinction between parties who appear with the aid of a lawyer, and those who do not (Article 5); in legal terminology, however, the description "unaided" ("unadvised") does appear,[1] referring to a person who is in need of aid, or to a person who is wrongly informed. This is undoubtedly connected with the absolute principle of equal rights declared in the constitution of the socialist states. According to the Constitution of the Peoples' Republic of Poland, its citizens possess equal rights irrespective of sex, birth, education, occupation, nationality, religion, or social position. Similar provisions are found in Article 14 of the Constitution of Albania, Article 71 of the Constitution of Bulgaria, Article 20 of the Constitution of Czechoslovakia, Article 33 of the Constitution of Yugoslavia, Article 6 of the Constitution of Hungary, and Article 123 of the Constitution of the Soviet Union.

Socialist scholarship, which considers the principle of equality to be one of the foundations of civil procedure, stresses that these provisions refer to the granting of actual, not nominal, equal rights, and that the guarantee of the realization of equal rights lies in the structure of the socialist civil procedure. It is assumed that the court cannot restrict its role to that of a passive arbitrator, and that the court must ensure that the equality of the parties is not affected by a difference in position which is a result

*Translated by Dr. Paul Bauer Weiss, Toronto, Canada

of economic conditions, education, or familiarity with the law.

The dialectical interpretation of the principle of equal rights has caused the concept of "poor" to disappear in civil procedure classifications; not only can a party without any means whatsoever expect waiver of costs,[2] but also a party who has means but who, because of the high cost of the dispute, is not in a position to pay the court costs, may obtain a full or partial waiver of costs without prejudicing the means of support of himself and his dependants (Article 113, s. 1, ZPO).[3]

The socialist ZPO treat the principle of access to the courts as one of the principles of civil procedure basic to the administration of justice. The principle is clearly expressed in Article 5 of the ZPO of the Soviet Socialist Republic,[4] according to which every interested party is entitled to turn to the court to demand protection for an injured or a disputed right. Article Article 7 OSNOW and Article 5 of the Russian ZPO stress the equal rights of all to justice, irrespective of birth, means, occupation, race and religion. Similarly, s. 3 of the Czechoslovakian ZPO (of December 4, 1963) states that everyone has the right to demand protection from the court if his rights are endangered. A similar principle is contained in ss. 2 and 57 of the Bulgarian ZPO, according to which the courts are required to decide all motions directed to them for protection of personal rights and for aid in the protection of these rights. This principle is also stated in s. 3 of the ZPO of the German Democratic Republic (G.D.R.).

The ZPO now current in the Peoples' Republic of Poland does not contain a principle similar to that of the Czechoslovakian ZPO (a similar provision was contained in Article 3 of the previous ZPO); however, the principle is an axiom which is the foundation of the Polish ZPO.

It is characteristic that the Polish ZPO place no restrictions on the assertion of a right by a foreigner (with certain exceptions which concern security for costs); and parties who live in foreign countries can assign matters concerning financial disputes to the administration of the Polish courts (Prorogation clause – Article 1104 of the ZPO).

The guarantee of the principle of access to the courts is shown in the forms of legal aid which are available:

1. The possibility of using *an uncomplicated and inexpensive "expiation procedure"* which can be introduced before a complaint is made (Article 313 of the Yugoslavian ZPO, s. 47 of the ZPO of the NRD, s. 67 of the Czechoslovakian ZPO, Articles 184-6 of the Polish ZPO). The Czechoslovakian ZPO also provides that the court is required to exercise a preventive function in order to prevent a dispute. To this end the court can use the means it considers suitable, but it may not use force.

2. *An extensive simplification of the transactions* connected with lodging a complaint. According to Article 141 of the Russian ZPO, the judge, after delivery of the complaint, discusses the essential contents of the complaint, explains which defences the respondent can raise, and demands details of evidence from the plaintiff. According to s. 94 of the Hungarian ZPO, a plaintiff who is not represented by a lawyer can deliver his complaint to the court orally. Article 188 of the Polish ZPO permits the plaintiff to read the complaint into the record in those situations where court costs have been waived. The court is required to consider whether or not the complaint is ineligible or unfounded. The Romanian ZPO also give a complainant living in a rural area the right to explain his statements for the record (Article 82).

Non-compliance with the formal requirements of the complaint does not automatically result in rejection, but, according to Article 130 of the Polish ZPO, the party is requested to remedy the defect within a week. An erroneous designation of the type of action (for example, "review" instead of "complaint") does not provide an obstacle to proceeding with the action. According to s. 95 of the Hungarian ZPO, the presiding judge has a duty to assist a party in remedying defects, and if the party resides in the court's district, he can be requested to appear before the court to explain the defects. The Romanian ZPO require the presiding judges to investigate defects in the complaint and to allow the plaintiff to remedy the defects in the proceedings (Articles 131 and 132). The Yugoslavian ZPO (Article 98) and the ZPO of the G.D.R. (s. 28) require the court to assist the plaintiff in remedying defects in the complaint. S. 41 of the Czechoslovakian ZPO require collaboration from the plaintiff during the hearing for the purpose of remedying any formal defects in the description of the action and clarifying the claims of the plaintiff (Article 471, ZPO). The rules which concern this type of proceeding apply to complaints arising out of working conditions or employment (for example, the many complaints that concern inventions). In addition, the provisions of the statute of October 24, 1974 concerning district courts for employment and insurance matters (G.Bl. No. 39 Poş. 231) provide for the collaboration of the court with the worker for the purpose of remedying formal defects (Article 43).

A court may alter a plaintiff's claim by joining a third party (who, in addition to or instead of the plaintiff, may have a cause of action). Such a possibility is provided for by Article 36 of the Russian ZPO, Article 196 of the Polish ZPO, s. 35 of the ZPO of the G.D.R., s. 96 of the Czechoslovakian ZPO, and s. 117 of the Yugoslavian ZPO.

3. *A limitation on provisions nullifying actions* where there is a lack of positive requirements or where procedural limitations are involved. The socialist ZPO have for the most part reduced these negative provisions. Lack of jurisdiction does not lead to a non-suit, but requires the court without jurisdiction to move the complaint to a competent court (Article 122 of the Russian ZPO, s. 95 of the Bulgarian ZPO, ss. 104–5 of the Czechoslovakian ZPO, s. 27 of the ZPO of the G.D.R., Article 200 of the Polish ZPO).

Even presentation of the complaint to an incompetent court (for example to the *Streitig* court instead of the *Nichtstreitig* court) does not result in a non-suit, as was the case before World War II, but requires the incompetent court to decide the matter itself (Article 201 of the Polish ZPO).

Impropriety of procedure, according to s. 104 of the Czechoslovakian ZPO, does not cause a rejection of the claim; but the court is required to direct the matter to the court of proper jurisdiction. The Polish ZPO require the court to refer the matter to the competent authority in matters concerning the claims of workers. In questions of other procedural requirements the provisions of s. 104 of the Czechoslovakian ZPO are typical: the court must waive corresponding orders so as to remedy any defects in prerequisites to the action which are capable of being remedied.

According to Article 191, s. 2 of the Polish ZPO, lack of court jurisdiction, inactivity of legal counsel, and lapse of official agents of a plaintiff organization can bring about rejection of the claim only if the defect of a court rule is not remedied within a time set by the court.

4. Cases which have a *variable jurisdiction* make it possible to lodge a complaint in the following categories:[5]

(a) In maintenance disputes, in the court where the plaintiff is resident (Article 118 of the Russian ZPO, s. 81 of the Bulgarian ZPO, s. 24 of the ZPO of the G.D.R., Article 32 of the Polish ZPO).
(b) In damage suits, brought about by physical injury or death of the provider, in the court where the complainant resides, or in the court where the injury occurred (Article 118 of the Russian ZPO).
(c) In disputes where damages are claimed, in the judicial district where the injury took place (Article 118 of the Russian ZPO, s. 87 of the Czechoslovakian ZPO, s. 85 of the Bulgarian ZPO, s. 20 of the ZPO of the G.D.R., Article 34 of the Polish ZPO).
(d) In contract disputes in which a place was specified to fulfil the obligations, in the court of this location (Article 118 of the Russian ZPO,

s. 20 of the ZPO of the G.D.R., Article 34 of the Polish ZPO).

(e) In disputes concerning employment conditions, in the court where the worker resides (s. 25 of the ZPO of the G.D.R.) or in the judicial district where the work was done or was to be done, or in the judicial district where the working location is (Article 462 of the Polish ZPO).

5. *Abolition of the requirement of counsel.* The requirement of counsel which existed before World War II was strongly criticized in the legal press. It was felt that this requirement hindered protection of the rights of injured parties in that the complainant had to bear counsel fees. Furthermore, this requirement made it more difficult to establish a direct relationship between the court and the parties, which delayed settlement of the matter.[6] These objections had an undeniable influence on the decision of the socialist legislators, although the chief cause was probably the introduction of the system of "double instance" in which the area court, with few exceptions, became materially competent for all disputes. According to this ruling, no distinction was made between minor matters and important matters so that parties were no longer required to have counsel in some matters and not in others.

If one nevertheless considers that the introduction of the "double instance" system and the abolition of the district courts (as in Poland) had as its goal justice for the broadest part of society, then the abolition of the requirement of counsel must be seen as a removal of the limitations which make access to justice more difficult. This did not mean that the value of the legal profession was not recognized. All socialist ZPO mention lawyers (Article 44 of the Russian ZPO, s. 20 of the Bulgarian ZPO, s. 25 of the Czechoslovakian ZPO, s. 3 of the ZPO of the G.D.R., Article 87 of the Polish ZPO). Scholars and legal administrators emphasize that counsel is an important factor in the administration of justice. Ensuring the assistance of counsel for parties in a civil proceedings is seen as a sign of socialist democracy, and the lawyer is useful as a translator of legal terminology.[7] Thus, in line with a movement towards access to justice for citizens there was a widespread increase in the availability of the aid of counsel in civil proceedings. This is expressed in the fact that counsel fees were reduced, and certain types of clients were provided with lawyers at a reduced fee.

The order of the Justice Minister of December 21, 1967, which concerned the fees for the work of the legal collective[8] (G. B1. No. 48 Pos. 241), directs in s. 4 that the fees of the legal collective are to be decreased by 30 per cent if:

1. the main source of income for the client is a disability, old-age, or family pension;
2. the dispute is a claim of a worker and has arisen from his employment, or which concerns a remedy for an injury which the worker has received at his place of employment;
3. the dispute concerns maintenance or a pension.

6. *The duty of the court to instruct.* The consequence of eliminating the requirement of having a lawyer is an increase in the activity of the court, especially in instructing parties who appear without a lawyer. Instruction about the procedure, the trial proceedings, the consequences of these proceedings, and the consequences of an omission are defined (Article 5 of the Polish ZPO). This duty is imposed upon the court by all socialist ZPO.

Article 14 of the Russian ZPO requires the court to explain rights and duties to the participants, to draw to their attention the consequences of instituting an action or of the omission of procedural requirements, and to instruct them on defence of their rights (compare Article 7 OSNOW and Article 155 of the Russian ZPO). This duty is set out almost identically in Pr. 2, s. 3 of the ZPO of the G.D.R. s. 5 of the Czechoslovakian ZPO places upon the court the duty of instructing citizens and organizations about their rights and duties, and requires the court to ensure that no one is injured as a consequence of ignorance of his rights. Such a duty is also imposed by Article 14 pt. III of the Bulgarian ZPO and Article 53 of the Hungarian ZPO, and is also set out in the single provisions of the ZPO, as, for example, Article 134 s. 2 of the Polish ZPO (according to which the parties when the claim is first filed are to be instructed that in case of an omission of notification of every change of address, the court will shelve the papers with the consequences of an adjournment).

Article 12 of the Polish ZPO requires the presiding judge to give the parties any necessary instruction and advice.

The Supreme Court of the Peoples' Republic of Poland stipulated, in a decision of the General Assembly of July 15, 1974, that this duty of the courts to instruct the parties "is closely related to the realization of the principle of a true equality of parties to the action" and that this instruction should be given to unaided persons who appear without counsel, and in matters of great social signifiance.

7. *Supervision of the action*; this can be undertaken for the purpose of asserting claims. It can consist of control of actions such as a withdrawal of the complaint, renouncing a claim, agreeing to a settlement, as well as to situations concerning the exceeding of a demand. The court's actions in

such matters are a type of legal aid. For example, withdrawal of the complaint, renouncing of a claim, or a settlement that is obviously in contradiction to the best interests of the complainant would bar the way to assertion of an injured right. In addition, if the court is able to make an award in excess of what the complainant demands, access to justice is greatly eased.

According to s. 34 of the Russian ZPO, the court cannot agree to a withdrawal of the claim or conclusion of a settlement agreement by the parties if they compromise the interests protected by law.[9] Even a settlement agreement is subject to the approval of the court to determine if it contradicts justice or social interests (s. 99). The Bulgarian ZPO refer to a confirmation of the settlement by the court, which shall ascertain if the settlement contravenes laws and the principles of social co-existence (s. 125).[10] On the other hand, the Polish ZPO require the court to deny a withdrawal of a complaint, renunciation of a complaint, or a settlement if they contravene justice of the principles of social co-existence, or when they clearly injure the interests of the party (Articles 203, s. 4, and 223, s. 4). Such an action by the court makes these actions void.

Two countries permit the court to award more than the complainant demands, or to vary the award. The Soviet ZPO allow a larger award to be made if it is necessary for protection of rights and for the legally protected interests of the state institutions and other organizations, or for cooperative, social, or civil interests (Article 37 OSNOW). The Polish ZPO, which recognize the principle *ne eat index ultra petita partium*, provide an exception for complaints which concern maintenance, working conditions, or damages arising from illegal conduct (Article 321, s. 2).

The court is also required in these cases to aid those who find themselves unquestionably in a worse practical or economic situation than that of their opponents.

8. *Setting a maximum for court costs.* The Socialist ZPO provides for relatively low court fees. The Soviet Union, the Peoples' Republic of Poland, and the G.D.R. require that the costs be in proportion to the value of the dispute. According to Article 82 of the Russian ZPO the costs of matters valued up to 30 Rubles reach 30 Kopecks, matters valued at 20-50 Rubles reach 50 Kopecks, matters valued from 50–500 Rubles are set at 2 per cent of the value, and matters valued at more than 500 Rubles are set at 6 per cent of the value. In the G.D.R. the costs of matters up to 100,000 Marks reach 5 per cent of the value (s. 165 of the ZPO). Above 100,000 Marks there is a surcharge of 0.5 per cent added. In the Peoples' Republic of Poland, because of s. 11 of the decree of the ministerial

counsel of June 13, 1967, on setting maximum fees in civil matters, the costs of a dispute valued up to 3,000 Zloty are 5½ per cent; up to 5,000 Zloty they are 6 per cent; and over 5,000 Zloty they are 6½ per cent. This progression is supported by the assumption that complainants in matters of slight value are not well-to-do, while in matters of greater value complainants may run a business and have corresponding financial means (in respect of these persons, the court can double the costs if the matter is complicated and demands greater action on the part of the court: s. 3 of the decree).

As appears from the above, court costs (see above for lawyers' costs) present no obstacle to asserting a claim in the socialist states. The socialist legislators have not entirely done away with court costs, the assumption being that the duty of paying court costs can prevent a rash of litigation; but the relatively low costs which are set do permit access to justice for a large number of people. It is characteristic that in many matters of great social significance, such as divorce and family disputes, the provisions of ss. 13-15 of the decree allow the court a free hand in setting costs within a relatively large scope (for example, in divorce matters, from 1,200 to 5,000 Zloty). The courts consider the economic position of the complainant when using this provision. Although the object of setting a minimum court fee is to make the parties reflect on whether or not to pursue the divorce, it must not make the assertion of rights impossible. One must here note the provisions of Article 103 of the Polish ZPO, s. 80 of the Hungarian ZPO, Article 145 of the Yugoslavian ZPO, s. 177 of the ZPO of the G.D.R., and s. 147 of the Czechoslovakian ZPO, which permit the court to levy against the parties and even their agents (or, as the Polish ZPO provide, even the witnesses and expert witnesses) the costs which have arisen because of their carelessness. These restrictions ensure that the complainant can rely on his rights to legal action not being misused.

9. *Waiver of court costs*, a typical form of legal aid. It is characteristic of some socialist ZPO that they provide for two forms of waiver of court costs: the statutory form and the judicial form. Statutory waiver includes situations of waiver *ex lege*. Persons who establish claims relating to working conditions or maintenance disputes are entitled to waiver (Article 80 of the Romanian ZPO, s. 63 of the Bulgarian ZPO, s. 68 of the ZPO of the G.D.R., and Article 11 of the Polish ZPO). According to Article 80 of the Russian ZPO, those who seek damages for physical injury are also entitled to statutory waiver.

Additionally, any citizen may demand a judicial waiver if it is warranted by his economic position (Article 80 of the Russian ZPO, s. 131

of the Czechoslovakian ZPO, s. 63 of the Bulgarian ZPO, Article 161 of the Yugoslavian ZPO, s. 84 of the Hungarian ZPO). Article 113 of the Polish ZPO makes waiver dependent upon presentation of a certificate from a governmental body certifying that the person requesting waiver cannot pay the costs without danger to his support or that of his family. The application can be made orally in the court of the applicant's residence (Article 114 of the Polish ZPO). According to Article 116 of the Polish ZPO, s. 85 of the Hungarian ZPO, s. 170 of the ZPO of the G.D.R., and s. 138 of the Czechoslovakian ZPO, an obvious lack of merit in the complaint is a ground for refusing the application for waiver.

Statutory waiver is interpreted broadly. Eligible matters include the claim of a society member for balance profits, claims arising out of working conditions, claims for alteration or abrogation of a bad report on an employee, claims of heirs for damages that arose in the course of employment, claims of students of a trade school, and claims of officers or soldiers.

The Supreme Court of Poland has stated that possession of a single family dwelling does not preclude cost waiver, and a person who is unemployed and has no income can still be recognized as eligible for waiver. A cost waiver, based on a principle of reciprocity, may also be available for foreigners (Article 1129 of the Polish ZPO, s. 181 of the ZPO of the G.D.R., and Article 443 of the Russian ZPO).[11]

An important result of cost waiver is the right to demand the appointment of a lawyer (Article 163 of the Yugoslavian ZPO, Article 17 of the Polish ZPO, s. 30 of the ZPO of the G.D.R.). In the Soviet Union, those persons who have many claims also receive the free aid of a lawyer. A cost waiver or reduction based on the economic situation of the client is permitted by a provision of the Ministerial Council of the Soviet Union of February 14, 1966.

The Polish ZPO carefully regulates the appointment of counsel for the persons who obtain a cost waiver; counsel is named on application of the party if the court decides that participation of counsel is necessary (Article 157 of the Polish ZPO).

The submission of a certificate from a state organization is statutorily required of the parties who obtain cost waiver *ex lege* (those whose claims arise from working conditions, maintenance claims, and affiliation proceedings); they must certify that they cannot bear the costs without endangering their own upkeep or that of their family. The court will appoint counsel if these conditions are confirmed.

The Bar Association determines which lawyer will be appointed.

(Appointment of counsel is dealt with in ss. 30 and 31 of the Czechoslovakian ZPO and, to a lesser extent, s. 171 of the ZPO of the G.D.R.)

The Polish ZPO do not specify who is to pay counsel fees; they grant the lawyer the right to collect only the honorarium and disbursements due him. Article 91 of the Russian ZPO empowers the court to award the fees to the Bar Association. Article 122 of the Polish ZPO gives counsel precedence over claims of third parties. If the applicant is unsuccessful, the lawyer receives no fee. Although the legislative intent was to encourage lawyers to represent those parties relieved of costs, and although the bar association gives great weight to counsel's conscientious performance of duties in this area, the gratuitous nature of legal aid presents a problem. In the G.D.R., it should be noted, lawyers who represent parties relieved of costs receive their fees from the state treasury.

Those who are released from the obligation to pay costs can, according to Article 188 of the Polish ZPO, read their complaint orally into the record.

If the cause of action for which a lawyer was appointed or cost waiver granted no longer exists, the court rescinds the cost waiver and the appointment of counsel (Polish ZPO and ZPO of the G.D.R.). If the party for whom costs were waived wins the action, the court is required to allocate court costs to the treasury (Article 121 of the Polish ZPO, Article 166 of the Yugoslavian ZPO, s. 148 of the Czechoslovakian ZPO, s. 63 of the Bulgarian ZPO and Article 91 of the Russian ZPO). According to the Polish ZPO, waived costs cannot be regained if the action was unsuccessful. The losing party can, however, be ordered to repay the costs of the other party if the latter had costs waived. According to Article 95 of the Russian ZPO, the losing party is required to repay the treasury for its outlays. Court fees need not be repaid.

10. The socialist ZPO provide for *the aid of a state lawyer* to be offered to the citizen, in order to ensure protection of civil rights (Article 29 of the Soviet OSNOW, Article 45 of the Romanian ZPO, s. 35 of the Czechoslovakian ZPO, s. 2 of the Hungarian ZPO, s. 7 of the ZPO of the G.D.R., and Article 17 of the Polish ZPO). The Bulgarian ZPO do not directly mention the protection of civil rights, but allude to governmental and social interests. The Yugoslavian ZPO, on the other hand, speak only of preventing the use of civil actions for illegal goals. The state lawyer only initiates a complaint if a social interest demands it; normally the parties are left to make their own claims, and the lawyer acts as an adviser. In Bulgaria and Poland the number of claims raised by the state lawyer is low (0.003 per cent and 0.5 per cent respectively). Permitting a state

lawyer to institute proceedings does not mean that the person for whom a claim was instituted loses control of the matter. The state lawyer cannot refuse a claim or conclude a settlement himself (s. Z A 76 3 of the Hungarian ZPO, Article 41 of the Russian ZPO, s. 35 of the Czechoslovakian ZPO, Article 56, s. 2 of the Polish ZPO).

The person for whom the state lawyer is acting can participate in the proceedings as a complainant (Article 56 of the Polish ZPO). If, however, the person himself takes no part in the proceedings, the judgment which dismisses the claim of the state lawyer wholly or in part is not binding for this person (Article 58 of the Polish ZPO).

11. *The participation of social organizations* in civil proceedings on behalf of a citizen is also provided for by many ZPOs. This right is contained in Article 30 of the Soviet OSNOW, and in Article 42 of the Russian ZPO which permits, in circumstances specified in the statute, initiating of claims by organizations of the state government, by trade unions, by state institutions and operations, and by single citizens on behalf of another in order to protect their rights and interests. Article 8 of the Polish ZPO permits initiation of a claim or participation in civil proceedings which carry out no economic activity. The Soviet law sets out a number of cases in which a social organization can institute an action; for instance, it can move to have set aside a contract which was concluded under deception, force, or threat (Article 58 of the Soviet civil code). Trade unions can appear in labour disputes (Article 151 of the labour code).

The Polish ZPO permit participation in civil actions only by workers' organizations named by the justice minister, and then only in disputes relating to working conditions, accidents, or occupational disease (Article 61 of the Polish ZPO).

Organizations acting for their members in civil proceedings are governed by the same rules of procedure as the state lawyers. They can also cite precedents. In addition, the societies can designate an agent in disputes concerning working conditions (Article 446 of the Polish ZPO); this agent then is a party to the proceedings. A similar right exists for family service organizations.

In practice, trade unions seldom participate in labour actions[12] because matters relating to working conditions are normally decided by so-called conflict commissions which have union representation. (The labour and social insurance tribunal hears appeals from the decisions of the conflict commissions.) Other types of organizations do not fully utilize their rights in the area of instituting claims and participation in actions.[13] Associations, trade unions, and other organizations also offer legal advice to their members.

In the G.D.R., representatives of work collectives and social organizations can participate in the action, if the court finds it necessary, in order to serve as expert witnesses or to simplify the proceedings (s. 4 of the ZPO of the G.D.R.).

According to s. 32 of the Czechoslovakian ZPO, only the national council (*Nationalrat*) has the right to institute proceedings if the social interest requires it; a social organization, on the other hand, may only participate in an already instituted action if it concerns a matter of social interest.

II

In a discussion of the forms of legal aid which are provided in the ZPO of the socialist states, one should stress the fact that a number of matters are actually referred to the competence of different social commissions, which means that jurisdiction on some matters is actually divided. This tendency is expressed most clearly in the Peoples' Republic of Poland; however, in the Hungarian Peoples' Republic nearly all civil matters came to be concentrated in court proceedings.

A division of jurisdiction in civil matters between the commissions and the courts was accomplished by expediting the citizen's access to the appropriate tribunal. The industrial conflict commissions, for example, hear disputes arising out of working conditions in industries employing at least 100 workers (Article 248 of the Polish labour code). The members of this commission meet with the foreman and the industrial council (Article 251). Thus the worker realizes that a dispute can be determined within the confines of his own industrial setting. There are some difficulties with this procedure, however, because the members of the commission are not independent, often are not acquainted with the legal problems, and there are difficulties in reaching a speedy resolution of the matter.

Similar provisions, which are accepted as principles of the industrial conflict commission, also exist in the principles of the social tribunals. In the Soviet Union the arbitration boards are active in industry, offices, housing commissions, street committees, immigration, and collective farms. They determine, among other matters, salary disputes involving less than 50 Rubles. The parties must have given their permission for a decision by a social tribunal. In Bulgaria, these social tribunals decide salary disputes up to a value of 20 Lewa. (However, 50 per cent of these tribunals are not active.)[14] In Yugoslavia, conciliators mediate labour disputes and give legal advice. In some republics (as, for example, in Macedonia), these tribunals determine minor village disputes. In the G.D.R. the social tribunals decide matters up to a value of 500 Marks. Circuit courts hear appeals from the decisions of the tribunals (s. 21, ZPO). In Romania, arbitration commissions act in conjunction with the executive committee of the Peoples' Council; they can arbitrate civil matters and, with the agreement of the parties, can decide matters up to a value of 10,000 Leu. In the Peoples' Republic of Poland social tribunals do not play a great role in civil matters; their activity is limited to reconciliation of the parties. Settlements concluded by the social tribunals or arbitration commissions give no right to execution, so that a party cannot enforce a decision. One characteristic of proceedings before the courts is the fact that parties are free to choose and are not bound.[15] Nevertheless these tribunals comprise a form of aid outside of the normal courts.

III

The social organizations in Poland are very active in the provision of legal advice and assistance.[16] The regulations of the Polish trade unions, which were accepted in December 1976 at the Congress of Unions, impose a duty on the unions to represent and protect the legal rights of all workers. The guidelines of the central council of the unions, dated June 12, 1975, relating to working conditions and legal aid, obliges the area council of the unions to provide legal advice and legal aid for the indsutrial council and the workers.

The regulations provide for social commissions on legal aid. Judges and lawyers, scholars and pensioners with legal knowledge are members of these commissions. Besides this commission, persons with legal training working in legal aid collectives with the regional trade union council and in area advisory centres are active. Legal aid includes informing the workers of their rights; intervention; representation of the worker before the conflicts commission, appeal courts and occupational and social insurance bodies.

In greater Poland in 1973 there were 3,110 complaints and applications and 1,117 processed; yearly about 6,500 instances of advice arise (in 17 matters claims were instituted).

Another active organization which delivers wide legal services is the

Polish committee of social welfare. According to s. 8 of the articles of association, this organization has as a goal advising in maintenance or support matters, chiefly families with many children, and older persons. Advice is given by an agent of the legal division, or where there is no legal division, by a member of the commission. In 1975, 6,350 disputes were handled (including 3,088 maintenance disputes). When necessary, the committee initiates claims or takes part in proceedings that have already been instituted. The committee also appoints its officials as agents of the complainant.

The Polish women's league delivers legal aid to women. It operates 300 centres in which 1,400 legally trained persons are socially active. Approximately 50,000 disputes are handled yearly (about 25 per cent of which are related to maintenance). Legal aid consists of oral advice, intervention, mediation, and aid in drafting claims. In 1975 the representatives of the women's league appeared in 500 disputes as agent during the course of the proceedings. Claims were instituted in a relatively smaller number.

The Society of Friends of Children operates no organized centres; however, the regional divisions give advice on social matters. Thirty-two adoption and welfare centres process adoption applications and participate in adoption proceedings. In difficult cases the representatives of the society appear as agents. Only in extraordinary cases does the society initiate claims.

The Polish Union of the Deaf also delivers legal aid to its members (s. 9 of its articles of association), but operates no legal aid centres. The organization is active in giving advice. This union does not restrict itself to legal advising, however, but it also mediates settlements.

The Union of the War Wounded of the Peoples' Republic of Poland, according to s. 2 of its articles of association, gives legal aid (drafting, assistance, and intervention) to members and to war-wounded nonmembers. Legal aid is given by legally trained members of the governing body and by co-operative regional bodies.

The main governing body of the union advises about 500 people yearly and gives other forms of legal aid, including drafting assistance and intervention. In individual cases and maintenance disputes, the union refers the matter to the court.

The Co-operative Anti-Alcohol Committee gives legal aid to families of alcoholics. This aid consists of legal advice, drafting claims in maintenance and divorce matters, referral of the alcoholic to social and medical services, and drafting documents in execution proceedings. The organization oversees the progress of the action, but does not actively participate.

Legally trained members of the regional centres and the co-operative economic units give advice in many cases jointly to the populace. The statute of December 19, 1963 concerning advocacy (G. Bl. No. 57 Pos. 309) foresees a development of co-operative legal aid offices. The provisions in this area were previously not realized.

The daily and weekly press in the socialist countries carry columns on legal advice and will answer questions by mail. Radio and television broadcast programmes which make the law more accessible to the general public, and legal organizations such as the Polish Jurists Union maintain a lecture circuit.

Notes and References

1. Decision of the Supreme Court of June 27, 1953, concerning the regulation which includes legal terminology and the practice for the use of Article 236 of the rules of practice in civil disputes.
2. Before World War II the Polish rules of practice made waiver of court costs dependent upon proof of complete poverty.
3. ZPO = Zivilprozessordnungen = Rules of Practice.
4. Principles of the civil procedure of the U.S.S.R. and the Union Republic.
5. I am mentioning only the cases which occur frequently – other than those mentioned here there are others that are specified for each country.
6. Especially disdained was the situation in which the district courts had to designate a complainant who had actually appeared as not appearing and permit a judgment *in absentia.*
7. So Gottfried Baumgartel sees the role of the lawyer.
8. A legal collective = Rechtsanwaltskollective.
9. According to s. 95 of the Czechoslovakian ZPO, the court can permit withdrawal of a claim if it is in contradiction to social interests.
10. The ZPO of the G.D.R. require the court to examine the settlement to see if it corresponds to the principles of socialist justice.
11. Provided for in the agreements which were concluded between the Peoples' Republic of Poland and the Soviet Union, Czechoslovakia, Hungary, Yugoslavia, the G.D.R. and Bulgaria concerning cost waiver.
12. From the information gathered by the author it appears that in greater Poland (one-sixth of the Polish territory) in 1975, seventeen complaints were raised.

13. From a questionnaire circulated by the author, it seems that only the women's league and the Polish committee of social welfare have raised complaints in some instances.
14. In 1972 in the Peoples' Republic of Poland there were 6,447 arbitration commissions in which (including penal matters) 72,002 matters were handled.

P. H. GROSS

South Africa

In South Africa access to civil proceedings is a question of both economics and race. Indigent whites[1] are at as much of a disadvantage in enforcing or defending their rights in civil legal proceedings as are coloureds, Asians or Bantu who are unable to pay the costs of litigation. A sizeable majority of indigent South Africans are non-white, and average standards of education are far higher amongst white than amongst non-white South Africans. The matter is further compounded by the fact that a significant number of Bantu continue to live in conditions of tribal life, posing quite different questions with regard to his access to ordinary courts.[2] Race, economics and cultural differences all play a role in determining the ease with which any individual South African may pursue a dispute in accordance with the general civil procedure of South African law.

A definition of legal aid[3]

> The organized rendering of legal services by advocates and/or attorneys, either in the nature of consultation and advice or in the nature of representation in court or before administrative tribunals, in civil and criminal matters, to persons who, through indigency, are unable to engage legal representatives.[4]

This definition concentrates on the problem of indigency. As a practical matter, this barrier to equal access to the courts may be removed by an efficient and effective legal aid system. In so far as racial, cultural, and other difficulties impeding the access of the individual to the courts and the law may be regarded as compounding the problem of indigency, they can be likewise remedied. If and in so far as these other difficulties represent barriers quite distinct from indigency they are, it is submitted, beyond the manageable scope of legal aid, which is submitted further, is an aspect of legal procedure.[5]

I shall therefore confine my attention to the problem of indigency without regard to racial differences.

The definition cited above emphasized the organized and systematic nature of legal aid. It follows that acts of charity by legal practitioners, as valuable as they might be, fall outside the definition of legal aid. Undoubtedly there have been many random acts of philanthropy by legal practitioners in South Africa; but it is clear that their very nature precludes their forming the basis of an organized approach to meet the need for legal assistance of those who cannot afford to pay. Other provisions of South African law have incidentally assisted indigents or have been patchwork attempts to cope with the worst breakdowns in the system of justice, but these have all fallen short of an organized and systematic rendering of legal help to those who cannot afford to pay for it.[6]

The legal aid bureaux commenced their operations in 1937, aimed at least in part to ease the problems of the many migrants from rural to urban areas.[7] A legally qualified legal aid officer was to be stationed at each bureau, and matters requiring litigation would be referred to members of a panel of local attorneys who rendered assistance free of charge. Over time an organizational pattern developed: the bureaux were funded by a government department, but the administration of the scheme was entrusted to the local Law Societies. Applicants for legal aid were required to be indigent and a flexible means test was administered at each bureau – the basic standard was the ability of an applicant to afford consulting a lawyer in private practice.

A variety of problems, the most serious of which was a shortage of funding, ultimately led to the collapse of this approach to legal aid.[8]

The Legal Aid Scheme of 1962 was to be administered by a government department and it envisioned the appointment of civil servants as legal aid officers. Matters referred by the legal aid officers to private practitioners were to be handled free of charge. Means test levels were to be determined locally. This scheme, however, never succeeded in getting off the ground.

Legal aid pursuant to the Legal Aid Act 22 of 1969[9]

Present day legal aid in South Africa is run as a scheme pursuant to the above Act and is financed by parliamentary appropriations. The Act sets out to establish a Legal Aid Board to provide legal aid for indigent persons and which is empowered, *inter alia*, to "fix conditions subject to which legal aid is to be rendered".[10] The constitution of the board is determined by the Act. The bench, the organized legal profession and a number of government departments, are represented thereon. Except where membership of the board is contingent upon holding a particular government post, all appointments to the board must be made by the Minister of Justice. The Act provides further:

> The Minister may, if in his opinion there are good reasons for doing so, at any time terminate the period of office of any appointed member or his alternate.[11]

The Act itself serves only as a broad outline, and the board is left with wide discretion. The directives of the board have been incorporated into the Legal Aid Guide,[12] which amounts to a set of rules made in terms of the Act and has the force of delegated legislation.[13] The provisions of the guide are therefore crucial to the scheme.

The scheme is administered by way of resolutions of the board carried out under the supervision of an officer of the board – the Director of Legal Aid. The core of the scheme, civil and criminal, is the presence at magistrates' courts of legal aid officers who are either employees of government departments or of the Legal Aid Board.[14] The legal aid officers consider whether applicants for legal aid qualify in terms of the guide for legal aid, and if they so qualify they are referred to attorneys in private practice, who have indicated a willingness to accept legal aid matters. Attorneys are empowered to brief advocates and both attorneys and advocates are remunerated[15] for legal aid work. The guide explicitly states that where practicable the applicant for legal aid is able to obtain the attorney of his choice.[16] Provision is made in the guide for recipients of legal aid to make a contribution towards the cost of the assistance.[17]

Legal aid is available to all indigents "relatively permanently resident" in the Republic of South Africa. The guide then includes the following provisions:

> If a legal aid officer is satisfied that an applicant is unemployed without sound reasons, or that he leads a dissolute or dishonest life, or that is

as a result of his own misconduct or neglect unable to bear the legal costs himself, no legal aid shall be rendered to him.[18]

Legal aid is rendered in all civil matters except certain specified types of cases[19] which include:

(c) . . . an action for compensation on the ground of defamation, insult, breach of privacy, seduction, adultery or the persuasion of a person to leave or stay away from his spouse;
(d) (an action) simply to prove paternity;
(e) . . . a law-suit to which the Board is a party.

The guide further provides:

If an attorney or advocate to whom an applicant is referred in connection with a civil case is of the opinion that
(a) the applicant's claim is of a trivial or vexatious nature;
(b) no real or substantial benefit will be attained by the rendering of legal aid;
(c) the applicant, had he not relied on legal aid, would not have enforced his rights because the costs involved would have been out of proportion to what he may achieve; or
(d) the application should not have been granted in terms of the Board's scheme;
such an attorney or advocate must refuse to render assistance and inform the Director accordingly.

Divorce cases are governed, in addition, by certain separate requirements.[20]

Provision is made in the guide for appeals against the refusal to grant legal aid and for the granting of legal aid in civil appeals. These provisions are, however, somewhat restrictive in nature.

A means test has been prescribed by the board and forms part of the guide.[21] The same test is applicable throughout the country without local variations. The basic consideration is "calculated income" which takes both income and assets into account. With regard to a married couple, the income and assets of both spouses are relevant and this provision applies to estranged spouses as well, except for matrimonial matters *inter se*, when the assets and income of the applicant only are considered. The means test determines ceilings for calculated income which vary as between different racial groups. Applicants whose calculated income exceeds the relevant ceiling do not, in general, qualify for legal aid.[22] As already mentioned, applicants who are eligible for legal aid are obliged to pay contributions.

Legal aid clinics at the universities[23]

While the administration of these clinics is independent of the Legal Aid Board the clinics are geared to performing the work which is a necessary preliminary to the granting of legal aid under the national scheme. Thus a case requiring legal aid is referred to the relevant legal aid officer of the national scheme but before this is done the matter is thoroughly investigated and the necessary preliminary steps are taken. The clinics operate in poor neighbourhoods from rent-free premises. The services of students are on a voluntary basis – students receive neither remuneration nor academic credits for their work. The management of the clinic is in student hands. Supervision is undertaken by members of the local side-bar[24] on a gratuitous basis. The clinics maintain friendly links with the university authorities and the Law Societies and are in regular contact with the national scheme.

Statistics[25]

The national scheme actually began its operations in 1971. For the period March 29, 1971 to February 20, 1973, a total of 4,312 cases were handled, of which 4,121 were civil. These civil cases were divided among the different race groups as follows:

Whites	2,237
Coloureds/Asians	1,253
Bantu	631

The majority of civil cases of whites were divorce actions. There are suggestions that the number of cases handled is on the increase; thus, it has been stated that for the year ending in March 1974, the board received 10,600 applications for assistance, of which all except 2,984 were accepted in some manner. In 1974–75 Parliament appropriated R370,000 to the scheme which reflects a substantial increase on prior appropriations.

The University of Cape Town also operates as a legal aid clinic. As of September 1974, some 2½ years after the clinic's inception, 992 cases had been dealt with. 31 per cent of all these cases were referred to legal aid officers of the national scheme, and 24 per cent were handled by students without requiring further assistance.

The main criticisms of legal aid in South Africa

This section will deal chiefly with the national scheme.

It is submitted that no coherent strategy has evolved, and that consequently the scheme suffers from a lack of government commitment. There has been an absence of any clear thinking on the direction and growth of the legal aid system. This results in legal aid being approached as a negative stopgap measure with the danger that increasing sums of public money will be spent without any firm idea of what is meant to be accomplished.

The statistics cited above are alarming, even given the comparative youth of the scheme. They suggest that the question may yet be posed whether South Africa has seriously begun to tackle the problem of providing legal assistance to indigents.

The Act itself, by providing only a bare outline, makes a flexible approach possible. Criticism may, however, be directed towards the Minister of Justice's wide powers in relation to the appointment of members to the board and the possible termination of their tenure. It is also regrettable that the Act does not deal with the position of a successful party to litigation, who does not receive legal aid, where the unsuccessful party was assisted by the legal aid scheme.

There is merit in certain provisions of the guide. For instance, we have already observed that legal practitioners are remunerated for legal aid work and that applicants should, in general, be able to obtain the attorney of their choosing. These regulations are praiseworthy in that they approximate the position of the legally-aided person with that of the fee-paying client. But the guide is essentially negative in tone and it nowhere contains any indication of the principles underlying the provision of a legal aid scheme. Further, the legal aid officers (whose performance is crucial to the scheme) are civil servants who are frequently combining legal aid with other work; the danger becomes real that their primary concern will focus on how to exclude potential applicants from the scheme rather than how to assist those who cannot afford their own legal representation. An example of this misplaced emphasis is to be found in the specific provision of the guide which enumerates certain possible abuses against which legal aid officers must be on their guard – these guidelines pertain, in essence, to the truthfulness of the applicant and the genuineness of his application for legal aid.[26] It is not disputed that there are likely to be individuals who will attempt to abuse a legal aid scheme. These abuses cannot go unchecked, without resulting in a waste of scarce resources. However, this legitimate and limited need to guard against exceptional cases of abuse must not assume an unwarranted importance. It may well be asked whether this specific provision in the guide was necessary or whether it would not have been preferable to leave the matter implicit and to the good judgment of legal aid officers.

The provision of the guide referred to above, that a person who is unemployed without sound reasons, or who leads a dissolute or dishonest life, or who as a result of his own misconduct or neglect cannot pay for his own lawyer, is ineligible for legal aid, deserves the most severe criticism.[27] The problems of interpreting this paragraph appear insurmountable; in addition, conflicts with the rules of evidence governing the admissibility of similar fact evidence may well arise.

Several types of civil cases are excluded from the ambit of the scheme.[28] It is proposed here to observe only the exclusion of cases to which the board is a party. In principle, legal aid aims to render affluence irrelevant in determining the quality and availability of legal representation. It is a corollary of this principle that the identity of the party opposing the legally-aided person is irrelevant. In principle, this exclusion is unsound in that cases may occur where a person will need legal aid if he is to pursue a dispute and the fact that the board is the opposing party should not alter matters. For instance, an applicant refused legal aid might wish to challenge the refusal by way of review by the Supreme Court. The provision in the guide is even wider in that it likewise denies legal aid to a person defending an action brought against him by the legal aid board.

The greater stringency with which applications for legal aid for divorce actions are sifted, referred to earlier, is founded on faulty principles.[29] It would be one thing to simplify divorce procedures to the point where lawyers were no longer used for these matters. It is another to make it more difficult for a poor man to be properly represented in these cases than it is for a rich man to be so represented. Moreover, the scheme, rather than the legally-aided indigent, decides that the enforcement, for instance, of a hire-purchase contract is more important than the right to dissolve a failed marriage. No one tells a fee-paying client, without sound legal reasons for doing so, which of his legal rights are relatively more or less important. If these attempted restrictions are a consequence of the need to utilize limited resources for other types of cases, then it would be well to make this point clear and to recognize the departure from principle involved in doing so.

It is submitted that the chief criticism of the means test is that its ceilings are inflexible. Moreover, there is no provision for regional variations. On both counts the present provisions compare unfavourably with their precursors. There is continual argument over the levels of the ceilings, but that should not obscure the fact that the ceilings are but means to an end – the end being the provision of legal assistance to those who cannot afford to pay for it themselves. It would be desirable to eliminate the racial differentiation contained in the means test ceilings; improvements may be forthcoming in this regard.

One of the chief failings of the scheme has been the almost complete absence of any publicity for its operations. This is particularly important when it is borne in mind that the benefits of the scheme have to be publicized to an indigent and relatively uneducated segment of the population – a segment of the population that does not automatically perceive a problem as a legal one. It cannot have been the intention of Parliament that the people for whom the benefits of legal aid are intended should be entirely unaware of its existence.

While state funding of a legal aid scheme is essential, it does not follow that state administration is essential or even desirable. The South African scheme illustrates both the rigidities of an over-centralized state-administered scheme and the failure to utilize fully the goodwill towards the scheme present in the profession and the universities; this is a consequence of the exclusive concentration of administration in the hands of the board.

It is a feature of the guide that a multitude of issues have to be referred to the Director of Legal Aid; this reference becomes a condition precedent to the *granting* of legal aid. On the question of administration, the English approach of entrusting administration to the organized legal profession has many advantages, not the least of which relates to the level of commitment of the profession to the scheme.

The chief problem with the student bodies has been the necessity to build on precarious foundations. The difficulty stems not from a lack of student interest but from the somewhat unreceptive national legal aid climate allied to the completely voluntary nature of the work done by the students.

The right to legal aid

A statement of the law on this question is brief: in civil cases there is no right to legal aid. There is, it is assumed, a right to compel the due observance of the Act and the guide but that would be putting an applicant's position at its strongest. South African law is a very long way from saying that a right to legal representation, whether it can be afforded or not, is a prerequisite to the proper determination of a civil matter. Indeed, even in criminal matters, there is no right to legal aid under the scheme. There is, however, an important right to counsel in the sense that the denial of access to counsel may result in a decision being reversed as a mis-trial. The cases concerned are all criminal, and the right does not extend to the case where an accused is permitted counsel but is unable to afford the costs of legal adivce. In capital cases there is a long-standing practice of appointing advocates[30] to represented undefended accused.[31]

It is submitted that the most likely developments in this sphere of the law will be on the criminal rather than the civil side. A practice which could be adopted with comparative ease would be to enquire of undefended accused whether they were aware of the legal aid scheme and had taken advantage of it.

The purpose of legal aid

The relationship between legal aid and law reform is complex. The primary funciton of a legal aid organization is to provide legal assistance to indigents. It is not a legal aid organization's function to attempt to create an alternative society. However, it is essential that legal aid recipients be represented with the same zeal that a private practitioner would use in representing his paying clients. The underlying aim is that indigency should not be a material factor in determining the quality or availability of the legal services which an individual may obtain. In the pursuit of this overriding objective, law reform, i.e., lobbying for changes in the substantive law, fighting court cases up to the highest court level etc. is permissible and desirable as an ancillary aim.

The primary focus of legal aid rests on the needs of the individual indigent. The aim is to place the individual indigent in a position approximate to that of the fee-paying client. To this end law reform work may be undertaken as an ancillary objective.

The corollaries of the principle are that the popularity of the client's case is irrelevant; that the identity of the opposing party is irrelevant; and that the higher the ratio of individuals benefited to cases fought, the better.

This approach is not lacking in what, with respect, may be termed authoritative support. Reginald Heber Smith wrote in 1919:

> The legal aid societies are not legislative bureaux, they have no political affiliations, and they are not vehicles for the promotion of any pet cause or panacea. Their primary work is confined to giving . . . the legal advice and assistance in individual cases which poor persons need. It early became apparent, however, that if they were to be effective in their fight against injustice, they must from time to time take a part in the formulation of remedial legislation.[32]

He continued:

> In the generality of its application, a case decision is as important as an act of legislature. It follow, therefore, that a proper and equitable decision may have as much effect in safeguarding the rights of the poor as a remedial statute. Precisely the same reasons which lead legal aid oganisations into legislative work lead them to seek final adjudication in proper cases.[33]

The English approach to legal aid is based on the individual rather than the group approach.[34] This is well suited to the English constitution and law and practice and has not prevented a number of leading cases being funded by legal aid.[35]

The law reform- and group-oriented strategy has been recently popularized as the hallmark of the OEO Legal Services Program in the U.S.A. This is not the place for a general discussion on the merits or demerits of this strategy other than to observe that even in the U.S.A. it has had a somewhat chequered history.

It is submitted that in South Africa, while there are admittedly appealing arguments in favour of a law reform strategy, such an approach in present conditions would be doomed to failure. To be adopted, a strategy must be viable. The viability of any national legal aid scheme in South Africa depends, as a *sine qua non*, on adequate state financing. It is one thing to persuade parliament to appropriate funds to prevent the injustice occasioned by a poor man being unable to afford a lawyer; it would be a matter of considerably greater difficulty to persuade the same parliament to appropriate funds to a scheme the object of which was the reform of society in a direction which may or may not be in accordance with the views of the majority of members of parliament. This preference for the individual approach takes realities into account but not for a moment does it entail pursuing the principles of legal aid with anything less than the utmost vigour. The primary purpose of legal aid, as set out above, allows immense scope, certainly in South Africa, for enabling individual citizens to lead less difficult lives. To achieve this very worthwhile purpose effectively the scheme must ensure: (a) that it does not alienate the state; and (b) that it operates with sufficient strength and dynamism to win and retain the confidence of the indigent section of the community, without which it cannot possibly be efficacious.

This is the problem of balance which those responsible for the management of legal aid in South Africa must keep continuously at the top of their priorities.

The use of lawyers in private practice versus the employment of full-time legal aid lawyers

Evidence at hand from the experience of the U.S.A. suggests that the employment of full-time staff legal aid lawyers carries with it advantages in terms of both effectiveness and efficiency as compared with the system of referring legal aid cases to lawyers in private practice (the "judicare" system). It is worth observing further that such advantages extend to the rendering of legal aid in rural areas.

South African legal aid operates, as has already been stated, on a judicare system. There are, however, no *a priori* grounds for supposing that the U.S.A. experience would be invalid in South African conditions. The problem is of a different nature, namely, that as a matter of practicality there is no consensus in favour of a change to the full-time staff system. Accordingly, our interest must lie in developing and modifying the existing system – at least for the time being.

That there is scope for very considerable improvement in the organization of the South African system has already been suggested. It is submitted that the path to be chosen lies along the lines of a system where administration becomes the responsibility of the organized legal profession.[36] Financing would remain a matter, in the main, for the state. The system would build on the abilities and goodwill that do exist in the profession and the universities for legal aid. Moreover the aim would be to remedy the criticism so aptly stated as follows:

> There is no corpus in South Africa of persons deeply involved in legal aid, or thinking of legal assistance, or working out poverty law programmes.[37]

It is unnecessary to await the coming of a full-time staff system in order to improve this situation.

Likewise, there is much which can be done given the present system to make legal aid far more accessible in real terms to those who need it. The problem of publicity has already been referred to. Certain measures adopted by student clinics have much merit. Thus these clinics operate, as already described, in poor neighbourhoods, and they are open outside of the clients' regular working hours. More flexibility and less identification with officialdom could do much to enhance the present national system. A full-time staff system is not a necessary prerequisite – the effective representation of the poor does not demand the *exclusive* representation of the poor.

A welfare right or part of the administration of justice?

We are here concerned with the role of the state rather than the role of the legal profession. Most governments have accepted the responsibility for public expenditure on welfare and social services projects. It is possible to justify legal aid expenditure as being another form of welfare expenditure. Governments, however, are even more committed to expenditure on the administration of justice. Legal aid may be thus justified as forming an integral part of the administration of justice in terms of the function it performs in making the law accessible to all and in providing representation for those for whom otherwise the complexities of the legal system would prove insuperable. It is again relevant to cite Reginald Heber Smith:[38]

> . . . the administration of justice might be likened to an automobile, in which the law represents the engine, the judge the control and the attorney the gasoline. To give to two men exactly the same type of car and supply one with gasoline and the other with none and then to expect a fair race is obviously preposterous.

Given the state financing of legal aid in South Africa, the question of whether it is to be justified in terms of the "welfare proof" or the "justice proof" becomes principally a matter of theoretical interest. To the extent that the idea of justice carries with it the idea of a right, while the context of welfare suggests the notion of privilege, this writer's preference is for the justice proof.

Conclusions

Within its proper sphere of application, namely, procedural legal inequality, a well-run legal aid system can accomplish much in the way of assisting harassed citizens to lead less difficult lives in accordance with law. These are meaningful (if limited) achievements and they should not be put at risk by a search for utopian solutions to problems of substantive law and national politics.

With regard to South Africa, my major proposal for the improvement of the legal aid system may accordingly be stated as follows:[39] building on the present framework, opting for a strategy geared towards individuals' needs and injecting the system with a strategic coherency and a commitment to dynamic growth.

Notes and References

1. The racial terminology used here follows that used in the current South African legal aid legislation. No comment whatsoever is implied as to its suitability or otherwise.
2. See R. S. Suttner, "African Civil Law-Special Legal Aid Problems" in *Legal Aid in South Africa* (University of Natal, 1974), p. 189.
3. The definition is the writer's. See, by the writer, *Legal Aid and its Management* (Juta, 1976), at p. 26.
4. The terms "advocates" and "attorneys" cover the situation where the legal profession is divided. "Advocate" corresponds to the English term "barrister" and "attorney" to the English term "solicitor".
5. There is of course no provision in South African law precluding persons from going to court on account of race.
6. Many but not all of these measures realte to criminal but not civil matters. An example of present relevance are the *in forma pauperis* proceedings under the Rules of the Supreme Court.
7. Since in part this migration represented a facet of the race relations problem, the provision of legal aid could assist the promotion of better race relations.
8. One bureau, the Johannesburg Legal Aid Bureau, survived and continues to operate.
9. Referred to herinafter as "The Act".
10. Sec. 3(d).
11. Sec. 4(3)(c).

12. Described hereinafter as "the guide", it is revised periodically and we discuss the revised form valid in 1976. See *Legal Aid and its Management*, *supra*, pp. 179-84 and Appendix X.
13. See Para. 4(1) read with Secs. 2 and 3 of the Act.
14. Paras. 4.4 and 4.5.
15. In general, remuneration appears to be reasonable.
16. Para. 20.1(c).
17. See Paras. 7.1 and 8 and Appendix C of the Guide.
18. Para. 10.2.
19. Para. 13.2.
20. Para. 18 and see also Annexure C of the guide.
21. Paras. 5-10 and Annexure B. Means tests are varied from time to time; we refer to the test valid in 1976.
22. Exceptional cases are covered by Paras. 10.1 and 8.1.
23. The model chosen for the ensuing specific remarks is that of the University of Cape Town legal aid clinic. By late 1975 legal aid clinics were operating at seven South African and Rhodesian universities – see P. Ellum, *Legal Aid Developments in South Africa: July 1973–June 1975* (University of Natal, 1975), at p. 39.
24. "Side-Bar" is a collective term for attorneys.
25. These are taken from "Legal Aid and its Management", *supra*, at pp. 190-2. The detailed sources are there set out.
26. Para. 36.
27. *Supra*, note 18.
28. *Supra*, note 19.
29. *Supra*, note 20.
30. But not attorneys to assist the advocates.
31. *R.* v. Mati 1960(1) SA 304(AD).
32. Reginald Heber Smith, *Justice and the Poor*, 1967 Memorial edition.
33. ibid., p. 206.
34. See Seton Pollock, *Legal Aid: the First 25 Years* (Oyez, 1975), at pp. 43-4, 106ff., 130-9.
35. Examples are: *Ridge* v. *Baldwin (1964) AC 40* and *Rookes* v. *Barnard* (1964) AC 1129.
36. See *Legal Aid and its Management*, *supra*, 23.2.4.1. The writer there adopts in principle the proposals of S. L. Gross in *Paper on Legal Aid and Advice* presented at National Law Congress, Kimberley, May 1966.
37. F. N. Kentridge, in *Legal Aid in South Africa*, *supra*, at p. 88.
38. *Supra*, note 32.
39. See *Legal Aid and its Management, supra*, at p. 226 and 23.1.1.

CARLOS DE MIGUEL Y ALONSO*

Spain

Introduction

Spanish law today defines free legal aid as the "defence of the poor" in the regulations to Articles 13 through 50 of the law of Civil Procedure of 1881. Its origins are very old; one important source is the *Liber iudiciorum*,[1] which prescribes as one of the duties of bishops the care of the poor and the unfortunate in legal matters; it also declares that the rich and the poor are equal in questions of litigation.[2] This orientation was followed in subsequent Spanish legislation. *Las Siete Partidas* (the Seven Laws) of Alfonso X the Wise[3] mention the protection of orphans, the poor, and the unfortunate in the judicial process. The prescribed remedy is adjudication by the King himself or by the usual judge of the needy person's domicile. In the New Compilation[4] and in the Newest Compilation[5] the guarantee of access to justice for widows, orphans, and persons without means is regulated by the express proviso that jurisdiction in these cases belongs to the Crown and to the Chancery, that is, to royal justice or to the territorial tribunals. In the first Law of Spanish Civil Procedure of 1855 this issue was dealt with under the rubric "defence for the poor" in Articles 179 to 200. This treatment has remained, with few modifications, in the present law.

*Translated by José Hernon Rima, Toronto, Canada, 1978.

I. Social categories which are considered marginal in relation to the civil law

The underprivileged

In Spain today[6] there is a right to receive free legal aid for all those citizens whose incomes do not exceed twice the minimum wage set by the Ministry of Labour. This means that persons earning less than 880 pesetas daily, 13,200 pesetas monthly or 158,400 pesetas annually[7] may enjoy the benefits of justice (with prior judicial approval) and are exempted from all legal expenses, taxes, tariffs and professional fees. This benefit is granted in a judicial hearing in which the petitioner must demonstrate that his earnings from all sources do not exceed the prescribed amounts.

Per capita income in Span in 1976 was 180,000 pesetas.[8] Hence, it can be assumed that many Spaniards are entitled to free legal aid. The latest judicial statistics available indicate that in 1972 there were 1,522 civil cases in which legal aid was requested, or 2.53 per cent of the 60,032 cases which were dealt with at the trial level. In 1973, there were 1,419 such cases out of a total of 56,352 at trial, or 2.51 per cent.[9]

The actual regulation of free legal aid in Spain for the underprivileged suffers from serious defects. The mechanics of exemption base the denial of legal aid on external signs of wealth, despite the fact that the applicant may fulfil all other legal conditions. Aid will be denied if the judges conclude that the applicant has earnings that are greater than the cutoff points mentioned above. The Supreme Court has formulated a wide interpretive doctrine on this matter. On the other hand, there are some indications that the value of the exemption itself is quite doubtful, since the recipient of legal aid is obligated to pay costs if he has assets with which to do so; he is not exempt from paying the costs of his own defence, provided that they do not exceed one-third of what he could have received as a judgment. This duty lasts for three years after the termination of the litigation if the recipient improves his economic condition in the meantime.[10]

The gypsies

The gypsies are a racial minority living on the fringes of Spanish society. Their number is estimated at approximately 200,000; 15,000 live in Madrid and Barcelona.

They arrived in Spain at the beginning of the fifteenth century; at the end of that century, in 1499, a decree of the Catholic kings appeared[11] ordering the exile of all gypsies without a recognized occupation. This provision was the first European law of a national character against the gypsies.

Various laws were directed against the gypsies after 1499 prescribing penalties for those not having a recognized occupation, selling without a proper licence, or wearing the gypsy costume.[12] It is, however, interesting to note the decree of Charles III of September 19, 1783, defending the gypsies because they were "not an evil race by origin or by nature, and do not come from any dangerous roots", and forbidding that they be called "gypsies" under the same penalties as existed for libel or slander.[13] However, this move towards tolerance proved to be an exception; a relatively recent provision recommended the "close surveillance of gypsies".[14]

In recent years there have been partly successful attempts to integrate the gypsies into the Spanish national context. The state has provided public housing and in 1965 the Church created the National Fund for Service to the Gypsies. A secular organization, the Civil Association for the Gypsy Presence, has recently been founded in Madrid. The general assembly of this association took place in June 1975; a major discussion dealt with the gradual movement towards a normal legal status for Spanish gypsies.[15]

In a typical Spanish gypsy community few cases ever reach the civil courts; rather, community dispute-resolution is preferred. When a gypsy demands that another gypsy perform some civil obligation, a selected group of members of the colony arrive at an arbitral decision based on equitable principles. This decision is generally accepted by both parties. In a dispute involving a gypsy and a non-gypsy, however, there may be no arbitration; the case may be heard before the competent tribunal, although few litigants opt for this alternative.

In labour disputes, the few gypsies who have disputed against a private or corporate employer can present their grievance without discrimination. Unfortunately, most gypsies work as temporary labourers, and this status often prohibits them from using the ordinary channels.

One of the most important functions of the diocesan secretariats is to instruct the gypsies about their rights as Spanish citizens so that they may gradually integrate themselves into Spanish society. However, given the ancestral characteristics of the race, this will be a difficult task.

II. Obstacles to access to the civil law

The costs incurred in Spanish civil procedure have been discussed elsewhere.[16] Such costs are retrogressive in nature. Paradoxically, an important matter is relatively less costly than a minor matter. In small claims, the costs incurred in the process frequently represent more than half the value of the dispute, while in actions for larger amounts the costs average about 8 per cent of the value.[17] This problem, seen in almost all procedural systems, brings to mind the observation of Laski mentioned by Silveira: in the majority of cases, justice is a luxury which cannot be allowed to the proletariat.[18]

The introduction of a system of free legal aid has, to a great extent, alleviated the last problem for the underprivileged. Once aid is granted, the applicant is exempt from all procedural costs,[19] except for the limitations already mentioned; the payment of costs if there are sufficient assets, payment of costs if they do not exceed one-third of the amount obtained by the recipient of legal aid as a result of the judgment, and the payment of costs if within a period of three years the economic situation of the litigant improves.[20] The latest Tentative Project for basis for the Code of Civil Procedure of 1970 attempts to modernize and expedite the granting of legal aid to the underprivileged, which is provided exclusively by the judicial institutions themselves.

The ignorance of the availability of legal aid for some citizens (such as for the gypsy minority), but taking into account the educational and cultural level of the average Spanish citizen, does not appear to be a serious obstacle to access to justice. Any person who wishes to pursue a matter concerning a civil complaint will normally seek legal advice, and the lawyer will advise the prospective litigant of the likelihood of legal aid being granted to him either as a plaintiff or a defendant.

Spanish civil procedure suffers from a general defect of excessive formalism that affects all social classes. This problem is less serious, however, for small claims, because the process is simpler and shorter than that dealing with large amounts. In this sense formalism is not as serious for the underprivileged as it is for the upper classes.

The length of the process is a pervasive obstacle in the Spanish civil procedure, as it is in many legal systems. The average duration of a typical trial involving a fairly large amount[21] in three levels (at trial in front of the trial courts, on appeal before the territorial court, and on final appeal to the first division of the Supreme Court) has been sixty-five months.[22] Like procedural formalism, this is not an obstacle only to the underprivileged but is a defect prevalent in Spanish procedure. Naturally, modern projects for reform attempt to simplify the process drastically so as to facilitate access to justice.

III. The condition of the underprivileged from the end of the eighteenth century up to the latest reforms and proposals for reform of the civil process

Throughout the history of Spanish law, attempts have been made to alleviate the plight of the poor by exempting them from the payment of legal costs. More specifically, with respect to legal representation and free legal aid, Lalinde indicates[23] that the professionalization and the formation of associations of lawyers permitted the development of bodies which specialized in defending the needy, thus creating the "poverty lawyer", a provision for payment of subsidies to counsel was created, along with a general obligation for all lawyers to rotate through the system. By a royal decree of 1771, King Charles III ordered the bar association to handle cases involving the poor in the court prison; a rotation system was set up.[24]

In 1835, an important provision was issued which regulated the powers of the trial judge, authorizing him henceforth to deal with all civil and criminal matters previously under the ordinary royal jurisdiction, including those that had been Crown cases, such as trials involving the poor. One of the most important duties of the judge was to "administer and cause the administration of complete justice to those who, according to the laws, are in the class of the poor, in the same fashion as to those who pay; taking care as well that in all litigation they should be defended and aided without any charge, as they should, by the lawyers and court officers".[25] The First Law of Civil Procedure of 1855 dealt with the question of free legal aid in Articles 179ff., and which, with few variations, appears in the Law of 1881, which is still in force.[26]

There have been few legislative modifications in the past one hundred years. The only important reform is that undertaken by R. D. Law of February 3, 1925, in which the concept of "middle poverty" was introduced; those whose earnings were between two and three times those of a local labourer were exempted from 50 per cent of their legal costs. Judicial discretion was strengthened by permitting the judge to disallow a petition for aid when the external signs indicated such relief would be improper. Subsidiary personal liability was also introduced, whereby the beneficiary of free legal aid became liable if the judgment stated that he had acted in bad faith.

It is interesting to note that the granting of free legal aid was better regulated in the Spanish legislation contained in the Code of Civil Procedure of the (then) Protectorate of Morocco of June 1, 1914. There a flexible and modern approach was followed, establishing that legal aid would be granted to those persons who were not able to pay the costs of litigation without difficulty.

Several attempts to reform the free legal aid system have been made in the past century.[27] In the Basic Proposals of Canalejas of 1889-91, in response to the possible abuses arising from the granting of free legal aid, supervision by the Public Ministry and the possible economic sanction of costs to the defence lawyer were proposed.

In the project of 1894, Minister Ruiz Capdepon proposed that the economically advantaged only be granted interim free legal aid; he also recommended that the cut-off point for the granting of legal aid be raised to three times the earnings of a labourer.

In 1918, the Count of Romanones proposed the introduction of a system which would entrust to the Public Ministry the exclusive representation and defence of the poor. This proposal also suggested enlarging the ambit of the benefits of free legal aid in relation to marital status and the family expenses of the individual petitioner.

In 1929, judicial discretion was increased to grant aid to those persons who did not find themselves in a position to pay the expenses of litigation; this proposal also attempted to grant the same benefits to the opposing party until the judgment was given.

The Basic Proposals of 1942 also attempted to equalize the position of the parties by proposing that free legal aid be extended to the opposing party until sentence had been passed. They proposed that aid be granted to those persons of "scarce means", but established no economic guidelines. The proposals also reinforced the principle that justice must be accessible to everyone, and that costs should be minimized.[28]

The Basic Proposals of 1966 include some new developments, among them appointing mixed commissions (legal, administrative, and other professionals) to grant, supervise, and revoke free legal aid. Their authority would extend to the exemption of expenses incurred by a party until the process is concluded, as well as the granting of aid to resident foreigners (Basic Proposal #19).

Finally, the Project of 1970[29] proposes that the fundamental principles of the law of free access to the court be implemented by a system of exemptions from judicial costs (establishing necessary safeguards so that the system is not used fraudulently or abused), and granting aid to all those persons whose resources do not allow them to pay the costs of litigation. The power to grant this benefit would be given to the judge or to the tribunal in charge of the main case.

The question of access to justice has long occupied Spanish jurisprudence. In attempting to summarize the most recent contributions to the subject, we will refer to the work done by the Professors of Procedural Law in the Academic Proposal of 1972:[30]

1. The concept of poverty is degrading and is in conflict with a just and Christian concept of a well-organized society;

2. A person who is eligible for free legal aid does not have to be "poor" in the popular sense of the term, that is, an absolute destitute, but "poor" in a legal sense;

3. Legally poor means that a person would be seriously economically affected if he had to pay some or all of the costs of prosecuting or defending at law;

4. It is therefore proposed that a different title be given to the system; instead of "defence for the poor", it should be called "free justice".

5. The power to grant this type of aid should remain in the courts, and not be given to an administrative body, although it is possible that some governmental decrees may grant the benefits to specific classes of individuals.

6. The present economic criteria are class-oriented, old-fashioned, and inadequate, and should be replaced by more flexible guidelines in order to grant aid to persons whose own and whose families' health, education, or welfare would be endangered by the obligation to pay legal expenses. Such considerations would replace the existing single criterion of the applicant's income. The granting authority would undertake a personalized analysis of the individual's situation and that of his family, taking into account human and ethical imperatives.

7. To assist the applicant in obtaining legal assistance a petition to the tribunal would be prepared containing a statement of the facts upon which the applicant's rights are founded so that the judge can determine the eligibility of those persons and try to interest the respective professional associations in providing a lawyer.

8. If the economic situation of the recipient changes for the better, he will be obliged to repay the costs of justice.

Historically, the Church and the Crown have cared for the poor, the needy, and the unfortunate; after the reform of 1835, this responsibility was given to the ordinary civil judge. There appear to be no institutions in Spain, private or public, which provide organized assistance to the underprivileged in defending their rights in strictly civil conflicts. However, legal aid has been granted by the Department of Public Welfare, charitable schools, savings banks and gratuity funds for widows and orphans, the Spanish Red Cross, the National Institute of Social Security, and charitable and educational foundations.[31]

In the text of the First Law of Civil Procedure of 1855 (Article 181), one of the benefits granted to the legally poor was that "a lawyer or solicitor shall be appointed for them, without their having an obligation to pay fees". The text of 1881, which is still in force, repeated this provision (Article 14) and added new provisions (Articles 40ff.) in which it is established that the poor may choose their lawyers or solicitors; if they do not exercise this right, one will be appointed for them. Thus, professional assistance for the underprivileged in Spanish law may arise either through an applicant's initiative (whereby a lawyer or solicitor accepts the request of the individual) or through compulsory assistance (whereby a professional is appointed at the government's initiative). Compulsory assistance is the object of quite detailed regulation (Articles 43ff.) covering those situations where the appointed lawyer finds the allegations of the underprivileged person to be baseless. The appointed lawyer can be excused, although there are safeguards which permit a thorough examination of the rights of the client. That examination may result in a decision that the position of the client is not sustainable, once the opinion of several lawyers of the professional association and even of the Public Ministry is heard. Compulsory assistance by means of the official rotation (among the lawyers who are registered with the professional association) is regulated today by the General Statute of the Professional Associations of Spain of February 3, 1947, which, in Article 25, establishes the right to a public defender for all persons who request and are granted legal aid.

As of the date of the statute, all the lawyers belonging to the association are included on this roster. This is an egalitarian system and an improvement over the previous system in which the lawyers who paid the highest contributions were exempted. Until very recently this compulsory assistance was gratuitous and the expense was accepted by lawyers as a charitable duty.[32] Article 26 of the 1947 statute provides that in important or difficult trials, there will be a special rotation among those lawyers with more than five years in practice.

Recently, the professional associations expressed to the government their dissatisfaction with the gratuitous nature of the system; as a result, in 1975, for the first time, 100 million pesetas were allocated in the national budget, and that figure was increased by another 200 million in 1976 to indemnify lawyers and solicitors who provide free legal assistance.[33]

Prior to the passing of the State Organization Law of January 10, 1967,[34] there was no express constitutional guarantee of the rights of Spanish citizens to access to the courts. Nevertheless, this principle was implicit in some constitutional provisions. Articles 3, 17 and 21 of the Code of Laws of the Spanish People of July 17, 1945, state that the law protects all Spaniards without distinction due to social class; the principle of equality before the law is included by reference to the doctrine that the protection of rights must be accomplished through the judicial system, guaranteeing the rights of the Spanish people to judicial protection.

The State Organization Law of 1967 states in Article 30 that all Spaniards will have free access to the courts. The statute reinforces this theoretical equality with the declaration that justice will be free for those without means. This wording has been criticized by Almagro because it does not refer to this concession as a right.[35]

The latest legislative approach to free access to the courts appeared in the proposals for the statutes approved by the Spanish Cortes (legislature) and enacted on November 28, 1974.[36] The draft document of the proposal (which was approved by the Commission of Justice on November 20, 1969) established that "everyone shall have free access to the courts of justice to enforce rights recognized by law. This enforcement cannot be denied or limited. The necessary institutions shall be created to ensure to all persons the capacity to prosecute and to defend themselves before the courts of justice".[37]

The bill sent by the government to the Cortes varied the preceding text slightly.[38] After discussion by the commission and in the Cortes, the following text was finally approved: "Everyone shall have, in accordance with the law, free access to the courts and tribunals to enforce rights which are recognized by law." Litigants who lack sufficient economic means will be relieved of costs and an adequate system will be established to ensure legal representation and assistance when required.[39]

IV Legal aid in Spanish labour relations

The labour process in Spain is one of the most efficient, economical, and rapid ways to obtain access to justice.

Labour jurisdiction in Spain[40] is considered an ordinary jurisdiction with a specialized clientele (workers, persons protected by Social Insurance or members of a beneficial association, on the one side; management and institutions which provide or assist in providing Social Insurance on the other) and by subject matter (individual or collective labour conflicts, issues concerning Social Insurance, labour organizations for mutual aid). Since the staff of the tribunals is drawn from the judges and attorneys involved in the ordinary justice system, we consider the labour jurisdiction to be an ordinary jurisdiction, but dealing with specialized individuals and issues.

The fundamental chracteristics of the process in the labour jurisdiction are efficiency, economy, and speed.[41] It is, therefore, the best way to obtain access to justice in Spain. Further procedural reform in other areas should take into account the principles used in the labour process for their possible application to civil procedure, which is both slow and expensive.

The labour process is primarily oral, and its basic principles are immediacy, free acceptance of evidence, no appeal, and publicity. No appearance by a lawyer or attorney is required, and procedural guarantees are given to solve rapidly and efficiently the individual or collective conflicts arising through the application of labour legislation. One of the important characteristics of the process is that it is gratuitous, which extends until the execution of the judgment (Article 12 of the 1973 revised text).

In labour conflicts the parties may appear on their own behalf or they may bring a representative. If a worker is to be represented by a lawyer or an attorney, he should communicate that fact so that the other party may also be represented, and if it is the company which intends to bring professional counsel, it must make that fact known to the worker so that a rotation lawyer may be appointed. In collective conflicts whose main objective is the application of a collective agreement, the law establishes that the litigation will be undertaken by a lawyer or by one of the workers or managers involved in the litigation.[42]

With respect to the defence of workers before labour tribunals, a special role has been fulfilled by the labour lawyers, a body of lawyers who provide assistance to the union. They exist in all the provinces of Spain and give assistance to workers in the labour law area, and are charged with representing and defending workers in labour litigation. Such labour lawyers are characterized as public functionaries, and their services are free when they defend and represent workers in individual or collective conflicts. Their salaries are paid by the Ministry of Labour Relations.

V. Aspects of social assistance and activism

Class actions and "pilot actions"

Class actions[43] are practically unknown outside of the common law countries. In Spanish law there is a parallel to the Italian *legittimazione per categoria* in matrimonial and incompetence hearings. In matrimonial disputes of a civil character in which an annulment is sought, legal standing may be granted to the spouses, to the Public Ministry, and to any person who may have an interest in the annulment.[44] This is comparable to the concept of a popular action[45] in which a person is given standing to act *quiquis de populo.*[46]

In actions concerning incompetence, legal standing is granted to the spouse and to the relatives of the presumed incompetent who may have rights of succession.[47] In actions for prodigality, the spouse has standing to initiate the action; and the statutory heirs of the prodigal party may participate in the action.[48]

With respect to "pilot actions" certain types of civil actions (such as proceedings for review by a higher court) can be initiated by the Public Ministry with the object of creating legal precedent, although the judgment does not affect the judgment given to the parties to the litigation.[49] Other possible examples of "pilot actions" can be found in the regulations of Spanish corporations; for example, the objection to social agreements, the creditors' meeting, and the regime for co-operatives.[50]

Possible alternatives for the provision of legal assistance

In the present Spanish law, legal assistance in Spain is provided by legal professionals (lawyers and solicitors) to whom the representation and defence of the underprivileged is entrusted by means of the official rotation system which was discussed earlier. To this date, there are no other types of public assistance available.

Several attempts have been made by lawyers' associations and law schools to organize free legal assistance in clinics located at law schools. These attempts have not been widespread. Such clinics would be desirable, if they could be organized efficiently.

The Public Ministry has participated in civil actions, as indicated by Fernandez Martin-Granizo;[51] some of its tasks are to defend the public interest; for example, in actions concerning inheritance, suspension of payments, matters of voluntary jurisdiction, or proceedings to record a title in fee simple.

The National Council of Internal Commerce and of Consumers, a department of the Ministry of Commerce, is charged with the protection and defence of the consumer.[52] This body operates through different consumer associations.

In the area of environmental protection, the government has created several administrative bodies, the most noteworthy of which is the Spanish Association for the Preservation of the Environment. Its mandate is to inform the government of actual or potential threats to the environment.[53]

Notes and References

1. Of the year 654, approved by the Council of Toledo on the reign of Recesvinto; Law XXVIII, Title I, Book II.
2. Law IX, Title III, Book II.
3. Finished in 1265, Law V, Book III, and Law XLI, Book XVIII, General Law III.
4. Of 1567, in the reign of Philip II.
5. Of 1805, in the reign of Charles IV.
6. February of 1977.
7. Law of March 26, 1977.
8. *Commentario sociológico. Estructura social de España*, Spanish Confederation of Savings Banks, Nos. 14-15, Madrid, April-September 1976, p. 96.
9. *Estadisticas judiciales de España*, Years 1972-73; National Institute of Statistics. Madrid, 1976, pp. 123 and 347.
10. Articles 36, 37, and 39 of the Law of Civil Procedure.
11. Royal decree of March 4, 1499, issued in Madrid by Ferdinand and Isabella. See "Libro de las bulas y pragmáticas de los reyes católicos", No. 150 of the Royal Laws, reproduced in facsimile, Institute of Spain, Madrid, 1973.
12. See all the contents of Title XVI of Book XII of the Newest Compilation which contains the provisions against the gypsies issued from 1499 to 1783.
13. Law XI, Title XVI, Book XII of the Newest Compilation. This provision that on the one hand helps protect the gypsies, by allowing their admission into any occupation, guild, or community without obstacles of any kind, and with serious penalties to those who deny

such admission to the gypsies, also establishes the type of persecution which might be termed "traditional" against those who continue in their nomadic life with more serious punishments than previously applied.

14. Article 4, Chapter 1 of the Second Part. Regulations for the different services of the Organization of the Civil Guard, Order of May 14, 1943, in which it is established that "The gypsies shall be closely surveyed, taking care to inspect all documents they produce, checking their particular identification marks, observing their costumes, inquiring as to their way of existence and into anything which may help establish an exact idea of their movements and occupations, inquiring as to their destination and their purpose."
15. According to Gutierrez Lopez, the Evangelical Movement of Brotherly Love – Spanish Gypsy Section, actually has seventy places of worship and 7,000 followers which are attended by 200 preachers, most of them gypsies (p. 83).
16. C. de Miguel, *Los costos y las costas en el proceso civil español*, p. 932.
17. Silveira, *La justicia inglesa de hoy*, trans. d'Alcalá-Zamora, *Rev. Faculty of Law of Mexico*, Vol. V, January–June, 1955, Nos. 17–18, p. 203.
18. In another later work we presented actions involving different amounts which allowed us to draw sad conclusions concerning this discouraging aspect of Spanish justice which can practically be extended to all procedural systems. C. de Miguel, *El acceso a la Justicia en el Derecho Español*, answers to questionnaire concerning "Access to justice: a program to study and improve dispute resolution in contemporary societies", created by Professors Johnson and Cappalletti, Valladolid, 1975, p. 23.
19. Article 14 of the Law of Civil Procedure. The recipients were entitled to the following benefits: free lawyer exemption from payment of all fees, exemption of deposits to file an appeal, free use of communications derived from judicial help and free advertisement in the official newspaper.
20. Articles 36, 37, and 39 of the Law of Civil Procedure, which makes us doubt the true efficacy of the present regulations on free legal aid.
21. In which amounts exceeding 500,000 pesetas are in contention, amounts impossible to calculate, or actions relating to political rights or honorary rights or related to the civil status of conditions of the individual (Article 483 of the Law of Civil Procedure).
22. C. de Miguel, "Consideraciones sobre la lentitud de los procesos

civiles y sus posibles soluciones", *Rev. Derecho Procesal Ibero-americano*, Madrid, 1971, p. 63.

23. Lalinde, Abadia, "Los gastos del proceso en el derecho histórico español", *Anuario de História del Derecho español*, Vol. XXXIV, Madrid, 1964, p. 406.
24. Law XV, Title XXVII, Book IV, Newest Compilation, Royal Decree of November 28, 1771.
25. Articles 2 and 36 of the Regulations for the Administration of Justice concerning ordinary jurisdiction of September 26, 1835.
26. The law of July 20, 1849, and the instructions of April 27, 1865, give legal aid to charitable organizations.
27. *Cronica de la codificación española*, 2, Civil Procedure, Ministry of Justice, General Commission for Codification, Madrid, 1972, pp. 157ff.
28. The fourth proposal of the 1944 proposals addresses these same questions.
29. "Anteproyecto de bases para el codigo procesal civil y ley reguladora de la jurisdicción voluntaria", text adopted by the general commission on Codification of the Ministry of Justice, on July 10, 1970, Project XVI, Nos. 59-60, in *Cuadernos Informativos* of the Ministry of Justice, Madrid, 1970, pp. 22 and 27.
30. Profesores de Derecho procesal de las Universidades Españolas, *Corrección y actualización de la Ley de Enjuiciamiento Civil*, Madrid, 1972, Vol. 1, pp. 49ff. and 195ff.
31. Instructions of March 14, 1899; R.O. of December 21, 1857, Law of June 29, 1880, Reg. of March 13, 1907, and Statute of October 13, 1931; Law of February 27, 1908; O. of August 12, 1955, etc.
32. Fernandez Serrano, *La abogacía en España y en el mundō*, 2nd edn, Madrid, 1955, Vol. 1, p. 236.
33. Item 143 of Chapter 4 of the budget of the General Directorship of the Ministry of Justice, approved in December 1974 for 1975 (Law 49/1974 of December 19) and in December 1975 for 1976 (Law 47/1975 of December 30). The budget for 1977 has been approved by Law 38/1976 of December 30, but a complete itemization could not be available to date although we assume that an amount greater than 200,000,000 could have been assigned.
34. Juan Montero Aroca, *Introducción al Derecho procesal, Jurisdicción, acción y proceso*, Madrid, 1976, p. 146.
35. Almagro Nosete, "El 'libre acceso' como derecho a la jurisdicción", *Rev. Faculty of Law of Madrid*, Vol. XIV, No. 37, Madrid, 1970, p. 96.

36. The proposals were supposed to be effected within a year. The difficult circumstances surrounding the political and legal climate in Spain in the last months and the severe criticism which was directed towards the proposals, demanded that the time limit be extended twice (Law of October 31, 1975, and of November 26, 1976). This task will probably not be accomplished until the formation of the new Legislative Assembly in accordance with the political reform.
37. Information pamphlets of the Ministry of Justice, No. 8, General Technical Secretariat, October 1970, p. 14.
38. Official Bulletin of the Spanish Cortes, No. 1309 of December 20, 1973.
39. In the summary of reasons it is stated that the principle of free access to the Tribunals of Justice understood as the right to present petitions to the state bodies specifically designed for that purpose, is one of the most important judicial guarantees, since the free access to the courts is considered by all civilized peoples as a fundamental right, which, ultimately, is based on the following concept: in a State of Law a petition for Justice constitutes an inalienable right of the individual, which cannot be denied to anybody as a means of obtaining the protection of the system. However, the concession of this subjective right is not enough; its realization must be ensured and to that end the state should establish the necessary mechanisms so that cultural or economic differences do not become a factual limitation of this right so intimately connected with personal dignity.
40. The most immediate antecedents of Labour Justice in Spain were the industrial courts created in 1908, the joint boards of 1926, the mixed juries of 1931, up to the creation of the labour courts in 1938. See Montero Aroca, *Los Tribunales de Trabajo (1908–1938) Jurisdicciones especiales y movimiento obrero*, Valencia, 1976. With respect to legislation applicable to these matters we cite the Book IV of the Labour Code and once the Labour courts were created, numerous decrees, which have been compiled in the revised text of July 4, 1958, later in the revised text of April 21, 1966, and finally in the revised text of August 17, 1973, in effect today, which contains 230 Articles.
41. The average duration of the labour procedure with no appeal is thirty-three days.
42. With respect to collective conflicts the latest provisions are the Law of December 19, 1973, and the Law of March 4, 1977.
43. C. de Miguel, "El acceso a la Justicia en el Derecho español", op.

cit., pp. 97ff.

44. Article 102 of the Civil Code.
45. Recognized in Spanish criminal procedure, Article 101 of the Law of Criminal Procedure of 1882.
46. Calamandrei, *Instituciones de derecho procesal civil*, trans. Sentis Melendo, Buenos Aires, Vol. 1, 1962, p. 279.
47. Article 214 of the Civil Code. The Public Ministry has legal standing on a compulsory fashion in cases of insanity and also when the indicated relatives do not exist, or do not exercise their legal rights, or are minors, or do not have the legal capacity to appear in court (Article 215 of the Civil Code).
48. Article 222 of the Civil Code. The Public Ministry has standing on its own or on behalf of a relative in exceptional cases when the relative is a minor or is incompetent.
49. Article 1782 of the Law of Civil Procedure.
50. Law of July 18, 1951, Articles 67, 69ff. and 122 ff.; Law of December 19, 1974, Articles 27 and 35.
51. Fernandez Martin-Granizo, *La posición del Ministerio Público en el proceso civil*, Spanish submission to theme 9 of this same International Congress of Ghent.
52. Decree of May 8, 1971, and Order of December 14, 1972.
53. Law of the Protection of the Environment of December 22, 1972; Decree of February 8, 1975, and Order of May 14, 1971.

JOEL F. HANDLER*

United States of America

I. Introduction

Organizations have been and continue to be the principal mechanism for defining the legal needs of the poor and unrepresented, for changing the legal consciousness of society, and for the recruitment and training of most lawyers in legal rights activities. In the process of formation and through their continual efforts to mobilize resources, organizations develop ideologies and define legal needs that attract lawyers and provide the focus for their work. The structured job opportunities which organizations provide are most important in directing young lawyers toward a continued career in these activities. The success of organizations in winning cases, obtaining publicity, and attracting public support, generates new organizations and other efforts to offer similar kinds of opportunities in the two major sectors of the legal profession – private practice and government.

II.A. Antecedents: traditional legal rights activities

In the legal profession in the United States, reduced fee work for the poor historically depended on the willingness of individual lawyers in private practice. In part, this was charity by lawyers; in part, it was an effort to justify the public service image of the profession. The reigning ideology

*This paper is a shortened version of a chapter in *Lawyers and the Pursuit of Legal Rights*, by Joel F. Handler, Ellen Jane Hollingsworth and Howard S. Erlanger (Academic Press, Inc., New York, 1978).

was that the legal system essentially worked well, but that some people needed better access to it. If these people could not afford fees of lawyers, it was the obligation of the profession to assist them without charging. Individual practitioners had the responsibility to make some of their time available to satisfy this professional obligation. No or low fee work for the indigent was called *pro bono* (from *pro bono publico*, for the public good).

When the American Bar Association and similar groups were organized at the state level in the late nineteenth century, canons of ethical conduct were defined. These canons were limited: they only mandated defense of indigent prisoners, and did not deal with obligations toward the indigent in civil disputes.[1] Moreover, even the obligation to prisoners was narrowly construed and often ignored.

During the latter part of the nineteenth century, some lawyers and bar associations turned their attention to creating a more organized method of handling the legal problems of the poor, as an alternative or supplement to the obligations of individual lawyers. The first legal aid society was established in 1876 in New York City as part of an organization that attempted to ease the transition for German immigrants in the United States. Within a few years, legal aid organizations were extended to other immigrants and indigents, although on a very modest scale.

During the first half of the twentieth century, the legal aid model spread slowly. The legal aid office was not intended to replace the activities of private lawyers on behalf of the poor as part of their professional obligations. In smaller cities two different types of organizations, with roughly the same effect, emerged. One was a lawyer referral program, where a part-time secretary put needy clients in touch with lawyers who were willing to be listed. The other was a program in which a lawyer undertook the work himself, or was responsible for a younger member of his firm who did the work. Either way, the lawyer in charge of a legal aid committee or a lawyer referral committee often held his position at the behest of the city or county bar association. Costs were low for both arrangements and were usually borne by bar organizations.

Partly to limit work load, but also for moralistic reasons, legal aid offices established guidelines concerning the types of cases they would accept. Family cases usually made up a large percentage of the service load, though divorces were handled only very reluctantly.[2] Adoption, bankruptcy, civil mental commitment hearings, juvenile proceedings, and administrative hearings were also often refused.[3] The second largest category of cases was landlord-tenant disputes, especially in major metropolitan areas. Consumer problem cases were numerous; they included installment purchases, repossession of merchandise, or fraudulent sales.

Legal aid emphasized service to individuals exclusively; there was no law reform or class action litigation, and only a minimal effort was made to uncover the problems of the poor and to sensitize society to their legal needs. Emphasis on individual services stemmed from the assumption that the law was just, that for poor people the problem lay not in the nature of the law, but in obtaining access to the law. Logically, the more lawyers who made time available to the poor (on an individual, one-to-one basis) the more likely it was that the legal system would operate fairly. However, offices were usually so poorly funded that they had to set very strict eligibility standards in order to keep down the caseload limit. They avoided community education or publicity so that their work schedules would remain tolerable. Studies have shown that for most legal aid clients, access to the legal system consisted of only one interview with a legal aid lawyer.[4]

Despite the obvious shortcomings of legal aid, it served an important public relations function for the organized bar. Quite often prestigious members of the bar lent their names and some of their time to legal aid, or to high level bar association panels concerned with it. Even if most lawyers had no time for legal aid, it won a definite niche for itself in the legal profession. For the criminally accused, representation has most often been through the assigned counsel system, which has been the dominant mode of providing such aid for over a century.[5] In this system, a practicing attorney is assigned to the defense by the judge, usually without compensation. There are variations in the crimes included in the system, in the point in the proceedings that the assignment is made, and in the method of selecting the lawyers. Generally speaking, young lawyers have welcomed assignments. If they were in small firms or on their own, assignments gave them experience and visibility; if they were in large firms, they provided a change from a business practice. More experienced lawyers, on the other hand, have usually tried to avoid assignments and, it was claimed, tended to give these clients a minimum amount of service. Needless to say, the quality of the assigned counsel system varies enormously.

Despite the shortcomings of the assigned counsel system, widespread alternatives have been slow to emerge. Although the first public defender office for the criminally accused was established in Los Angeles County in 1910, until 1960 the growth of defender programs with salaried lawyers working exclusively in defense of criminally accused indigents was very slow, even in comparison with the growth of legal aid societies. In 1917 there were five defender programs; in 1947 there were only twenty-nine (including four legal aid societies doing substantial criminal work), and of these twenty-nine, thirteen were in two states. By 1960, ninety such programs existed, and three basic organizational patterns had emerged: public defenders defined by statute and paid by public funds; public-private programs with some funds from the private sector; and programs with all financing from private sources (usually bar associations). The dominant pattern, however, was public – more than 75 percent of defender funding came from tax sources, as opposed to the 7 percent that legal aid organizations received from public sources.[6]

In sum, although there had developed a long tradition of charitable legal work for the poor, and although this tradition was supported by the elites of the profession, it remained in fact in the backwaters of the profession. Legal aid offices and defender programs were few in number, and even when they became more numerous they were poorly financed; they were staffed either by lawyers looking for alternatives to private practice or by those seeking security from a competitive society. With few exceptions, young, activist, social-minded lawyers would not join legal aid or defender programs.

Nevertheless, from the time they were first formed, legal aid and public defender programs were an important reform, because they at least began the broadening of the delivery of legal services. They provided an organizational setting for traditional legal rights activities which supplemented the *pro bono* efforts of private practitioners. These legal aid efforts were paternalistic, moralist, and limited in the services that were delivered. The organizers conceived of their role as handling problems that were thrust upon them, not as seeking out the problem of the poor. Partly because of the dissatisfaction with traditional legal rights activities, legal services programs and a major expansion of the defender efforts were initiated in the middle 1960s. On the other hand, as we shall see, traditional legal rights activities were not replaced in the 1960s; they continued to grow.

II. B. Antecedents: early aggressive legal rights activities

About the same time that these first steps were being taken to expand traditional legal representation for the indigent, major efforts were being made in the use of litigation to achieve broad social reforms. The most influential early organizations pursuing this strategy were civil rights organizations, particularly the National Association for the Advancement of Colored People. The NAACP, founded in 1909, relied heavily from the very beginning on the use of test case litigation – and with great success. Through a series of cases, the NAACP brought to the attention of the courts (and through the courts, the larger society) the existence, nature, and legal implications of racial discrimination. As a result of NAACP cases, the United States Supreme Court invalidated anti-black voting restrictions (1915),[7] housing segregation ordinances (1917);[8] and other anti-black laws. These cases attracted a great deal of support, both white and black, to the organization. The membership of the NAACP expanded rapidly (there were 30,000 members in the 1920s). However, in spite of this growth and the continuing stream of legal activity, the legal staff remained small.[9]

In 1939 the NAACP established the Legal Defense and Educational Fund, Inc. (popularly known as the "Inc. Fund"), not only to handle its own legal work but also to work with other civil rights groups on civil rights cases. The Inc. Fund, with its small staff (three lawyers in the middle 1940s and only nine in 1963) fought numerous test cases in a wide range of areas (education, voting rights, housing and restrictive covenants, transportation and public accommodations), and continued to win. By 1952, the Inc. Fund had won thirty-four of thirty-eight cases argued before the U.S. Supreme Court. The regular staff was assisted by volunteer attorneys throughout the country, though it bore most of the load itself, especially prior to 1960.[10]

Inc. Fund achieved its greatest fame in *Brown* v. *Board of Education*,[11] which was followed by successes in cases involving segregation in buses, golf courses, bathhouses, courtrooms, voting, marriage, public accommodations, and housing, as well as other state activities. In this era of the Warren Court, it seemed as though in every year following the *Brown* decision reformers could count on not one but several Supreme Court decisions on behalf of the disenfranchised of American society. A great many of these cases were class actions, a model of social reform that was openly encouraged by the court itself. As the court saw it, ". . . [U]nder the conditions of modern government, litigation may be the sole practicable avenue open to a minority to petition for redress of grievances."[12]

It would be difficult to overestimate the influence of the Inc. Fund class action litigation strategy on the subsequent development of legal consciousness and of legal rights activities. United States Supreme Court victories had an enormous appeal. At the stroke of the judicial pen, so it seemed, legal rights and legitimacy were given to disadvantaged groups.

The executive and legislative branches of government, thought to be hostile and indifferent to the claims of blacks and other minorities, appeared to be circumvented. The style and location of the litigation were very important in influencing lawyer recruits. Young, motivated lawyers would work with the leaders of the organization, and their legal work would be in the prestigious federal courts, often at the appellate level. The legal training of young lawyers and the law school conception of the role of law and lawyers in social reform concentrated on appellate court litigation. The Warren Court and the NAACP litigation seemed to be the perfect example of what law, lawyers and legal education were all about.

As we shall see, this model of class action law reform strategy became the single most important influence in the development of Office of Economic Opportunity (OEO) Legal Services, consumer and environmental law, and public interest law. It became the popular standard for measuring the quality and effectiveness of other legal rights activities. In time, it also became the focus of political attacks on legal rights activities.

The other principal civil rights and civil liberties organization was the American Civil Liberties Union. The ACLU emerged in 1920 as the successor organization to the American Union Against Militarism, the Bureau for Conscientious Objectors, and the National Civil Liberties Board. During the 1920s, the ACLU was concerned with censorship, deportation, harassment of the International Workers of the World and other labor groups. Gradually, branches of the ACLU were created in the nation's largest cities, loosely coordinated through a national office with slender resources.[13] Few branches retained attorneys; most of the work was done by volunteer attorneys (both members and outsiders). Because of a lack of funds and a strong organizational base, the work of the ACLU prior to 1960 consisted mainly of filing *amicus* briefs rather than direct litigation. Nevertheless, the ACLU did considerable civil liberties work in times that were generally not sympathetic to such work.

For a brief period, the National Lawyers Guild also influenced reform work done by lawyers. Organized in 1937 as a nationwide professional organization counter to the American Bar Association, the guild enjoyed a period of success; it fell on hard times in the 1940s and 1950s during its long fight to avoid being placed on the Attorney General's list of subversive organizations. Although it was ultimately successful in remaining off the list, membership declined steadily and the guild's influence virtually disappeared until the late 1960s. Whatever its organizational problems, the Guild's activities in protection of dissidents and in other civil liberties problem areas were an important factor in the emergence of a reformist, socially activist community in the legal profession.

III. Legal rights activities in the 1960s: the emergence of aggressive legal rights as a major theme

The activity, spirit, beliefs, and symbols of the New Frontier of the Kennedy administration encouraged the idea that law could be used on behalf of the unrepresented. Much of the activity of the administration was based on the assumption that the institutions of American society could be activated and reordered to achieve social justice: government agencies could and should serve as protectors and advocates of the down-trodden (the Civil Rights Division of the Justice Department and VISTA (Volunteers in Service to America), for example); private groups of various types could save the cities, change the power structure of the South, and end nuclear testing, to mention only a few objectives. The individual citizen, working in social reform organizations, was seen as capable of affecting the machinery of government and the future of society. The thrust of these beliefs was twofold: that government agencies could spearhead reform and that citizen action should be taken against parts of government that were reluctant to change society.

A. Civil rights and law reform

As the legal profession – especially young lawyers – came to grips with the spirit of the early 1960s, there was really only one applicable historical model. Traditional legal aid had never seriously been considered as a workable means of restructuring society. Government service had also fallen into disfavor as a result of the Eisenhower years and the reluctance of government to respond to the most burning social issue of the day – civil rights for blacks.[14] Test case litigation of the ACLU type continued to attract its small group of adherents, but this kind of social reform work was either too traditional or too professionally antiseptic to capture the spirit of the decade. The ACLU functioned largely within the established legal profession, as a conscience rather than as a challenge. Appellate criminal and civil liberties litigation often attracted lawyers only interested in the chance to win an appeal, irrespective of the nature of the case; this type of disinterested, highly professional appellate work was not the stuff of which social movements were made.[15]

The early part of the 1960s belonged to civil rights for blacks; the model was the NAACP and the Inc. Fund. Eventually, a number of strands were bound together in the 1960s – civil rights, civil liberties, poverty law, environmental protection, consumerism. But for at least the first half of the decade, the civil rights movement was the most conspicuous area of activity for reformed-oriented lawyers. Moreover, civil rights activity set a tone for other legal rights activities organizations, and established an influential pattern.

During the years of desegregation campaigns, voter registration drives, and sit-ins, civil rights groups faced an acute shortage of legal help. Few lawyers in the South would represent blacks in these kinds of matters; and those who did so suffered severe reprisals.[16] The NAACP had only limited funds and personnel. This shortage of legal manpower meant that a movement or campaign could be effectively controlled or slowed if its leaders could be jailed or otherwise halted through the legal system. The fact that the civil rights leader could ultimately win in the courts was irrelevant if legal help was unavailable. In response to this urgent need for legal help, three organizations of lawyers and law students were created between 1963-65: the Law Students Civil Rights Research Council (LSCRRC), the Lawyers Committee for Civil Rights Under Law (LCCRUL), and the Lawyers Constitutional Defense Committee (LCDC).

After a 1963 summer experience in the South assisting civil rights lawyers, ten northern law students established the Law Students Civil Rights Research Council. The purpose of the organization was to make available large number of law students for civil rights work. During 1964, chapters were founded at many law schools; members worked both in the South and in their school communities in a variety of capacities. It is difficult to estimate how many law students were "interns," as they were often called, during the early and middle 1960s, but they helped popularize student activism in the law schools they attended.[17]

The Lawyers Committee for Civil Rights Under Law was formed in 1963 in response to a plea by President John Kennedy and Attorney General Robert Kennedy, urging the legal profession to create an organ to address itself to social upheaval and other problems connected with the enforcement of civil rights. There was no difficulty in recruiting more than 200 prestigious lawyers for committee membership. The first act of the program was to send volunteer lawyers into the South for two- to three-week periods, but later LCCRUL staffed a permanent office in Jackson, Mississippi, and worked with other civil rights attorneys already on the scene.[18] Sizeable chapters were created throughout the country, emphasizing test case litigation. In later years, the organization broadened its concerns while it continued to recruit and train young lawyers interested in civil rights work.[19] In part because of the visibility of its creation and in part because of the professional prominence of early participants, LCCRUL attracted considerable attention and was recognized as a vehicle for bringing high-powered talent to focus on social impact litigation.

Thus, the early 1960s witnessed the emergence of aggressive legal rights activities pressing into the trouble spots of discrimination. The effort was primarily through voluntary organizations; the subject matter was civil rights for blacks; and the basic strategy was law reform litigation, following the lead of the NAACP and the Inc. Fund.

B. OEO Legal Services and its antecedents: the struggle between traditional and aggressive legal rights

Just as it appeared that adequate legal assistance might be available for civil rights organizations, a displacement of enthusiasm occurred as the war on poverty drew the nation's attention away from the civil rights movement.[20] By 1965, a program for lawyers had been added to the war on poverty, and for many lawyers the focus of attention became not the quality of legal defense of southern blacks, but representation of the poor. Although for a few years in the mid-1960s the two movements of civil rights and the poor seemed to dovetail, by 1967 it was clear that whereas civil rights law had previously been "in", poverty law seemed to some extent to have replaced it.[21]

Poverty law, as expressed in OEO Legal Services, had its structural roots in the Ford Foundation's Grey Areas programs, in the President's Committee on Juvenile Delinquency, and most important, in Mobilization for Youth (MFY) in New York City. All of these programs were efforts to reach the poor and other disenfranchised groups and, by offering them new or different resources or tools, increase their participation in the mainstream of American life. Mobilization for Youth was the most famous program. Conceived as an experimental application of a theoretical analysis of the roots of delinquency. MFY primarily was concerned with youth employment and training program for the area in New York City below 14th Street on the East River. Shaped largely by the ideas of Richard Cloward and Lloyd Ohlin of the Columbia School of Social Work, MFY was known – and attacked – for its fairly modest efforts related to militant self-assertion of the poor.[22]

Service projects involving a staff of 300 workers,[23] began in 1962 in four major divisions: educational services, employment services, services to individuals and families, and community development (including services to groups). Legal services was added as a fifth division in 1964, with the following aims: (1) direct service to and referral of clients; (2) legal orientation for MFY staff, clients, and community leaders; and (3) use of law as an instrument of social change.[24] It was the third goal that was the most important for MFY. To implement its commitment toward social reform, MFY's legal component considered the test case as the primary vehicle for creating new law as well as for establishing the rule of law in the administrative processes of welfare programs. The most important legal needs of the poor were thought to be those that concerned their relations with public service programs such as welfare and housing. Also of concern were certain aspects of criminal law (pre-trial representation of youth, especially), consumer problems, and developing coordination between social workers and lawyers.[25] Though MFY's legal program initially had only four attorneys and a down-town location, it rapidly increased its staff, established ties in neighborhoods and built a very large caseload. Almost from its inception, the MFY program was involved in bitter controversy as to what extent community organization was appropriate.

Edward Sparer's energetic direction of MFY's legal unit, Jean and Edgar Cahn's 1964 article[26] suggesting the ways in which neighborhood law firms might be structured to respond to the needs of the poor, and the 1964 Conference on Law and Poverty, held in Washington, D.C., all contributed to the development of a general feeling by late 1964 that the federal government should make a sizeable investment in adding a legal services component to the war on poverty programs.[27] Moreover, it was argued that to be consistent with the goals of the war on poverty, federally-funded legal services were to be aggressive and client-oriented, and would stress social change through litigation.

The issue was immediately joined between the traditionalists and those who argued for aggressive legal rights. Initially, the controversy over the goals and style of legal services focused on what role existing legal aid societies and local bar associations would have in the new program. Both the American Bar Association and the National Legal Aid and Defenders Association (NLADA) were hostile to the massive funding of new legal organizations if carefully shepherded existing legal aid societies were to be passed over. Their argument was a simple one: more than 200 legal aid societies (or committees or similar organizations) already existed, and there was no reason not to build on their strength by allowing them to apply for new funding as Legal Services programs. Critics of legal aid[28] pointed out the faults of legal aid societies and warned that no program associated with them could accomplish the general law reform objectives stated for Legal Services. Legal aid societies, they claimed, were too cautious, too service-oriented, too supportive of the establishment and the *status quo*, too inexperienced in dealing with the kinds of cases that really mattered, too accepting of the structure of the law and its injustices, and too tied to local influences – in short, too traditional.[29] The compromise was that legal aid societies could apply to be Legal Services units but would not be considered automatically entitled to Legal Services grants. At the same time, lawyers not affiliated with a legal aid society could apply for funding in the same local area. Their application would be considered alongside that of the legal aid society; one might be funded, or both. NLADA immediately undertook a campaign to instruct legal aid societies in how they might obtain the federal money, and applications began to flow.[30]

The other compromise related to the role of the bar and the extent to which the local bar association had to approve a program before it would be funded. Understanding on this point differed, but clearly many lawyers and commentators believed a veto power existed. Early critics of Legal Services and of the legal aid model doubted that the goals of the war on poverty could ever be realized if the bar retained this degree of control over legal services.[31] Although the ultimate question of whether a local bar association had a veto was never fully resolved, it was generally agreed that some kind of bar endorsement was necessary for federal support. Another manifestation of bar influence was the requirement that roughly half the governing board for a legal services program had to be lawyers.

In return for these concessions, and as the culmination of a half-century of support for the general idea of aid for the indigent, the American Bar Association in February of 1965 passed a statement of approval and support for the new Legal Services program. The sanction and continuing support of the ABA was invaluable to Legal Services, particularly as it acted to influence otherwise doubtful bar associations. It was generally acknowledged that most local bar associations were at least somewhat hostile to the idea of Legal Services. And the more the Legal Services unit departed from the legal aid model, the greater the likelihood of hostility. The ABA's role in defending Legal Services – both from local bar association attacks and from political attacks – became very important.[32] No doubt part of the ABA support of Legal Services stemmed from the desire of the profession to protect itself from interference by outsiders, but as the years passed the ABA became more generally supportive of the content and achievement of Legal Services.[33] The issue of the responsibility of the lawyer to a client, removed as far as possible from outside pressure, motivated the ABA toward support of Legal Services, so long as the program put no obstacles between professional and client. Local lawyers could be community resources to ensure reliability in program activity.

Understandably, in the early days of Legal Services, the stress was more on getting programs funded and underway than on agreement as to purposes of Legal Services. According to Philip J. Hannon, in the early days of OEO about half the grants went to existing legal aid societies and most of the first Legal Services budget was allotted to local bar associations or bar-sponsored groups of lawyers.[34] By the end of 1965, about twenty-seven projects were in operation[35] and seven regional offices had been established. In 1967, approximately 1,200 lawyers were working in approximately 250 different projects, with 850 offices.[36] The number of attorneys employed by Legal Services grew steadily until 1972, with peak size being somewhat over 2,000. Similarly, the number of projects increased until 1972, when there were about 280. Funding, which had begun at a level of $27 million in fiscal 1966, grew to $71.5 million by fiscal 1972, and then stood still. In effect, Legal Services was held at this level until 1976, when the program was reorganized at the national level and funding was increased.

Many organizational changes occurred in the early Legal Services years. As the number of programs increased, the number of regional offices grew from seven to ten. Back-up centers that engaged in research and appellate litigation in specific problem areas such as health, housing, and juvenile delinquency were established (although in a few instances they were created to support programs in a certain geographical area or state rather than in a specific policy area). There were continual efforts to rationalize the operation of field offices. In the early days of Legal Services, when there had been great urgency to establish programs, some very small programs – one-attorney offices in many cases – were funded. In subsequent years, many smaller offices and branch offices were closed or merged. In metropolitan and highly urbanized areas, programs were encouraged to combine so as to meet the range of urban problems more effectively. The amount of program turnover, unfortunately, cannot be measured – some programs that were terminated had never even opened; some were merged; others were restructured under new names. At the top of the Legal Services bureaucracy, there was also considerable personnel turnover. Between 1965 and 1972, there were seven directors; the average stay was only a bit more than a year, and the pattern for other top administrators was similar.

Legal Services offices, in most cases, had the benefit not only of the lawyers directly employed by them but also of the assignement of lawyers who were holders of Reginald Heber Smith ("Reggie") fellowships and of VISTA lawyers. The Reggie program, begun in 1967, grew from an entering class of fifty to 250 a year. Almost all Reggies were assigned to neighborhood Legal Services offices, usually for a one-year period, but later for a second or third year if the Reggie so wished. Not surprisingly, many Reggies remained in programs as staff attorneys when their fellowships ended. Since Reggie fellowships were prestigious and paid a salary higher than most regular Legal Services jobs, they were usually a source of recruitment of special talent. After 1970, the Reggie program increasingly recruited minorities, which carried implications for minority representation in neighborhood programs as well. In much smaller numbers with with much less pay and shorter assignements, VISTA lawyers also supplemented the staff of Legal Services programs. VISTA, often called the domestic Peace Corps, recruited people of all ages and skills to work in different human service delivery systems. Lawyers in VISTA had assignments to many types of organizations other than Legal Services, but local Legal Services offices often had VISTA volunteers who were not lawyers.

Although the conflict over whether Legal Services was to be traditional or aggressive was settled by compromise, initially, by the decision to receive and fund applications from existing legal aid societies and programs with a heavy bar influence, the early leadership of Legal Services pushed hard for an aggressive program. The degree of emphasis on law reform quickly became the single most important question in the development of Legal Services. Divisions over the wisdom of a law reform strategy were not necessarily along liberal-versus-conservative lines; there was also the question of practicality. Vigorous law reform might be too much for local bar associations and the local establishment to swallow, jeopardizing support at the local level. There was also the problem of allocation of scarce resources – the more law reform work an office did, the more it might have to turn away service cases. There were disagreements about which approach would serve the needs of the poor best and about the types of problems each approach was best suited for. By the spring of 1967 law reform had emerged as the dominant official ideology of OEO Legal Services and became a specific aspect of program evaluation. The national office of Legal Services and the regional offices lent their efforts towards increasing the amount of law reform work. All of these areas of activity proved extremely difficult to foster. It was one thing to tell programs that they would be evaluated in terms of their efforts to achieve particular goals; it was quite another to implement the findings of the evaluation.

Ironically, while the political fight was going on over the future of law reform in Legal Services, doubts were being raised by Legal Services lawyers, among other, concerning the efficacy of law reform. The argument was made that law reform, almost by definition, was inappropriate and unattainable within the Legal Services program framework: that no matter how aspiring and energetic the lawyers, they usually failed in their law reform work. What did it really matter if agency or state rules about welfare dependency were overturned by a test case? The state or agency had enormous administrative discretionary authority and could eventually outmaneuver the Legal Services clients and attorneys, so that the overall practices remained the same.[37] When law reform work was visible and successful, the political repercussions were enormous. The Reagan-Murphy attacks on Legal Services in 1967 and 1969 were prompted by the suits against various state agencies and programs filed by the California Rural Legal Assistance program.[38] In many other states and communities, politicians and bar groups treated Legal Services programs with thinly disguised hostility.

Though the immediate threats to Legal Services posed by Reagan and Murphy were blunted, there were other political attempts to curb the law reform activities of Legal Services. There were efforts to regionalize and weaken the program by putting Legal Services under the authority of Community Action Program (CAP) regional directors of state governors. Initially, Legal Services had been created as a semi-autonomous program within the Community Action Program of OEO. The arrangement was imperfect and, on occasion, unworkable; for example, when CAP promoted decentralization of Legal Services programs, and supported lay administration, with Legal Services personnel playing only advisory roles. Some state governors and agency heads thought that more state or local control of programs would effectively control law reform suits against public authorities. Although CAP leaders and state governors had little in common, they did agree on the desirability of regionalization of legal Services and won the backing of OEO leaders. The political troubles intensified when Donald Rumsfled, as head of OEO, pushed hard for regionalization. This move was thwarted, but one of the casualties was Terry Lenzner, the National Director of Legal Services, who was very popular with the law reform elements in the program. Morale in Legal Services reportedly sank and the political warfare continued. Legal Services had to fight vigorously every year for budget increases, and the amounts requested by the program were severely reduced.[39] Eventually, the shape and composition of a national corporation to run Legal Services and the nature of restrictions on law reform and other political activities of Legal Services offices emerged as the main political issues.[40]

Another criticism was that law reform had jaundiced the prospects of Legal Services by affecting recruitment patterns. Law reform, as an ideology, appeared to be very important in recruitment to Legal Services. The possibility of doing law reform and appeals work added to the glamour of a Legal Services position, and it has been argued that this attracted graduates of elite schools who were solely interested in doing law reform and appellate work. Critics held that participation by these elites had a number of drawbacks: (1) law reform was too heavily emphasized; (2) lawyers from non-elite law schools were discouraged from doing law reform work; and (3) graduates from elite schools left after short tenure, thereby posing serious problems for programs that hoped to maintain some continuity of law reform work. The argument here is much like that applied to participation of law-elites in civil rights work: they left very large gaps when they returned to their normal settings, and organizations suffered greatly. According to this argument a more realistic, and more satisfying, work plan should de-emphasize law reform work and seek better kinds of service work, or, alternatively, recruit different personnel.[41]

In July 1974, after several years of bargaining, the various conflicting forces at the national level were able to compromise their differences over Legal Services and produce a new governing statute called the Legal Services Corporation Act. Legal Services are to be run by an eleven-person board of directors appointed by the President of the United States with the advice and consent of the Senate. A majority of the board must be lawyers admitted to practice. The statute contains a number of attempts at restricting the more controversial aspects of Legal Services: there is an attempt to cut down on law-reform litigation; the back-up centers are to be restructured; the corporation itself can undertake research, training, and clearinghouse activities, but cannot contract out any of these functions and cannot engage in litigation on behalf of clients. The intent is to keep research under the direct control of the board and prevent any activism. Another restriction on the corporation forbids contracting with "any private law firms which expend 50 percent or more of their resources and time litigating issues in the broad interests of a majority of the public", i.e., public interest law firms.

The Legal Services Corporation is directed to issue rules and regulations governing the activities of lawyers in its employ. Some of these restrictions include prohibitions against participation in public demonstrations, picketing, or civil disturbances; violations of court injunctions; "any political activity"; any voter registration activity; transportation of voters or prospective voters; the incitement of litigation; training programs "for the purpose of advocating particular public policies or encouraging political activities"; legal assistance for desegregation of schools, or to procure non-therapeutic abortions, or to challenge violations of the selective services or armed forces laws. In addition, local offices are required to solicit the local bar associations for staff positions and to give preference in hiring to local qualified persons.

It is uncertain how this new statute will be administered and what effects it will have on the future of Legal Services. The membership of the board and the leadership of the corporation indicate that integrity, quality, and independence of Legal Services were strongly and effectively supported by the organized profession and other influential political actors. Leading critics of Legal Services, including a former Congresswoman, were kept off the board. The chairman of the board is Roger Cramton, Dean of Cornell Law School, former head of the Administrative Conference; the President of the Corporation is Thomas Ehrlich, Dean of Stanford Law School; and the Executive Vice President is Clinton Bamberger, the first head of OEO Legal Services and former dean of Catholic Law School. These three influential people should be able to lead Legal Services out of the political wilderness of the Nixon years. They are sympathetic, energetic supporters of Legal Services. One of their first acts was to find a way to save the back-up centers, one of the more prominent symbols of law reform.

Although future directions of Legal Services are not clear at this time, a few general points can be made. The organization of Legal Services at the national level with its strong bar association support indicates that the program will most likely continue in the future; it seems to have won its battle for survival and barring a dramatic change in political climate, it is unlikely that future elected politicians will try to kill or seriously damage the program. At the minimum, the program will continue with at least its present level of support. Whether its supporters can gain increased levels of support is unknown.

C. Public defenders: a traditional program that didn't change

At the same time that the federal government was undertaking a sizeable investment in lawyers for the civil problems of the indigent through Legal Services, defender programs were beginning to grow rapidly both in number and size. By and large, defender programs were built on the base established prior to 1960. Although there has been more concern with appellate work in the last decade, there was no centralized administration for defender programs advocating reform activity. The problem of service-versus-reform among defenders was never very significant.

Defender programs began to improve after the 1963 Ford Foundation grant for the National Defender Project (NDP). The project was an effort to increase the number of programs, to improve operations, and to win greater acceptance of defender programs as the best method for defending the indigent criminally accused. The NDP included the funding of seventy-three projects at several levels – in small counties, large metropolitan centers, statewide, and some at the federal level – as well as different working arrangements: with law schools, through legal aid societies, and through private defender organizations.[42]

In 1961, defender programs existed in only three percent of the counties of the nation and served only about one-quarter of the population; by 1973, 650 defender programs were providing services in 28 percent of all United States counties, reaching two-thirds of the population. In addition, sixteen states have organized and funded defender services at the state level.[43] The NDP and the Supreme Court decisions mandating the provision of lawyers for indigents in the criminal justice system[44] served to focus attention on defender programs. In large urban programs, in particular, changes have included increased staff, more use of volunteers, students, paralegals, and investigators; better funding; more appeals work; more office specialization; more training; and improved procedures for working with clients. Although the number of programs and size of some have increased, a recent NLADA Defender Survey revealed that only one-half of the existing 650 systems are really offices with staff attorneys or other staff. The other systems have only one lawyer, unassisted. Approximately five thousand lawyers are providing defender services in state courts throughout the United States; of these lawyers, half are part-time.[45]

There have been some developments in the defender programs that in some ways parallel the development of Legal Services, and in other ways are a reaction to Legal Services. A small number of defender offices in the country became high-prestige law reform offices that attracted a great deal of publicity and recruited staff from social-reform-oriented elite young lawyers. Positions in these offices were considered, for a time, to be as desirable as positions in the best Legal Services offices. The other attraction of defender positions had to do with the growing disenchantment and radicalization of some young lawyers that occurred in the late 1960s. As the Vietnam War escalated and the "counter-culture" developed, some young lawyers began to work more and more in draft, drug, and political cases. For increasing numbers of lawyers, criminal law practice (with overtones of social and political reform) became more attractive, and the public defender's office became the training ground. However, on the whole, the defender program grew in size but did not change much in orientation; it remained basically traditional.

D. A panorama of other efforts

Contemporaneous with the growth of Legal Services, organizations engaged in legal rights activities in the voluntary sector and in the profession also continued to grow, taking different positions along the traditional-aggressive continuum. Aggressive legal rights activities, however, seemed to be dominant.

1. Aggressive independent organizations

Just as the voluntary organizations, particularly the NAACP, Inc. Fund and, to a lesser extent, the ACLU, set the pace in the early 1960s, it was voluntary organizations (and to a lesser extent, some types of private organizations) which provided the cutting edge of aggressive legal rights activities in the second part of that decade. The most prominent were organizations developed by Ralph Nader, foundation-supported public interest law firms, and law communes.

Nader's premise was that unrepresented consumers could defend themselves if more information were made available to them, and if they organized to determine and implement their collective will. Investigation and exposé were the key ingredients for the dissemination of information. Goals were enforcement of neglected legislation, passage of new legislation, and alteration of practices by public or private authorities. Nader had great appeal for young lawyers. He was a lawyer himself and, although he called on other professionals for particular kinds of expertise, he felt that the aggressive lawyer as a problem-solving generalist was best suited for his crusade. There was also a substantive attraction. The civil rights movement was waning, at least for whites. Some young lawyers were also seeking alternatives to OEO Legal Services; some were anti-government. Nader was anti-big business – he was for the little person, the consumer, the victim of giant public and private bureaucracies. Nader's movement represented a facet of participatory democracy: little people could get together and with a skilled, sympathetic lawyer make their voices heard. Working for Ralph Nader combined missionary zeal and camaraderie, self-sacrifice, independence from government, business, or private law practice, a vision of a new, democratic society, and for most, an exciting professional life in Washington. By the late 1960s, the appeal of Nader organizations to law graduates rivaled the drawing power of Legal Services. To many, Nader organizations seemed much more reform-oriented than Legal Services, which had no case-by-case service activity. There was the attraction of working exclusively with like-minded people with a great deal of organizational autonomy and no outside political interference. Another attraction was that since the organizations were small, the workers were also the principals. Extremely low salaries did not seem to hinder recruitment.

Nader organizations have been well known for their use of research teams whose findings have been widely published. The reports for the most part on the failings of federal regulatory agencies. In addition to organizations more or less directly under his control, some organizations in which Nader has a strong interest are financially independent, and several former Nader lawyers have started their own organizations, which function with varying degrees of autonomy. Most of Nader's organizations have operated on very modest amounts of money from the General Motors settlement,[46] Nader's fees for appearances and speeches, from small foundation grants, and from donations to Public Citizen, Inc. By 1974, Nader or Nader-type organizations had emerged in the areas such as auto safety, aviation, health research, corporate responsibility, land use, water cleanliness, food safety and standards, women's issues, science, and citizen action. Public interest research groups had been founded in a number of states, often through university student support.

There is a large amount of transition in Nader organizations. The staffs are small and often are supported by only small amounts of money.[47] Despite this, most groups include at least one lawyer, with volunteers, students and other professionals playing an important part in the larger projects. The focus of each group may change somewhat with the preferences of staff members; in several instances parent groups have spawned satellite organizations as departing personnel have created new groups.

With the formation of independent public interest groups in many states, often relying on student workers, the Nader thrust is quite decentralized. The formal appurtenances of organization have never been of great interest to Nader and his coworkers. What they have been concerned about is the institutionalization of advocacy for consumers – whether that advocacy is expressed in private study-research groups, or by sub-units in bureaucracies charged with consumer responsibilities.

In the late 1960s, groups of social reformers began to feel that the lack of representation suffered by blacks and to consumers applied more generally throughout American society. In particular, it was felt that the government regulatory agencies that were supposed to represent the public interest often failed to do so, and that they were captives of the special interests that they were supposed to regulate. The idea that there was a need to represent the unrepresented – to represent the public interest – before government agencies received its first strong sanction in a 1966 Court of Appeals decision involving a Federal Communications Commission license renewal proceeding.[48]

In this proceeding, the United Church of Christ sought to represent groups of blacks as listeners. The Court granted the group the right to present their case on the ground that the FCC no longer effectively represented listener interests. This ruling was applicable for many kinds of groups before many different government agencies. The term "public interest" began to be used to express the idea that the problem of inadequate representation applied through all sectors of society. In the late 1960s public interest law firms emerged, firms in which salaried lawyers worked to secure more citizen rights *vis-à-vis* government, at first mainly in consumer and environmental problem areas, and later with poverty and the problems of minorities. Public interest law firm work was almost entirely test-case law reform.

The importance of public interest law is that it represented another distinct phase in the growth and development of aggressive legal rights activities. It presented to young, socially-minded lawyers new areas of interest and new organizational settings. Just as OEO Legal Services appeared to present an alternative to civil rights work, public interest law appeared to replace Legal Services as the cutting edge of social reform.

In addition to foundation-supported firms, some private law firms identified themselves as public interest law firms. A very few of these private public interest law firms support themselves solely from public interest law work – that is, they have sufficient "public interest" clients (like the Sierra Club) that pay fees. These firms might also obtain grants for specific projects. Most private public interest law firms have a mixture of regular clients and public interest clients. Lawyers in such firms tailor their caseload in order to do a considerable amount of free or low-fee work on cases that they define to be in the public interest. Most often these firms are wholly dependent on regular client fees for income. The total number of these lawyers in these firms is small, perhaps only about 100.[49]

In a sense, the law commune is a radical version of the private public interest firm. Communes attempt to limit their work to kinds of cases or clients along radical political and ideological lines, charging for their work only if clients have funds. The overriding aim of the communes is political activism, rather than the traditional practice of law. The usual – and preferred – clients are criminal defendants, political activists, radicals, and students.

The organized bar has also engaged in efforts which, although not as aggressive as those of non-bar groups, have had a law reform orientation. Best known is the public interest law firm funded by the Beverly Hills Bar Association. Several other bar associations are presently considering, or have already started, similar projects, although how aggressive or traditional these projects will be is uncertain. Also, the American Bar Association recently approved a special committee report strongly supporting public interest law, and the LCCRUL has continued its earlier concentration on law reform.

2. Service-oriented independent organizations

Another type of organization, generally more traditional than the bar-sponsored groups discussed above, has emerged in several cities. Lawyers have been organized by ghetto or foundation organizers to provide volunteer legal services; these services may be supported by the lawyers themselves, by large private law firms, or occasionally by small subsidies from local bar associations. Community Legal Organizations (CLO) of New York City, founded in 1968, uses volunteers and employs several staff lawyers on a full-time basis.[50] Chicago Volunteer Legal Services, founded in 1964, grew to 250 attorneys by 1973.[51] The more aggressive Chicago Council of Lawyers was founded in October of 1969 and grew to more than 1,200 members.[52] The Council of New York Law Associates, founded in 1970, acts primarily to disseminate information about *pro bono* activity, and only secondarily as a service organization or in an investigative capacity. With about 1600 members, the New York Council has become somewhat more action-oriented in the last two years, but it remains more of a clearinghouse than anything else.[53] Councils were also formed in Washington and San Francisco. Several other communities have or have had rather similar programs, varying in size, in type of preferred clientele, and in kinds of cases handled; overall, their emphasis is on one-to-one case service and not on law reform work. However, we suspect that at least some of these lawyers have been influenced by aggressive legal rights ideology. Certainly large numbers of professionals have become involved in these service organizations, which provide a structured setting for the delivery of traditional typing services.

3. Regularized *pro bono* activities by large private firms

Most *pro bono* work is carried on by individual practitioners and is of a traditional nature. In some large firms, however, *pro bono* activity is organized. Around 1968 it was widely believed by many hiring law firms that the best law graduates were not interested in traditional firm jobs and that they would seek jobs in Legal Services, or similar activities, unless traditional firms had attractive *pro bono* programs in which they might participate.[54] Although the actual deflection of talent away from private law firms was probably small, it is clear that some Legal Services programs were successful in attracting very able people. Law firms concerned with hiring the best people therefore had an incentive to create an in-house program for *pro bono* work.

Evidence suggests that the *pro bono* interest of traditional firms is on the wane. Perhaps, as suggested by some critics, there was no real commitment on the part of traditional law firms, and once the competition from OEO Legal Services declined, their interest in offering non-traditional alternatives to new associates slackened. It is also reported that applicants for jobs in traditional firms are no longer inquiring about *pro bono* opportunities. If true, this change in professional orientation may be the result of a softening job market for lawyers, or may reflect a more general decline in interest in social reform.[55] The *pro bono* programs of law firms have varied in the extent to which they depart from traditional service patterns, but their very existence has meant more opportunity for lawyers to deal with the problems of the underrepresented.

Summary and conclusions

Our concern has been to indicate the wide variety of activities that are a part of efforts by the legal profession to increase the availability of legal representation. In describing these legal rights activities and how they have emerged from the traditions of the profession, I have emphasized the roles of organizations, especially Legal Services. I have also indicated how these organizations have been related to broader social reform activities of the 1960s.

By the late 1960s and early 1970s, legal rights activities had expanded into a large variety of organizations. Both traditional and aggressive organizations served the legal needs of the poor and the unrepresented, but aggressive organizations played a much different role in the development of legal needs. The essence of these organizations was to chart out new areas, to uncover problems, to define them in terms of legal needs, and to sensitize the country to these issues. They were a creative force in the development of legal consciousness on behalf of the poor and the unrepresented, and in this respect they functioned very differently from traditional legal rights organizations which were more or less content to respond to the demands thrust upon them.

Organizations also performed another crucial role – the recruitment, training, and cycling of lawyers interested in pursuing careers in legal rights activities. Young lawyers interested in pursuing legal rights careers had a choice of working in government, in the voluntary sector, in private practice, or in Bar Association organizations; moreover, within each of these settings, they could select organizations that were aggressive, traditional, or a mixture of both. In short, there has been growth in a number of different directions. Although organizations engaged in aggressive legal rights work have been the most prominent – at least in terms of publicity and controversy, if not in results – there has also been a steady growth in mixed and traditional organizations. Legal rights activities have developed into a rich and variegated enterprise, with a wide array of full-time and part-time opportunities for participation. The conclusion that I draw is that legal rights work is a growing, dynamic field in which, over time, structures will emerge – some to disappear, some to survive. What others have described as waning and waxing of interest in legal rights activities is a more subtle process: a substitution and broadening of interest in such work, with different organizations highlighted at different times.

Notes and References

1. Canons of Professional Ethics, adopted by American Bar Association, 1908.
2. Martin Mayer, "The Idea of Justice and the Poor", *Public Interest*, 8 (Summer 1967), p. 97.
3. National Legal Aid and Defender Association, *Annual Report of the President* (September 1964).
4. Mayer, "The Idea of Justice and the Poor", *Public Interest*, 8 (1967), p. 101.
5. Stuart S. Nagel, "Effects of Alternative Types of Counsel on Criminal Procedure Treatment", *Indiana Law Journal*, 48 (1973), pp. 404-26; Bennett G. Hornstein, "Effective Indigent Criminal Defense Services in Nebraska State Courts", *Creighton Law Review*, 7 (1973), pp. 1-26; Lee Silverstein, *Defense of the Poor in Criminal Cases in American State Courts* (Chicago: American Bar Foundation, 1965).
6. Emory Brownell, *Legal Aid in the United States* (Rochester, N.Y.: Lawyers Cooperative Publishing Co., 1951), p. 35.
7. *Guinn* v. *U.S.*, 238 U.S. 347 (1915).
8. *Buchanan* v. *Warley*, 245 U.S. 60 (1917).
9. August Meier and Elliott Rudwick, eds., *Black Protest in the Sixties* (Chicago: Quadrangle Books, 1970), pp. 3-4; Charles Flint Kellogg, *NAACP: A History of the National Association for the Advancement of Colored People*, Vol. 1: 1909-1920 (Baltimore: Johns Hopkins Press, 1967), pp. 9-42.
10. NAACP Legal Defense and Education Fund, Inc., *The Quiet Revolution* (May 1969), p. 6; Michelle Washington, "Constance Baker Motley: Black Women, Black Judge", *Black Law Journal*, 1 (Summer 1971), p. 1973.
11. 347 U.S. 483 (1954).
12. *NAACP* v. *Button*, 371 U.S. 415 (1963).
13. Donald O. Johnson, *The Challenge to American Freedoms: World War I and the Rise of the American Civil Liberties Union* (Lexington, Ky.: University of Kentucky Press, 1963), p. 53.
14. A conspicuous exception to the low regard in which social reform-oriented lawyers held government work was the Civil Rights Division of the Justice Department, created in 1957. The Attorneys General of the 1960s (Robert Kennedy, Nicholas Katzenbach, Ramsey Clark) and the heads of the Civil Rights Divsion (Burke Marshall, John Doar, Stephan Pollak) were leaders who attracted many young, dedicated

lawyers interested in civil rights. In 1965 there were eighty-six lawyers in the division; by 1970, there were 136. Most of the litigation brought by the Civil Rights Division was in education, but large numbers of cases were also filed in the areas of public accommodations, interference with civil rights, employment, and housing.

15. Jonathan D. Casper in *Lawyers Before the Warren Court: 1957-1966* (Urbana, Ill.: University of Illinois Press, 1972) points out that lawyers who were either "group advocates" or "civil libertarians" were sensitive to broad issues in the areas of reapportionment, loyalty-security, and civil rights, but that lawyers presenting criminal justice litigation were interested in winning, not in broad issues.
16. Barbara Carter, "A Lawyer Leaves Mississippi", *Reporter*, 28, No. 1 (May 9, 1963), p. 33; Daniel H. Pollitt, "Timid Lawyers and Neglected Clients", *Harper's*, 229 (August 1964), pp. 81-6; John Honnold, "The Bourgeois Bar and the Mississippi Movement", *American Bar Association Journal*, 52 (March 1966), pp. 226-32. The Congress for Racial Equality (CORE) had most of its legal work done free by the New Orleans black firm of Robert Collins, Nils Douglas, and Lolis Elie, although the amount of work was far greater than the firm could handle. August Meier and Elliott Rudwick, *CORE: A Study in the Civil Rights Movement, 1942-1968* (New York: Oxford University Press, 1973), pp. 115, 151.
17. Law Students Civil Rights Research Council, *In the American Tradition* (Fall 1972).
18. Vern Countryman and Ted Finman, *The Lawyer in Modern Society* (Boston: Little, Brown, and Co., 1966), pp. 576-7.
19. F. Raymond Marks, *The Lawyer, the Public and Professional Responsibility* (Chicago: American Bar Foundation, 1972), pp. 126-37.
20. Michael Harrington's book, *The Other America*, published in 1962, focused national attention on the problem of the American poor. By 1964, poverty had become a national issue. President Johnson proclaimed the war on poverty, and Congress passed the Economic Opportunity Act of 1964, which created the Office of Economic Opportunity (OEO) to administer and coordinate federal anti-poverty efforts.
21. Richard C. Leone, "Public Interest Advocacy and the Regulatory Process", *Annals of the American Academy of Political Science* (March 1972), pp. 46-58.
22. Edgar S. and Jean C. Cahn, "The War On Poverty: A Civilian Perspective", *Yale Law Journal*, 73, No. 8 (July 1964), pp. 1317-52.

23. Henry Heifetz, "Introduction", in Harold H. Weissman, ed., *Justice and the Law* (New York: Association Press, 1969), p. 23.
24. Michael Appleby, "Overview of Legal Services", in Weissman, ibid., p. 36.
25. Charles Grosser, "The Need for a Neighborhood Legal Service and the New York Experience", *Proceedings of the Conference on the Extension of Legal Services to the Poor, Nov. 12-14, 1964* (Washington, D.C.: Government Printing Office, 1964), p. 74.
26. See note 22.
27. See note 25 above.
28. See Jerome Carlin, Jan Howard, and Sheldon Messinger, "Civil Justice and the Poor", *Law and Society Review* 1, No. 1 (November 1966), pp. 9-89.
29. A. Kenneth Pye, "The Role of Legal Services in the Anti-poverty Program", *Law and Contemporary Problems* (1966), pp. 211-49.
30. ibid., at pp. 224-6.
31. Eric W. Wright, "Competition in Legal Services Under the War On Poverty", *Stanford Law Review*, 19 (February 1967), pp. 579-92.
32. A. Kenneth Pye and Raymond F. Garraty, Jr., "The Involvement of the Bar in the War Against Poverty", *Notre Dame Lawyer*, 41, No. 6 (1965-66), pp. 847-52.
33. "What Price Professionalism?" *American Bar Association Journal*, 56 (December 1970); "A Cloudy Legal Services Picture", ibid., 57 (March 1971); "Toward Better Legal Services", ibid. (September 1971).
34. Philip J. Hannon, "The Leadership Problem in the Legal Services Program", *Law and Society Review*, 4, No. 2 (November 1969), p. 242; E. Clinton Bamberger, Jr., "The Legal Services Program of the Office of Economic Opportunity", *Notre Dame Lawyer*, 41, No. 6 (1965-66), pp. 847-52.
35. Pye, ibid., at 230.
36. There are no precise data on either the number of attorneys employed or projects funded for the early years of Legal Services. Programs that were funded did not always open, much less continue. And while program grants were partially determined on the basis of the numbers of attorneys to be employed, slots were often unfilled.
37. Joel F. Handler, "Controlling Official Behavior in Welfare Administration", *Calif. Law Review*, 54 (1966), 479; Harry P. Stumpf, "The Failure of Legal Services: Or, Let Them Clean Out Cellars", unpublished paper delivered to the Conference on the Delivery and

Distribution of Legal Services, State University of New York at Buffalo Law School, 11-12 (Ocrober 1973), p. 4; Samuel Krislove, "The OEO Lawyers Fail to Constitutionalize a Right to Welfare: A Study in the Uses and Limits of the Judicial Process", *Minnesota Law Review*, 58 (1973), pp. 211-45. For a different view, see Lawrence A. Sullivan, "Law Reform and the Legal Services Crisis", *California Law Review*, 59 (1971), pp. 1-28.

38. Fred J. Hiestand, "The Politics of Poverty Law", in Bruce Wasserstein and Mark J. Green (eds.), *With Justice for Some* (Boston: Beacon Press, 1970), pp. 160-89.
39. Richard Pious, "Congress, the Organized Bar, and the Legal Services Program", *Wisconsin Law Review* (1972), pp. 418-46.
40. ibid.; Walter Karabian, "Legal Services for the Poor: Some Political Observations", *Univ. of San Francisco Law Review*, 6 (April 1972), pp. 253-65.
41. Burt W. Griffin, *Proceedings of the Harvard Conference on Law and Poverty* (Harvard Law School), March 17, 18, 19, 1967 (Cambridge, Mass., 1967), pp. 31-3.
42. *Legal Aid Briefcase*, 26, No. 2 (Feburary 1968), pp. 97-144.
43. National Legal Aid and Defender Association, *The Other Face of Justice: A Report of the National Defender Survey* (1973), p. 13.
44. The 6th Amendment to the U.S. Constitution requires that "[I]n criminal prosecution, the accused shall enjoy the right . . . to have the Assistance of Counsel for his defence." Beginning in the late 1950s, the Supreme Court began to interpret the passage as requiring the provision of counsel to indigents at various stages of the criminal prosecution. *See*, e.g., *Gideon* v. *Wainwright*, 372 U.S. 335 (1963) (counsel required in noncapital felony prosecution); *Argersinger* v. *Hamlin*, 407 U.S. 25 (1972) (counsel required for misdemeanor prosecution where penalty may include imprisonment); *In re Gault*, 387 U.S. 1 (1967) (juveniles have right to counsel in juvenile proceedings); *Miranda* v. *Arizona*, 384 U.S. 436 (1966) (indigents have right to appointed counsel during police interrogation.
45. ibid., pp. 14-15.
46. The GM lawsuit was a suit Nader brought against GM for invasion of privacy. Shortly after Nader's *Unsafe at Any Speed* appeared in 1966, GM began an intensive investigation into Nader's personal life, including having him followed by private investigators. GM hoped its investigation would reveal that Nader had some unsavory personal habits, which might diminish Nader's credibility. The resulting lawsuit was

settled out-of-court for $400,000.

47. For perspectives on organizational structure and function, see Luther P. Gerlach, "Movements of Revolutionary Change", *American Behavioral Scientist*, 14, No. 6 (July, August 1971), pp. 812-35.
48. 359 F.2d 994 (D.C. Cir. 1966).
49. Charles R. Halpern and John M. Cunningham, "Reflections on the New Public Interest Law: Theory and Practice at the Center for Law and Social Policy", *The Georgetown Law Journal* 59 (May 1971), pp. 1095-126.
50. Douglas E. Rosenthal, Robert A. Kagan, and Debra Quatrone, *Volunteer Attorneys and Legal Services for the Poor: New York's CLO Program* (New York: Russell Sage Foundation, 1971).
51. Interview with staff Chicago Volunteer Legal Services.
52. Interview with staff Chicago Council of Lawyers.
53. Interview with staff The Council of New York Law Associates.
54. *Wall Street Journal*, September 26, 1968: "While most law students still do strive to get a lucrative job with a corporation or a firm or a traditional Government post, an increasing number are opting for low paying jobs that they consider more challenging and . . . 'socially rewarding' . . . those that are choosing to stay away from Wall Street are often the brightest students." In the same tone, as recently as May 29, 1972, a *Wall Street Journal* article reported: "The hiring partners in most firms agree that they get many more questions about opportunities for public service work from law school seniors interviewed today than in the past. Young lawyers themselves say such opportunities play an important role in their decisions to join a given firm."
55. ibid., December 1973.

VITTORIO DENTI

An International Overview on Legal Aid

This report will discuss general trends rather than analyse in detail the rules which regulate legal assistance to the underprivileged. A few preliminary remarks are necessary to the understanding of these trends.

Legal assistance, as it is currently understood, is the result of a development of the concept of legal systems. Beginning at the end of the nineteenth century, the mere formal right to legal protection developed into a more substantial equality of parties before the courts.

Prior to this development, legal assistance to the poor had always had a connotation of charity, whether it was provided by private religious organizations, by the public authorities (such as in the proceedings *in forma pauperis* of the English law), by public assistance bodies (such as the *Avvocatura dei Poveri*, the public attorney for the poor, which existed in some Italian states before the unification of Italy). According to this approach, the poor were not regarded as individuals experiencing economic difficulties, but were assigned to a rigid social class governed by rules which may have met the needs of the poor, but which also hindered movement out of the class. These are the characteristics of the English "poor law" which grants legal assistance to the indigent as a social class which, by definition, does not have the same rights as the ruling class.[1]

The increasing appeal of social ideologies at the turn of the century prompted the development of legal aid services in three directions: (1) legal assistance became a duty related to the professional status of lawyers who, according to the system first introduced in France[2] and subsequently adopted by other European countries (e.g., *assistance judiciaire, gratuitio patrocinio*), were expected to offer their services free of charge to the poor; (2) closely related social groups developed group-related forms of legal assistance, which then were extended to all underprivileged people (e.g., the legal aid societies in the United States which were first formed in immigrant groups); (3) public intervention in legal assistance developed; aid was offered mainly through local administrative bodies (e.g., public defender offices in the United States, public advice bureaux in Europe).

"Legal socialism", an ideology which was developed by the Austrian scholar Anton Menger, exerted the strongest influence on the administration of justice in Europe. According to Menger's theories, the inequality of the parties before the court could be eliminated if the judge were given the power to assist the party who is socially weaker. The court thus departs from its passive role and takes an investigatory initiative, assembling and presenting proof in order to better understand the material facts. This concept was first put into practice in the 1895 reform of the Austrian law of civil procedure. This reform, which was chiefly the work of Franz Klein, subsequently influenced many other important reforms in Europe.[3] The judge has been given *ex officio* initiative powers with respect to evidence in those proceedings where one of the parties is economically weak (such as in labour conflicts or in small claims). The reforms accomplished by the socialist countries also reflect this trend.

After World War II, political evolution in the democratic states led to a concept of providing assistance for the poor within the framework of the welfare state. The major reforms in legal aid were prompted by a number of factors. First, the traditional liberal concept of the civil lawsuit as a structure of formal guarantees was increasingly challenged. Even those legal systems that were slowest to abandon the adversary system in civil proceedings have been forced by growing social demands to introduce more and more exceptions to their procedure. Thus, within the scheme of the ordinary traditional civil proceeding, certain categories of conflicts (such as labour disputes) are singled out and handled by a different procedure (e.g., by giving the judge *ex officio* powers such as those that resulted from the concept of legal socialism). Alternatively, the traditional system may be modified by creating special judicial bodies (such as the English tribunals, or the American administrative agencies) which are not restricted to ordinary legal procedures and which are characterized by their wider powers.[4] This has also led to the creation of simpler small claims proceedings, characterized by lower litigation costs, speedy procedures and the equitable and conciliatory powers of the judge.[5] Secondly, the persistence of the adversary system in ordinary proceedings emphasizes the need for guarantees of true equality between the parties, it is necessary that the weaker party have an adequate opportunity to present his evidence and argument to the court. This need corresponds to the traditional concept of proceedings which stresses the neutrality of the judge as opposed to any active and direct involvement. Maintaining the adversary system demands that the parties be able to carry out their defence effectively; this requires assistance by counsel.[6] The concept of the right to counsel as an aspect of legal aid developed after World War II. It was codified in such international treaties as the European Convention for Human Rights. The decisions of constitutional courts have put increasing emphasis on the right to counsel in criminal matters, and, more recently, in civil matters as well. Generally, in countries having a written constitution, the right to counsel is directly or indirectly embodied in constitutional principles. The Italian Constitution of 1947 (Article 24) and the Japanese Constitution of 1946 (Article 32) recognize this right directly, while the Constitution of the German Federal Republic (Articles 101 and 103) and the Constitution of the United States (14th Amendment) recognize the right indirectly. The most important examples of the evolution of this right can be found in the decisions of the United States Supreme Court. Since the 1938 decision in *Johnson* v. *Zerbst* (304 U.S. 458), the Supreme Court has stressed the constitutional right of indigent defendants to be assisted by judicially appointed counsel. In the 1963 case of *Gideon* v. *Wainwright* (372 U.S. 335), the indigent's right to appointed counsel was extended to state actions, and in 1972 *Argensinger* v. *Hamlin* (407 U.S. 25) provided for publicly paid counsel whenever the defendant was subject to imprisonment. In 1971, in *Boddie* v. *Connecticut* (401 U.S. 371), the Supreme Court extended these guarantees to civil proceedings whenever the intervention of the court is required to protect individual rights (as in divorce cases).[7] Finally, the welfare state has become more socially oriented, as is reflected in the constitutions drawn after World War II. The most important task of the state is perceived to be the removal of all obstacles which prevent the attainment of true equality between citizens. The poor are thus no longer assisted as members of a segregated class. Social justice through civil justice is the goal of all the reforms which, beginning with the English *Legal Aid and Advice Act* of 1949, have shaped the recent development of legal assistance in modern states.[8]

Before analysing the trends of legal aid systems in the second half of this century, it should be recalled that the treatment of this problem has been greatly influenced by the legal profession. With the exception of the socialist countries, where the legal profession has become a public service, lawyers have retained their nineteenth-century bourgeois tradition. This has influenced the attitude of the legal profession towards the development of legal assistance. Lawyers have retained the principle of neutrality towards the values involved in legal conflicts. According to the traditional approach, the lawyer should work only to win the case by applying the law in his client's favour, disregarding any broader social or economic implications. This purely technical interpretation of the lawyer's function results directly from the kind of education provided by law schools. Lawyers receive a strictly legal education with little or no emphasis on economics, history, or sociology.[9]

Lawyers have stubbornly defended the private character of their profession, and have rejected attempts to create a public position for legal assistance. This attitude was apparent in the United States when the first public defender offices were established early in this century, and it persisted until the creation of public legal assistance centres within the Legal Services Program, which was begun in 1964. The same attitude prevailed in Italy at the beginning of the century when several bills were drawn up aimed at creating staff attorney offices for the indigent. In England the proposal by labour lawyers to set up public legal advice centres as provided for in the *Legal Aid Act* of 1949 has been strongly opposed.[10]

The legal profession has resisted legislative efforts to broaden the duties of lawyers beyond the traditional role of acting as counsel in individual cases. The profession has been reluctant to see its role expanded to include informing the underprivileged of their rights and promoting legislative and administrative reforms to ease the economic and social problems of the underprivileged. The traditional role has been upheld by retaining the rules of lawyers' ethics within the framework of a personal lawyer-client relationship, and by opposing any change in the canons. The picture began to change in the 1960s when reform movements led to the birth of a new type of lawyer – the public interest lawyer. These lawyers see the economic and social advancement of the underprivileged as an integral part of legal assistance.[11]

The resistance of the legal profession to these new trends is still very strong. In particular, any plan to turn the legal profession into a public service is still strongly opposed, while the intervention of the state is accepted only in so far as it is a method of paying for private lawyers' fees with public money. This attitude is also shared by some constitutional courts. For example, the Austrian Constitutional Court, in a decision of December 19, 1972, ruled against the existing law on legal assistance on the ground that the provision of free services by private lawyers to the indigent violated the principle of equality.[12]

A number of sociological studies on the relationship between poverty and justice have been carried out in several countries. The contributions of the London School of Economics and the American Bar Foundation in this area are particularly important.[13] The welfare state model and the expansion of the U.S. anti-poverty program have led to the awareness that legal assistance is essential to achieving upward social mobility. In particular, the investigations performed have drawn attention to a series of factors which still hamper progress.

The poor lack information about their rights and how to enforce them. They are often not even aware of statutes designed to protect their interests such as those dealing with housing and welfare. Moreover, this lack of information is often accompanied by a suspicion of the administration of justice and legal systems which have long been considered repressive and inflexible.

Frequently the poor live far from the centre of large cities (where most lawyers' offices are located); this, along with inflexible working schedules, makes it difficult for them to consult a lawyer in case of need. This is also true in rural communities in isolated areas. A social and cultural gap exists between lawyers and the poor. Besides differences in economic status and level of education, factors such as race, nationality or recent immigration also play a major role. Within a poor community, there are often minorities further hampered by communication problems arising from language, customs, and religious beliefs. Finally, it is becoming increasingly clear that legal protection for the underprivileged does not simply mean solving individual disputes; only special statutes and administrative measures can solve the difficult problems of housing, education, employment and welfare.

In light of the studies mentioned above, the need for justice acquires a clearer definition: it is no longer simply the need to be represented by a lawyer, but rather the need to be assisted at various levels during the course of a legal action. In this context, legal advice has come to be regarded as a basic form of social assistance.

Sociological studies have also yielded data on the cost-benefit ratio of different types of legal assistance, such as private lawyers, staff attorneys, etc. In addition, they have shown that the poor generally resort to counsel with respect to traditional legal problems.

With the exception of the socialist countries (which will be considered separately), three basic trends emerge in viewing the overall picture of legal assistance in contemporary countries:

Legal assistance must ensure equality before the court; this objective is realized through the granting of free counsel by means of coverage of the lawyer's fee by public funds, the introduction of a system of prepaid legal services as a form of public or private insurance,[14] or gratuitous services by private lawyers.

The services rendered by private lawyers are of public and social interest and are to be delivered within the framework of a wider assistance programme directed or controlled by public bodies. This view would not completely rule out assistance on a private basis (such as the assistance afforded by some workers' unions to their members.[15]

Legal assistance is part of a broad range of social services. According to this concept, the goal of social advancement should, in principle, be more effectively reached by public centres operating within a general plan for a more advanced concept of social justice.[16]

These three trends should be examined separately, although they are not always mutually exclusive. In fact, the traditional models of legal assistance often exist alongside the more advanced forms.

The first trend, which is certainly in line with the laws of civil procedure in liberal countries, can be found in the legal systems which have maintained practically unchanged the scheme of legal assistance introduced in the second half of the nineteenth century. Those schemes were based on the lawyer's moral obligation to render free services to indigent litigants; special committees established the requirements of an eligibility for free assistance; and a preliminary inquiry into the likelihood of a favourable outcome was held. This view of legal assistance as a lawyer's duty has remained practically unchanged in countries such as Italy, Spain and Belgium where the nineteenth-century legislation has been retained. In other countries, changes have recently been made which have led to the introduction of direct or indirect coverage of lawyers' fees. In addition, recent statutes (e.g., the French statute of 1972)[17] provide for partial assistance in payment of litigation costs. All these reforms involve direct payment of fees to the lawyer by public funds; however, proposals for some indirect compensation have been put forward. For example, the Austrian statute of 1972 has solved the problem created by the decision of the constitutional court (which held that the provision of free services to the indigent violated the principle of equality) by allocating public money to increase lawyers' insurance and social security funds. All these systems allow the professional associations to retain a great deal of autonomy in deciding which forms of legal assistance to use and in supervising the effectiveness of services rendered by lawyers. In fact, even in countries such as Germany and France, where some forms of free legal advice have been introduced, there is no socially-oriented public service. There are only bar associations which offer advice on an occasional and therefore limited basis. The solution preferred in these countries is the provision of free civil justice, a goal which is sometimes attained by private forms of insurance which cover legal expenses. This approach is favoured by many professional associations even in countries such as the United States,[18] where legal aid has had a long and difficult evolution. On the other hand, it is understandable that lawyers attempt to avoid any public control of their professional activity. Such control is unavoidable if the state takes upon itself the task of paying the legal expenses of the poor. It should also be remembered that the traditional attitude of the legal profession is to resist the introduction of any form of assistance which goes beyond the solution of technical problems connected with individual cases and which attempts to establish a link between legal aid and social improvements.

The second trend envisages private lawyers' services within the framework of a system which includes the activity of public bodies. The reforms carried out in England after 1949, in the Canadian province of Quebec in 1972, and in Sweden after 1973, clearly fall within a broader system of social assistance, where provision of legal assistance is only one of the basic tasks of the state. What has been accomplished up to the present is still a long way from a National Legal Service, comparable to the British National Health Service, but the concept underlying the two programmes is the same. The incomplete development of these programmes is a result of the opposition of lawyers who are unwilling to accept any form of public control, and also of the economic crisis which has led to drastic cuts in public assistance funds from the beginning of the 1970s. An important example of this trend is the English *Legal Aid and Advice Act* of 1949, a flexible scheme which allows partial innovations at varying times. Even now the English legal aid system does not include all the forms of assistance envisaged in the initial scheme; it does not yet provide for any kind of representation before most administrative tribunals and no public assistance bureaux have yet been created. On the other hand, a recent alliance between legal advice bureaux and citizens' advice bureaux is regarded as evidence of the effectiveness of the scheme. In addition, legal centres and neighbourhood law centres have been set up by local administrations in accordance with the basic principle of assistance put forth by the Society of Labour Lawyers, which advocates an extension of both the degree and basis of legal assistance.[19] In England, the obstacles to the completion of this programme are difficult to overcome. From the beginning the legal aid programme has been administered by the Law

Society, the association of English solicitors, which has acted mainly in its own interests. As a result, proposals have been made to administer legal aid by an independent public body unconnected with the government; it is hoped that this arrangement will overcome the conflict between the public interest and the private interests of the members of the Law Society.[20]

The Swedish Act of 1973, although one of the most advanced legal assistance laws in Europe, is a compromise between the traditional model of services rendered by private lawyers and the need for legal assistance available through public offices. The Swedish reform regulates the activity of thirty state-supported public law offices under the supervision of regional governments as well as assistance given by private lawyers. Those who need legal assistance may choose either the private practitioner or the public law office; neither system has a monopoly, although it was assumed that the underprivileged would benefit more from a public service created specifically for the purpose of giving legal aid than they would from advice given by private lawyers.

The solution adopted in these countries is basically a compromise between legal aid through the private bar and assistance by public law offices. If public legal advice systems are aimed at solving the immediate problems, then they too view assistance as the solution of an individual problem in a given situation and fail to take into account the legal needs of the underprivileged as social beings. Legal assistance is closely related to the right to counsel, and too often the problems outside the courtroom are disregarded.

The most significant example of the third trend outlined above is represented by the United States Legal Services Program, the most advanced legal aid programme in capitalist countries. This program was put into effect between 1964 and 1974 within the framework of the Office of Economic Opportunity (OEO) created by the Johnson administration for the purpose of fighting poverty.[21] The programme was devised by experts who had spent several years investigating the need for justice, and who were convinced that the true social assistance of the underprivileged would call for a modification in the traditional lawyer–client relationship. Neighborhood Law Firms were set up in poor neighbourhoods in large cities and in rurual areas; legal assistance was provided on a part-time or full-time basis by lawyers whose salaries were paid by public funds. According to the philosophy of the programme,[22] the activity of the centres was to be advertised among the target group by means of an information network (public debates, leaflets distributed in the streets, ads on local radio and television stations). Mobile offices were also used to take the advice centres as close to the poor as possible. This activity, which contrasted sharply with the traditional reserve of the legal profession, provoked many ethical problems which were challenged in court by bar associations.

The programme was intended to initiate strong law reform activity. Test cases on matters relevant to the needs of the poor were brought to court. This technique frequently instituted class actions to enforce rights belonging to a large group. Actually, many decisions of the United States Supreme Court concerning civil rights and social equality were the result of actions brought by the OEO lawyers. This law reform activity was combined with actions aimed at bringing about legislative and administrative changes in favour of the poor in areas where intervention was most dramatically needed – housing, welfare, urban policy. For this purpose, citizens interested in these problems were also organized into pressure groups which attempted to influence federal, state and local administrations.

The programme was also characterized by the direct participation of community representatives in the running of the legal assistance centres. This kind of participation, which was unique in the history of legal assistance schemes, was recognition of the need for community participation.

The American Legal Services Program was faced with strong opposition because of the innovations it introduced. This opposition reached its peak with the direct attack by the then vice-president of the United States, Spiro Agnew.[23] His main targets were the progressive political aspects of the programme (the actions in defence of the poor were often brought against public administrations). The Nixon administration supported these criticisms, and withdrew financial aid, resulting in the dismantling of the programme. In 1974 it was replaced by the Legal Services Corporation, a private organization supported by public funds. This corporation, which adopted a more restrictive attitude towards social action and reform, is governed by rules which limit legal assistance and which exclude the categories of disputes involving overtly political issues.[24] There has been an attempt to bring legal assistance back within the traditional framework, but it is too early to say whether the Carter administration will give support to those who had supported the original OEO programme.

To further demonstrate the significance of the OEO experience in the evolution of legal assistance in the United States, it should be noted that this programme was part of a multifaceted legal aid pattern which is the consequence of the different systems adopted by various states, as well as of the survival of private legal assistance organizations. Along with the traditional legal aid societies which have maintained their private structure and which operate mainly in large cities, these are programmes based on payment of private lawyers' fees by public funds (Judicare) which are reminiscent of the English legal aid. The choice between these two types of assistance (staff attorney or compensated private counsel) is often presented as a technical choice, based on efficiency and cost criteria.[25] But the choice is also a political one, since the activity of public offices is founded on the concept of legal assistance as a social right, rather than the solely individualistic approach of traditional systems.

The socialist countries

The situation in socialist countries must be examined separately, since the problem of the right to counsel is seen in a different perspective; even the concept of "underprivileged" cannot be clearly defined.

The basic principle of socialist legal systems is the attainment of substantial equality through simple, free procedures which enable all citizens to assert their own rights quickly and at no cost. According to a principle common to the procedural codes of all socialist countries, the judge is to assist all parties by intervening in the drafting of the complaint (which can be presented orally) and by giving appropriate directions during the proceedings. This is a duty, not a discretionary power of the judge; and in some systems its violation may lead to the invalidation of the proceedings.

According to the socialist system, the assistance of counsel in civil actions is not compulsory: as a consequence, the problem of providing counsel for persons unable to pay for a lawyer does not arise.[26] Moreover, hiring a member of a bar association is fairly easy since fees are low, and can be reduced even further if necessary.

Legal expenses are also treated differently in socialist countries. Exemption is granted not in relation to the economic status of the parties but *a priori* for given categories of conflicts (labour, alimony, damages for work accidents, etc.). Individual exemptions can be granted on the discretion of the judge, on the basis of economic conditions. A similar discretionary evaluation is made by the chairmen of the collective of attorneys upon a request for free legal assistance.

The organization of lawyers into public offices provides legal advice on a general basis.[27] The group of attorneys must offer free oral advice to all those who ask for it, while for written advice a small fee is charged. It should be emphasized that the judge himself fulfils an advisory function, since he is obliged to assist all parties throughout the proceedings.

Finally, socialist countries meet the need for more accessible systems of justice through public bodies peculiar to these countries. For example, the public prosecutor can bring civil actions on behalf of an individual if the individual is unable to act because of economic constraints. Social organizations such as trade unions can also intervene in the proceedings in support of a party; and there are social courts, which are special jurisdictional bodies entrusted with the resolution of minor disputes. There has been a recent tendency in the socialist countries to increase the parties' responsibility in the proceedings.[28] This trend increases the need for counsel in civil proceedings, thus extending the tasks of lawyers' organizations as far as legal assistance to economically weak parties is concerned.

The developing countries

The problems of legal aid in the developing countries deserve special attention. In these countries, it is necessary to reconcile the restructuring of the legal system with the concept of access to justice for the majority of the population which is still bound to dispute settlement through tribal or customary law.[29]

Developing countries have directed their reform attempts towards reducing the pluralism which exists in the administration of justice and in substantive law. This implies a restriction of customary law, which is itself an obstacle to the access to justice for the poor. The centralization of courts and the rationalization of the law require more professional judges and the assistance of a lawyer.

Professional specialization stresses the need for legal aid. At this point, however, there is a danger of the monopolization of counselling by the few lawyers available, who are mainly concentrated in the capital cities.

On the other hand, the cost of a truly efficient legal aid system would be unbearable for these poor countries. As a consequence, legal aid on a universal basis is not yet feasible, at least as far as civil cases are concerned. It has correctly been observed that an efficient legal aid system requires a high national economic standard, a relatively small proportion of poor people, the availability of many lawyers willing to perform a socially-oriented activity, the independence of courts, and the existence of constitutional principles regulating fundamental guarantees in the administration of justice. The absence of these conditions in developing countries indicates that access to justice can be attained not through the introduction of legal aid schemes such as those found in Western countries, but by eliminating the need for representation by counsel. This means simpler procedures, initiative powers for the judge with respect to the course of the proceedings and to the assembly of evidence,[30] and the creation of special conciliation boards and greater utilization of small claims courts. The maintenance of legal pluralism and of traditional dispute settlement techniques typical of the customary law is regarded as necessary to a certain extent.[31]

It should also be noted that similar problems have to be faced in developed countries where there are still areas of underdeveloped population (such as the aboriginal communities in Australia).

Summary

The picture emerging from a study of the evolution of legal assistance in the contemporary world is highly differentiated and reflects the political positions of diverse societies. The reforms carried out in capitalist countries show basically homogeneous trends, since they all move from the assumption, derived from the liberal ideology, that *de facto* inequality of access to justice is principally due to the lack of adequate legal assistance. Reforms thus aim at improving the existing assistance systems and extending their benefits not only to the poor, but to the lower middle class, for whom the cost of legal assistance remains too high.

In most systems there is a distinction between legal aid systems based on services rendered by private lawyers who are paid out of public funds, and systems based on the creation of public offices of counselling and advice which include part-time or full-time salaried staff attorneys. The first model is generally regarded as closer to the traditional values of the legal profession, and thus more individualistic, while the latter is more socially-oriented and views the accessibility of justice as a social right. However, the establishment of public legal assistance offices does not always reflect an acknowledgement of the legal problems of the underprivileged; it may be preferred simply because of its lower cost. From this standpoint, the experience of the OEO Legal Services Program in the United States, in spite of all its limitations, remains a relatively unique phenomenon – one of the great hopes of the 1960s – which has not outlived its times.[32]

On the other hand, attempts to reform the system in capitalist countries by widening the scope of legal assistance are often viewed with distrust; some observers feel that there is little point in improving access to justice when the law which is enforced in the courtroom reflects the interests of ruling classes and operates against the lower classes who have no control over the means of production. Social inequality should therefore be eradicated through laws capable of drastically modifying existing social structures.[33]

In the socialist countries the problem of access to justice is dealt with by public legal aid offices and by creating simple and informal proceedings, characterized by auxiliary powers of the judge, the public prosecutor, and social organizations. In the developing countries, as we have seen, the attempts made at restructuring the law have often resulted in a wider gap between justice and the people: the administration of justice should therefore follow the route of conciliatory procedures, thus decreasing the need for professional lawyers.

In conclusion, the overall picture allows the discussion of trends only within homogeneous systems[34] and reflects political and ideological differences.

Notes and References

1. On the historical evolution of this problem, see Abel-Smith and Stevens, *In Search of Justice: Law, Society and the Legal System*, London, 1968; Levitan, *The Great Society's Poor Law*, Baltimore, 1969.
2. The first organic French law on legal assistance dates back to 1851: see Solus and Perrot, *Droit judiciaire privé*, I, Paris, 1961, p. 960; Pellettier, "Legal Aid in France", *Notre Dame Lawyer*, 42 (1967), 627.
3. On the influence exerted by Menger on the Austrian reform, and on Franz Klein's work, see the recent paper by Langer, "Rechtsuchender und Richter in Österreich", *Jur. Zeit.*, 32 (1977) 376. On the role of Anton Menger within the framework of legal socialism, see the recently published book by Willdrodt v. Westernhagen, *Recht und Soziale Frage. Die Sozial- und Recht-philosophie Anton Mengers*, Hamburg, 1975.
4. This evolution in the concept of legal proceeding is discussed in detail by Cappelletti in "Social and Political Aspects of Civil Procedure. Reforms and Trends in Western and Eastern Europe", *Mich. L. Rev.*, 69 (1971), 847.

5. On this subject, see Ison, "Small Claims", *Mod. L. Rev.*, 35 (1972), 18.
6. The problem is discussed by Goodpaster, "The Integration of Equal Protection, Due Process Standards, and the Indigent's Right of Free Access to the Courts", *Iowa L. Rev.*, 56 (1970), 223 and by Adams, "Toward a Mobilization of the Adversary Process", *Osgoode Hall L.J.*, 12 (1974), 569.
7. See Cappelletti, "Legal Assistance and Modern Constitutionalism", in Capelletti, Gordley and Johnson (eds.): *Toward Equal Justice: A Comparative Study of Legal Aid in Modern Societies*, Milan, 1975, p. 64.
8. This subject is discussed in particular by the reformers who set up the OEO Legal Services Program in the U.S. See Cahn, "The War on Poverty: a Civilian Perspective", *Yale L.J.*, 73 (1974) 1317; Carlin, Howard and Messinger, "Civil Justice and the Poor: Issues for Sociological Research", *Law and Soc. Rev.*, 2 (1966) 9; and, lastly, Gordley, "Legal Aid as a Welfare Right", in the volume *Toward Equal Justice*, p. 109.
9. For a discussion of the problem see, for example, Geck, "The Reform of Legal Education in the Federal Republic of Germany", *Am. J. Comp. L.*, 25 (1977), 86.
10. On these attitudes of the legal profession, see Countryman and Finman, *The Lawyer in Modern Society*, Boston, 1966; Zander, *Lawyers and the Public Interest. A Study in Restrictive Practice*, London, 1968; Auerbach, *Unqeual Justice: Lawyers and Social Change in Modern America*, New York; Bloomfield, *American Lawyers in a Changing Society*, Cambridge, Mass., 1976.
11. On the figure of the public lawyer, see Cappelletti, "Governmental and Private Advocates for the Public Interest in Civil Litigation: A Comparative Study", *Mich. L. Rev.*, 73 (1975), 793; Rabin, "Lawyers for Social Change: Perspective on Public Interest Law", *Stanf. L. Rev.*, 28 (1976), 207.
12. The decision of the Austrian Verfassungsgerichtshof can be found in Cappelletti, Gordley and Johnson, *Toward Equal Justice*, 721.
13. With regard to England, see Abel-Smith, Zander and Brooke, *Legal Problems and the Citizen*, London 1972 and Morris *et al.*, *Social Needs and Legal Action*, London, 1973. For the United States, see the review by Rumi Paroni, "Studi e ricerche sull'assistenza legale ai non abbienti negli Stati Uniti", *Sociologia del Diritto*, 1974, p. 171.
14. On this form of assistance, see the investigation carried out by

Pfennigstorf, *Legal Impense Insurance. The European Experience in Financing Legal Services*, Chicago, 1975.

15. On legal assistance by trade unions, see, e.g., Latta and Lewis, "Trade Union Legal Services", *Brit. Journ. Ind. Rel.*, 12 (1974), 56.
16. The various ways of delivering legal assistance are discussed in Johnson, "Alternative Methods of Delivering Legal Services to Low-Income Persons", in Cappelletti, Gordley and Johnson, *Toward Equal Justice*, p. 136.
17. On the French reform of 1972, see Oppetit, "L'aide judiciaire", *Rec. Dalloz, Chr.*, 1972, 41; Danses, "Reform des Armenrechts in Frankreich", *Juristenz.*, 1976, 208.
18. See, for example, the *National Conference on Prepaid Legal Services*, sponsored by the American Bar Association in 1972.
19. On the English experience, see the comprehensive work by Pollock, *Legal Aid. The First 25 Years*, London, 1975.
20. On the subject, see the *Evidence* presented to the Royal Commission on Legal Services by the Society of Labour Lawyers in July 1977, and the *Evidence* presented to the same Commission by M. Zander in September 1976.
21. The American experience is described in detail in Johnson, *Justice and Reform. The Formative Years of the OEO Legal Services Program*, New York, 1974.
22. The Guidelines for Legal Services Programs can be found in Cappelletti, Gordley and Johnson, "Toward Equal Justice'., p. 453.
23. See Agnew, "What's Wrong with the Legal Services Program", *Am. Bar Ass. J.*, 58 (1972) 930 and the answer by Falk and Pollock, "What's Wrong with Attacks on the Legal Services Program", ibid., 1287.
24. On the subject, see Green, Keyser and Nadas, "Depolitizing Legal Aid: A Constitutional Analysis of the Legal Services Corporation Act", *Cornell L. Rev.*, 61 (1976), 734. Apparently, since the beginning of Carter's administration, the limitations provided for by the Legal Services Corporation institutive law have been *de facto* not implemented.
25. See, for example, Cole and Gremberger, "Staff Attorney v. Judicare: A Cost Analysis", *J. Urb. Law*, 50 (1973), 705.
26. See Stalev, "Fundamental Guarantees of Litigants in Civil Proceedings: A Survey of Laws of the European Peoples Democracies", in the volume edited by Cappelletti and Tallon, *Fundamental Guarantees of the Parties in Civil Litigation*, Milan, 1973, p. 389.

27. On the nature of professional organizations in the Soviet Union, see Stepsovskii, "The Legal Standing of Soviet Collegia of Attorneys", *Soviet Law and Gov.*, 15 (1977), 28.
28. See Fasching, "Entwicklungstendenzen in Zivilprozessrecht der sozialistiche Staaten Osteuropa", *Zeit. f. Rechtsvergl.* 10 (1969), 98; Neval, "I fondamenti dell'attuale diritto processuale e civile ungherese", *Riv. dir. proc.*, 1972, 775.
29. On the problems of legal services in Africa, see Dunning, "Legal Systems and Legal Services in Africa", in the volume *Legal Aid and World Poverty. A Survey of Asia, Africa and Latin America*, New York, 1974, p. 21.
30. On the need for an "activist role of the Courts", similar to the "judicial activism" of customary procedure, see in particular Bush, "Modern Role for Customary Justice: Integration of Civil Procedure in African Courts", *Stanf. L. Rev.*, 26 (1974), 1124. On the same subject, see also Smith, "Man and Law in Urban Africa: A Role for Customary Courts in the Urbanization Process", *Am. Bar Ass. J.*, 58 (1972), 33.
32. See Cramton, "Promise and Reality in Legal Services", *Cornell L. Rev.*, 61 (1976), 670.
33. The contrast between the *liberal* and *radical* approaches to the problem of access to justice is emphasized in Levinson's review of Auerbach ("Unequal Justice", op. cit.) in *Vand. L. Rev.*; 29 (1976), 1487. With regard to the radical approach, see the papers collected in the volume edited by Lefcourt, *Law Against the People*, New York, 1971; in particular, by Lefcourt, see "Lawyers for the Poor Can't Win", ibid., 123. With reference to *civil law* systems, see Rasehorn, *Recht und Klassen. Zur Klassenjustiz in der Bundesrepublik*, Darmstadt u. Neuwied, 1974 and Wassermann, *Justiz im sozialen Rechtsstaat*, Darmstadt u. Neuwied, 1974.
34. An example of this kind of study is Baumgärtel, *Gleicher Zugang zum Recht für Alle*, Köln, 1976.

Biographical Details

Baumgärtel, Gottfried – Professor of Law and Director of the Institute for Procedural Law at the University of Cologne, Germany

Boman, Robert – Professor of Law, Uppsala University, Juridiska Institutionen, Uppsala, Sweden

Denti, Vittorio – Professor of Law, Faculty of Jurisprudence, University of Pavia, Pavia, Italy

Epstein, Judd A. – Faculty of Law, Monash University, Clayton, Victoria, Australia

Gross, Peter Henry – Barrister, London England, 61 Kensington Gardens Square, London W.2.

Handler, Joel F. – Professor of Law, University of Wisconsin Law School, Professor and Institute Fellow, Institute for Research on Poverty, University of Wisconsin Law School, Madison, Wisconsin

König, Bernhard – University Professor in the Department of Law (Civil Proceedings) University of Innsbruck, Austria

Kojima, Takeshi – Professor of Law at Chuo University, Higashinakano Hachioji-City, Tokyo, Japan, Associated with the Institute of Comparative Law in Japan.

de Miguel, Carlos – Professor of Civil Law at the University of Valladolid, Valladolid, Spain

Onate, Santiago – Professor of Law, University of Mexico, Mexico City, Mexico

Partington, Martin – Lecturer in the Law Department at the London School of Economics, London, Great Britain

Pradel, Jean – Professor of the Faculty of Law and Social Sciences at the University of Poitiers, Institute of Criminology, Poitiers, France

Reyntjens, Filip – Vice Dean of the Law Faculty at the National University of Rwanda, Butare, Rwanda

Song, Sang Hyun – Professor of Law, Seoul National University and Former Dean of the Law School, Seoul National University, Seoul, Korea; Visiting the Faculty of Law, Harvard University 1978-79

Vigoriti, Vincenzo – Professor of Comparative Procedure at the University of Florence, Associated with the Institute of Comparative Law, Florence

Weiss, Paula B. – L.L.B. 1979 Osgoode Hall Law School of York University, Dawnsview, Ontario, Canada. Ph.D. in German from Cornell University

Wengerek, Edmund – Professor of Law at the Adam Mickiewicz University, Poznam, Poland

Zemans, Frederick H. – Professor of Law of Osgoode Hall Law School of York University, Dawnsview, Ontario, Canada; Visiting academic at the Law Department, London School of Economics, London, Great Britain, 1978-79